INSIDERS' GUIDE® TO
YELLOWSTONE & GRAND TETON

HELP US KEEP THIS GUIDE UP TO DATE

We would love to hear from you concerning your experiences with this guide and how you feel it could be improved and kept up to date. Please send your comments and suggestions to:

editorial@GlobePequot.com

Thanks for your input, and happy travels!

INSIDERS' GUIDE® TO

YELLOWSTONE & GRAND TETON

EIGHTH EDITION

BRIAN HURLBUT

INSIDERS' GUIDE

GUILFORD, CONNECTICUT
AN IMPRINT OF GLOBE PEQUOT PRESS

All the information in this guidebook is subject to change. We recommend that you call ahead to obtain current information before traveling.

INSIDERS' GUIDE ®

Copyright © 2011 Morris Book Publishing, LLC

Editor: Kevin Sirois
Project Editor: Lynn Zelem
Layout Artist: Kevin Mak
Text Design: Sheryl Kober
Maps: XNR Productions, Inc. © Morris Book Publishing, LLC

ISSN 1539-6584
ISBN 978-0-7627-6477-8

Printed in the United States of America
10 9 8 7 6 5 4 3 2 1

CONTENTS

CONTENTS

CONTENTS

ABOUT THE AUTHOR

Brian Hurlbut is a journalist and freelance writer living in Big Sky. He began hiking around the Adirondack Mountains of upstate New York as a young boy, but the lure of the high peaks was eventually too much. In 1993, a year after graduating from the State University of New York at Buffalo, he packed his belongings into a microscopic Nissan Sentra and headed west. He landed in Missoula, where he continued his graduate studies in journalism at the University of Montana and began to explore the state's vast physical and cultural geography. Since then he has hiked in most of Montana's mountain ranges and visited many of the region's small towns, immersing himself in everything the Treasure State has to offer. Brian spends most of his free time in the outdoors and is particularly interested in backpacking, traveling, backcountry snowboarding, and history. His work can be seen regularly in publications around the region, and he is often on stage as a drummer in a local rock-and-roll band. He lives in Big Sky with his wife and two children.

ACKNOWLEDGMENTS

Writing a book is a challenging and time-consuming task, one that cannot be possible without the help of many individuals and organizations. Writing and updating this Insiders' Guide has been a tremendous experience for me, one that I certainly will never forget. I owe my gratitude to many.

First and foremost, I would like to thank my first editor, Erika Serviss, for giving me the opportunity to be an insider, and all of the subsequent editors I have worked with. My first coauthor and friend, Seabring Davis, was a tremendous help, taking the time out of her busy day for brainstorming sessions—usually involving large amounts of coffee. I need to thank my wife, Lindsie, for being a fun and supportive travel companion. The various chambers of commerce used in this book were extremely helpful. An extra special thanks goes out to Donnie Sexton at Travel Montana and Dax Schieffer at Big Sky Resort. My parents, of course, were extremely supportive of this opportunity and were a big help in many ways. I would also like to thank my sister, Diane, whose various excursions with her family in the outdoors continue to motivate me to get out there and write—and to try to keep up with her.

Lastly, I would like to add that I am extremely grateful to be able to live in such a beautiful place. The Yellowstone region is like no place on earth, full of friendly people and incredible scenery—a place I'm proud to call home. Writing this book served as a reminder of just how lucky I am.

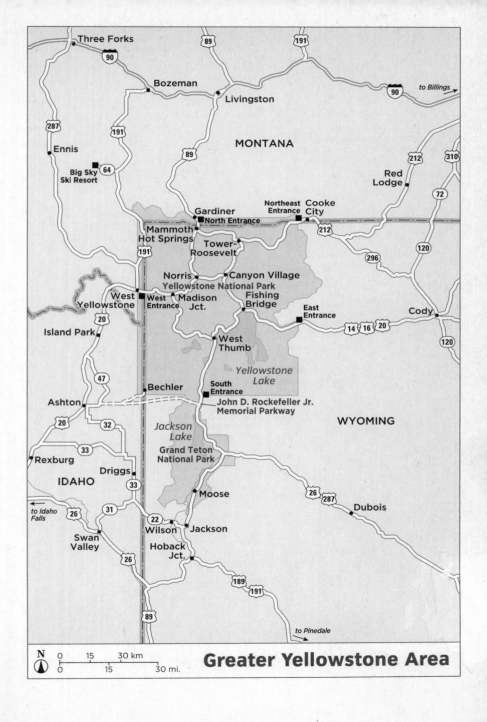

Greater Yellowstone Area

Three Forks

90

89

191

Bozeman

Livingston

90

to Billings

287

191

MONTANA

Ennis

89

64

Big Sky
Ski Resort

212

310

Red
Lodge

72

Northeast
Entrance

Cooke
City

Gardiner
North Entrance

212

Mammoth
Hot Springs

191

Tower-
Roosevelt

296

120

Norris

Canyon Village

Yellowstone National Park

West
Yellowstone

West
Entrance

Madison
Jct.

Fishing
Bridge

East
Entrance

Cody

20

Island Park

West
Thumb

14 16 20

120

47

Yellowstone
Lake

Bechler

South
Entrance

Ashton

John D. Rockefeller Jr.
Memorial Parkway

WYOMING

20

32

Jackson
Lake

33

Rexburg

Grand Teton
National Park

Driggs

IDAHO

33

Moose

26

287

Dubois

to Idaho
Falls

26

31

22

Wilson

Jackson

Swan
Valley

Hoback
Jct.

26

189

191

89

to Pinedale

N

0   15   30 km

0   15   30 mi.

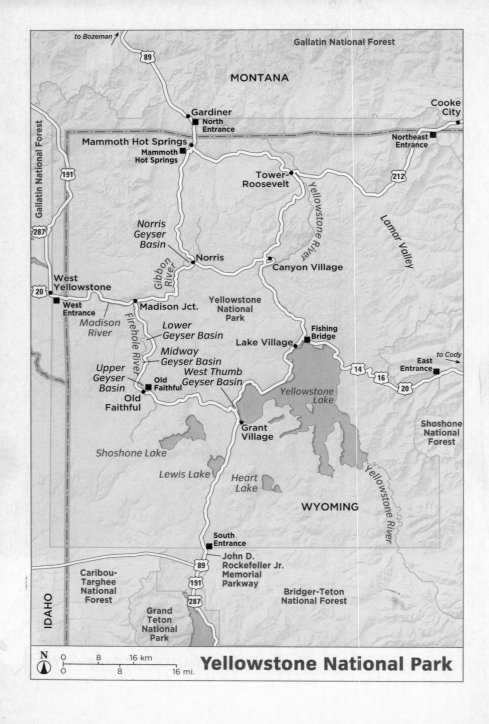

to Bozeman

89

Gallatin National Forest

MONTANA

Cooke
City

Gallatin National Forest

191

287

Gardiner
■ **North
Entrance**

Mammoth Hot Springs ■

Mammoth
Hot Springs

Northeast
Entrance ■

212

Tower-
Roosevelt

*Norris
Geyser
Basin*

Yellowstone River

Lamar Valley

Norris ■

West
Yellowstone

■ Canyon Village

20

West
Entrance ■

Madison Jct. ■

*Madison
River*

**Yellowstone
National
Park**

*Lower
Geyser Basin*

Fishing
Bridge ■

Lake Village ■

Firehole River

Gibbon River

*Midway
Geyser Basin*

*West Thumb
Geyser Basin*

East
Entrance ■

*Upper
Geyser
Basin*

■ Old
Faithful

14

16

to Cody

Old
Faithful

*Yellowstone
Lake*

20

■ Grant
Village

Shoshone Lake

Shoshone
National
Forest

Lewis Lake

*Heart
Lake*

WYOMING

Yellowstone River

■ South
Entrance

89

191

287

John D.
Rockefeller Jr.
Memorial
Parkway

IDAHO

Caribou-
Targhee
National
Forest

Bridger-Teton
National
Forest

Grand
Teton
National
Park

N

0   8   16 km
0   8   16 mi.

Yellowstone National Park

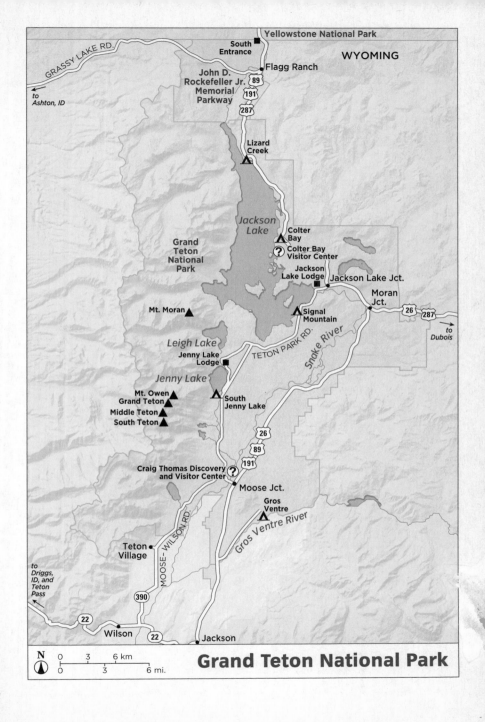

Grand Teton National Park

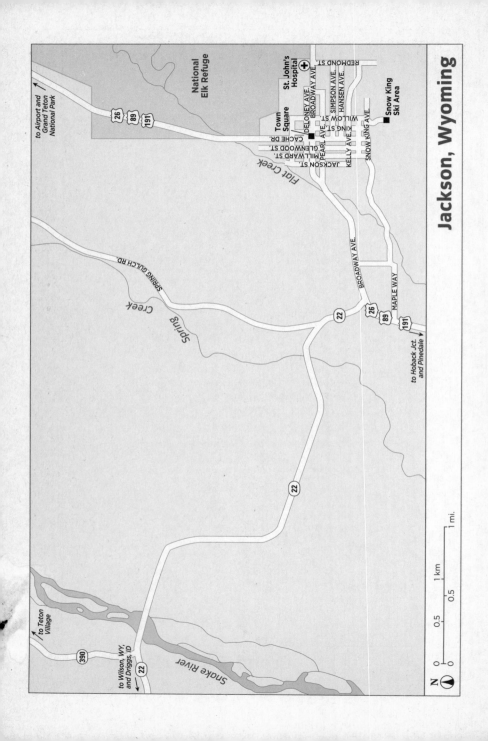

Jackson, Wyoming

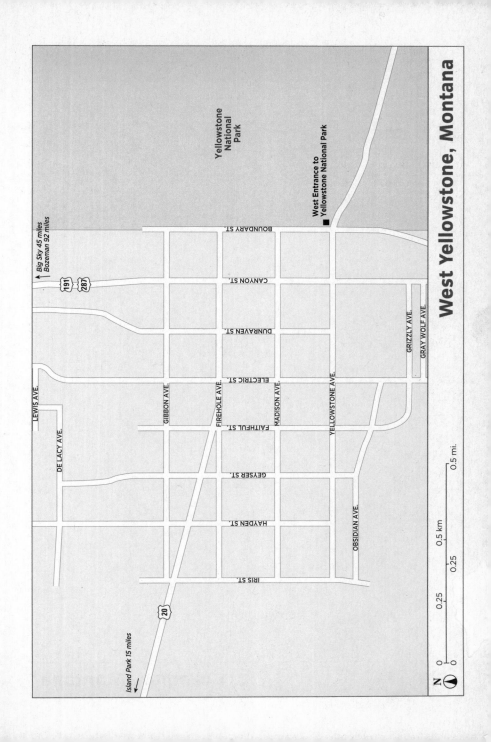

West Yellowstone, Montana

Yellowstone National Park

West Entrance to
Yellowstone National Park

Big Sky 45 miles
Bozeman 92 miles

191 287

20

Island Park 15 miles

BOUNDARY ST.
CANYON ST.
DUNRAVEN ST.
ELECTRIC ST.
GEYSER ST.
HAYDEN ST.
IRIS ST.

LEWIS AVE.
DE LACY AVE.
GIBBON AVE.
FIREHOLE AVE.
FAITHFUL ST.
MADISON AVE.
YELLOWSTONE AVE.
GRIZZLY AVE.
GRAY WOLF AVE.
OBSIDIAN AVE.

N

0   0.25   0.5 km

0   0.25   0.5 mi.

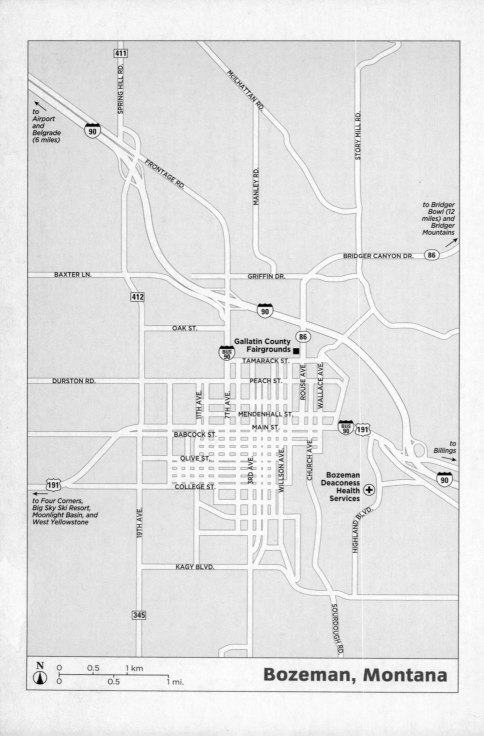

Bozeman, Montana

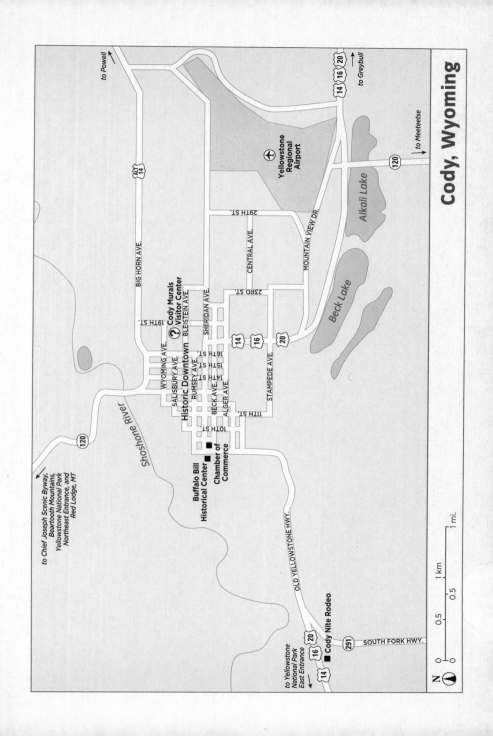

Cody, Wyoming

HOW TO USE THIS BOOK

Whether this is your first or 40th trip to the Greater Yellowstone region, this book is designed for you. If it's your first time, I hope that you'll discover many of the places described in here, from Yellowstone's hidden haunts to an out-of-the-way restaurant that serves up the best burger you've ever had. And for those travel veterans, I hope you'll find something that you've overlooked before, a new discovery that will make this trip even more memorable.

Each year, I log thousands of miles driving throughout the region. From winter snowboarding trips to Red Lodge and Cody to fall canoe excursions in Grand Teton National Park, I'm constantly searching for that next inclusion for the book—and checking other establishments to make sure they are still up to par. It's a rough job, I know, but it's all in the name of accuracy . . . and a good road trip.

The book is set up for easy trip planning and navigation. After a brief overview of the geographic area, the **Getting Here, Getting Around** chapter will highlight all of the transportation options. The **History** and **Our Natural World** chapters will make you a roadside expert as you drive around, giving you an idea of how this part of the world was formed, settled, and developed.

Much of the book is written around the individual gateway towns encircled by the two national parks. Depending on where you start and end your journey, you'll most likely visit several of the nine towns listed in the book. Each chapter will give you a general overview of the town's history, culture, and feel, and list specific recommendations on lodging, eating, camping, and shopping.

Yellowstone and Grand Teton are also treated as "towns" in their individual chapters—that is, if you are looking for lodging, dining, and information about the parks, read these chapters. If you're looking for scenic hiking trails or the best fishing streams, that information will be in a different chapter with the corresponding subject heading. So, if you want information about cross-country skiing in Yellowstone, check the **Winter Sports** chapter, if you want to know where the best whitewater rafting is around Jackson, check the **Fishing & Water Sports** chapter.

Likewise, the **Attractions** chapter includes Yellowstone and Grand Teton—specifically the features that I think travelers should see—as well other highlights from around the region. Some of these will be things most people will have heard of, but others are identified for those who want to get off the beaten path and explore the area a little bit.

Throughout the book you'll also find listings accompanied by the ✳ symbol—these are our top picks for attractions, restaurants, accommodations, and everything in between that you shouldn't miss while you're in the area. You want the best this region has to offer? Go with our **Insiders' Choice.**

HOW TO USE THIS BOOK

To make the book even more informative, I've highlighted interesting tips and useful knowledge in breakout text with the **i** symbol. There are also dozens of longer pieces that delve a little more deeply into certain subjects, identified as **Close-ups** throughout the book.

Moving to the Greater Yellowstone area or already live here? Be sure to check out the blue-tabbed pages at the back of the book, where you will find the **Living Here** appendix that offers sections on relocation, real estate, education, health care, retirement, and media.

Like any guidebook, I've done my best to include what I think is the best throughout the region. Undoubtedly, things change over time, and places change owners or management. If you're out there and you see something that I should include—or not include, for that matter—please let me know. After all, even as long as I've lived here I'm still up for new discoveries. In my opinion, that's what Greater Yellowstone is all about.

AREA OVERVIEW

The Yellowstone and Grand Teton region is one of contrasts. From the geothermal pools and rugged peaks of Yellowstone National Park to the warm, dry summers and cold, snowy winters, contrast is everywhere. It is what makes this region so interesting to visitors and residents alike and is one constant in this ever-changing environment. While here you'll drive on flat, straight roads and winding mountain passes. You'll have mountain ranges on your left and farmland on your right. It can be hot and steamy during the day and bone-chilling cold at night, and you might have the best meal ever at an out-of-the-way cafe in a town you never thought you'd be in. This is contrast, and people here live by it, right down to how they feel about their environment and land.

Exploration is another theme of our region. From Lewis and Clark's epic journey in the beginning of the 19th century and the first expedition to Yellowstone in 1866 to the millions of tourists who flock here each year, exploration is at the heart of Yellowstone Country. But you don't have to stay on the beaten path. Some of the area's greatest charms are hidden—from small towns to lesser-known trails to scenic backroads, all of which will leave a lasting impression on anyone who visits. And don't forget the friendly people, all of whom want to help you in your own quest for exploration.

THE LAY OF THE LAND

For our purposes the Yellowstone region is defined as the area surrounding Yellowstone and Grand Teton National Parks. This is a large area, yes, but you'll soon find out that all of it is worth exploring—even if it means coming back again and again.

From north to south the region extends close to 200 miles; from east to west it is nearly 150. But the great thing about such a large area is that there is always something, or somewhere, to explore.

From its inception as the country's first national park in 1872, the 2.2 million acres of Yellowstone have been one of the world's most popular destinations. With 10,000 thermal features, abundant wildlife, miles of hiking trails, and hundreds of lakes, streams, and waterfalls, Yellowstone is a nature lover's paradise that sees more than four million visitors a year.

Grand Teton National Park, created in 1929 and expanded in 1950 to include the Jackson Hole portion, offers more than 300,000 acres of some of the most dramatic scenery in the world. With peaks rising above the valley floor to nearly 14,000 feet, the Teton Range's famous silhouette will never leave your memory, and neither will the lakes, trails, and scenic byways.

Because of these two parks, tourism is at the center of what we call "gateway towns," places you can use as your base camp for exploring the region. All of these towns offer everything a visitor needs to stay for a day, a week, a year, or more for the person wishing to relocate. We will cover the following Montana gateway towns: Bozeman, Big Sky, Livingston, Gardiner, West Yellowstone, Red Lodge, and Cooke City. In Wyoming we cover Cody and Jackson, and we include Idaho's Driggs and Island Park. As we want to keep you informed of all of the little gems around the gateway towns, we give information on smaller towns, such as Ennis, which we included in the West Yellowstone chapter. We have decided to leave out larger cities, such as Billings, Montana, and Idaho Falls, Idaho, other than including them as options for starting and ending your visit.

i When you get here, pick up a few free road maps of Montana, Wyoming, and Idaho. These maps will have roads that a larger travel atlas may leave out, and many are worth driving on. They will also have information on campgrounds, historic sites, and other points of interest. Free maps can be found at visitor centers, airports, and chambers of commerce.

These gateway towns swell in the summer with busloads of visitors, and in the winter skiers and snowmobilers flock here eager to see the park as few have. These same towns are quiet in the off-season, giving locals a chance to rest a little and the occasional visitor a different atmosphere altogether.

But again, contrast is here. While tourism may be the driving force behind these towns, each offers a different look into what makes the Yellowstone region so special. Annual events, arts and music, outdoor adventures,

great dining, history—these towns have it all, whether they are on the map or not. Music festivals, museums, and art shows abound, including Bozeman's Sweet Pea Festival of the Arts, Jackson's Grand Teton Music Festival, and Cody's Buffalo Bill Historical Center. Even the smallest of towns will have plenty going on, offering a glimpse into what living here is really like. For us it is a place where folks still talk about community, where the landscape dominates the soul, and where hard times are made easier by the surrounding beauty. Simply put, people choose to live here for all the same reasons people want to visit.

THINGS TO REMEMBER

1. **Plan ahead**—Millions of people flock to the area in the summer, so plan accordingly. Book your accommodations (including campsites) early, and always have another option. If big crowds aren't your thing, do some research and pick out a smaller town to stay in and less-traveled trails to hike. You may even want to visit the area in one of the shoulder seasons, spring or fall. During this time most of the crowds have dispersed and room rates are significantly lower. However, check for closures—roads and services—if you choose this option.

2. **Be careful!**—Whether driving on a winding road or hiking on a backcountry trail, be alert to possible dangers. On roads, watch out for wildlife and heed large trucks and recreational vehicles, and constantly adjust your driving to the conditions. On trails, remember that wildlife is just that—wild—and do not approach anything you may encounter. Check with rangers in the

parks and forests to find out what to expect on a trail, and know what to do in case of an encounter. Precaution is the key here, and the more you know, the better and safer you'll feel.

3. **Tread lightly**—Much of this region is pristine and removed from human intrusion, and we want to keep it this way. Be aware of rules and heed them. For example, leaving the marked boardwalks around Yellowstone's geothermal features is a no-no, and doing so can be dangerous. Stay on marked trails, don't switchback, and use a zero-impact ethic. Remember that everyone has the same privilege to enjoy the area.

4. **Respect**—From wildlife to locals, make sure to be considerate of your surroundings. When watching wildlife, don't get so close that you disturb the natural actions, and refrain from making loud noises. Even the most streetwise wildlife—like the roaming elk in Mammoth and Gardiner—can be extremely dangerous. Be courteous to the locals. They are here to make sure your visit is enjoyable. Do your best to let them know they're appreciated.

5. **Have fun**—If you keep all of this information in mind, your visit will be an enjoyable one. It's a chance for many to do things they may have never thought of—swim in a mountain lake, glimpse a grizzly bear, stand in snow in August—and remember it for the rest of their lives. Take lots of pictures and read about the area's history; visit local museums and out-of-the-way attractions. But most of all, keep a smile on your face as you enjoy our area. We'll be smiling back.

GETTING HERE, GETTING AROUND

The Greater Yellowstone region encompasses three states, and the variety of ways to get here is equally impressive. The changes over the past century have made getting to this once remote area easier on the itinerary—and wallet. Once you're here, though, you'll need to remember just how big the area is and plan accordingly. Our roads are often windier and hillier than most, making for scenic but sometimes slow driving. And believe it or not, traffic can exist in even the most remote places. Visit either Yellowstone or Grand Teton National Park in summer and you will often see vehicles backed up along the roads as tourists take pictures of the wildlife. Small towns may not offer all the services you require, and long stretches can go by without services at all. All of this may make your trip take a little longer, but no one here will mind. This is the West, and life creeps along just a little bit slower than most other places.

Weather is the other major factor to consider when traveling in this region. Whatever your mode of transportation, it can be affected by quickly changing conditions. Even in summer, high altitudes and cool weather can mean snow. Take this into consideration, and always give yourself some extra time.

With all this in mind, the Greater Yellowstone region offers all modes of transportation, from airplanes to snowcoaches, and many choices of where to begin and end your trip. Modern methods of travel have made getting here and getting around easier. All the airports described here are within a few hours—or miles—of Yellowstone Country, and there are plenty of scenic byways that allow you to see much of the region in a single trip. Whatever method you choose, just remember that getting to your destination is half the fun.

BY AIR

Seven airports regularly serve the Greater Yellowstone region: They are located in Salt Lake City, Utah; Bozeman, West Yellowstone, and Billings, Montana; Jackson and Cody, Wyoming; and Idaho Falls, Idaho. There are no distinct advantages for any one of these, although the Jackson Hole airport is the most centrally located. However, a higher price may make up for this smaller airport.

Either way you will most likely rent a car to drive around the region, and all are worthy options for starting and ending your trip. If you prefer, the proximity of these airports allows for a nice change of pace—you can easily fly into one and out of another. There are also regional airports in Butte, Helena, and Missoula, Montana; and in Pocatello, Idaho.

GALLATIN FIELD AIRPORT
850 Gallatin Field Rd., Belgrade, MT
(406) 388-8321
www.bozemanairport.com
Gallatin Field is Bozeman's airport, even though it is located 8 miles west of the city in the small town of Belgrade. The beautiful airport is a great representation of the Montana post-and-beam architectural style and has a friendly feel. Its small size makes getting in and getting out easy, and Delta, United, Horizon, Frontier, and Allegiant, all serve Gallatin Field. Rental cars are available in the terminal from Alamo (406-388-6694), Avis (406-388-4091), Budget (406-388-4091), Enterprise (406-388-7420), Hertz (406-388-6939), and National (406-388-6694). Karst Stage (800-287-4759) offers ground transportation from the airport, and you can get a taxi by calling All Valley Cab (406-388-9999). The airport was significantly expanded in 2010.

To get to Bozeman, make a left out of the airport onto Frontage Road. Stay on this road for about 7 miles; it will take you right into the city. The easiest way to get to Yellowstone from the airport is to make a right out of the airport exit; then turn left onto Jackrabbit Lane. This road will turn into US 191 and take you right to Big Sky and West Yellowstone and the west entrance of the park. Well-marked signs at the airport's exit will point you right toward the park or Bozeman.

IDAHO FALLS REGIONAL AIRPORT/ FANNING FIELD
2140 Skyline Dr., Idaho Falls, ID
(208) 529-1221
This airport serves Allegiant, United, and Delta airlines. Most flights go through Denver, Salt Lake City, and Boise before touching down in Idaho Falls. You can rent cars in

the terminal from Avis (208-522-4245), Budget (208-522-8800), Hertz (208-529-3101), or National (208-522-5276). Mountain States Express (800-652-9510) can take you from the airport to Jackson Hole for $35.

JACKSON HOLE INTERNATIONAL AIRPORT
Jackson, WY
(307) 733-7682
www.jacksonholeairport.com
This small airport with a spectacular backdrop is located northeast of the town, within the boundaries of Grand Teton National Park. It is serviced by American, United/United Express, Delta, and SkyWest airlines. Daily buses run to and from the Jackson Hole airport via Idaho Falls and Salt Lake City. Schedules change with each season, but you can check times and dates by calling (800) 652-9510. Alltrans (800-443-6133) also has daily shuttles to Jackson, Grand Targhee, and other areas around Yellowstone.

Rental cars from Alamo (307-733-0671), Avis (307-733-3422), Hertz (307-733-2272), and National (307-733-0671) are available at the airport. Dollar (307-733-2206) and Thrifty (307-739-9300) are located in downtown Jackson but offer free airport pickups. When you exit the airport, heading north will lead you to Moose Junction, at which point you can choose your route through the park. Heading south on US 191 out of the airport will take you right into the center of Jackson.

LOGAN INTERNATIONAL AIRPORT
1901 Terminal Circle, Billings, MT
(406) 247-8609
www.flybillings.com
Located about 130 miles from the northeast entrance to Yellowstone National Park, Billings is Montana's largest city, with about

100,000 residents. Flying into Logan is kind of a hair-raising experience, as it is perched above the city on the Rimrocks, a shelflike rock band that drops off precipitously in several spots. Montana's largest airport services more than 300,000 passengers a year on Horizon, Delta, Frontier, Northwest, Allegiant, and United airlines. Great Lakes Aviation flies to several smaller Montana cities. Car rentals from Avis (406-252-8007), Budget (406-259-4168), Hertz (406-248-9151), and National (406-252-8700) are available at the airport. You can also call City Cab at (406) 252-8700 or Yellow Cab at (406) 245-3033.

There are a few options to get to Yellowstone National Park from Billings. To get to the northeast entrance of the park at Cooke City, head west out of Billings on I-90 and turn south on US 212. This will take you through Red Lodge and over beautiful Beartooth Pass, topping out at around 11,000 feet, before descending toward Cooke City and the park. Allow about four hours if you choose this route. You can also continue west on I-90 to Livingston, Montana, about 120 miles from Billings. At Livingston, head south on US 89 toward Gardiner and the north entrance to the park. This route shortens the driving time considerably, and in winter it's the only option, since Beartooth Pass is closed from mid-Oct through the end of May. Call the Montana road report at (800) 226-7623 even during summer, as inclement weather can close roads.

i If you're flying in from another country or the other end of the United States, try the Salt Lake City International Airport. Flights and car rentals may be significantly cheaper, and Yellowstone Country is only a few hours away by car.

SALT LAKE CITY INTERNATIONAL AIRPORT
776 North Terminal Dr., Salt Lake City, UT
(801) 575-2400
www.slcairport.com
This airport, the largest in the Yellowstone region, handles more than 22 million passengers per year and serves nine major airlines: American, Continental, Delta, Frontier, JetBlue, SkyWest, Southwest, United, and US Airways. Rental cars from Advantage, Alamo, Avis, Budget, Dollar, Enterprise, Fox, Hertz, National, and Thrifty are available at the airport, and calling the number above can connect you with all of these.

There are several shuttle options to choose from if you are not renting a car. The Salt Lake airport (801-575-2400) offers numerous shuttles into eastern Idaho towns. The Salt Lake Express (800-356-9796) has up to a dozen shuttles a day going to various towns in Utah, Idaho, and Wyoming. Recently the company updated their fleet by adding brand-new Mercedes vans. Mountain States Express (800-652-9510) offers shuttles from the Salt Lake airport to Jackson Hole for about $70 one-way.

If you're renting a car at the airport and driving to Jackson, the quickest way is I-15 north out of Salt Lake City to Idaho Falls; then US 26 right into Jackson. In good weather this should take about five hours. In summer, exiting I-15 at Brigham City to US 89 north will take you on a longer, more scenic route. Take US 89 north to Montpelier; then take US 30, also known as the Bear Lake–Caribou Scenic Byway, to Soda Springs, Idaho; then take ID 34 (the Pioneer Historic Byway) to Freedom, Wyoming; then north to Alpine and on to Jackson via US 26. This route is not recommended in winter, but in summer it is well worth the extra time. The gorgeous road takes you through the northern tip of the Wasatch National Forest, past Bear Lake and Mead Peak (10,541 feet), and along the Salt River to Palisades Reservoir. Make sure to call the Wyoming (307-772-0824) and Idaho (888-IDA-ROAD) road reports for up-to-date information on conditions and closures.

i Don't rely on your cell phone in the Greater Yellowstone area. Although service is continually getting better, the high mountains and narrow canyons often block signals, and antenna towers can be few and far between.

YELLOWSTONE AIRPORT
1515 Gallatin Rd., West Yellowstone, MT
(406) 646-7351, (800) 453-9417
SkyWest provides daily scheduled air service to West Yellowstone from June through Sept, and you'll find rental cars available from Avis (406-646-7635) and Budget (406-646-7882). Although open only during summer, this high-elevation airport (6,642 feet) gets good business from its three daily SkyWest flights and from private pilots.

YELLOWSTONE REGIONAL AIRPORT
3001 Duggleby Dr., Cody, WY
(307) 587-5096
www.flyyra.com
Cody's airport is located just a few minutes from downtown, approximately 52 miles from the east entrance to Yellowstone. It is serviced year-round by Delta and United. Rental cars from Budget, Hertz, and Thrifty are available in the terminal. The east entrance to Yellowstone National Park is reached by taking US 20 west from Cody.

BY TRAIN
You won't find any direct service to the gateway towns, but **Amtrak** does offer service to Salt Lake City, Utah; Laramie, Wyoming; and Idaho Falls and Pocatello, Idaho. Depending on the route, connecting services may be provided by train, motorcoach, van, or taxi. Call Amtrak at (800) USA-RAIL.

BY BUS & SHUTTLE

ALLTRANS, INC.
P.O. Box 96, Jackson, WY 83001
(307) 733-3135, (800) 443-6133
www.jacksonholealltrans.com
Alltrans offers airport shuttles, taxis, and charters, as well as single-day and multiday tours of the Grand Teton area. Alltrans meets every flight at the airport and also offers shuttle service to the Grand Targhee ski area.

BUFFALO BUS TOURING CO.
429 Yellowstone St.,
West Yellowstone, MT
(406) 646-9564, (800) 426-7669
www.yellowstonevacations.com
Buffalo Bus has daily, narrated sightseeing tours of Yellowstone Park and offers free pickup at motels and campgrounds around West Yellowstone. This is also the home of Big Sky car rentals.

GREYHOUND LINES
(800) 229-9424
www.greyhound.com
The closest Greyhound bus stops are in Wyoming at Powell and Cody, near the east entrance of Yellowstone. In Montana, Greyhound serves Billings, West Yellowstone, Livingston, and Bozeman, and in Idaho at Island Park, Idaho Falls, Pocatello, and Ashton.

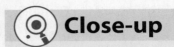 **Close-up**

The Beartooth Highway

Few roads in the country rival the majestic beauty of the **Beartooth Highway**, which runs from Red Lodge to Cooke City, Montana. The highway opened in 1936, and it remains an engineering marvel. Topping out at a dizzying 10,946 feet, the highway winds its way through high-alpine country with stunning views in every direction.

To reach the highway, drive south of the small community of Red Lodge on US 212 or east from the northeast entrance to Yellowstone Park. Red Lodge's downtown shops, restaurants, and attractions aren't this western town's only draw. It is also home to Red Lodge Mountain ski resort, one of the state's major ski areas, and numerous bed-and-breakfasts and other lodging options (see the Red Lodge chapter in this book).

From Red Lodge, nestled in the Beartooth Range at around 5,500 feet, the high-way begins to climb with a series of sharp switchbacks. There are numerous turnouts that provide panoramic views and spots for larger vehicles to pull over and let others pass. Driving on this road is slow going, but for good reason. The hair-raising road drops off steeply in several spots.

For campers, Ratine and Sheridan campgrounds just south of Red Lodge offer numerous sites along Rock Creek, one of the major drainages originating from the large cirque to the south. Here you'll see the charred remains of the 2000 Willie Fire, named for country singer Willie Nelson, who happened to be performing in Red Lodge the day the fire broke out.

As the highway continues to rise, you'll cross into Wyoming and eventually come back into Montana. At the first border, stop your vehicle where you can to get a great view of the alpine sage fields and the Bear's Tooth, a pointed jutting rock that is a landmark on the southwestern horizon. Granite Peak, Montana's highest at 12,799 feet, is also in the distance, and dozens of lakes and snowfields dot the horizon.

You'll also pass the site of the Red Lodge International Ski Race Camp and the Beartooth Freeride Camp, a permanent snowfield used for summer training. The top of the pass is also popular for backcountry skiing and snowboarding, as many diehards flock to the Rock Creek and Gardiner Headwalls when the highway is open. Most likely there will be patches of snow at the top into late summer; you can watch expert diehards cruising down the slopes.

Cresting the top of the pass, you'll see far into the mountains of Wyoming and Yellowstone National Park. The Top of the World store offers lodging, gas, food, and other services, and numerous opportunities for hiking exist. The Beartooth Loop National Recreation Trail, Beartooth Butte, and Beartooth Falls are all worth explor-ing. Campgrounds on this side of the pass include Island Lake, Crazy Creek, and Fox Creek. The highway descends to follow the Clark's Fork of the Yellowstone River, past the burned areas of the devastating 1988 fires, through the old mining town of Cooke City, and terminates at the northeast entrance of Yellowstone National Park. Of course, you can also drive the road in the opposite direction described here.

The weather can change instantly, and snow can close the road even in summer. Typically the road is open Memorial Day through the middle of Oct. Call the Montana road report at (800) 226-7623 or the Wyoming report at (888) 996-7623.

KARST STAGE

511 North Wallace Ave., Bozeman, MT
(406) 388-2293, (800) 287-4759
www.karststage.com

This charter motorcoach company offers year-round service to West Yellowstone, Big Sky, and Mammoth Hot Springs from the Bozeman airport and the surrounding area. In winter Karst runs an early-morning shuttle between West Yellowstone and Big Sky. Karst has two locations, one in downtown Bozeman (above) and one at the airport.

SKYLINE BUS

P.O. Box 160099, Big Sky, MT 59716
(406) 995-6287
www.skylinebus.com

Skyline is a free bus service that provides a link between Bozeman and Big Sky. Schedules depend on the season. Skyline also has routes between Big Sky's Canyon, Meadow, and Mountain Villages.

SOUTHERN TETON AREA RAPID TRANSIT (START)

P.O. Box 1687, Jackson, WY 83001
(307) 733-4521
www.startbus.com

The START bus is a public bus service offering year-round transportation around Jackson and to and from Teton Village, where the ski area is located, as well as the Teton Valley in Idaho and the Star Valley in Wyoming. Fares are free for in-town service and $3 for the trip to Teton Village, with children age eight and younger riding free with an accompanying adult. The bus has ski racks in winter and bike racks in summer. You can also find discount booklets available at most motels.

SNOWCOACHES

XANTERRA PARKS AND RESORTS

P.O. Box 165, Yellowstone National Park, WY 82190
(307) 344-7311
www.travelyellowstone.com

This company offers daily snowcoach and snowvan tours to Old Faithful from Mammoth, West Yellowstone, and the south entrance, as well as trips from Mammoth and Old Faithful to Canyon. Prices run about $90 round-trip.

i If you're renting a car in the winter, you may want to consider a four-wheel-drive vehicle. Winter roads around the region can get nasty in a hurry, and many of the region's out-of-the-way places require travel on primitive roads. Also, don't wait until your gas tank is near empty to fill up. Smaller towns have limited services and are often spaced far apart.

YELLOWSTONE ALPEN GUIDES

555 Yellowstone St.,
West Yellowstone, MT
(406) 646-9591, (800) 858-3502
www.yellowstoneguides.com

Yellowstone Alpen Guides offers guided tours daily from West Yellowstone to Old Faithful or the Grand Canyon of the Yellowstone on 10-passenger heated, traditional snowcoaches. The tours make many stops along the way, including opportunities for viewing geysers, paint pots, and wildlife. The adventurous can bring along cross-country skis and take a few side trips. Biscuit Basin is an option on the Old Faithful tour that allows members of your group to ski the easy 2.5 miles along the Firehole River through the Upper Geyser Basin right to Old Faithful while the rest of your group continues by snowcoach.

HISTORY

A land of contradictions, a spectacular pageant, a world incomprehensible ... a wonderful gift to men from a benign God—all this and more.

—Olin Wheeler, 1914

Yellowstone National Park has been dubbed "America's best idea," "the great American experiment," and "Wonderland." Because it is all of these things, it continues to fascinate, unite, and sustain millions of people today, as it has for centuries. Those of us who live in and love the Greater Yellowstone Area—that vast stretch of land ringed by blurry borders within Idaho, Montana, and Wyoming—are continually pulled by the paradox of Yellowstone Park as a place to be preserved and protected, yet promoted.

Long before the idea of a national park existed, the Yellowstone region was revered by Native Americans. This land was essential for hunting and gathering and splendid enough to inspire spiritual practices. They considered Yellowstone a sacred gift.

Likewise, when early explorers and, later, white settlers came to the area, Yellowstone left them awed. Its beauty and abundance were too incredible to be consumed by industry or development; we knew this even before understanding its magnitude. This undeniable truth eventually led to the creation of Yellowstone National Park in 1872 and subsequently brought hordes of other people who wanted to experience the wilderness.

In that way Yellowstone National Park shaped its corner of the West, becoming a hub for tall tales of the frontier, for industry, and for population. At a time when America was still creating itself, the eerie geysers, impossibly tall mountains, and sheer vastness of this region gave our country identity—the opportunity to say, "There is no place like this anywhere else on the planet." And this is true. In Yellowstone we found the undiscovered and embraced its wildness as a place to live and cultivate new communities, new traditions, and new ideals. From Yellowstone our country gained its most long-standing legends: the explorer, the cowboy, and the rugged individualist.

OVERVIEW

Two hundred years have passed since the first white travelers discovered the region, and people continue to come here to gawk, study, commune with nature, and capitalize on the awesome treasures Yellowstone holds.

Our methods may be different in modern times, but in a way the sentiment is much the same as early inhabitants who revered and utilized the riches of this land. At the heart of Yellowstone's influence is its power to inspire a sense of place.

Today's Greater Yellowstone Area encompasses roughly 18 million acres of land. With Yellowstone and Grand Teton National Parks at its core, the area includes seven national forests and three national wildlife refuges, plus thousands of acres of private lands.

Because this region is so huge, diverse, and complex, in this chapter we'll highlight how Yellowstone's history relates to the region and its individual communities.

EARLY RESIDENTS

Today 25 different American Indian tribes incorporate Yellowstone into their tribal history or culture. With this, the area surrounding what is now known as Yellowstone National Park could have been called "the land of many tribes." The Sioux, Bannock, Shoshone, Crow, Blackfoot, Kiowa, Nez Perce, Flathead, and Assiniboine nations valued the land of "Yellow Stone" or "Smoke from the Ground" for its abundant hunting grounds inhabited by bison, bighorn sheep, and elk, among other animals. The area's hot springs were used for spiritual rituals, and several tribal deities resided in some of the mountains of Yellowstone Country—the Absarokas, the Gallatins, and the Tetons.

Although many tribes made annual hunting and foraging forays to the region, no single group claimed exclusive territorial rights to the area. Several tribal territories did overlap with Yellowstone's boundaries, such as the Crow to the east near Billings, Montana, and present-day Cody, Wyoming, and the Blackfoot to the west near Three Forks, Montana. But because of the harsh winters and rugged terrain, this mountainous region was considered uninhabitable.

Historically, the Sheepeaters (a band of the Shoshone) were the only known year-round residents here. Archaeologists speculate that the Sheepeaters may have migrated from the Great Basin to the intermountain area of Montana and Wyoming as early as AD 1200. Reports from the earliest Euro-American explorers indicate that the Sheepeaters hunted bighorn sheep and were well known for the high-quality bows they made from the sheep's horns. Additionally, the historic shelters called "wickiups" found throughout Yellowstone were undoubtedly made by the Sheepeaters.

Although early American explorers claim to have discovered the "unknown wilderness," it was more accurately American Indian homes, gardens, and hunting territory.

Even the name "Yellowstone" is derived from American Indians, according to historian Aubrey Haines. The Minnetaree Indian expression *Mi tsi a-da-zi* translated is "Rock Yellow" or "Stone Yellow" and is thought to refer to the yellowish sandstone bluffs that border the Yellowstone River near present-day Billings.

OPENING THE WESTERN FRONTIER

Both the French and the Spanish had interests in the land now considered Greater Yellowstone. Early Euro-American explorers reported a land of abundant wildlife and vast natural resources. Although most of the area was unexplored, there was no doubt the land was valuable.

In the end it was President Thomas Jefferson who claimed this region as American soil when he signed the Louisiana Purchase in 1803. The United States bought the rights to 828,000 square miles of uncharted land west of the Mississippi River from France for $15 million. Jefferson had big plans to develop a trade route from St. Louis,

Missouri, to the Pacific and to further American power through land ownership. Critics of Jefferson saw the Louisiana Purchase as a waste. But the visionary president knew that the acquisition would change the course of American history, further cultivating the image of democracy with the fact that there was enough land for every man.

By 1804 Jefferson had enlisted Meriwether Lewis and William Clark to lead the Corps of Discovery into this newly acquired territory. The expedition's primary goal was to locate a waterway that could be used as a northwest passage to transport goods across the continent. (At the time the only way to ship commodities was by way of Cape Horn.) Lewis and Clark were also sent to make contact with American Indian peoples and to survey this vast, new property. Their travels crossed much of what would later become the states of Idaho and Montana.

Historically, the Lewis and Clark Expedition left an indelible mark upon the development of the West, but technically it was considered unsuccessful because they were unable to locate a viable trade route to the Pacific. What Lewis and Clark did do is plant the seed of opportunity on the western frontier. They reported a wealth of furs and timber stores for potential development.

Ironically, the Corps of Discovery's efforts skirted around today's Yellowstone, bringing them within 50 miles of Mammoth Hot Springs. It was actually John Colter, an original member of the Lewis and Clark Expedition, who discovered the awesome geysers and hot springs of the region in 1807. Colter had joined a hunting party, hoping to establish a fur-trading relationship with area Indians. He spent three years hunting and trapping, and his travels took him on an epic 500-mile trip from the Bighorn River, along the Shoshone River near present-day Cody into Jackson Hole. From there he traversed Teton Pass and came into Idaho's Teton Basin until he apparently headed on to the Yellowstone Plateau through Cooke City and back into the Bighorn Basin. Finally in 1810 Colter returned to St. Louis, Missouri, with tales of great steaming valleys, geysers that shot hundreds of feet out of the earth, and more beaver than any one man could trap.

Despite the fact that Colter's tales of a steaming, bubbling, boiling land were met with disbelief, people listened intently to the confirmation of abundant trading and trapping opportunities. A new economic boom began in America: the mountain man era of fur trading. If St. Louis was the gateway to the West, then Yellowstone was its heartland.

From the 1820s through the 1930s, demands for fashionable beaver-skin hats fostered the fur-trading industry. Most notably, the Rocky Mountain Fur Company and the Hudson Bay Trading Company dominated in Idaho, Wyoming, and Montana. Highly competitive Canadian, American, and English fur-trading companies vied for beaver pelts, which were worth as much as $6 apiece. Some trappers even vowed to trap areas into "deserts" before allowing anyone to infringe on their territory.

These rugged opportunists etched out their own culture in the wilderness. They endured hardships of the climate, fought unfriendly Indians, and lived most of the year in solitude until rendezvous. Rather than establishing formal trading posts, mountain men gathered annually at designated sites such as Red Lodge, Montana, or Jackson Hole, where they would sell their furs and trade for supplies. Rendezvous was also a social event, where they drank, caroused, gambled, swapped stories, and feasted.

i In August 1877 the Nez Perce's Chief Joseph led 800 men, women, and children and 2,000 horses through Yellowstone National Park in a desperate attempt to reach Canada. At the end of his 1,500-mile flight, which included 18 engagements and 4 major battles, Chief Joseph made his famous speech: "Hear me, my chiefs! I am tired. My heart is sick and sad. From where the sun now stands I will fight no more, forever." He was only 40 miles from the Canadian border.

With the influence of mountain men, the door of this untouched frontier was open. Such legendary names as Jedediah Smith, Jim Bridger, Don MacKenzie, Nathaniel Wyeth, David Jackson, William Sublette, and Maj. William Ashley still dot the landscape of the Northern Rockies in the form of towns, mountain ranges, and other usages. These men paved the way for many of the routes that would later be used in the settlement of the western frontier. About the time the beavers were disappearing in the 1840s, mountain men traded in their traps for positions as guides to the steady stream of pilgrims traveling to California in search of gold and rich farming land. Famous overland passages such as the Oregon Trail brought a flood of more than 500,000 settlers in what became the greatest overland migration this country has ever known.

MINERS & SETTLERS

From the coast of California to the high hills of Idaho, the cries of "Gold! Gold! Gold!" resounded. Throngs of fortune seekers journeyed through the Yellowstone region, first to California and Oregon in 1848 and gradually into the interiors of Montana, Wyoming, and Idaho. Here and there prospectors hit pay dirt outside the present-day park. In 1863 gold was found—lots of it—to the north in Virginia City, Montana. The rush continued in this region until 1870, when a group of miners staked their claims on a gold strike in Cooke City, Montana.

Recklessly, miners chipped at the frontier, settling in camps that later became official towns. Gold strikes became scarce as supplies were depleted, and people found other ways to eke out a living. Many settlers realized the futility of gold mining and made their living instead by supplying goods to miners. A few others raised cattle, while still others opened hotels, saloons, and stores.

It was providence that shielded the heart of Yellowstone Country from gold discoveries. Protected by high, unpassable mountain ranges, it remained relatively unexplored and uninhabited until the late 1860s. But accounts of the area's other treasures trickled back to Washington, D.C.

EXPLORING YELLOWSTONE

It is a testimonial to Yellowstone's spectacular wonders that three "discovery" expeditions were required before the American public would believe such a place existed. Even journalists refused to print stories of ghostly geysers and steaming valleys for fear of being dubbed liars. In the end, exploring parties of 1869, 1870, and 1871 each played an integral role in revealing Yellowstone to the world.

Persistent rumors of unfathomable curiosities led three prospectors from Diamond City in Montana Territory (near present-day Helena) into the wilds of Yellowstone. In September 1869 these men, known as the Folsom-Cook-Peterson Expedition, left to explore the area near the headwaters of the Yellowstone River. They spent 36 days exploring and mapping the region and were astounded by what they saw. When they stumbled upon the Grand Canyon of the Yellowstone, Charles Cook wrote, "It seemed to me that it was five minutes before anyone spoke." Upon their return they wrote a magazine article about their experiences and suggested the area be preserved for its natural wonders.

By the next year excitement over Yellowstone was feverish. The Washburn-Langford-Doane Expedition left Bozeman in August 1870 to further investigate the region. This group spent a month exploring the present park, naming many of its features, including Old Faithful Geyser. Following the expedition's return, Nathaniel P. Langford (an employee of the Northern Pacific Railroad, which would play a prominent role in advertising the future park) traveled to the East Coast to promote their "discovery." Dr. Ferdinand Hayden, then head of what would become the US Geological Survey, was in one of the Washington, D.C., audiences. Intrigued by Langford's story, Hayden petitioned Congress for a $40,000 grant to outfit a government party to explore Yellowstone Country.

The Hayden Expedition spent many months in Yellowstone during the summer of 1871 and confirmed much of what Washburn's party had found. The group of about 30 men included artist Thomas Moran and photographer William H. Jackson. Their visual images were the proof needed to confirm Yellowstone's existence. It was their work that tipped the scales in favor of the world's first national park in the eyes of Congress . . .

CREATING A NEW IDEAL

If there were any pure intentions in the creation of Yellowstone National Park, they stem from the sheer awe felt by explorers when they first experienced the geothermal features of the area. Amidst the smell of sulfur, the eerie spouting, steaming earth seemed otherworldly and sparked wonder in the men who first laid eyes upon it. And although no one person can be credited for creating Yellowstone, it was Ferdinand Hayden, following his 1871 expedition, who first approached Congress with the idea of setting aside this chunk of land.

At the time there was substantial debate within Washington about what to do with the land they considered "worthless" because its climate was too harsh to be utilized for farming or ranching. They considered exploiting it for timber and mining but did not yet have a way to access the expanse of property or to affordably transport their goods. The suggestion of a national park seemed preposterous and wasteful in an era where conservation wasn't practiced.

The first hurdle Hayden had to clear was making people believe in the astounding "wonders and curiosities" that made the proposed two million acres of land worthy of preservation. Since photographer William Jackson and artist Thomas Moran had accompanied the expedition, their works were presented to Congress. Historians attribute the artful representations of Moran's paintings as a key factor that clinched the national park deal.

The next obstacle was funding for this proposed park. For this, Hayden had help. Following the creation of Yellowstone, the railroad barons of the Northern Pacific hoped to lay tracks into Yellowstone Country, bringing curious tourists to see the sights of this wild place. The collective thinking of park supporters at the time was that Yellowstone would support itself through fees paid by concessionaires, who would build hotels, and by tourists, who would pay entrance fees. With the agreement that Yellowstone National Park would not require federal funding, Congress passed the bill.

On March 1, 1872, President Ulysses S. Grant signed the National Park Act and created a new ideal for American wilderness.

MAKING TRACKS

While the depths of America's wild lands were being explored, railroad companies were frenetically racing to lay tracks across it. The Union Pacific Railroad was first, completing its transcontinental railroad in 1869. Not to be outdone, investors in the Northern Pacific Railroad turned their interests toward discoveries in Yellowstone, hoping to be the first to access it.

The railroad's influence reaches back to the actual exploration of Yellowstone Country, beginning with Nathaniel Langford's connection to the Northern Pacific Railroad when he accompanied the Washburn Expedition. In fact it was partially the lobbying of railroad supporters such as Minnesota governor William Marshall (Langford's brother-in-law) and Judge William Darrah Kelley that helped push the National Park Act through Congress in 1872. It was no coincidence that only the year before, the federal government had issued a series of railroad land grants on which to continue the newly established transcontinental rail system to encourage western settlement. What railroad barons saw in Yellowstone was a hugely profitable tourist destination. The idea was for the Northern Pacific (other smaller lines had similar interests) to haul in visitors along tracks leading right to attractions such as Old Faithful and the Grand Canyon of the Yellowstone.

Although advances toward developing Yellowstone as a "summer resort" came to a standstill for a decade due to Northern Pacific's financial difficulties, by 1882 the idea of building a railroad to service attractions inside Yellowstone's boundaries was refueled. The best evidence of this was the construction of a branch line from Livingston, Montana, to Cinnabar, just 3 miles from the national park's Gardiner entrance. This multimillion-dollar investment was made with the intention of continuing the tracks through the actual park. But it would be a long time before the railroad would even come close to attaining its goal.

Throughout the next decade railroad monopolists and Yellowstone supporters within Congress debated over the railroad's intent to develop Yellowstone National Park. The first stone of opposition to railroad development within the boundaries of Yellowstone Park was thrown by Gen. P. H. Sheridan in 1882. After a summer of vacationing in Yellowstone, Sheridan succeeded in convincing the secretary of the interior to forbid the building of any railroad within the park. This began the "Yellowstone war," as historian Aubrey Haines called it in his book *The Yellowstone Story*.

Despite clever and aggressive efforts by railroad lobbyists who approached the Yellowstone railway project from every angle, including the attempt to access mining claims along Yellowstone's northern border, near Cooke City, they were consistently defeated in Congress. One of Yellowstone National Park's biggest supporters was Sen. George Vest, who said, "allowing any railroad to enter Yellowstone would end in the destruction of the Park." While the Northern Pacific lost to park supporters, it was still integral in the promotion and success of Yellowstone National Park.

The park branch line eventually extended to Yellowstone's northern entrance in 1903 and was marked by President Teddy Roosevelt's dedication of the Roosevelt Arch for the "benefit and enjoyment of the people." For the next three decades, railroad interests tapped into every aspect of Yellowstone, from its management practices, stage transportation, and lodging to national advertising campaigns. The Burlington Northern, Northern Pacific, Oregon Short Line, and later the Chicago Milwaukee and St. Paul railroads all invested money in regional depots. Both the Sacajawea Inn in Three Forks, Montana, and the Gallatin Gateway Inn outside Bozeman are testaments to the railroad marketing of Yellowstone. Trains made it possible for hundreds of wealthy travelers to experience "Wonderland" in style. After traveling thousands of miles, passengers disembarked and would often stay overnight in a railroad luxury hotel before being carted off by stage for the "grand tour" of Yellowstone's wonders. Explorations of the park thrived until automobile travel finally replaced trains after World War II.

As it turned out, railroad spur lines originally built to access coal-mining areas later became the major entrances to Yellowstone National Park. Without the railroads there would be no Cody, Wyoming, or Livingston, Red Lodge, West Yellowstone, or Bozeman, Montana. Public access to the park and to the western frontier eventually solidified the railroad's success.

THE GRAND TOUR

While debates over access to Yellowstone raged in Washington, the park was left to its wildness. Without real roadways or formal tour guides, the park was mainly accessible by horseback or on foot. In fact, the park's first superintendent, Nathaniel Langford, refused to issue leases to a number of entrepreneurs who proposed building hotels because there were no roads to access them. (Historians claim he denied other concessionaire ventures because he was in cahoots with the Northern Pacific Railroad.)

By the turn of the 20th century, railroad travel opened the gates of Yellowstone National Park to throngs of wealthy tourists. They traveled long distances from the East and West Coasts first to the Northern Pacific Railroad's outpost in Cinnabar, Montana. Those early tourists purchased a five- or six-day travel package from the railroad and were shuttled along the Grand Loop Road.

From Cinnabar visitors embarked on a rough and dusty stagecoach ride to Gardiner's north entrance into the park and on to Mammoth Hot Springs. The National Hotel at Mammoth was the first to offer luxurious accommodations in the park. It served as home base for the "grand tour of Wonderland." After a night's stay at Mammoth and a tour of the terraces, folks were herded into 11-person coaches, assigned a driver, and sent on their way. Stagecoach drivers were barraged with questions from the tourists, and though most did right by their guests, others spun yarns about the wonders of the park just for fun. But these guides brought tourists to the edge of the Grand Canyon of the Yellowstone and to the foot of the major geyser basins throughout Yellowstone for six glorious days before returning to Mammoth and then the train terminal at Cinnabar.

Until 1891, when the modern Fountain Hotel was built in the Upper Geyser Basin, travelers were subjected to the simplest of rustic accommodations. The lavish grand hotels built at Lake Yellowstone and Canyon replaced the rustic Firehole Hotel, where the rooms held two beds and had canvas walls. Even that was an improvement over other accommodations in which guests slept shoulder to shoulder on plank floors in hotels with broken windows.

Because these early tourists were accustomed to luxury, concessionaires knew the rustic accommodations wouldn't be accepted for long. With the opening of the Fountain Hotel—with its steam heat, electric lights, and hot baths—a new precedent was set for lodging within Yellowstone. All the new hotels were equipped with formal dining areas and grand rooms for lounging, reading, and socializing. The majestic Old Faithful Inn opened in 1904 as the pinnacle of Yellowstone's hotels with its massive Douglas fir and native stone construction.

> **i** Yellowstone National Park is home to the world's greatest concentration of geothermal activity.

The grand tour of Wonderland continued this way for 30 years. As a result, the park remained largely an elitist vacation spot, because train travel was so expensive. But all that changed in 1915 when automobiles were first permitted to tour Wonderland independently.

TRAFFIC

In a sense, by making Yellowstone accessible to just about everyone in America, the automobile restored the democratic intentions upon which the park was founded. When the gates opened in 1915, more than 50,000 mostly middle-class Americans flooded Yellowstone National Park. Honking their horns, vehicles lined up 100-deep at the entrance gates. After that, visitation numbers climbed steadily for the next 15 years.

Unlike the upper-class railroad tourists who had packed trunks full of fine clothing to dress for dinner and dancing, these working-class people loaded up a gaggle of relatives into the Ford and headed for the park. Following a route from St. Paul to Bozeman mapped out by the Minnesota Automobile Association, the slow-moving cars inched along with washbasins, tents, pots and pans, chairs, bedding, and a couple of spare tires strapped on top. They followed a string of platter-sized orange signs marking the rough rural roads that would later become today's Interstates 90 and 94.

Inside the park, Model Ts blocked attractions and the sighting of a bear or bison from the road was enough to jam up traffic. Objections were raised (mostly from the park concessionaires, who were losing money) about the effects of automobile traffic within the park. Some said it would lead to the ruin of the whole place. It took only a year for the noisy automobiles to oust outdated stagecoaches and horse-drawn carriages; the three former transportation companies were outraged.

With the automobile came change and reorganization. In 1916 Stephen T. Mather, director of the newly formed National Park Service, streamlined concession operations when he designated the Yellowstone Park Transportation Company as sole provider of transportation. Frank M. Haynes, who owned several hotels and other businesses, was told to sell his operations and become the photographic concessionaire; and the Yellowstone Park Hotel Company merged with Wylie Permanent Camps to be the only hotelier in the park. Each was asked to contribute 4 percent of its gross profits to the National Park Service for the leases. The changes were not easily accepted, but in the long run concessionaires provided better service for the public.

ORDER IN THE WILDERNESS

Since Yellowstone was theoretically set aside for the benefit of the public good, it seemed natural that it would be governed by civilians. The secretary of the interior appointed civilian superintendents from 1872 until 1886. This new creation of the government came with no instructions or manual to maintain its pristine state, and early managers struggled to maintain order.

Because of his Washington connections, Nathaniel Langford became the park's first superintendent and held the post from 1872 to 1877. An absentee manager in this unpaid position, he made only three visits to Yellowstone and filed one report during his tenure. Otherwise, the park was unguarded, unregulated, and unmaintained. Yet it had been discovered, so it was at the mercy of squatters and vandals. Hunters brazenly poached elk by the thousands; would-be concessionaires camped at major attractions; tourists stuffed rocks, logs, and clothing into geysers and then poured soap into them to get them to blow; they skinny-dipped in hot springs and hauled home whole petrified trees as souvenirs.

Yellowstone's second superintendent, Philetus W. Norris, saw a monument that was underfunded and neglected. For his part, Norris reasoned with Congress, saying Yellowstone would forever falter if there were no roads leading to its attractions. He received enough money to map out the early portion of the Grand Loop Road. He served until 1882, when he was ousted for supporting a railroad through the park.

i Greater Yellowstone encompasses the intersection of three wild western states: Idaho, the most populous with more than 1.5 million people; Montana, with around 975,000; and Wyoming, the ninth-largest in the nation geographically, with only 530,000 residents.

By 1886 Yellowstone National Park had been branded with scandals. News of visitors victimized by stagecoach robberies, rampant poaching, shameless bootlegging, and destruction of geothermal formations reached Washington. Congress was so fed up that it refused to allocate funds for that year. This action in turn stirred vengefulness from park employees, who trashed public facilities and even started numerous forest fires.

Yellowstone had gone amok. There were grumblings within Congress that the national park idea was a failure and even talk of abolishing Yellowstone. The Department of the Interior pulled its trump card: It called in the US Cavalry.

When Capt. Moses Harris rode into Mammoth Hot Springs with his Troop M on August 20, 1886, he immediately relieved Superintendent Wear from his duties and restored order to Yellowstone. This began a 30-year era of military administration in Yellowstone. Although the enlisted men endured great public criticism, their presence restored the park's integrity and saved it from ruin.

By World War I the military was needed for other, more pressing national situations. That and the fact that the national park system had grown to 30 national parks and monuments throughout the country called for the creation of an agency to manage these special places. On August 25, 1916, Congress created the National Park Service, and two years later the cavalry left Yellowstone.

The Yellowstone Park left to the National Park Service was now a full-fledged business. Unlike the soldiers, whose job it was to prosecute poachers, bootleggers, and robbers, the rangers were there to manage people. They greeted cars at entrance gates; investigated accidents; patrolled popular areas on foot, on horseback, and on motorcycles; maintained public buildings; managed wildlife problems; administered first aid; and conducted interpretive talks about Yellowstone. From 1919 to 1929 visitation numbers jumped from about 62,000 to 260,000 people, and the 71 park rangers struggled to maintain order.

Into the 1930s and World War II, Yellowstone seriously suffered from the impacts of the Great Depression and wartime America. Visitor numbers were so low that concessionaires boarded up their facilities and left. Our first national park fell into severe disrepair. When tourists finally returned to Yellowstone in droves, no one was prepared. By 1948 more than one million people visited Yellowstone, tipping it into a new era of tourism.

Since its creation the National Park Service has persevered in its impossible task of balancing the preservation of Yellowstone with the needs and desires of visitors. Then, as now, NPS administrators work under the demands of tight federal budgets, changing politics, and ever-increasing visitation.

FROM GREAT IDEA TO GREATER YELLOWSTONE

Even as Yellowstone became more of the "pleasuring ground" it was set aside to be,

concern for the health of the park heightened. While tourists reveled in the natural curiosities of Yellowstone, they did little to preserve it. Campsites and attractions were littered with trash, observation areas were built to watch park rangers feed garbage to bears, and debris was tossed into mud pots or geysers. Gradually Yellowstone began to show signs of duress, and the National Park Service experimented with how to maintain the park's natural integrity.

i **The Yellowstone fires of 1988 remain the largest in the park's history. Burning from mid-June through Oct, the blaze ate up 1.4 million acres of Yellowstone. But more than 20 years after the legendary fires, scientists continue to study nature's regeneration and learn more about forest ecosystems.**

Ironically, because of Yellowstone's aesthetic and recreational appeal, gateway communities to the park have created an isolated wilderness troubled by problems of wildlife overpopulation (grizzly bears, wolves, elk, and bison), overgrazing (elk and bison), and predator conflicts with human pursuits (wolves versus cattle and sheep ranching). These conflicts have historically escalated and at times created a climate of resentment and polarization among recreationists, environmentalists, scientists, ranchers, developers, and politicians. Yet the lives affected most by these issues are Yellowstone's plants and animals. Because they know no boundaries and don't abide by state or federal laws, they are caught in the middle of human battles about public access, mining, ranching, noxious weeds, nonnative species infiltration, disease, and forest fires—to name a few.

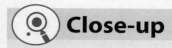 Close-up

From Tribe to Tribe

Bozeman, Montana's history is a short one. The town's beginnings reach back only to its founding in 1864. The Gallatin Valley's history, where Bozeman sits, however, is ancient. As historian Phyllis Smith wrote in her book *Bozeman and the Gallatin Valley: A History:*

"The first migration through the Gallatin Valley may have occurred more than 30,000 years ago after small groups of hunters from Asia tentatively crossed a 56-mile-long land bridge to this hemisphere, now underwater as the Bering Strait. As these early travelers tracked mastodon, caribou, mammoth, and giant bison with wide-spreading horns, they may have watched small horses and camels traveling in the opposite direction to Asia. They passed along grassy corridors through towering glaciers and filtered slowly down the eastern face of the Rockies along what is sometimes called the Old North Trail. They seldom went into the mountains to hunt because the remaining glaciers blocked their passage. They avoided the high plains as well because they felt vulnerable without forest cover."

This purported migration was a slow population process for North America. Hunting and gathering tribes moved methodically and at a pace that would accommodate a large group of women and children. Approximately 12,000 years ago, paleontologists believe that other small bands of hunters ventured to this continent after hearing legends about the plentiful game and abundance of clean water.

"We don't know who the people were that lived here thousands of years ago and even who they turned into isn't known," said Walter Fleming, professor for Native American Studies at Montana State University in Bozeman.

About 5,000 years ago the Gallatin Valley's weather patterns gradually changed. It became a barren high desert in a drought that lasted approximately 2,000 years. A people from the southwest, accustomed to such conditions, ventured into the region, wrote Smith. They trapped small animals and foraged for plants to survive that long dry period. Fleming claimed that it is difficult to know the cultural habits or lifestyle of these early people because any artifacts of their existence have long since decayed.

The most significant remains of a native people in this area date from about 4,000 years ago along the Madison River. The valley's climate had shifted again, presumably bringing it to a state much like today's. Traces of an early village remain in the form of about 100 circles of boulders lining the river and marking temporary lodges. Pieces of primitive tools and weapons were found in this area as well as points, chips, and frag-

---

As one of the last intact ecosystems, Yellowstone is an experiment not only of federal policy but also of nature. During its tenure the National Park Service has tested both boundaries, often learning from mistakes. NPS employees have stocked Yellowstone waters with exotic nonnative fish; fed bears for visitor entertainment; nearly brought on the extinction of bison and later bred them; implemented the "let-burn" forest-fire policy to the extreme that two-thirds of Yellowstone was charred in the fires of 1988; and exterminated the gray wolf and then in 1995 reintroduced it.

As early as 1882 Yellowstone was a place of conflict and controversy. Following a tour through Yellowstone with President Chester

ments of knives made mostly of basalt and occasionally obsidian or jasper. According to Smith, other early camps existed in the valley, the most notable in Kelly Canyon.

Additionally, the famous Madison Buffalo Jump is estimated to have been used by those same people who laid camp along the Madison River. This 30-foot cliff is located just 7 miles south of Logan. "For possibly 4,000 years or more, these early Gallatin Valley people utilized the steep cliffs generally associated with the high plains country to force grazing bison to run to their death over the drop," according to Fleming. More recently, dating from the 1500s, the cliffs were used by the Flathead, Crow, Blackfoot, and possibly other High Plains Indian tribes.

"This valley was an important crossroads for tribes heading into the plains to hunt buffalo," Fleming explained. "You really can't say this was one single tribe's territory because all tribes crossed through and fought in this area. Tribal lore refers to it as a common hunting ground, which implies some kind of mutual agreement that no single tribe could exert its control over it."

On the fringe of several tribal territories, such as the Crow and the Blackfoot, Fleming said, the Gallatin Valley became disputed territory in the 1850s with the advent of white settlement and railroad surveys. The first Fort Laramie Treaty was passed in 1851, promising the land to the Blackfoot, but new treaty signers reneged in 1855 and changed the Gallatin Valley to open territory. According to Smith, the three forks and the Gallatin Valley were named "common Indian hunting grounds for 99 years." This new treaty ultimately allowed wagon trains following overland routes such as the Bozeman Trail to cross directly through essential tribal hunting territory, despite Indian protests saying the traffic would alter their way of life entirely. This route, which crested at 5,500-foot Bozeman Pass, later became known as "the Bloody Bozeman," because of conflicts with Indian warriors. Ultimately, the trail was abandoned for less dangerous routes.

A new migration began in the 1860s and continued through the turn of the 20th century as trappers, traders, explorers, and prospectors opened up the western frontier. These new people brought customs and cultures that were different from those of early Gallatin Valley inhabitants. As the railroads solidified this region's change, existing tribes were pushed to different boundaries of the West. By the 1870s almost all Indians were placed on reservations. Wheat fields replaced rolling grassland and hunting grounds, cattle eventually replaced bison, and houses replaced tepees. The Gallatin Valley, like so many other parts of the West, became the single territory of white settlers.

Alan Arthur, Gen. Phil Sheridan suggested that the national park's boundaries should be doubled to protect wildlife. Even then it was evident that Yellowstone National Park's boundary lines were drawn when there was little knowledge of ecosystems or animal migration patterns. That lack of knowledge has resulted in an ongoing debate over park management and the ecological value of land bordering the park.

The Greater Yellowstone concept took root in 1917 when a 1,200-square-mile addition to the south of Yellowstone National Park was proposed. Congress nearly passed the bill, which would have included land from the Absaroka Range ridge to the

Buffalo Fork of the Snake River, then west, just south of Jackson, Leigh, and Jenny Lakes, including some National Forest Service land. But when the ranching community caught wind of it, they protested the move and urged the Wyoming Legislature to oppose the bill. The debate continued for a decade, tangling US courts with political twists and turns regarding grazing leases and paranoia over too much federal land control.

Finally someone tried a new approach. Sen. Gerald Nye proposed a bill not for the expansion of Yellowstone Park but for the creation of a whole new park: Grand Teton National Park. Echoing sentiments expressed by General Sheridan almost 40 years earlier, Nye outlined the new park boundaries around the dramatically beautiful Teton Mountains, which were too steep and high for livestock. Congress passed it with flying colors on February 26, 1929.

Encouraged by this, John D. Rockefeller Jr. also wanted to keep the whole area outside Jackson Hole protected from commercial development. He formed the Snake River Land Company and purchased 35,000 acres of land (worth $2 million) from area residents. He offered to donate the property to Grand Teton National Park but was thwarted by congressional and local opposition. Again the issue of national park expansion went to the courts.

A man accustomed to getting his way, Rockefeller wouldn't have it. In 1943 he told President Franklin Roosevelt that he would happily sell the land on the open market. Roosevelt was moved to action. He set aside the 221,000-acre Jackson Hole Monument by presidential decree.

Roosevelt's decision set fire to a new war that was battled out in congressional and legislative sessions for nearly another decade.

Congress passed a bill abolishing the decree, but Roosevelt vetoed it. Then the state of Wyoming sued the Grand Teton National Park superintendent—and lost. Finally Congress cut funding for the monument's maintenance. At last, in 1950 a compromise was reached. It included allowances for lifetime grazing leases, permanent family homes, and monetary compensation for displaced land owners. But that same year the Jackson Hole Monument and Grand Teton National Park lands were combined.

Consequently the founding of Grand Teton National Park stands as a historic victory for American wildlands. In addition, the creation of the National Forest Service in 1905 and the Wilderness Act of 1964 are hallmarks in our country's conservation history, which began with the Yellowstone story. When so much of the world is being urbanized, we can turn to the legacy of lands preserved for beauty and splendor.

BEYOND BORDERS

Side by side with economic growth, Yellowstone Park has fostered its own environmental movement. Rumblings of the controversial Greater Yellowstone Ecosystem concept cropped up in the 1970s. A biological study proved that the Yellowstone grizzly bear range extended over more than five million acres (only two million were contained within the park). The term implies that Yellowstone's health can only truly be sustained if it is managed like an ecosystem extending beyond its formal borders to maintain the long-term viability of its natural processes. The idea was heavily promoted by the Greater Yellowstone Coalition, a prominent conservation group based in Bozeman, Montana. The mention of Greater

Yellowstone Ecosystem was once considered fightin' words. With time, however, the concept of an interconnected ecosystem seemed logical and has attained a certain level of common acceptance. That acceptance, however, has been hard won and has brought Yellowstone Park to the brink of disaster more than once.

In 1990, for example, the Church Universal and Triumphant, a religious group headquartered near Gardiner, wanted to tap a geothermal feature on its land bordering the park. Concerned because thermal areas in the United States and other countries have been ruined by outside intrusion of connected systems, authorities studied the problem. They determined that tapping geothermal features outside the park could damage the geothermal features inside it. They denied the religious group access, and almost 10 years later the same parcel of land was purchased by the federal government to prevent the situation from occurring again.

Additionally in 1990 a proposed open-pit gold mine near Cooke City threatened to leak mining tailings into the Clarks Fork of the Yellowstone River and Soda Butte Creek and potentially further infringe wildlife habitat. The Noranda, Inc., mining company estimated a $600 million return in precious metal from the proposed site and promised high-paying jobs. Cooke City residents were divided, and debate over the issue raged until 1996. After flying over the New World Mining District bordering Yellowstone, President Bill Clinton cut a deal with the mining company. He traded $65 million worth of federal land for Noranda's mining rights.

These examples are neither the first nor last controversies spurred by Yellowstone National Park. As residents of the Greater Yellowstone, we struggle with the dilemma of how best to preserve our park. The realities of population, pollution, tourism, and industry repeatedly bring us to a threshold where we must ask ourselves, "How will we continue to reap the benefits of Yellowstone while preserving its wild amenities?" Some say the answer is to limit entry into Yellowstone National Park, others say it should be privatized to better fund its preservation, and still others say it's fine the way it is. Like the paradigm that exists inside park boundaries, outside we grapple with issues of loving this place to death.

GATEWAYS

Since its inception Yellowstone was intended to be the economic hub of the region, and in this sense it is a success. If Yellowstone had never been designated an attraction as the world's first national park, there would have been no long-term motivation for railroads to extend tracks out here, no reason to transport goods, and no reason to advertise the wonders of the area to the masses. Nineteenth-century buzz phrases like "Manifest Destiny" and "westward expansion" have been replaced with today's "diversified economy," but no matter what you call it, these are the bricks that built the gateway towns of the West. And Yellowstone National Park is the cornerstone of our greater community.

Indeed, it was economics that brought Yellowstone to our collective attention, although many of us don't like to think of it this way. Undeniably, without Yellowstone National Park it is difficult to say whether the communities along its borders would even exist today. The boom-and-bust economies of mining and logging fostered Cody, Wyoming; Cooke City, Montana; and Island Park, Idaho, to name a few, but it is the natural beauty of Yellowstone and its surrounding area that fosters long-term economic health. The forests, rivers, and wildlands encompassed by the national park ideal employ thousands of people in the region. Yellowstone intrinsically connects us as a benefactor and a commodity.

The towns that make up the Greater Yellowstone Area are divided by individual cultures, whether through ventures in agriculture, triumph in natural resource industries, endeavors in recreation or environmental protection, or forays into art. Yet there is a pervasive knowledge that no one industry can solely sustain a viable economy in this part of the West. Yellowstone's millions of visitors contribute to the financial fuel keeping these gateway towns alive, while the park's preservation guarantees a certain quality of life in our towns. You'll see that the entire region, consciously or not, is wholly bound and marvelously intertwined in the same story of beauty and natural wonders that have drawn people here for centuries.

YELLOWSTONE'S PAST IS OUR FUTURE

Surely our people do not understand even yet the rich heritage that is theirs. There can be nothing in the world more beautiful than the Yosemite, the groves of giant sequoias and redwoods, the Canyon of the Colorado, the Canyon of the Yellowstone, the three Tetons; and our people should see to it that they are preserved for their children forever, with their majestic beauty all unmarred.

—Theodore Roosevelt

Out of the national park experiment, the Greater Yellowstone Area emerged. Within our collective tristate community, we are both divided and connected by Yellowstone's wonders, yet the truth of Greater Yellowstone continues to grow. Finally we are realizing that this area is interconnected—towns and wilderness; waterways and valleys; grazing lands and conservation properties; animals and people; past and present. What we will do with this knowledge remains to be seen, but cooperative efforts between unlikely partners, such as mining companies and conservationists or developers and environmentalists, continue to emerge. Our communities are revamping city plans to include open space, wildlife migration corridors, and natural habitat. With the help of private conservation groups such as the Jackson Hole Land Alliance, the Montana Land Alliance, and the Nature Conservancy, we are preserving more valuable acreage for aesthetic and environmental qualities than ever before.

i For more details on the park's history, read *The Yellowstone Story* by Aubrey L. Haines.

The West continues to be the fastest-growing region in the United States. Some towns have seen their populations jump 50 percent in the past two decades, and with that growth come new issues. But most of us are here for the love of the land and lifestyle.

Because of the national parks and the natural beauty that surrounds us, we concern ourselves with what we will have to pass on to the coming generations. In Yellowstone there is a reverence for the actual spirit upon which our country was founded—the frontier of possibility that says anything can happen, if you believe in it.

OUR NATURAL WORLD

We are blessed here in Yellowstone Country with some of the most unspoiled, unparalleled, and beautiful land in the world. Many landscapes and features look the same to us as they did when the first settlers moved through the area in the early 1800s. Much of the same wildlife still roams the area, many of the same forests still stand, and many of the same trails crisscross the region.

Most people who call this area home are in touch with their surroundings. It isn't the same as living in the concrete jungle, where you occasionally have to look up to see blue sky. Here the vast landscape constantly encompasses you and it is omnipresent—a factor in every aspect of our life: recreation, economy, and politics.

The mountains are sure nice to look at and are reason enough to live here for most of us. But what's out there to someone who hasn't been here before? More than just trees, animals, and rocks, that's for sure.

THE LANDSCAPE

A constant theme in this book and our daily lives is contrast, and the landscape is no different. If need be, Yellowstone Country can be broken down into two divisions: **mountains** and **valleys.** You'll notice as you drive around that roads will travel across valleys, up mountains, and down again. Take, for example, the drive from Ennis to Livingston, Montana: You begin in the Madison Valley, where the Madison River cuts through the Tobacco Root Mountains and the Madison Range; from there you'll cross the latter and drop into the Gallatin Valley. Continuing east, up over Bozeman Pass and down into Livingston takes you through the upper end of the Gallatin Range. Once you're in Livingston, the Paradise Valley stretches between the Gallatin and Absaroka Ranges, and the cycle continues. You can be on flat land or up near the clouds, all in a matter of 80 miles. Isn't it beautiful?

Of course, there's water, too. Miles of blue-ribbon trout streams and loads of pristine alpine lakes ensure the region's popularity among outdoor lovers. The area's rivers—the Snake, Madison, Yellowstone, and more—and the mountains and valleys they run through are the result of a complex geologic history.

Most of the region's geologic features were formed by movement of the earth. Thirty to 80 million years ago, the area's mountains were created along a fault when two of the earth's plates collided, sending rock in all directions. The exception is the Tetons, which stretched skyward only two to three million years ago from massive earthquakes. The Tetons' granite peaks were exposed when the ground cracked, lifting the west side up and dropping the east side down nearly 24,000 feet. After millions of years of erosion, what's left are some of the oldest rocks on earth. In fact, a thin layer of rock on top of Grand Teton National

Wildlife Views

If you're staying in or around Big Sky, you should be able to see lots of wildlife. As you turn off of US 191 and head toward the ski resort, scan the rocky mountainside on the right side of the highway for bighorn sheep. You'll enter a large meadow just a little farther up the road where you can often spot elk, moose, and eagles. On the east side of US 191, just past Big Sky, elk roam the meadows surrounding the Gallatin River nearly every morning in winter, along with an occasional moose. If you don't have any luck with these spots, keep your eyes open while going up the chairlifts at Big Sky Resort. Bald eagles have been spotted soaring above the slopes.

Park's Mount Moran—12,605 feet above sea level—was once part of a layer that now lies buried nearly 5 miles below the valley floor.

i The large stands of aspen trees you'll see around the region are havens for wildlife. Look for woodpeckers, owls, and ruffed grouse hovering around branches of the white-barked trees, and keep an eye out for elk, moose, and deer foraging on plants and bark on the ground.

As the earth's giant masses of molten rock continued to thrust upward, the peaks you see today stretched up through the surface to create this dramatic landscape. Some of these peaks were buried under miles of thick ice during an era of cold climates and massive snowfall. Eventually these snow accumulations turned into glaciers, massive rivers of ice that gouged and carved out the present-day valleys. The result of all of this activity is broad river basins flanked by mountains—just the type of scenery our region is known for.

Incidentally, **glaciers** still permeate some of our region's mountains. Although not the behemoth size of the past, they are evidence of ice ages that this area went through—the most recent occurred only about 13,000 years ago. Although most mountain ranges have them, glaciers are most easily found in the Tetons, the Wind Rivers, and the Beartooths. These fluctuate with the temperature and annual snowfall. As the earth is warming, these glaciers recede little by little each year.

Yellowstone National Park was created by a series of volcanic eruptions, the biggest of which occurred about 600,000 years ago. Big is an understatement here, as the blast is estimated to be as much as 10,000 times greater than the Mount Saint Helens explosion of 1980. The Yellowstone explosion spewed gases and hot ash across the continent, with some fragments landing more than 1,000 miles away.

What's left is a **giant caldera**—the cylindrical cone of the volcano—that continues to erupt through the surface in the form of geysers, bubbling cauldrons, hot springs, and fumaroles. And yes, Yellowstone was also covered by ice at one time. In fact, geologists theorize that as much as 90 percent of the park was buried under 3,000 feet of ice between 20,000 and 25,000 years ago.

Yellowstone is renowned for its **geysers,** even though they account for only about 3 percent of geothermal activity. A geyser is an underground hot spring that ejects steam and water on a regular basis. Below the geyser is a narrow rock chimney fed by a constant supply of superheated water. The water wants to boil into steam but doesn't have room, so it has no place to go but up. Since steam has a much greater volume than water, the increasing pressure causes the water and steam to erupt out of the earth and into the air. The most famous geyser in the park is **Old Faithful,** named for its reliable eruption about every 81 minutes.

Mud pots, also called mud volcanoes or paint pots, make up some of the more interesting features in the park. These bubbling cauldrons are formed far below the earth when rising steam dissolves the surrounding rock into a watery, claylike substance. The clay bubbles and spits when it reaches the surface, with bigger bubbles meaning more steam is being forced through. On the surface, the edges of these formations are colored by minerals. Yellow is formed by sulfur deposits, while oranges, reds, browns, and blacks come from iron sulfides and oxides. The resulting colorful mix is what gives mud pots their alternate name—paint pots.

i Using Cooke City, Montana, as your base gives you access to hundreds of alpine lakes amidst the backcountry hiking trails of the rugged Beartooth Mountains. Fed by glaciers, these lakes are crystalline, pristine, and the color of sapphires.

A **fumarole** is like a geyser running low on water. What little amount of water there is converts to steam immediately after hitting the boiling point, sending the rising steam up through a small vent in the ground. Listen closely and you'll hear the steam hissing as it comes up to the surface.

You'll also see a variety of **hot springs** and **pools** around the park. Mammoth has the most dramatic—the water deposits calcium carbonate (limestone) as it trickles down marblelike terraces, creating beautiful, colored sculptures in the earth. Small hot pools can be found all over the park, usually in brilliant shades of blue or green. It looks like these would be great for soaking, but be careful. Most of them are scalding hot and the ground around them is extremely fragile. Stay on the park's boardwalks that pass nearby these geothermal features.

FLORA & FAUNA

Coupled with the dramatic mountain landscape is a plant and animal community that composes one of the largest protected natural areas in the United States. The Greater Yellowstone Ecosystem stretches across our entire region and is home to an awesome variety of species, from miniature wildflowers and animals to old-growth conifers and large ungulates—elk, deer, and moose.

The national parks are where you'll see the most wildlife. Bison, elk, deer, coyotes, and bald eagles will cross your path the most, and keen observers will have no trouble spotting moose, trumpeter swans, pronghorns, and others.

Most of the lower elevations around our region are almost desertlike and composed of sagebrush, grasses, shrubs, and wildflowers. Areas like the Teton Valley floor—made up of coarse, rocky soil with very few large trees—support squirrels, badgers, pronghorns, sage grouse, hawks, and eagles. Around June a variety of wildflowers burst with the bright colors of summer.

You'll notice while driving around our region that there is a lot of water—rivers, creeks, and lakes. These areas support

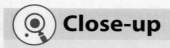 **Close-up**

Sure Things

You say there's no such thing as a sure thing? Well, in Yellowstone Country that's not entirely true in regard to wildlife viewing. Patient observers can almost always find their favorite animal, and the list below will help guide you to areas where the chances are greater.

- Everybody wants to see **elk.** Royal and majestic, these large ungulates frequent our region and never fail to impress. Just inside the north entrance to Yellowstone National Park at Mammoth, elk wander around and mingle with visitors. In fall, big bulls can be seen lying in the lush grass between the roads. The National Elk Refuge just north of Jackson Hole is home to as many as 10,000 elk during winter. See the Attractions chapter for details on the refuge.

- You should have no trouble seeing **bison** in Yellowstone. A full day of driving around the park's main roads should net you more than one sighting, and you may even have to stop your car to let them pass. If you're driving south from Bozeman on US 191, a drive back on the Spanish Creek Road will let you gaze upon media mogul Ted Turner's private herd. Look for the sign to Spanish Creek on the highway about 5 miles after you enter Gallatin Canyon.

- Your best chance to see a **wolf** may be in the winter, when packs will travel Yellowstone National Park's Lamar Valley in search of a good meal (usually a fallen elk). Huge herds of elk invade the valley floor looking for food, and wolves, in turn, hunt the elk. Bring a good set of binoculars and scan the elk herds and the valley floor, particularly in the morning.

- **Coyotes** are smaller than wolves but just as interesting to watch. If you're driving around Yellowstone or Grand Teton, coyotes can often be spotted walking swiftly along the roadside, hurrying to their next meal. You can also find them wandering around river basins and open meadows.

- If you're staying in or around Big Sky, you should be able to glimpse some **bighorn sheep.** As you turn off US 191 and head toward the ski resort, scan the rocky mountainside on the right side of the highway. Occasionally the sheep will cross the road and stop traffic, allowing you a rare close-up view of this amazing animal.

- Driving along the Snake River in Grand Teton National Park from the Jackson Lake Dam south to Moose affords opportunities to see **bald eagles, ospreys,** and **great blue herons.**

- Most people associate **pelicans** with tropical climates, but the American white pelican thrives around Yellowstone Lake in Yellowstone National Park and at the Snake River's Oxbow Bend in Grand Teton. Look for bald eagles here, too.

water-dependent wildlife such as moose, beaver, muskrat, swans, ducks, ospreys, and eagles and offer excellent viewing opportunities. The Lamar Valley in Yellowstone National Park is a great example. Here you're likely to see bison, eagles, ospreys, elk, and an occasional wolf all within a matter of miles, and perhaps even a grizzly bear roaming the valley floor.

Lodgepole pine trees—found on the lower elevations of hillsides and on the valley floor—harbor bears, elk, deer, coyotes, porcupines, owls, woodpeckers, and golden eagles. Just about any hiking trail in our region will take you through this type of forest, a veritable jungle of interesting plants and active animals. Consequently this is bear country. Stay alert when hiking and camping, and obey all rules of food storage and waste disposal.

At higher elevations subalpine fir, spruce, and other conifers take over, with the trees getting smaller and more sparse the higher you climb. Moose, mule deer, and the elusive mountain lion live here while bears and elk can occasionally wander up. You'll see lots of birds, including nuthatches, chickadees, golden eagles, grouse, and flycatchers.

Above tree line, the elevation of which varies depending on where you are, the land seems inhospitable to living things. But look closely and you'll find a vast community of hardy plants and animals that call this country home. In summer you can find patches of such colorful wildflowers as phlox, glacier lilies, and forget-me-nots, as well as marmots, golden eagles, bighorn sheep, and mountain goats. Grizzlies can also wander high in the spring, digging for a good meal of glacier lily bulbs.

WILDLIFE-WATCHING TIPS

Looking for wildlife is one of the best things about Yellowstone Country, but there are

---

Dinosaur Fossil Central

Montana is one of the world's hotbeds for finding dinosaur fossils, thanks to the way the landscape was created. As the mountains were beginning to form and the dinosaurs were starting to die off, sediment sloughed off the rising slopes to create a layer over their remains. Glaciers then scoured the plains, removing much of the sediment that buried the dinosaurs and leaving fossils near the surface of the largely undisturbed land. Bozeman's Museum of the Rockies (see the Attractions chapter) has exhibits detailing the region's rich paleontological past.

---

rules. Remember that they were here first and you're usually on their turf.

- Before your visit do some research on the area's wildlife. Find out about their habitat and what time of day they are out and about. This will give you a good idea of where to go when you're here.
- Try not to startle animals. Generally most won't even notice you're nearby and will continue going about their business, until you get too close. Carrying a set of binoculars and a telephoto lens for your camera is a good idea. Never approach wildlife, and never feed any animal.
- The best times of day to see wildlife are in the early morning or late evening— feeding time for most animals. Look for the signs with the brown-and-white binoculars logo and the words WILDLIFE VIEWING AREA, which signal roadside turnouts with viewing opportunities.

YELLOWSTONE NATIONAL PARK

Each year approximately three million visitors travel here from all over the world. While it is still fairly remote, the area makes its geysers, hot springs, waterfalls, and wildlife accessible to everyone. The number of visitors Yellowstone draws proves that it is a priceless resource not for its economic value but for its intrinsic natural beauty.

With more than 1,200 miles of trails and 466 miles of public roads, you can experience Yellowstone on or off the road. You are only limited by what you want to see and how much time you want to spend here. One thing is for sure, you can't see it in just one trip. So whether you tour the park hopping from campground to campground, in the comfort of the historic hotels, or via the backcountry, enjoy every moment and plan on coming back. Above all, no matter how you experience Yellowstone, respect this national treasure by obeying park rules and regulations for your safety and the preservation of Yellowstone for future generations.

Unless otherwise indicated, all listings in this chapter are located in Yellowstone National Park.

OVERVIEW

The creation of Yellowstone National Park was an expansive act uniting unprecedented philanthropic and political intentions. But it almost didn't happen.

At the time, there was lackluster support from the federal government for the proposal to designate 2.2 million acres of land as the world's first national park, despite reports from three exploratory expeditions in 1869, 1870, and 1871 stating that no other region was as rich in beauty and natural wonders.

Congress argued over the "worthlessness" of the Yellowstone area. Devoid of substantial timber, minerals, and other resources, the property was deemed "useless." With most of the land located above 7,000 feet, it was considered too barren for agriculture or settlement and therefore not economically viable. On top of all this, some skeptics doubted the reports of the area's geysers and abundant wildlife.

That all changed, however, when the members of Congress saw Yellowstone's beauty for themselves through the work of artist Thomas Moran and photographer William Henry Jackson, who documented the scenery for the Hayden Expedition in 1871. Moran's watercolors depicting the dramatic yellow, orange, and red walls in the Grand Canyon of the Yellowstone and other sketches of the area dispersed any doubts about the region's majesty.

A mere seven months later, Congress passed the legislation that made Yellowstone National Park a reality. When President Ulysses S. Grant signed the park bill on March 1, 1872, it was a precedent-setting moment in history for our nation and the world.

Today it doesn't take as much convincing for people to believe that Yellowstone is a wondrous place.

ENTERING THE PARK

Entrances to Yellowstone National Park are generally open to automobile traffic from mid-Apr or May through the first of Nov. The road from Gardiner to Cooke City is open year-round to auto traffic, but from about Nov 1 until the end of May, the road dead-ends in Cooke City. Depending on the weather the Beartooth Highway closes in mid-Oct. The Chief Joseph Highway from Cody to the intersection with the Beartooth Highway (US 212) remains open throughout the winter. In mid-Dec, when the park reopens for winter recreation, snowmobiles and snowcoaches line up at the west entrance to travel approximately 150 miles of groomed roads.

Once inside the park, expect to travel park roads slowly, since most are winding two-lane highways. The routes mostly circle around the center of the park past major attractions and through villages equipped with an array of tourist amenities. Park roads are easy to navigate, since they are well marked and generally named for the attractions they lead to and from, such as the Mammoth–Tower Junction Road, Mammoth–Norris Road, or the Madison–Old Faithful Road. The main roads are dubbed the Grand Loop, Lower Loop, and Upper Loop. Most tour operators offer trips on all three routes.

WEST ENTRANCE
West Yellowstone, MT
More than one-third of the park's visitors travel through the West Yellowstone gate annually, making it the No. 1 entrance. This

---

Yellowstone National Park Entrance Fees

- $25 per vehicle
- $20 per individual motorcycle or snowmobile
- $12 per individual (hiker, bicyclist, skier, or snowcoach passenger)
- Free admittance for children age 16 and younger

All passes provide entrance to both Yellowstone and Grand Teton National Parks for seven days. You can purchase an Interagency annual pass good for most national parks and recreation sites in the United States for $80, or an annual pass good for only Yellowstone and Grand Teton for $50. The Interagency Senior Pass offers additional benefits, including discounted camping fees, for a one-time fee of $10 to US citizens or permanent residents over 62 years of age.

---

is probably because of its accessibility by three main routes: US 20, US 191, and US 287. Expect to wait in line first thing in the morning at this entrance during peak season in summer or winter. The town of West Yellowstone, adjacent to the park, is packed with motels, campgrounds, restaurants, and attractions of its own.

SOUTH ENTRANCE
Via Grand Teton National Park
Being greeted by the Teton Mountains jutting up seemingly out of nowhere makes this

YELLOWSTONE NATIONAL PARK

one of the most scenic routes to enter Yellowstone. The second most used entrance, it is accessed by the north–south highway traveling through Grand Teton National Park.

NORTH ENTRANCE
Gardiner, MT
The historic, 50-foot Roosevelt Arch still marks the original entrance to Yellowstone. It is the park's only gate that is open to automobile traffic year-round, but the road dead-ends in Cooke City, 57 miles to the east. The third most popular gate in the park, it is grounded by the small western town of Gardiner. With the Yellowstone River cutting through town, Gardiner is a scenic stopover before starting into the park. The road begins to wind quickly after this gate and offers great views of the Absaroka Range.

EAST ENTRANCE
US 20, WY
This entrance is not as easy to access as some of the more popular gates, but given the surrounding scenery it makes for a wonderful beginning to a trip through Yellowstone. The stretch of highway between Cody, Wyoming, and the east gate was dubbed "the most scenic 50 miles in America" by President Theodore Roosevelt. Bordering the park boundary is historic Pahaska Tepee, once Buffalo Bill Cody's hunting lodge, which offers all-in-one lodging, gas station, convenience store, and guest ranch. Winter months are popular with cross-country skiers, since the entrance is open to automobiles only during summer.

NORTHEAST ENTRANCE
Silver Gate/Cooke City, MT
During the summer, visitors entering at this gate from US 212 will have just been over Beartooth Pass—the highest point of the

preceding Beartooth Highway. But in winter this entrance becomes a cul-de-sac for skiers and snowmobilers, since this is as far as the National Park Service is able to plow the road. The tiny hamlet of Silver Gate, located about 1 mile from the northeast gate, shuts down during this time, but nearby Cooke City bulges with hearty visitors. The 300 residents of Cooke City endure nine months of winter and offer simple, year-round attractions for tourists (see the Cooke City chapter for details).

VISITOR CENTERS

The cornerstone of information, Yellowstone National Park's visitor centers anchor curious travelers who want to experience everything the park has to offer. Many of them are treasure troves of park legend and lore, and all of them offer current details on hiking trails, interpretive programs, and park road closures. Most have nearby amenities such as shopping, refueling, and dining that are generally open from the last week in May to the first week of Sept. (We've noted those that stay open longer.) An extensive bookstore, specializing in Yellowstone-specific publications, is located at each center. Operated by the nonprofit **Yellowstone Association** (www.yellowstoneassociation.org), proceeds from book purchases help support educational, historical, and scientific projects. The Yellowstone Association has contributed more than $12.1 million to the park since it was founded in 1933.

ALBRIGHT VISITOR CENTER AND MUSEUM
Mammoth Hot Springs
(307) 344-2263
Located within the historic Bachelor's Quarters at Mammoth Hot Springs, the Albright

Center is an integral part of today's park headquarters. Not only do the center's cheery rangers answer all your questions, they can also direct you to the center's extensive research library and rare-book room. The rangers offer regular naturalist tours starting on the facility's front steps and direct you toward informative movies about Yellowstone's history, which are shown every half hour.

Once the location of Fort Yellowstone, Mammoth's historic stone buildings now house the offices of National Park Service employees. Besides the administrative buildings, Mammoth has a hotel, cabins, campground, a bar, and two restaurants operated by Xanterra, the park's main concessionaire. Other Mammoth amenities include a gas station, post office, and ice machine. This is also where you can obtain special camping, boating, and fishing permits for backcountry use.

*CANYON VISITOR CENTER
Canyon Village
(307) 242-2550

This is one of the busiest visitor centers in the park. Tucked into a horseshoe-shaped complex, this is a full-service stop for fuel, food, camping gear, and shopping. You can find anything you may have forgotten at the two curio stores, post office, and gas station. You'll also find a restaurant, cafeteria, fast-food places, a hotel, cabins, and a campground. Laundry facilities and showers are attached to the campground office. What's most attractive about this center, however, is the extensive bison exhibit—it's worth wading through the crowds to view it.

In 2006 a new visitor center was unveiled with more room, updated services, and, most important, the permanent exhibit of Yellowstone's supervolcano. For the first time, park visitors will see, hear, and learn how the Yellowstone volcano, its geysers and hot springs, and geologic history shape the distribution and abundance of all life found here. Explore these ideas on the first floor through a room-sized relief model of Yellowstone that illuminates and describes the park's volcanic eruptions, lava flows, glaciers, and earthquake faults. From the second-floor view, visitors can hear Native American tribes associated with the park interpret the park's geology from their tribe's perspective. There's also a 9,000-pound rotating globe illustrating global volcanic hot spots and one of the world's largest lava lamps illustrating how magma rises by heat convection.

FISHING BRIDGE MUSEUM AND VISITOR CENTER
North Shore of Yellowstone Lake
(307) 242-2450

The view alone is worth a stop at this visitor center, which is located on the north end of Yellowstone Lake. Housed in a historic building designed by renowned Yellowstone architect Robert Reamer in 1929, this center showcases exhibits on Yellowstone's birds, wildlife, and lake geology. Services here are not as extensive as other centers, since it's located in grizzly country. But you will find a convenience and curio store, RV park, a gas station, a lunch counter, and shower and laundry facilities. Backcountry permits can be obtained from the ranger stations nearby at Lake and Bridge Bay.

GRANT VILLAGE VISITOR CENTER
Grant Village
(307) 242-2650

This center's extensive exhibit about the 1988 Yellowstone fires will make your tour through some of the charred forests in the park more interesting. The film, which plays throughout the day, details what to look for as the forest regenerates, and it explains this natural process that occurs every 250 to 400 years. Located on the west shore of Yellowstone Lake, Grant Village facilities include one convenience general store, a post office, showers, a laundry facility, and an ice machine. You'll also find motel-style lodging and a large campground by the lake. You must register and purchase a permit at the center's office if you plan to camp in this part of the park.

NORRIS GEYSER BASIN MUSEUM
Norris Geyser Basin
(307) 344-2812

Don't confuse the stone building on the hill above the Norris Geyser Basin with a visitor center. The building you're looking for is the small log structure across the way. Inside you'll find an interesting collection of information on geothermal features in the park. We recommend stopping here before venturing into the basin. The Museum of the National Park Ranger is just up the hill. Housed in the former Norris Soldier Station, the 1908 structure is a historic landmark. A 25-minute video chronicles the development of the ranger profession. From June through Sept informative ranger-led programs are based here. Call for a schedule or check the *Yellowstone Today* newspaper.

✳OLD FAITHFUL VISITOR CENTER
Old Faithful Geyser
(307) 344-2750

After a decade of fund-raising and two years of construction, the new Old Faithful Visitor Education Center opened during the 2010 summer season. The $27 million building

features exhibits and programs to help visitors understand and appreciate geysers, hot springs, and other hydrothermal features in Yellowstone. The building also contains an auditorium, research library, multi-purpose classroom, and educational bookstore. Huge, floor-to-ceiling windows provide an up-close view of the Old Faithful geyser, and the building earned a gold certification in Leadership in Energy and Environmental Design (LEED). More than 2.5 million people are expected to visit the center each year. The center is open from May to Nov each year.

ACCOMMODATIONS
Hotels, Motels & Cabins

Staying in Yellowstone National Park is half the fun of visiting the area. Several of the hotels date from the park's early forays into tourism, and their architecture and location tell much about that era. These hotels are not just places to sleep, they are pieces of history to experience and relive. Imagine being among the first visitors to stay at the Lake Yellowstone Hotel or the Old Faithful Inn at the turn of the 20th century.

Of course not all the rooms in Yellowstone are quaint slices of history. With 2,500 rooms, including 1,232 cabins, the park offers a diverse array of accommodations from luxurious suites to rustic cabins. What you should know about Yellowstone's lodging is that the hotels were never intended to be the main attraction, so in some cases the accommodations are downright simple. When you read that Roosevelt Lodge's cabins are "rustic," indeed, they are. Heated only by a woodstove and with communal bathrooms, some would consider the tiny, barrack-style log buildings akin to roughing it in a campground. But that's all part of the experience. Remember that Yellowstone is a place of natural wonders, so none of the hotel rooms have TVs, and only a few have private phones. Some folks might consider this a drawback, but look at it instead as a way to get back to basics—read a book, sit by the fire, enjoy this time to talk with your family and friends, get outside. Some of the rooms in motel-style facilities are simply places to lay your head for the night, and the truth is that after a full day of sightseeing in this wondrous country, that's probably all you will need.

Remember that although the area is still somewhat remote, it isn't undiscovered. To ensure that your vacation is hassle free, make lodging reservations as soon as possible. Millions of people visit the area each year and sometimes it will feel very hectic, particularly if you are scrambling to find a place to sleep—be it campsite, luxury suite, or motel room.

Most facilities are open only during summer months, except the Old Faithful Snow Lodge and Mammoth Hot Springs Hotel, which also accept reservations from mid-Dec through early Mar. The park offers early-bird specials for spring bookings and also for autumn; these are considered the shoulder seasons, when the number of visitors thins out. All park accommodations are operated by Xanterra Parks and Resorts. They accept all major credit cards.

For reservations at all park hotels and cabins, call **Xanterra Reservations** at (866) 439-7375 or book online at www.travelyellowstone.com.

Price Code

Some rates are based on availability. The average nightly rates for two adults are based upon that establishment's lowest price during the most expensive season (primarily summer). Accommodations accept all or most major credit cards, unless otherwise noted.

$. . . . . **Less than $100**
$$ . . . . **$100 to $155**
$$$ . . . . **$155 to $200**
$$$$ . . . . **More than $200**

CANYON LODGE AND CABINS $–$$$
Canyon Village
(307) 344-7311, (866) GEYSERLAND

Constructed in the 1950s and 1960s, the Canyon Lodge offers some standard hotel-type rooms along with cabins that sleep from two to five people. All the cabins have private bathrooms. The main lodge has an activities desk in the lobby, along with restrooms, a lounge, a gift shop, and several dining options. Separate from the main lodge, two other buildings, Cascade Lodge and Dunraven Lodge, offer more updated accommodations decorated with lodgepole pine furniture and western influences. Built in 1992, the 30 hotel-style rooms in Cascade each have two double beds. The three-story, 44-room Dunraven was built in 1998 and features rooms with your choice of one or two double beds. There are a few wheelchair-accessible rooms with a double and a single bed in each as well.

Canyon Village is centrally located in the park but serves primarily as an ideal place from which to explore the Grand Canyon of the Yellowstone. The bustling village hosts plenty of traffic and people. The community has a visitor information center with a convenience store, a post office, and a photo shop. Open from early June through Sept 1.

YELLOWSTONE NATIONAL PARK

GRANT VILLAGE $$
Grant Village
(307) 344-7311, (866) GEYSERLAND

Named for President Ulysses S. Grant, who signed the legislation to create Yellowstone National Park in 1872, Grant Village is located in the southeastern portion of the park. Built in 1984, it is one of Yellowstone's newer lodging options and offers regular, motel-style accommodations. Six two-story complexes house 50 rooms each, all with two double beds and private bathrooms. You'll find two restaurants, a lounge, a gift shop, and a laundry facility nearby. This village is a pickup and drop-off point for Yellowstone Park Tour buses and an ideal location from which to explore Yellowstone Lake and Grand Teton National Park. Open mid-May through early Oct.

LAKE LODGE CABINS $-$$$
Lake Village
(307) 344-7311, (866) GEYSERLAND

The Lake Lodge Cabins are a more affordable alternative to the grandeur of Lake Yellowstone Hotel, with all the perks of a great lakeside location. Only paces from the convenience of a gift shop, cafeteria, laundry facilities, and the shore, these cozy cabins create a great family atmosphere. The massive log lodge offers a rocking-chair view of the lake. It is also an ideal perch for watching an early-morning moose or deer tiptoe through the yard. The huge fireplace, the focal point of the lodge's expansive lobby, beckons guests to cozy up with late-night cocktails and good books. Each of the 186 Western and Frontier cabins encircling the lodge sleeps two to five people, all in one main room with various bed configurations. You are only a stone's throw from the Bridge Bay Marina, headquarters for scenic cruises, guided fishing trips, and boat rentals. Open mid-June through early Oct.

✳LAKE YELLOWSTONE HOTEL AND CABINS $$$
Lake Village
(307) 344-7311, (866) GEYSERLAND

The Lake Hotel will captivate your whimsical side when you first see this historic building. Huge white columns reach up to the sky on the front porch facing the vastness of Yellowstone Lake. The hotel entrance's high arching ceilings will remind you of a classic period of elegance. The hotel was a shoebox building when it was constructed by the Northern Pacific Railroad in 1891. A 1920s remodel by Seattle architect Robert Reamer transformed the place to its present beauty. He drew in details like the blue tile fireplace and the sweeping staircase, but probably the best attribute of this classic hostelry is the sunroom looking out at the lake. You could spend most of a morning or late afternoon contemplating life from the comfort of an antique wicker chair in the enclosed sunroom. A cool glass of lemonade or sweet ice tea will make it even better.

In the 1980s this grand hotel and its 194 guest rooms underwent a 10-year restoration project that eventually landed it on the National Register of Historic Places. The old rooms are spacious, with high ceilings and private bathrooms. The newer rooms, built in the 1980s, follow suit. Most have two queen-size beds. There is one presidential suite. The 110 cabins are painted a buttery yellow to match the main hotel, and all feature private bathrooms as well. The hotel and cabins are open mid-May through the end of Sept.

MAMMOTH HOT SPRINGS HOTEL $$–$$$
Mammoth
(307) 344-7311, (866) GEYSERLAND

For early visitors who traveled by train to the nation's first national park, Mammoth Hot Springs was where it all began. Built in 1911 and completed in 1937, Mammoth is a testament to the day when only the wealthy could afford to visit Yellowstone. This stately hotel is located just 5 miles from the north entrance of the park and is accessible throughout the year by car. Most rooms have two double beds, and there are two suites. In addition to hotel rooms, the complex has 128 cabins, which mostly have two double beds. Some have communal facilities with toilets and showers instead of private baths, and the hot tub cabins are popular in the spring and fall.

Its location makes Mammoth ideal as a base for day trips into the nearby Lamar Valley for wildlife viewing and of course to explore the terraces of its namesake, Mammoth Hot Springs. During winter Mammoth is the starting point for adventures, including snowcoach rides, snowmobiling, and cross-country skiing.

Mammoth Hot Springs is the official park headquarters and was once Fort Yellowstone when the US Army was in charge of the park. Today the original stone structures built by the military house administrative offices for the National Park Service. The hotel is situated across from the Albright Visitor Center. You'll find fine dining at the Mammoth dining room and a pleasant atmosphere in the adjacent lounge. Sunday brunch in the Mammoth dining room is one of the best things about staying here; don't miss it. At the other end of the building is a fast-food outlet. There is also a novelty store

on-site. Mammoth is a pickup and drop-off point for Yellowstone Park Tour buses. Open mid-May through early Oct and late Dec through early Mar.

OLD FAITHFUL INN $$$
Old Faithful
(307) 344-7311, (866) GEYSERLAND

Of all the places in Yellowstone, this hotel has the most character. Walking through the 85-foot-high lobby, you feel the history of old Yellowstone greet you, whispering its memories from the high gnarled pine balconies overlooking the lobby. The huge roughstone fireplace and its restored wrought-iron tower clock have been the centerpiece of the room since the hotel was built in 1903–04. Designed by famed Yellowstone architect Robert Reamer, Old Faithful Inn is filled with custom detail, including wrought-iron door handles, light fixtures, and even the numerals for guest rooms. It is a prime example of a building style called "parkitecture," referring specifically to structures built in America's national parks. It took 1,500 men to build this log-and-stone structure that now stands as a testament to the ingenuity of the western spirit.

i **Over the past century, thousands of visitors had set their watches by the clock at the Old Faithful Inn. Little did they know that the 80-year-old clock had been missing time for decades. But in 2000 the historic clock tower was restored, and the clock now chimes on the hour. Ask about tours of the clock tower and the inn at the front desk.**

Originally the inn housed 146 guest rooms and was equipped with electricity, water, and steam heat—a rarity in that era.

YELLOWSTONE NATIONAL PARK

Today the remaining 75 rooms are much like they were at the turn of the 20th century. With the great public spaces for lounging and people watching, the actual sleeping quarters are small and dimly lit with a dangling bulb— the only thing missing is the chamber pot. Down the hall you'll find restrooms, showers, and two rooms with elegant claw-foot bathtubs for soaking. But during peak summer months the odds are against a relaxing soak; you're more likely to have other guests banging on the door. In the newer wing, 250 somewhat larger, brighter rooms are equipped with the "luxury" of private bathrooms. Several of the older balcony rooms, which are larger suites overlooking the geyser basin in front of the inn, are so sought after they're reserved two years in advance. In all, the inn has 327 rooms ranging from two single beds to two double beds.

Situated next to the famous Old Faithful Geyser, you won't spend much time in your room anyway. Take a stroll along one of the paths winding through the geyser basin just a few hundred yards from the inn. Or settle into one of the chairs on the outside balcony of the hotel and take in all the beauty. In addition to the formal dining room, the Old Faithful Inn houses a fast-food outlet, ice-cream counter, espresso cart, lounge, and gift shop. You'll also find a gas station and general store nearby. The park's tour buses pick up passengers here as well. Open early May through mid Oct.

i During winter herds of bison, elk, pronghorn antelope, deer, and bighorn sheep migrate down to the warmth of the thermal basins in Yellowstone for easier grazing in the open valleys, making it a spectacular time of year to view wildlife.

OLD FAITHFUL LODGE CABINS $$
Old Faithful
(307) 344-7311, (866) GEYSERLAND
Built to accommodate the overflow of guests wanting to stay near the famous Old Faithful Geyser, these cabins and sleek stone lodge were built in the 1950s. The lodge houses a gift shop, two snack shops, a cafeteria, and an espresso cart. The 132 cabins are classically practical, barrack-style structures. The rooms range from those with two singles to two double beds. Forty-seven rooms have private bathrooms, while everyone else uses the communal bathrooms scattered throughout the complex. Open mid-May through mid-Sept.

OLD FAITHFUL
** SNOW LODGE $$–$$$$**
Old Faithful
(307) 344-7311, (866) GEYSERLAND
Completed in 1999, this huge timber-frame structure is a much-needed addition to Yellowstone's lodging options. Architecturally the Snow Lodge is the modern counterpart to its neighbor, the Old Faithful Inn. It is an impressive heavy-timber structure with wrought-iron accents, custom-designed furniture, and turn-of-the-20th-century light fixtures. High vaulted ceilings, a massive native-rock fireplace, picture windows, and deep cushioned chairs in the lobby invite you to hunker down by the fire on a cold winter night. All rooms have built-in armoires, some have window seats, each has two double beds, and there isn't a room with a bad view in the whole hotel. An additional 34 cabins feature two double beds and bathrooms. A family restaurant and a gift shop are on the premises. Open early May through early Oct and mid-Dec to early Mar.

ROOSEVELT LODGE CABINS $$
Located at Tower Junction, Yellowstone National Park
(307) 344-7311, (866) GEYSERLAND

This historic lodge and cabins are located near President Theodore Roosevelt's favorite camping spot. Built in 1908, the lodge and barracks-style cabins are tucked beneath the trees. Roughrider units have wood-burning stoves but no private bathrooms. Communal bathing facilities are scattered throughout the cabin area. The Frontier cabins come with the luxuries of private bath and propane heat. But in actuality, all the cabins qualify as "rustic." From the ambling front porch of the lodge, you almost feel as if you've been transported back to the Old West, sitting in a rocking chair as the evening air grows cooler. Inside is a large lodgepole pine family-style dining room. Staying here truly feels like a step back in time. Stagecoach and horseback rides are available and can take you to the corral, where a wholesome real western cookout is offered nightly. Roosevelt Lodge activities fill up quickly; it's best to book well in advance. Open early June through early Sept.

Campgrounds & RV Parks

Yellowstone National Park has 11 campgrounds and one RV Park, for a total of 2,145 campsites. Seven sites are operated on a first come, first-served basis and require no reservations. The other five—Madison, Canyon Village, Grant Village, Bridge Bay, and the Fishing Bridge RV Park—contain more than 1,700 spaces that may be reserved in advance by calling **Xanterra Reservations,** the main park concessionaire. Call (307) 344-7311 or visit the website at www.travelyellowstone.com. Same-day reservations can be made by calling (307) 344-7901 or inquiring at a hotel activities desk.

i Xanterra Parks and Resorts offers special discounts for reservations made during "shoulder seasons"—autumn and spring. Go to www.travelyellowstone.com for details.

You'll find at least minimal amenities such as tables, fire grills, drinking water, and flush or pit toilets at every campground. The reservation campgrounds generally have more amenities, including firewood for sale, showers, and laundries. They are often conveniently located near general stores, post offices, restaurants, and gas stations.

For backcountry camping you must obtain a permit from a visitor center or ranger station. Advance reservations for overnight camping in the backcountry cost $15. For more information call (307) 344-2160.

Price Code
Prices below represent rates per night.

$ . . . . **Less than $14**
$$ . . . . **$14 to $19**
$$$ . . . . **More than $19**

BRIDGE BAY CAMPGROUND $$
West Thumb–Fishing Bridge Road

Don't be shocked if you wake up with an uninvited bison tromping through your camp. Despite Bridge Bay being the largest of Yellowstone's campgrounds, the bison still roam the area and share their territory with thousands of people each summer. The main feature here is Yellowstone Lake and the adjacent marina (see the Attractions chapter). At the marina you can launch your boat, enjoy a scenic cruise, or take a guided fishing trip on the lake. With 432 regular and four group sites, this campground sprawls along the lakeshore. Open from late May through Sept, Bridge Bay is a reservations campground. You'll find firewood sold here, flush toilets, an RV dump station, and boat access. Everything else you need can be found just 3 miles to the south at Lake Village.

CANYON VILLAGE CAMPGROUND $$
Canyon Village

Canyon Village is the most centrally located of all Yellowstone's campgrounds. It offers such easy driving access to nearly all the park's major attractions—from Yellowstone Lake to Mammoth Hot Springs to Old Faithful—you may want to call this home for the duration of your trip. From here you can drive in a different direction each day and get a whirlwind view of Yellowstone. Canyon is open from early June to early Sept and reservations are required. This full-service campground's 272 spaces are within walking distance from the actual Canyon Village. There you can stock up on gifts, groceries, and any outdoor gear you might have forgotten. Take a break from camp cooking and choose from the number of dining options, including a huge lunch counter, fast-food counter, cafeteria, and full-service dining room. Showers, laundry, and flush toilets are available at the campground.

FISHING BRIDGE RV PARK $$$
East Entrance Road

There isn't exactly a sign here that says no tents allowed, but the fact is that only hard-sided RVs are welcome to camp at this area near Fishing Bridge and Yellowstone Lake. These 344 sites, open from mid-May through early Oct, feature a general store, laundry, pay showers, electricity, water, and sewer hookups. The maximum RV length is 40 feet. The Fishing Bridge RV Park's central location makes it ideal for exploring the lower portion

of the park, but it is a place where you must be cautious storing food because it's smack in the middle of bear country. It is also close to the Pelican Valley trailhead, which leads to incredible hiking. Call ahead for reservations.

GRANT VILLAGE CAMPGROUND $$
Grant Village

Grant Village is a good staging spot for day trips into geyser and lake countries. The 425 campsites ramble along the shore of Yellowstone Lake and are an easy bike ride away from the geyser basin at the West Thumb. You'll find a laundry, showers, a dump station, a gift shop, a gas station, and a post office at Grant Village. This is a reservations campground open from late June through Sept.

INDIAN CREEK CAMPGROUND $
Norris–Mammoth Road

Obsidian Cliff, the Mammoth Terraces, and the Boiling River are just a few of the attractions you can access easily from this small campground. Wake up early and jump in the car to drive a couple miles down to the Boiling River trailhead and stroll about a mile to a natural hot spring that melts into the icy Gardner River to create the perfect temperature for a relaxing soak. Indian Creek doesn't take reservations, and since it is only 8 miles south of Mammoth Hot Springs and National Park Service headquarters, the spaces fill up quickly. Situated in an open meadow where bison and elk graze nearby, its namesake Indian Creek flows through the campground. Within walking distance is Sheepeater Cliff, the former home of the Sheepeater band of Shoshone Indians, Yellowstone's only resident tribe. Indian Creek is open from early June until mid-Sept. Firewood is sold here.

✳LEWIS LAKE CAMPGROUND $
South Entrance Road

Situated above Lewis Lake—renowned for its trout fishing—this campground is open from mid-June to early Nov on a first-come, first-served basis. It is a fine halfway point for exploring Yellowstone's lake country and Grand Teton National Park. These 85 campsites are hard to come by during peak season, so mark your claim early in the day. A boat launch in the campground offers access to Lewis Lake.

MADISON CAMPGROUND $$
West Entrance Road

This campground is often called Madison Junction, because it is near the confluence of the Madison, Gibbon, and Firehole Rivers. Located just 14 miles from the West Yellowstone entrance and 16 miles north of Old Faithful, Madison Campground is a prime location for exploring geyser country. You can see a good portion of the area at a leisurely pace in three or four days. And if fishing is your love, you can't beat the proximity to such beautiful, highly fishable rivers. Within biking or hiking distance, you'll find the turnoff for the one-way, 2-mile Firehole Canyon Drive, where you'll see several cascades and waterfalls up close.

Although there are 277 campsites, this campground still manages to feel peaceful and enclosed by the forest. Every night at the amphitheater, a naturalist presents programs on such topics as the bison, mountains, geology, or hiking in the park. More in-depth material is available at the adjacent log-and-stone building, a former ranger station that now serves as a small information station where you will find educational books for sale. Madison Campground, a reservation campground operated by Xanterra, offers a sanitary dump station and flush toilets and sells firewood. Madison is open from early May to late Oct.

MAMMOTH CAMPGROUND $
Mammoth Hot Springs

Located at the base of a winding road, this is one of the most popular campgrounds in Yellowstone. Its 85 campsites are full from Memorial Day to Labor Day. At the top of the hill are Mammoth Hot Springs and the National Park Service headquarters. It's an easy walk, though somewhat perilous because the path is dusty and easy to slip on. But wear some walking shoes and leave the car behind to explore the Mammoth complex, including the Albright Visitor Center, where you'll find exhibits on the controversial Yellowstone wolves, historic photos, and an interesting film on the history of the park. From there you'll want to walk up to the Mammoth Terraces and follow the boardwalk through stacks of sculpturesque mineral deposits (see the Attractions chapter). Mammoth is the only year-round campground in the park. During the summer months it's ideal for a one- or two-night stay. Camping sites are available on a first-come, first-served basis.

NORRIS CAMPGROUND $
Mammoth–Norris Road

With only 116 campsites, Norris Campground is one of the park's smaller campgrounds. That's a good thing, because the location is nice enough that you just might want to linger here a bit longer. The campground sits at the edge of a wildflower-covered meadow where elk graze in the summer months. Within walking or biking distance is the Norris Geyser Basin, as well as several hiking trails. To the north of the

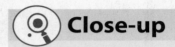 **Close-up**

Pedaling Yellowstone National Park

You may be able to cover more ground by driving Yellowstone in the comfort of an air-conditioned car, but there's also a lot you can miss. On a bicycle, however, every mile you rack up is earned and unforgettable. More than 300 miles of road are available to cyclists within Yellowstone. From short day rides or weeklong tours from one entrance to another, autumn is the best time to hop on two wheels in the park. Though July and Aug are typically the most popular months to bike in the park, Sept and Oct are even better because the days are clear and cool. Summer tourist traffic slows, making it easier to access trails without crowds and creating a safer atmosphere for road biking as well. Snowy roads and mountain passes prevent bicycling from Nov through Mar. Yellowstone launches spring by closing to auto traffic from Apr 1 through 20.

Bicycling through Yellowstone is a rewarding experience, but planning in advance is essential. This type of trip is not for beginners or the faint of heart. Distances between developed areas are long, and some of the most notable climbs range in elevation from 5,300 to 8,860 feet. Some favorite climbs, such as Craig Pass (8,261), Sylvan Pass (8,530), and Dunraven Pass (8,859), require extra time, energy, and food. If you're attempting a long ride crossing mountain passes, things to consider are camping reservations, packing extra food and water, bringing clothes that can be layered for any type of weather, and carrying supplies for bicycle repairs.

Though experiencing the wonders of Yellowstone on a bike is like nothing else, there are rules, according to the National Park Service. Bicyclists on public roads are required to obey the same traffic regulations that apply to motorized vehicles. Bikes are not allowed on most park trails or in backcountry areas, and service roads are closed to bikes unless otherwise specified. All riders must have a white light on the front and a red light or reflector on the rear of their bikes during times of low visibility. And riding abreast on a public road is prohibited.

Beyond that, safety and common sense also factor into the quintessential bike trip in the park. Road conditions predate today's bicycling popularity, to say the least, so Yellowstone's roads are narrow and rough, and they typically don't have a shoulder. Always ride single file. Be aware of heavy traffic and wide recreational vehicles near Old Faithful, Mammoth, and other major points of interest throughout the park. Remember that traffic swells highest from midmorning to late afternoon.

Despite obvious hazards that exist everywhere for cyclists, Yellowstone by bike is a way to see the park at your own pace. Smell the air, feel the sun on your face, work a little harder to see the view at the top. It's a worthwhile experience that will stick with you forever.

OFF-ROAD BICYCLING ROUTES

Mammoth area

- The abandoned railroad bed paralleling the Yellowstone River between Gardiner and the park boundary at Reese Creek; 5 miles.

- Golden Gate service road between Golden Gate and Joffee Lake; approximately 1.5 miles.
- Mammoth service road beginning at the top of the hill on the Old Gardiner Road above Mammoth and running northwest to the telephone microwave station; 1.5 miles.
- Swan Lake gravel pit road, 6 miles south of Mammoth; approximately 1 mile.
- Superintendent's campground road, adjacent to the entrance to Indian Creek Campground; 0.4 mile.

West entrance

- Riverside trail from entrance area to Barns Road; 1.4 miles.

Old Faithful area

- Lone Star Geyser Road from the Grand Loop Road to the Lone Star Geyser parking lot; 2 miles.
- The paved trail beginning in front of the Lower Hamilton Store at Old Faithful to Morning Glory Pool; 2 miles.
- Fountain Freight Road, located 6 miles north of Old Faithful; 5.5 miles.
- Daisy Geyser cutoff to Biscuit Basin. Abandoned service road; 1.4 miles.
- Natural Bridge Road near Bridge Bay; 1 mile.
- The old roadbed near the lakeshore between Lake Hotel and where the roadbed joins the main road south of Lake Junction; 1 mile.

Tower–Lamar areas

- Mount Washburn service road, from the Chittenden Road parking area to the summit of Mount Washburn; 3 miles.
- Old Chittenden service road, between Grand Loop Road and Tower Falls campground; 2 miles.
- Rose Creek service road behind the Lamar Ranger Station; 1 mile.

NOTE: Many routes are best suited to mountain bikes. Call (307) 344-2109 for more information.

campground, you'll find open meadows and Whiterock Spring. Then to the east follow Solfatara Creek through a large burned area. From there it's an uphill climb to Ice Lake. For a short walk and a little company, head to the Museum of the National Park Ranger, at the edge of the meadow. Former park service employees rotate through this old ranger station and educate visitors with historical anecdotes that paint a colorful picture of the past. Each evening a naturalist gives presentations at the Norris Campfire Circle near the "C" Loop.

Norris is within easy driving distance of the Grand Canyon of the Yellowstone and the geyser basin below Madison. To the north, Mammoth Hot Springs is only 21 miles away, with many attractions along the way. Give yourself a few days to see the diverse sights in the area. Amenities include flush toilets and firewood for sale. Open from mid-May to late Sept. Reservations are not accepted.

i If you are longing for a more extensive educational experience in America's first national park, the Yellowstone Institute offers 80 field courses throughout the year. The classes last anywhere from one day to one month and cover everything from wildlife photography to wolf watching in the Lamar Valley. Call for a catalog of classes at (307) 344-2293 or visit their website, www.yellowstoneassociation.org.

PEBBLE CREEK CAMPGROUND $
Northeast Entrance Road

To get away from the crowds, seek out this small, shady campground just 10 miles southwest of the northeast entrance at Silver Gate. With Pebble Creek running through the campground, there isn't a bad choice among these 32 campsites. This is a nice spot to regroup and relax before hitting the road again to tour the rest of the park. With access to Pebble Creek Trail, this is a nice location for a good day hike. Pebble Creek Campground is open from mid-June through Sept and is a nonreservation campground.

*SLOUGH CREEK CAMPGROUND $
Northeast Entrance Road

Slough Creek could easily be called the "Wildlife Watcher's Campground," with its proximity to the Lamar Valley. Tucked in a lush drainage just a mile from the main road, the rolling hills and open meadows surrounding this campground easily qualify it as Yellowstone's most beautiful. Eight miles northeast of the Tower–Roosevelt Junction, this is a quiet area known for its lack of crowds and unbelievable fishing (see the Fishing & Water Sports chapter). Located on the northern edge of the Lamar Valley, you are likely to see moose in spring; coyotes, trumpeter swans, and birds of prey in summer; and elk and bison in autumn. Some of Yellowstone's wolves are frequently sighted in this area; ask park rangers if they know of any perches you can seek out to catch a glimpse of these elusive creatures on your own. Also only a half-mile from camp is the Slough Creek trailhead, which leads to the park's northern boundary. Slough Creek's 29 campsites are situated in prime grizzly habitat, so take extra precautions in storing food and garbage. Bring everything you need for cooking and cleaning up, as there are no frills at this first-come, first-served campground. Slough Creek is open from late May to late Oct.

TOWER FALL CAMPGROUND $
Tower–Roosevelt–Canyon Road

This conveniently located campground is popular because of its access to amenities, hiking, and organized activities at Roosevelt Lodge. Staying here is more like summer camp than roughing it. Though they are hidden in the trees, these 32 campsites are located directly across from a gift shop and only 3 miles from the Tower–Roosevelt Junction. Hiking trails abound. The most popular leads to 132-foot Tower Falls, a breathtaking waterfall that tumbles between columns of rocks. Another begins at the campground entrance and travels 3 miles up Tower Creek. There are several other trails near the Tower–Roosevelt Junction. One of them, the Yellowstone Picnic Area Trail, follows the Grand Canyon of the Yellowstone for about 2 miles. Open from May to early Oct, campsites fill up fast on a first-come, first-served basis.

RESTAURANTS

Price Code

Prices represent meals for two people, excluding beverages, tip, and tax.

$ . . . . $10 to $19
$$ . . . . $19 to $27
$$$ . . . . $27 to $35
$$$$ . . . . More than $35

✳GRANT VILLAGE DINING ROOM $$
Grant Village
(307) 344-7311

This is a great spot to grab a delicious and reasonable meal. Popular dishes include artisan mac and cheese, slow-roasted prime rib, and bison meatloaf. There is also a decent wine list and dessert menu, and the adjacent Seven Stool Saloon is a cozy spot to grab a drink. Reservations are required for dinner, but the dining room is also open for breakfast and lunch. Also in Grant is the Lake House Restaurant, which serves spruced-up pub fare in a picturesque setting that overlooks the lake. The Lake House is one of the best breakfasts in the park—mainly due to its supreme location by the water.

LAKE HOTEL $$$
Lake Village
(307) 344-7311

With piano music in the background and chandeliers and candles casting warm light across this elegant dining room, there is one word that captures the scene: romantic. In the 1920s guests were required to dress for dinner—coattails for men and silk dresses for women. Supper was served at six o'clock sharp and offered a prix fixe, European-style menu. Today you can choose whatever you fancy from this seasonal menu, although the elk medallions are the restaurant's hallmark. And although formal dress is not a requirement, why not make it just a little more special? Whatever you wear, savor the time, come hungry, and order several courses— be lavish. Before your meal, opt for a cocktail and lounge in the sunroom. The menu and wine list are extensive. The hotel recommends reservations. There is also a cafeteria at the nearby Lake Lodge.

MAMMOTH HOT SPRINGS HOTEL $$
Mammoth
(307) 344-7311

The dining room at Mammoth Hot Springs is the kind of place where you might enjoy a high tea. It's spacious and grand; at a glance it seems prim, as if you should sit up straight and be careful not to use the wrong fork. But the atmosphere is actually very casual, with a menu that reflects its clientele—a cheeseburger for the kids, wild Alaskan salmon for the light eater, and prime rib for the hungry. Wine or mixed drinks are available to complete your meal. Mammoth is a popular dining spot because, like the pioneers, many tourists today begin and end their Yellowstone visit here. The winter months, Dec 21 through Mar 2, bring a lot of locals to the dining room. The restaurant is also open from the first week in May through mid-Oct. Reservations are accepted. The General Store and the Terrace Grill provide snacks and lighter fare.

OLD FAITHFUL INN $$$
Old Faithful
(307) 344-7311
At the turn of the 20th century, when there wasn't another restaurant for hundreds of miles, Old Faithful Inn offered formal dinner service and dancing. The band played from the Crow's Nest some 50 feet above the lobby. The scene isn't quite as formal these days, but the knotty-pine furniture and decor still take you back to the Old West era. Today's menu is contemporary, offering Rocky Mountain trout, honey-lemon chicken, and fettuccine with mushrooms, artichoke hearts, and olives. And though it's not necessary to break out your best attire like the early visitors, one thing you can do is take your time dining here as they did. Old Faithful has a full bar and a reasonable selection of wines. The restaurant, which suggests reservations, is open approximately May 1 through mid-Oct.

OLD FAITHFUL SNOW LODGE $$
Old Faithful
(307) 344-7311
The digs are new, but the food is hearty and traditional. Such comfort-food staples

as chicken-fried steak, meat loaf, and fried chicken are some of your options in this relaxed western setting. Nightly dinner specials start at $12.95. The grand picture windows, cathedral ceilings, and pine chairs adorned with wildlife carvings make an easy atmosphere. The Old Faithful Snow Lodge opens and closes with the park, serves liquor and wine, but does not accept reservations in the restaurant.

ROOSEVELT LODGE $$
Located at Tower Junction, Yellowstone National Park
(307) 344-7311
Barbecued ribs are the house specialty, whether you nosh on them at the table of the family-style dining room or outside at the picnic tables after a wagon ride. Either way the atmosphere is like a dude ranch, with huge platters of potatoes, meat, and green beans passed around the table. You can almost imagine yourself among gruff Teddy Roosevelt and his Rough Riders sipping whiskey and smoking pipes on full bellies. These days, however, in addition to the massive rib-eye steaks and juicy prime rib, you'll also find some lighter salads, pasta dishes, and fish specials on the menu. One thing is certain: A good old American cheeseburger tastes a little better when you're sitting in this turn-of-the-20th-century log dining room. Roosevelt is open only during summer, mid-June through Sept. Reservations are not accepted.

**ROOSEVELT OLD WEST DINNER
  COOKOUT $$$$**
Tower and Roosevelt Areas
(307) 344-7311
This family favorite lets you ride a horse or wagon to a real old west cowboy cookout,

complete with made-to-order steak, baked beans, potato salad, and cornbread muffins. Rides go through sagebrush flats, forests, and meadows to the cookout site, where guests are treated to buffet-style dinner. Fire-roasted coffee is offered, and a cowboy singer provides entertainment. And if that isn't enough, the cobbler served for dessert is some of the best in the West.

SHOPPING

GENERAL STORES
Various locations throughout the park
General Stores, formerly Hamilton Stores, have served park visitors since 1915. In the early days these general stores catered to the needs of their wealthy visitors and carried hard-to-get beauty products just for the ladies. Today, as a Yellowstone concessionaire, the shops carry camping and fishing equipment, film, groceries, sundries, and souvenirs. In some locations, such as Tower Falls and Lake, you'll find a comparatively limited menu of food, supplies, and gifts.

Other areas with greater visitor numbers, like Canyon, sell everything you might need for camping, cooking, traveling, and more. In some of the older locations, such as Fishing Bridge and Old Faithful, you can dine at the lunch counter. In addition, the stores at Fishing Bridge, Old Faithful, and the Canyon Nature Shop all have on-site, one-hour photo processing.

YELLOWSTONE ASSOCIATION BOOKSTORE
100 Chittenden House, Mammoth
(307) 344-2293
www.yellowstoneassociation.org
The thing you should know about this bookstore is that proceeds from any book you purchase go to the Yellowstone Association, a nonprofit organization that helps Yellowstone National Park with funding, research, and interpretive projects. You'll find an extensive selection of park- and nature-related books, many from regional authors. You'll find books on birds, animals, hiking, fishing, geology, history, geysers, and more.

GRAND TETON NATIONAL PARK

Today more than four million visitors see the majestic beauty of 310,000-acre Grand Teton National Park each year, whether by car or motor home or from the top of a 13,000-foot peak and the shore of a hidden backcountry lake. Visitors from all over the world marvel at the awe-inspiring Tetons, rising 7,000 feet off the valley floor. It's not a huge park, and that's one of its strengths. You can explore nearly every nook in a few days, from the miles of awesome hiking trails to the numerous alpine lakes and abundant wildlife. And for those who prefer driving around, the park's easily navigated roads offer views in every direction. Of course the going may be slow, as you'll most likely want to stop at every turnout to get that postcard-perfect photograph; by the end of your trip, you're sure to have plenty of those.

Unless otherwise indicated, all listings in this chapter are located in Grand Teton National Park.

OVERVIEW

Grand Teton National Park celebrated its 60th anniversary in 2010, but its controversial history dates back to the 1800s. The Teton region first received government protection in 1897, when Congress created the Teton Forest Reserve, made up of land not included in the creation of Yellowstone National Park in 1872. As early as 1917 bills were floating around Congress to create a much larger sanctuary, and three attempts to federalize land around Jackson Hole were defeated by local residents. In 1926 John D. Rockefeller Jr. toured the park with Yellowstone National Park superintendent Horace Albright, who thought that the area's beauty would be spoiled if something wasn't done quickly. Rockefeller agreed, and his legacy would be left on the park a few years later. In 1929 the central peaks of the Tetons and lakes at their eastern base officially became Grand Teton National Park, one-third of its present-day size.

Still not satisfied with the size of the park, Rockefeller began buying property through the Snake River Land Company—35,000 acres of farm and ranch land—between 1927 and the mid-1930s. His goal was to donate the property and expand the park, but congressional and local opposition was tough. Rockefeller finally forced the issue by threatening to sell his holdings on the open market in 1943. President Franklin D. Roosevelt responded immediately by declaring the 221,000 acres of the Snake River Basin— nearly the entire remaining valley—as the Jackson Hole National Monument. This was a clever move, since it didn't require congressional approval as did the creation of a national park.

The controversy didn't end there, however. Wyoming residents felt betrayed (most didn't want the park expanded) and sued Grand Teton National Park's superintendent, but they lost. Congress passed a bill abolishing the monument, but Roosevelt vetoed it. Finally, in 1950 the Jackson Hole National Monument officially became part of Grand Teton National Park. And in 1972 Congress dedicated a 24,000-acre parcel of land in the northern part of the park in honor of Rockefeller and named the highway from the south boundary of Grand Teton to West Thumb in Yellowstone for him.

As former Grand Teton National Park superintendent Jack Neckels wrote in a special anniversary publication, "The struggle for present-day Grand Teton National Park required decades of compromise and defined new horizons in park preservation. Today's park represents conservation through compromise and preserves a more complete ecosystem."

At the pinnacle of the ecosystem is the mountain range itself, located on a fault line that erupted with massive earthquakes two to three million years ago. The mountain block uplifted on the west side of the fault and the valley block dropped down to the east. That's why the mountains shoot straight up from the Jackson Hole Valley floor while they taper off to the west as the foothills of the Teton Valley. Glaciers finished sculpting the mountains, gouging out deep canyons between the high peaks and forming basins occupied today by lakes Leigh, Bradley, Jenny, and Taggart. Jackson Lake is what's left of a massive river of ice that covered most of Yellowstone National Park 25,000 years ago, and the Snake River now flows through its glacial moraines toward Jackson Hole.

The range itself is perhaps the most recognizable and photographed in the world, and its silhouette can be picked out from more than a hundred miles away on a clear day. The bent and jagged formation of the

Grand Teton—named by French trappers of the Hudson Bay Company, part of "les trois Tetons," meaning "the three breasts"—pokes up to 13,770 feet and is surrounded by the "cathedral" of peaks: Nez Perce, Middle Teton, Mount Owen, and Teewinot Mountain. Mount Moran, the highest and most recognizable peak on the northern end of the range, tops out at 12,605 feet. It was named by Ferdinand Hayden for Thomas Moran, who traveled with the 1871 Hayden Expedition into Yellowstone and Pierre's Hole on the west side of the Teton Range.

Besides the mountains, Grand Teton National Park is also known for its wildlife. The center of the ecosystem is the adjacent National Elk Refuge, a 23,754-acre winter refuge for up to 10,000 elk, but the park is also home to moose, bison, mule deer, pronghorn antelope, beavers, birds, mountain goats, bighorn sheep, coyotes, black bears, and grizzly bears. In addition, wolves released in Yellowstone National Park in 1995 have migrated between the two parks. Remember to report all wolf and bear sightings to a park ranger, and always respect the wildlife you encounter—don't put yourself in any danger and keep a safe distance away. Most important, never feed any animals.

ENTERING THE PARK

Grand Teton only has three entrance stations. If you're coming from Yellowstone, you'll travel the John D. Rockefeller Jr. Memorial Parkway south through Flagg Ranch, along Jackson Lake, and toward Colter Bay.

If you're entering the park on the east side from Dubois, you'll pay your admission fee at the Moran entrance station, a few miles inside the boundary of the park. The road splits here, and turning right will take you 5 miles to Jackson Lake Junction and the

Jackson Lake Lodge. Heading left will guide you 18 miles along the Snake River toward Moose Junction.

Coming from the south, you won't hit an entrance station until you drive north on Teton Park Road, which can be found by turning left at Moose Junction. Teton Park Road is the park's main thoroughfare, running along Cottonwood Creek and Jenny and Jackson Lakes.

Laurance S. Rockefeller Preserve Center

The park's interpretive center, the **Laurance S. Rockefeller Preserve Center,** is a great place to get out and walk around. The 1,106-acre preserve, which opened in 2008, features 8 miles of scenic trails that let visitors experience the area's vibrant riparian community. A 2.5-mile loop rewards hikers with views of Phelps Lake and the Teton Range, while more than 5 miles of secondary trails wander through remote areas of the preserve and to a series of overlooks along a glacial ridge. There is also a 0.3-mile accessible trail for those with limited mobility. The preserve is located on Moose–Wilson Road, 4 miles south of Moose, and once served as a summer retreat for the Rockefeller family.

You'll also find an entrance fee on the less-traveled Moose–Wilson Road (WY 390),

which is a summer route from Wilson to Moose Junction. No motor homes or trailers are allowed on this road once you enter the park boundary, and the road is closed from Nov 1 to May 1.

Another dirt road, the Grassy Lake Road, starts in Ashton, Idaho, and connects with the Rockefeller Highway at Flagg Ranch. There's no entrance station here, but the road makes for a beautiful drive into the park. It's not recommended for RVs, however, and is closed during winter.

The entrance fee is $25 per vehicle, good for seven days in Grand Teton and Yellowstone National Parks. Single hikers and bicyclists get in for $12, while motorcycles are $20 each. If you'll be in the area longer than a week or you are planning to return within a year, consider an annual pass. It's $80 and allows entrance to most US national parks and recreation sites for a full year. And if you're over 62, a $10 Interagency Senior Pass allows lifetime entrance to all national park system areas. A Winter Day Use Pass is just $5 per day; it is available from mid-Dec through Apr 30 in Grand Teton National Park only.

Grand Teton is open during winter, but not all services are available. The Teton Park Road is closed to motorized vehicles from the Taggart Lake trailhead north to Signal Mountain on Nov 1. You can drive on US 26/89/191 all the way to Flagg Ranch, but farther travel is prohibited. The unpaved portion of the Moose–Wilson Road is also closed, as is the Grassy Lake Road from Ashton to Flagg Ranch. All other main roads are open. Unplowed park roads are open to snowmobiles ($15 entrance fee required) when conditions allow. Refer to the following individual sections on building and service closures.

In the Park

US 89/191 runs through the entire park from north to south, from the town of Jackson up to Yellowstone National Park and out its west entrance. In Grand Teton the road forks right at Moose Junction and continues along the Snake River to the Moran Junction. Here US 26/287 goes east out of the park and US 89/191/287 heads west to Jackson Lake Junction, then north toward Yellowstone. It sounds confusing, but looking at the map will set things straight.

Picnic in the Park

The map you receive at the park's entrance station shows several picnic areas around the park. A few choices include the Signal Mountain Summit and Overlook, which has tables at a central high point in the Jackson Hole Valley, and the Cottonwood Creek Picnic Area, where you can learn about the forest's life cycle by reading interpretive signs. The String Lake Picnic Area, located on a spur road northwest of Jenny Lake, offers beautiful lake vistas and a great view of the Cathedral Group of Teton peaks.

Teton Park Road is where you'll find all park visitor centers and most services. Make a left at Moose Junction and follow the signs toward Moose, Jenny Lake, and Jackson Lake. The road skirts Cottonwood Creek and Jenny Lake before winding around Jackson Lake and reconnecting with US 89/191/287 at Jackson Lake Junction.

There are other smaller, less-used roads in the park. Refer to park maps for their exact location.

VISITOR CENTERS

COLTER BAY VISITOR CENTER
Colter Bay Village
(307) 739-3594
This is the main point of activity on the north end of the park. The center offers the same services as the Craig Thomas Visitor Center, as well as a marina, campground, RV park, and several lodging options. The center houses the Colter Bay Indian Arts Museum, which features the spectacular assemblage of American Indian artifacts from the David T. Vernon collection. From June to Sept the museum offers interpretive activities, such as craft demonstrations by tribal members and ranger-led museum tours, to enhance appreciation of American Indian culture. Hours are 8 a.m. to 5 p.m. from early May to late May; 8 a.m. to 7 p.m. from late May to early Sept; 8 a.m. to 5 p.m. from early Sept to early Oct. The center is located 0.5 mile west of the Colter Bay Junction of US 89/191/287.

☀CRAIG THOMAS DISCOVERY AND VISITOR CENTER
Moose
(307) 739-3399
This beautiful 22,000-square-foot building, the park's first new visitor center in more than 30 years, was finished in 2007. Formerly called the Moose Visitor Center, it features natural history exhibits, a bookstore, guided walks and talks, restrooms, telephones, a post office, permits, a relief map of the park, and an introductory video. The center is open year-round with normal business hours and extended hours in the summer. It is located 12 miles north of Jackson in Moose.

FLAGG RANCH INFORMATION STATION
Flagg Ranch
(307) 543-2327

While not a full-fledged visitor center, the Flagg Ranch Information Station offers audiovisual programs and backcountry and boating permits and has a ranger on duty to answer questions. The station is located 15 miles north of Colter Bay on US 89/191/287 and is open daily from early June through early Sept from 9 a.m. to 3:30 p.m.

JENNY LAKE VISITOR CENTER
Jenny Lake

This small visitor center is located on the Teton Park Road 8 miles north of Moose Junction. You'll find basic park information, a small store, geology exhibits, and GTNHA publications for sale. The visitor center is close to the South Jenny Lake trailhead and boat dock and the well-known Jenny Lake Lodge. The center is open 8 a.m. to 5 p.m. from mid-May to early June; 8 a.m. to 7 p.m. from early June to early Sept; and 8 a.m. to 5 p.m. from early Sept until it closes in late Sept or early Oct.

✳LAURANCE S. ROCKEFELLER PRESERVE CENTER
Moose–Wilson Road
(307) 739-3399

This new interpretive center opened in 2008 and is the first platinum-level Leadership in Energy and Environmental Design (LEED)–certified building to be constructed in the national park system. Eight miles of woodland trails wind throughout the 1,106-acre preserve, and the 7,500-square-foot visitor center features information, ranger-guided walks and talks, audiovisual exhibits, a seating area with fireplace, and restrooms. The

trails are open all year, while the center is open 8 a.m. to 6 p.m. from mid-June to late Sept.

ACCOMMODATIONS
Hotels, Lodges & Cabins
Price Code
Some rates are based on availability. The following codes indicate the average nightly rates for two adults. Accommodations accept all or most major credit cards unless otherwise noted.

$ . . . . Less than $50
$$ . . . . $50 to $100
$$$ . . . . $100 to $200
$$$$ . . . . More than $200

COLTER BAY VILLAGE $
Colter Bay
(307) 543-3100, (800) 628-9988
www.gtlc.com

Colter Bay Village offers a variety of accommodations as well as a full-service marina, two restaurants, laundry facilities, a grocery store, gift and apparel shops, corrals, and service stations. The 208 Colter Bay log cabins are nestled in the woods around Jackson Lake and feature many sizes and configurations that sleep up to six people. The cabins are pretty rustic—some are original settlers' cabins—but most have a complete bath with shower. No kitchen facilities are available, and the cabins don't have a phone, TV, or radio. Colter Bay also offers something unique—tent cabins made of canvas and logs. Each has an outdoor grill, wood-burning stove, two double-decker bunks (no bedding), and a picnic table. Restroom facilities with hot running water are included—showers are available for a fee—and sleeping bags, cots, and bedding may be rented at a central utility building. There are also 112 RV spaces and a large campground for tents only. Open from the end of May through Sept.

DORNAN'S SPUR
RANCH CABINS $$$$
200 Moose St., Moose
(307) 733-2522
www.dornans.com

Dornan's is a small, family-owned resort with eight one-bedroom and four two-bedroom duplexes. The cabins are attractively furnished with lodgepole pine furniture, and the bedrooms feature queen-size beds with down comforters. Each cabin has a kitchen and a living/dining area as well as a covered porch and BBQ grills during the summer. There are no TVs or phones in the cabins. Cabins are available all year, and the complex includes a grocery store, deli, gas pumps, restaurants, and gear rentals.

GRAND TETON CLIMBERS' RANCH $
(307) 733-7271
www.americanalpineclub.org

Membership to the American Alpine Club (AAC) is required to stay at this rustic ranch. Located a mere 3 miles south of Jenny Lake and 4 miles north of the park headquarters in Moose, the Grand Teton Climbers' Ranch offers the most affordable and accessible lodging for individuals visiting Grand Teton National Park. Formerly the Double Diamond Ranch, the AAC was granted a concessionaire's permit in 1970 to operate the Climbers' Ranch to provide mountaineers and their families with overnight accommodations without the congestion and time limitations of public campgrounds.

The Climbers' Ranch offers dormitory-style accommodations in small log cabins that sleep four to eight people each. Constructed in the 1920s and 1930s, the ranch contains a cook shelter (including dish- and pot-washing facilities), toilet facilities and hot showers, a small mountaineering library and lounge, and limited storage space. Climbers must supply their own sleeping bags, pads, cooking equipment, food, towels, and other personal gear. To minimize impact on the surrounding environment, tent and trailer camping is not available at the Climbers' Ranch. Please do not leave pets, which are not allowed in the cabins, unattended at any time.

Lodging is on a first-come, first-served basis, although the ranch now offers online advance reservations. There is no limit to the number of nights you may stay, and you may pay for several nights in advance. Once you have paid for a night's stay, space can be held for you if you plan an overnight trip. The ranch asks, however, that you clear your bunk to make space for others during your nights away. A limited amount of locker space is available. Lodging at the Climbers' Ranch is $8 per night per person for AAC members, and $16 for nonmembers.

The Climbers' Ranch is usually open from early-June through mid-Sept. Office hours are 8 a.m. to 10 p.m. daily. Call after June 1 for information, or write to P.O. Box 57, Moose, WY 83012.

i Grand Teton National Park is home to the largest bird in North America. The trumpeter swan weighs 20 to 30 pounds and lives in the valley year-round in quiet open water.

JACKSON LAKE LODGE $$$
Jackson Lake
(307) 543-3100, (800) 628-9988
www.gtlc.com

This magnificent lodge is a full-service hotel located in the heart of Grand Teton National Park on a bluff overlooking Willow Flats with a spectacular view of the Teton skyline and Jackson Lake. There are 348 guest cottage rooms on either side of the main lodge building and 37 rooms in the lodge itself. Standard cottage rooms have two full beds and a private setting. View cottages have private balconies where you can watch the Teton sunset each evening. View rooms in the main lodge have a huge picture window that frames the mountain range and lake. In keeping with the national park location, none of the rooms have TVs or radios, and all are comfortably furnished with a western decor.

The main lodge features 60-foot picture windows with breathtaking views as well as a collection of Indian artifacts and western art. You'll also find apparel and gift shops and a small newsstand that sells national papers and local reads such as the *Jackson Hole Guide* and the *Jackson Hole News,* as well as film, magazines, and snacks. You can enjoy a beverage and appetizers in the Blue Heron cocktail lounge, which features an amazing outdoor patio. The Pioneer Grill has counter service for light meals, snacks, and soda-fountain treats, while the Mural Room offers Rocky Mountain walls filled with historic murals. Other guest facilities include a business center, espresso station, heated outdoor swimming pool, horseback riding, bus tours, float trips, service station, and a medical clinic. The lodge is open from mid-May through mid-Oct, and a two nights' deposit is required.

✳JENNY LAKE LODGE   **$$$$**
Jenny Lake
(307) 733-4647, (800) 628-9988
www.gtlc.com

Jenny Lake Lodge offers a bit of luxury in a charming Old West setting. In the shadow of the Tetons, the lodge overlooks one of the park's prettiest sights, Jenny Lake. Thirty-seven rustic but elegant cabins surround the main lodge and come complete with handmade log furniture, covered deck, and telephones on request—but no radio or TV. The spacious and recently renovated main lodge has a sitting area with books and games for guests to enjoy. Breakfast and dinner as well as horseback riding and bicycle usage are included in the room rate. Dinners feature five courses served in the log-cabin elegance of the main dining room, which also hosts locally famous Sun night buffet dinners. Jackets are appreciated during dinner in the lodge. The lodge is open from June through early Oct. A three-night deposit is required.

Ancient Peaks

Towering more than a mile above the Jackson Hole Valley, the Grand Teton rises to 13,770 feet above sea level. Twelve Teton peaks stretch above 12,000 feet, high enough to support a dozen mountain glaciers. In contrast to the abrupt eastern face, the west side of the range slopes gently, highlighting the angle of tilt of the rectangular block of the earth's crust. The Teton Range is the youngest of the Rocky Mountains but displays some of North America's oldest rocks.

SIGNAL MOUNTAIN LODGE   **$$–$$$**
Inner Park Road
(307) 543-2831
www.signalmountainlodge.com
Lakeside suites, log cabins, and motel rooms are offered from early May to early Oct at the Signal Mountain Lodge, located on the shores of Jackson Lake a few miles south of the Jackson Lake Junction on Teton Park Road. Fireplaces are included in some rooms, and the lodge also features a restaurant, coffee shop, gift shop, and water-sports rentals. The Aspens restaurant offers fine dining, while you'll find lighter fare at the Trapper Grill and Deadman's Bar.

Guest Ranches

Price Code

$	Less than $85
$$	$85 to $115
$$$	$115 to $150
$$$$	More than $150

FLAGG RANCH RESORT   **$$$$**
John D. Rockefeller Jr. Memorial Parkway
(307) 543-2861, (800) 443-2311
www.flaggranch.com
Built in 1916, this cowboy-style ranch welcomes visitors during the summer to its location on the Snake River between Yellowstone and Grand Teton National Parks. While at the ranch stay in cozy log cabins, comfortably furnished with either two queen-size or one king-size bed. Each cabin has a private bath, telephone, coffeemaker, and patio with rocking chairs. Book early here for summer, as there is limited lodging between the parks. Summer season lasts from mid-May to mid Sept.

MOOSE HEAD RANCH   **$$$$**
P.O. Box 214, Moose, WY 83012
(307) 733-3141
www.mooseheadranch.com
Guests at the Moose Head stay in modern log cabins, nestled among the pine and cottonwood trees of its location on the east fringes of the park. The ranch offers weeklong family summer vacations with a wide variety of recreation opportunities. The Snake River flows through the ranch, and Moose Head also has stocked trout ponds. Guests eat family-style in the main lodge. The ranch is open from early June to late Aug and accommodates up to 40 guests.

✳TRIANGLE X RANCH   **$$$$**
2 Triangle X Ranch Rd., Moose, WY
(307) 733-2183
www.trianglex.com
Four generations of the Turner family have operated the historic Triangle X since 1926, offering visitors to Grand Teton National Park a chance to stay in an original homesteader cabin nestled it the heart of the Tetons. Choose from one-, two-, and three-bedroom cabins, and all of them have a nice porch to sit on after a long day and watch the sunset over the mountains. The cabins have a rustic feel but provide enough modern amenities to feel comfortable. The Triangle X is an authentic working dude ranch, and summer activities center around horseback riding. In the winter the ranch offers easy access to snowmobiling, cross-country skiing, and snowshoeing. Peak times in the summer require a minimum of a week stay, two nights in the winter. The ranch is located 26 miles north of Jackson and 32 miles south of Yellowstone National Park.

Campgrounds & RV Parks

Grand Teton National Park has five National Park Service campgrounds within its boundaries, for a total of 905 sites. Jenny Lake Campground is for tents only; all others accommodate tents, trailers, and RVs. All campgrounds have modern comfort stations but do not have utility hookups (there are others not operated by the park that do), and NPS campgrounds operate on a first-come, first-served basis. Advance reservations are not accepted. The fee is $17 to $19 per night, with a 14-day limit at all but Jenny Lake, where the limit is seven days. Doubling up on campsites is not permitted, and there are no overflow facilities. Fill-up times are listed below for individual campgrounds.

Free backcountry permits for overnight trips can be obtained at the Craig Thomas or Colter Bay Visitor Centers or the Jenny Lake Ranger Station. You can reserve backcountry campsites in advance—Jan 1 until May 15—by calling the park at (307) 739-3600. The fee is $15 per reservation. Campfires are prohibited except at designated sites, depending on fire danger.

Group sites for 10 to 75 people are available at Gros Ventre and Colter Bay Campgrounds. Organized youth, religious, or educational groups may use these sites, but advance reservations are required. The nightly use fee is $3 per person, plus a $15 reservation fee. Reservation requests for group sites only should be made between Jan 1 and May 15 by writing Campground Reservations, Grand Teton National Park, Moose, WY 83012, or by calling (800) 628-9988 All other reservations can be booked online at www.gtlc.com.

Price Code

Prices below respresent rates for one night.

$................. **Less than $12**
$$ .... **$12 to $24**
$$$ .... **More than $24**

COLTER BAY CAMPGROUND $-$$
Colter Bay Village

This 350-site campground is located near the greatest number of park services, including gas, food, stables, self-guiding nature trails, and a marina. There are laundry and showers as well as propane and RV dumping stations. The campground usually fills up by noon and is located on US 89/191/287 on the shores of Jackson Lake. It's open from late May to late Sept.

COLTER BAY RV PARK $$$
Colter Bay Village
(307) 543-3100, (800) 628-9988

This RV park is operated by the Grand Teton Lodge Company and offers 112 trailer spaces, each with sewer, electrical, and water connections and a picnic table. Most sites are pull-throughs and shaded, and showers are available for a fee. Expect to pay $2 more for vehicles more than 38 feet long.

*FLAGG RANCH CAMPGROUND $$$
Flagg Ranch
(307) 543-2861, (800) 443-2311
www.flaggranch.com

Flagg Ranch has a wooded campground near the Snake River with great views of the surrounding mountains. It features 175 tent and RV sites, with showers, laundry facilities, fire pits, and picnic tables. RV sites are pull-throughs. Prices are for one or two people, with each additional adult paying $5. Reservations are strongly recommended for summer.

Snow can linger on Teton trails into Aug, making for slippery spots in many areas. Be extra careful when crossing snowfields. In addition, the weather can turn wintry in a hurry at higher elevations. It's always a good idea to pack extra clothes, food, and water when going out for a day hike—even if it's a short one.

GRAND TETON PARK RV RESORT AND CABINS $$$
US 26/287, Moran
(307) 543-2483, (800) 563-6469
This is the closest year-round RV park near Grand Teton, located 1 mile east of the park in Moran. There are 120 RV sites with full services and 60 tent sites available during summer. Other amenities include a pool, recreation room, and laundry facility.

GROS VENTRE CAMPGROUND $–$$
Gros Ventre–Kelly Road
This 355-site campground, the largest in the park, is located on the banks of the Gros Ventre River in the southeast corner of the park. It's open from early May to mid-Sept, and it's usually the last campground to fill up. There's an RV dump station but no hookups. Five group sites are available as well. To get here, take a right at the Gros Ventre Junction upon entering the park from the south; you'll see the site a few miles ahead on the right.

JENNY LAKE CAMPGROUND $–$$
Teton Park Road
Since this tent-only campground is located in the most popular part of the park, its 50 sites fill up early, usually by 8 a.m. It's open from mid-May to late Sept. The campground is located next to numerous hiking trails, and a small store is nearby.

Boating Permits

There are several regulations that you must follow when boating in Grand Teton National Park. Motorized-craft use requires a $20 seven-day permit or a $40 annual permit. Nonmotorized-craft use requires a $10 seven-day or $20 annual permit. To float the Snake River, you must register your craft with the National Park Service and obtain a $20 annual permit. Motorized-craft use is permitted only on Jackson, Jenny, and Phelps Lakes. Nonmotorized craft are allowed on Bearpaw, Bradley, Emma Matilda, Jackson, Jenny, Leigh, Phelps, String, Taggart, and Two Ocean Lakes. Permits can be purchased at the Craig Thomas and Colter Bay Visitor Centers.

A regulation passed in 2010 states that boaters are required to purchase an annual Aquatic Invasive Species decal. Costs for the decal are $10 for motorized watercraft registered in Wyoming, $30 for motorized watercraft registered in other states, $5 for nonmotorized watercraft owned by Wyoming residents, and $15 for nonmotorized watercraft owned by nonresidents.

LIZARD CREEK CAMPGROUND $–$$
US 89/191/287
This is the most northern of the NPS campgrounds, located on the edge of Jackson Lake just south of the park boundary. There are 60 sites, many of which are walk-in sites. Early in summer there is access to the lake,

but by mid-Aug the water level is so low that there is no water nearby. The campground is open from early June to early Sept. It usually fills up by 2 p.m.

i Each campground in the park has a nightly ranger presentation during summer, including slide shows and storytelling sessions. Programs are usually offered between 7 and 9:30 p.m. Check the park's newspaper, *Teewinot*, for information on times, locations, and topics.

SIGNAL MOUNTAIN
CAMPGROUND $-$$
Teton Park Road
This scenic campground features 81 sites on the shores of Jackson Lake, with direct views of the Tetons. There's also a dump station for RVs, and nearby you'll find a gas station, marina, and restaurants. Sites usually fill up by 10 a.m., and the campground is open from mid-May to early Oct.

RESTAURANTS

Price Code
Prices represent meals for two people, excluding beverages, tip, and tax.

$.................. **Less than $19**
$$ .... **$19 to $27**
$$$ .... **$27 to $35**
$$$$ .... **More than $35**

THE BLUE HERON $
Jackson Lake Lodge
(307) 543-2811
Open mid-May to mid-Oct, the Blue Heron offers all your favorite latte, espresso, cappuccino, and coffee drinks from 6 to 10 a.m.

The Blue Heron opens for lunch at 11 a.m., serving appetizers and a fine selection of mixed drinks, wine, and beer in a panoramic setting. On nice days you can enjoy the Blue Heron's outdoor patio, and nightly live entertainment is offered during summer. The lounge is open until midnight.

CHUCKWAGON RESTAURANT $$
Colter Bay Village
The Chuckwagon is a great place to take the family, as it has a special menu just for kids. Steaks and homemade pastas are the specialties here, and dinner includes a bottomless salad bowl. The breakfast buffet is a great way to start your day, and lunch includes an extensive sandwich and salad menu. Breakfast is served from 7:30 to 10 a.m., lunch from 11:30 a.m. to 2 p.m., and dinner from 5:30 to 9 p.m. The Chuckwagon has a full bar, does not accept reservations, and is open from early June to early Sept.

JENNY LAKE LODGE
DINING ROOM $$$$
Jenny Lake Lodge
(307) 543-3300
The rustic main lodge at Jenny Lake and its accompanying dining room are park favorites and are open June through early Oct. The log structure is the perfect place to enjoy the renowned cuisine for breakfast, lunch, and dinner. Breakfast and the six-course dinner are a fixed price and included in the room rate for lodge guests. Lunch is served a la carte. Besides the innovative dishes and extensive wine list, the dining room is known for its outstanding Sun buffet dinner, featuring enough food selections to last a week. Reservations are required for dinner and breakfast, and jackets are appreciated on men for dinner.

JOHN COLTER CAFE COURT $
Colter Bay Village
This little cafe at Colter Bay is a great place to go for a quick meal or a snack. Open 6 a.m. to 10 p.m., the cafe's breakfast features pastries, breads, and packaged items; pizza, deli sandwiches, and fresh salads make up the lunch menu. Everything here can be packaged to go for a picnic or lunch on the trail, and beer is available. The cafe is open from early June to early Sept.

LEEK'S RESTAURANT $$
North of Colter Bay
(307) 543-2494
Leek's—located on the main park road just north of Colter Bay—offers Italian favorites: specialty pizzas, calzones, pasta, and sandwiches, served with a great view of Jackson Lake and the Tetons. An outdoor patio makes for great summer dining, and snacks, desserts, and draft beer are available. Leek's is open 11 a.m. to 10 p.m. from early June to early Sept.

THE MURAL ROOM $$$$
Jackson Lake Lodge
(307) 543-2811, ext. 1911
Artist Carl Roters's historic murals aren't the only things to look at in the Mural Room. A 100-foot picture window offers dramatic views of the Tetons and serves as a backdrop for diners enjoying Jackson Lake Lodge's finest cuisine. The Mural Room serves breakfast, lunch, and renowned dinners. Hours for breakfast are 7 to 9:30 a.m., lunch hours are noon to 1:30 p.m., and dinner is served from 5:30 to 9 p.m. Reservations are strongly recommended for dinner. The Mural Room is open mid-May to mid-Oct.

> **i** Free, ranger-led naturalist programs and walks take place each day during the summer from the Colter Bay, Craig Thomas, and Jenny Lake Visitor Centers and other locations around the park. Check the latest *Teewinot* for schedules and events. From late Dec to mid-Mar, ranger-led snowshoe hikes and other winter activities depart daily from the Craig Thomas Discovery and Visitor Center. Reservations are required; call (307) 739-3399.

PIONEER GRILL $
Jackson Lake Lodge
(307) 543-2811
The laid-back Pioneer Grill—open from mid-May to mid-Oct—serves breakfast, lunch, and dinner in a classic, soda fountain–style diner. Breakfast includes traditional hot and cold selections; sandwiches, burgers, and salads are served for lunch. Dinners are served until 10 p.m., but you can get cold sandwiches, beverages, and ice cream until 10:30 p.m. The Pioneer hosts the Pool Grill and Barbecue—next to the lodge's heated swimming pool—during July and Aug. Sandwiches, pizza, and burgers are served from 11:10 a.m. to 3:30 p.m., with the all-you-can-eat western barbecue buffet featuring charcoal-broiled steaks, chicken, ribs, and all the fixings, lasting from 6 to 8 p.m. Reservations are required for the barbecue. The Pioneer Grill also offers box lunches to go. Just place your order at the take-out window the evening before your departure.

SHOPPING

There aren't many places to actually shop in the park—you go to Jackson for that—but stores at Moose, Colter Bay Village, Signal

Mountain Lodge, Flagg Ranch, Jackson Lake Lodge, and South Jenny Lake all sell basic camping supplies, groceries, gifts, film, and ice.

Colter Bay has the biggest selection of goods and services during summer. The **General Store,** open from 7:30 a.m. to 9:30 p.m., sells everything mentioned above, plus Grand Teton apparel and sporting goods, including a complete line of fishing tackle and backpacking supplies. The **Colter Bay Marina Store,** open from 7:30 a.m. to 8 p.m. daily during summer, offers scenic cruises, canoe and boat rentals, fishing equipment and licenses, and guided fishing trips. Film, apparel, postcards, and reference books are also available here.

The **Jenny Lake Store,** located near the Jenny Lake Ranger Station, offers camping supplies, apparel, postcards, film, gifts, groceries, and ice daily from 8 a.m. to 7 p.m. during summer. You'll find the same stuff— as well as guided Snake River trips, fishing tackle, and licenses—at the **Moose Village Store,** located across the street from the national park headquarters. Hours are 8 a.m. to 6 p.m. daily during summer.

The **Jackson Lake Lodge** houses several shops. An apparel shop featuring casual sportswear and outdoor leisure wear is open from 8 a.m. to 10 p.m. The Grand Teton Shop, also open 8 a.m. to 10 p.m., provides a wide assortment of sweatshirts, T-shirts, reference books on the area, and souvenirs. The newsstand sells newspapers, film, magazines, candy, stamps, sundries, and postcards and offers 24-hour film processing from 7:30 a.m. to 10 p.m. You'll also find a good-size gift shop, featuring a large collection of American Indian crafts and jewelry and local art and photography. The store also sells liquor, beer, and wine and has a small sporting-goods section. It's open from 8 a.m. to 10 p.m. daily during summer.

In the **Signal Mountain Lodge,** the **Needles Gift Store** offers gifts, accents, and styles with a western flavor, while **Timbers** has cowboy and western duds and home furnishings.

You can help support the health of Grand Teton National Park at most of the above-mentioned shops by buying the custom products developed by the **Grand Teton National Park Foundation** (GTNPF). This private nonprofit organization is dedicated to raising money for projects that protect, preserve, and enhance the park; the foundation doesn't receive government support. So look for Jackson, the **Teton Bear Cub,** within the park as well as in retail stores throughout Jackson, Wyoming. If you've got a sweet tooth, seek out **Outlaw Fudge** at motels and resorts in Jackson Hole. Outlaw Fudge Company donates $1 from the sale of every box of fudge. Also drink Grand Teton Water, bottled locally by the **Grand Teton Water Company;** 100 percent of profits go to the GTNPF.

Buying books can help maintain the treasures of Grand Teton National Park. The **Grand Teton Natural History Association** operates **interpretive and educational bookstores** at the five visitor centers within Grand Teton National Park, on John D. Rockefeller Jr. Memorial Parkway, and in the Targhee and the Bridger-Teton National Forest outlets, as well as the National Elk Refuge information center. When you purchase something at the association store, profits are donated to support visitor programs. Call the Grand Teton Natural History Association at (307) 739-3403 or check out www .grandtetonpark.org for more information.

NIGHTLIFE

The park is a quiet place to be when the sun slips behind the Tetons. Other than the occasional howling coyote or bugling elk, you can hear live music nightly during summer at the **Blue Heron Lounge** in the Jackson Lake Lodge. **Dornan's** (307-733-2415) in Moose has live local and national acts performing year-round. To get there turn left at Moose Junction; then make your first right. Dornan's is just down the road next to the Snake River.

The real nightlife scene is in Jackson. Refer to the next chapter for more information.

JACKSON

Ask anybody around these parts what their favorite town is and many will answer "Jackson." Perhaps more than any other place in Yellowstone Country, Jackson combines all the elements of past and present to create a unique, vibrant destination for visitors to explore during all four seasons.

Jackson, the southern gateway to Grand Teton and Yellowstone National Parks, provides visitors a spectacular introduction to the scenery of the region. It's a bustling place during summer, when it can seem like everyone you see on the streets is from somewhere else. Busloads of visitors come here from all over the world to enjoy a real western town with modern clothes on. And this is one of the reasons it's so popular: You can get a vacation with a western flair while enjoying the amenities of an upscale destination—renowned restaurants, top-shelf lodging, and exquisite boutiques.

Unless otherwise indicated, all listings in this chapter are located in Jackson, Wyoming.

OVERVIEW

If you're confused about the name of the town—Jackson or Jackson Hole—you are not alone. The two terms are used interchangeably these days, but technically, Jackson is the major town within the 80-mile-long valley that is called Jackson Hole. The ski area is also called Jackson Hole—which adds to the confusion—so for this book all references to the town will be given as Jackson.

Only about 9,000 people call Jackson home, and 2,000 of them came here within the past 10 years. Nearly 20,000 people live in Teton County, which is one of the most expensive places to live in the country. It can be a hard place to live, since real estate costs have skyrocketed and most jobs are in the service sector, but the locals stay here for one reason: the mountains. Jackson truly is a mountain town and the birthplace of climbing in North America. Just as early settlers were lured to the valley for the profits of the fur trade, climbers were lured to "the Hole" in the hopes of becoming the first to scale some of the continent's most challenging peaks.

Of course, this led to skiing and the creation of **Jackson Hole Mountain Resort** in Teton Village, a separate community about 12 miles north of Jackson. Containing some of the wildest terrain and some of the deepest powder you'll find anywhere, the resort is a major destination for skiers from all over the world. Young and adventurous ski bums flock here to take any job available just for the chance at catching one of the ski area's epic powder days. Many area businesses also have a "powder clause," meaning that getting work done on a day with more than 6 inches of new snow will be put on hold—until the mountain gets tracked up.

It's not hard to see why the locals love it here. Looking at the Tetons every day will do something to you, something that can't be described. The majestic skyline of a Teton sunset is incomparable. You can gaze at the snowcapped peaks for hours and not get bored but only more amazed as you ponder the way the rocks stretch up more than 7,000 feet from the valley floor. You'll wonder how people can actually scale the Grand Teton—13,770 feet of jagged, twisted rock—and what would possess them to do so. There's no straight answer, really, but climbers say the mountains just beckon them to stand on the top.

The younger population keeps the town from getting too stuffy. Jackson's not all about high-priced galleries and boutiques—there are numerous quaint, out-of-the-way cafes, shops, and bars that are part of the local heritage and show off the town's lesser-known side. Nightlife abounds, with lots of live regional and national acts performing around town, and the après-ski scene is one of the most lively around. In short, there's always something fun going on.

It's hard to decide which season is best in Jackson, as each one offers so many different colors—in the scenery and in the town. Summer means blue sky, balmy temperatures, and hiking. In winter the snow-drenched Tetons seem even more impressive, and the skiing and snowmobiling are world-class. Fall is full of warm days, cold nights, and the bright gold leaves of aspen trees, ready to shed as the chill of winter sets in. Spring is a special time where the beauty of the valley comes alive with brilliant wildflowers and bustling wildlife. And events like the Fall Arts Festival, the Stage Stop Sled Dog Race, the spring's Old West Days, and the annual Teton Valley Balloon Festival keep Jackson's vibrant atmosphere kicking all year long.

The best way to describe Jackson is that it has a great vibe. In summer it can feel a little hurried, but the friendly locals never let the busy atmosphere get them down. After all, many of them work hard to make money for the coming winter so that they can enjoy the benefits of the ski resort without having to work that hard. Walk in any pub or shop and everybody is in a great mood. People on the streets are friendly and say hello as you walk past. Ask questions and you'll get answers. The vibe will certainly do one thing: make you want to come back—maybe even in a different season.

Several outlying towns contribute to the lively atmosphere of the Teton region. Driggs and Victor, Idaho, and Pinedale, Wilson, Alpine, Hoback Junction, and Teton Village, Wyoming, all play a role, and you'll find them mentioned in this chapter.

ACCOMMODATIONS

Hotels & Condominiums

Price Code

Some rates are based on availability. The following codes indicate the average nightly rates for two adults. Rates below are summer (regular season) rates. Winter rates in downtown Jackson hotels are often significantly cheaper, while Teton Village rates may be more expensive during ski season and cheaper during summer. Accommodations accept all or most credit cards, unless otherwise noted.

$	Less than $75
$$	$75 to $100
$$$	$100 to $150
$$$$	More than $150

JACKSON

THE ALPINE HOUSE $$$$
285 North Glenwood St.
(307) 739-1570, (800) 753-1421
www.alpinehouse.com

The quaint Alpine House—a cozy, country-like inn in the heart of downtown—offers 22 individually decorated guest rooms, each with a private bath and most with fireplaces, TV, and phone. The rooms are light and airy and include down comforters, plush towels and linens, bathrobes, and European antique furniture; suites and whirlpool tubs are available. The latest additions to the lodging at the Alpine House are four two-bedroom cottages and one studio cottage, situated along Flat Creek one block from the current inn 2 blocks from the Town Square. The cottages have kitchens, flat-screen TVs, fireplaces, king-size beds with down comforters, Wi-Fi, and outdoor patios. The two-bedroom units sleep up to five people, while the studio unit can sleep up to three.

The "little spa" offers relaxing treatments for men and women. In the dining room choose from the overwhelming selection of gourmet breakfast entrees (don't miss out on the Rocky Mountain eggs Benedict with smoked trout), and in the evening a sizable list of wines is available. Owners Hans and Nancy Johnstone are both former Olympians—Nancy was on the US biathlon team and Hans was on the Nordic team—who take every measure to make sure your visit to their Scandinavian oasis is an enjoyable one.

i To see what's happening around town, pick up a copy of *Tempo,* published every Wed in the *Jackson Hole Guide.* You'll find information on movies, music, art exhibits, theater, and food, as well as television listings. The guide costs 50 cents.

AMANGANI RESORT $$$$
1535 North East Butte Rd.
(307) 734-7333
www.amangani.com

Located near the southern tip of Grand Teton National Park, this 40-suite hotel is built into a cliff overlooking the Teton Range and the valley below. Rooms range between $500 and $1,500 per night, with king-size beds, fireplaces, and minibars in every room. For the guest who prefers extensive luxuries, this resort is consistently rated among the country's finest hotels. The dining room serves an Asian-fusion version of western cuisine, featuring many wild game options.

ANGLERS INN $$$
235 North Millward St.
(307) 733-3682, (800) 867-4667
www.anglersinn.net

Handmade lodgepole furniture, locally made wrought-iron lamps, knotty-pine accents, and fine art by Jackson Hole artists complete the illusion of staying at a riverside fishing camp, but the Anglers Inn is located within walking distance of all downtown shops, restaurants, and galleries. The 28 rooms feature coffeemakers, microwaves, queen-size beds, cable TV, and air-conditioning. Winter rates are substantially lower, making the Anglers one of the best values in town.

ANTLER INN $$$
43 West Pearl St.
(307) 733-2535, (800) 483-8667
www.antlerinn.com

The Antler Inn is located just a block from the town square, which means you can walk to just about anywhere in downtown Jackson from this reasonably priced and full-feature hotel. The two-story building was recently remodeled and offers comfortable rooms with a western decor, some available with stone fireplaces. A large indoor hot tub is on the premises, and a complimentary ski shuttle is offered during winter.

ANVIL MOTEL $$$
215 North Cache St.
(307) 733-3668, (800) 234-4507
www.anvilmotel.com
The Anvil is the skier's motel because of its in-room ski racks and on-site waxing room. Built in 1991, the Anvil is located a block from the town square and offers refrigerators, microwaves, cable TV, free local phone calls, and an outdoor hot tub. A free continental breakfast is included.

BUCKRAIL LODGE $$
110 East Karns Ave.
(307) 733-2079
www.buckraillodge.com
The Buckrail is located near the base of Snow King Resort and offers 12 beautifully appointed cedar log rooms with cathedral ceilings and a western decor. The spacious, parklike grounds feature a large outdoor hot tub and mature spruce and aspen trees. All rooms include guest-controlled electric heat, two beds, a sitting area, writing desk, wireless Internet, and expanded-cable TV with a flat screen. Furniture is all native western pine. The walls feature original prints from local artists, and abundant lighting is provided by custom-designed fixtures.

COWBOY VILLAGE LOG
CABIN RESORT $$$
120 South Flat St.
(307) 733-3121, (800) 962-4988
www.cowboyvillage.com
Staying at Cowboy Village is a great way to combine convenience with the rustic charm of a log cabin. Located within walking distance of the town square, Cowboy Village offers 82 individual log cabins with kitchenettes, full baths, air-conditioning, cable TV, phone, queen-size beds, barbecue grills, and covered decks. You'll also find two on-site Jacuzzis and a complimentary continental breakfast in the morning. A free ski shuttle is offered in winter. If you will be in the Moran area, try the Cowboy Village at Togwotee, (800) 543-2847. It's 17 miles from the park's east entrance.

ELK REFUGE INN $$$
1755 North US 89
(307) 733-3582, (800) 544-3582
www.elkrefugeinn.com
You can look for elk from your balcony at the Elk Refuge Inn, located across from the National Elk Refuge, 1 mile north of town. The inn has 24 comfortable rooms, 11 of which have full kitchens. All rooms have phones, cable TV, full baths, high-speed Internet, and a private patio. There are picnic tables and barbecue grills for summer cookouts, along with a fenced pasture for horses and ample trailer parking for hunters.

FOUR SEASONS AT
JACKSON HOLE $$$$
7680 Granite Loop Rd., Teton Village
(307) 732-5000, (800) 914-5110
The Four Seasons, which opened in 2006 at the base of Jackson Hole Mountain Resort, is the finest hotel-type slopeside lodging option in Teton Village, with 124 guest rooms—including 18 suites and 32 condominium residences. Opulence is around every corner, such as the amazing outdoor pool and hot tub complex, the full-service spa, and the original, hand-picked artwork that adorns the walls of the entire resort. Dining is especially inviting—the Westbank

Grill pairs distinctive flavors with local ingredients for an elegant take on breakfast, lunch, and dinner, while the Lobby Lounge is a comfortable spot for appetizers and a cocktail. The ski-in/ski-out Peak restaurant offers a modern, sophisticated twist on the traditional American steak house and is a lively spot for lunch, après ski, and dinner. All rooms are generously sized and feature natural wood and stone finishes and comfortable, residential-style furnishings, as well as high-speed Internet, DVD players, down linens and pillows, a minibar, bathrobes, and either a mountain, courtyard, or valley view. To top it off, the staff at the Four Seasons will accommodate your every need—and do so with a smile on their faces.

*HOTEL TERRA $$$$
3335 West Village Dr., Teton Village
(307) 739-4000, (800) 631-6281
This eco-friendly hotel is located in the heart of Teton Village and offers 132 rooms with a modern, hip atmosphere. You won't find any log furnishings here—the decor has more of an urban flair, with flat screen TVs, iPod docking stations, organic cotton sheets, high-speed Internet, inlaid gas fireplaces all set around contemporary western design features and rich tones and textures. The LEED-certified building also houses the Chill Spa and an infinity pool on the third-floor terrace, as well as the excellent Il Villaggio Osteria Italian restaurant and a small cafe. All of this—combined with an accommodating staff—makes the Hotel Terra one of the coolest places to stay in the area.

INN ON THE CREEK $$$$
295 North Millward St.
(307) 739-1565, (800) 669-9534
www.innonthecreek.com

If it weren't for the small sign in the river-rock front of this small hotel, you might think it's someone's house, especially because of its location on the more quiet, north side of town. Therefore, the Inn on the Creek is geared more toward couples looking for a romantic getaway than vacationing families. Each room features down comforters, TV and VCR, robes and slippers, queen-size beds, and breakfast served in your room. Deluxe rooms with Jacuzzis and rock fireplaces are also available, and there is an outdoor Jacuzzi for guests.

JACKSON HOLE CENTRAL
RESERVATIONS $$$
Teton Village
(888) 838-6606
www.jacksonholewy.com
If you want to stay on the mountain at the Jackson Hole Mountain Resort, your best bet is to give Jackson Hole Central Reservations a call. Choose from a variety of properties, including vacation homes, condominiums, and cabins. Vacation homes range from two to six bedrooms, and you can get one with just about any amenity you want, including hot tubs and washer and dryers. Condominiums range from reasonably priced one- and two-bedroom units (Tensleep/Gros Ventre, Sleeping Indian, Nez Perce) to three- and four-bedroom luxury (Moose Creek, Snowridge, Timber Ridge, Wind River). The new slopeside Granite Ridge Cabins offer two bedrooms, deck, hot tub, washer/dryer, and single-car garage. By calling Jackson Hole Central Reservations, you can also rent rooms at the Snow King Resort, Grand Targhee Ski and Summer Resort, the Jackson Hole Racquet Club, the Jackson Hole Lodge (downtown), and the Spring Creek Ranch.

THE LEXINGTON AT
JACKSON HOLE $$$$
235 North Cache Dr.
(307) 733-2648, (888) 771-2648
www.trapperinn.com

The Lexington, formerly called the Trapper Inn, offers nice rooms in downtown Jackson at a reasonable rate. Located one block from the town square, the completely redesigned hotel offers well-appointed rooms with new furniture, cable TV with HBO, full baths, coffeemakers, refrigerators, and microwaves. A new indoor swimming pool and hot tub are among the first things visitors will notice.

RENDEZVOUS MOUNTAIN
RENTALS $$$$
3610 N. Moose Wilson Rd., Wilson
(307) 739-9050, (888) 739-2565
www.rmrentals.com

Named for the 10,450-foot summit of the Jackson Hole Mountain Resort, Rendezvous has rented budget to deluxe properties around the valley for more than 30 years. Choose from cabins, vacation homes, and condominiums in Teton Village, Teton Pines, Granite Ridge, and the Aspens at the Jackson Hole Racquet Club.

*RUSTIC INN AT JACKSON HOLE $$$
475 North Cache Dr.
(307) 733-2357, (800) 323-9279
www.rusticinnatjh.com

Formerly called Wagon Wheel Village, this in-town seven-acre resort has been completely remodeled with a fresh, western design and a slightly upscale feel. The Rustic Inn offers 75 new, luxury log cabins with large private decks, in addition to 70 remodeled historical cabins. Accommodations range from double queens with fireplaces to deluxe and superior king and queen cabins. Most cabins feature fireplaces, flat-screen TVs, down linens, sitting areas, and coffeemakers. Amenities include a heated outdoor pool, outdoor Jacuzzi, spa, gym, Wi-Fi, and a free winter ski shuttle. The complimentary breakfast is the best in town. The adjacent lobby lounge features a Mediterranean-inspired tapas-style menu, an extensive wine list, outdoor patio, and a cozy atmosphere. Pets are not allowed at the Rustic Inn.

RUSTY PARROT LODGE & SPA $$$$
175 North Jackson St.
(307) 733-2000, (888) 739-1749
www.rustyparrot.com

This beautiful, three-story log hotel is located just a short walk from downtown and is one of Jackson's finest in-town hotels. The hotel houses the Body Sage Day Spa, one of the top day spas in the country, and the entire lodge has been featured in such national publications as *Travel & Leisure, Bon Appétit, In Style,* and *Gourmet.* The luxuriously appointed rooms feature handcrafted log furniture, goose-down comforters, terry-cloth robes, and an oversize bath. Some rooms also have fireplaces and/or whirlpool baths. Breakfast—included in the price—is nothing short of incredible, with a changing menu that often features world-class dishes such as Russian eggs Benedict with smoked trout, spinach, and caviar. Old favorites such as French toast are also offered, as well as juices, fresh fruit, and homemade granola and pastries.

SNOW KING RESORT $$$
400 East Snow King Ave.
(307) 733-5200, (800) 522-KING
www.snowking.com

Wyoming's first ski resort has 250 year-round guest rooms, suites, and condominiums for

rent 6 blocks from downtown Jackson. Condominiums include one- to four-bedroom
units. Rooms include coffeemakers, 27-inch
TVs, and queen-size beds, and guests can
also enjoy the swimming pool and an outdoor hot tub. The Atrium restaurant serves
breakfast, lunch, and dinner, and the Shady
Lady Saloon has occasional live entertainment. Summer visitors can take advantage
of Snow King's alpine slide—a wild ride,
similar to a waterslide without the water,
where you control your own speed down
the mountain through woods and wildflowers. And, of course, winter visitors can enjoy
Snow King's 1,571 vertical feet of skiing and
the area's only snow-tubing park.

✳TETON PINES RESORT $$$$
Teton Village Rd.
(307) 733-1005, (800) 238-2223
www.tetonpines.com
This luxury property is located on the road
to the Jackson Hole Mountain Resort and
Teton Village and boasts amenities such
as indoor tennis courts, cross-country skiing trails, a health club, and a golf course.
Condominium rooms include his and her
bathrooms, microwave, wet bar, and more,
while individual townhomes are even a step
up from that. Each one has three bedrooms
with a king-size bed, three and a half bathrooms, a full kitchen, washer/dryer, fireplace,
two decks, and an attached one-car garage.
Some townhomes feature a hot tub.

TETON VALLEY CABINS $$
388 East Ski Hill Rd., Driggs, ID
(208) 354-8153, (866) 687-1522
www.tetonvalleycabins.com
Teton Valley Cabins, formerly the Intermoun-
tain Lodge, is a great place to stay if you're
doing most of your skiing at Grand Targhee,

as the lodge is located on the road from
Driggs to the ski hill (hence the name of
the road). Deluxe cabins have kitchenettes,
queen beds, phones, and TVs, while standard
cabins have just a small fridge and micro-
wave. There are also bunk cabins that sleep
up to six. All cabins are set up like duplexes
with a shared porch; two allow pets. Ameni-
ties include a large indoor hot tub to soak
in after a day on the hill, wireless Internet,
a horse corral, coffeemakers, and laundry
facilities.

TETON WEST BEST WESTERN $$$
476 North Main St., Driggs, ID
(208) 354-2363, (800) 528-1234
www.bestwesternidaho.com
Kids age 12 and younger stay free at the
Teton West, which offers 40 nicely decorated guest rooms with queen- or king-size
beds, cable TV, and some with Jacuzzi baths.
Hotel amenities include an indoor pool and
hot tub and a free continental breakfast,
and a conference room that seats up to
50. It's located right on ID 32, Diggs's main
thoroughfare.

THE VIRGINIAN LODGE $$$
750 West Broadway Ave.
(307) 733-2792, (800) 262-4999
www.virginianlodge.com
This large, single-story hotel is on the west
end of town near the Albertson's shopping
center and the turnoff to Teton Village. One
hundred and seventy nicely sized rooms
look out over the Virginian's big courtyard,
where an outdoor heated pool is flanked
by a year-round 15-person hot tub. Jacuzzi
suites are available, too, if you don't want
to walk outside for a soak. The Virginian also
houses a restaurant, saloon, liquor store, and
convention center, as well as an RV park with

pull-throughs, cable TV, electric hookups, and a dump station.

THE WORT HOTEL $$$$
50 North Glenwood St.
(307) 733-2190, (800) THE-WORT
www.worthotel.com

On the corner of Broadway and Glenwood in downtown Jackson stands the historic Wort, one of the town's landmark and most recognizable hotels. Named one of the "54 Great Inns of America" by *National Geographic Traveler* magazine, the three-story Wort stands out for its elegant Swiss-chalet look—easy to pick out among Jackson's western-style buildings. The adjacent Silver Dollar bar often features live entertainment and is a popular gathering spot for locals and visitors. The hotel's main dining room serves excellent continental cuisine with a western flair.

Guest Ranches & Lodges

Price Code

$.................. Less than $85
$$ .... $85 to $115
$$$ .... $115 to $150
$$$$ .... More than $150

BENTWOOD BED
 AND BREAKFAST $$$$
4250 Raven Haven Rd.
(307) 739-1411
www.bentwoodinn.com

Lee and Deborah Clukey offer five rooms in their large, award-winning log cabin bed-and-breakfast, nestled in three acres of stately cottonwood and pine trees and only a few casts away from the Snake River. The 5,800-square-foot home was built in 1995, utilizing many logs salvaged from the Yellowstone fires of 1988. Every nook of

the Bentwood is impressive, from the slate entry and the three-story living area to the 30-foot floor-to-ceiling river-rock fireplace. A cozy library is stocked with classics and best sellers, and a baby grand piano awaits the musical guest. Four of the rooms have Jacuzzi tubs, and each is decorated in its own unique style. All rooms are exquisitely furnished, and Deborah's homemade breakfasts and baked goods will roust you out of bed each morning. The Bentwood is located between Teton Village and Jackson, 6 miles from the ski resort. Rates here are based on double occupancy, with a $50 fee for each additional person. The Bentwood is a non-smoking establishment.

BOULDER LAKE LODGE $$$$
P.O. Box 1100, Pinedale, WY 82941
(307) 537-5400, (800) 788-5401
www.boulderlake.com

Nestled in the foothills of the Bridger-Teton National Forest and surrounded by mountains of the Wind River Range is Boulder Lake Lodge, where families have enjoyed true dude-ranch vacations for generations. Part of an original early 1900s ranch homestead, Boulder Lake features modern guest rooms with private baths. A main lodge offers opportunity for visiting and relaxation in front of a huge fireplace, and ranch-style meals are served three times a day. Nearby activities include fishing, hiking, horseback riding, and hunting. Guided trips are available.

THE SASSY MOOSE INN $$$
3859 Miles Rd.
(307) 733-1277, (800) 356-1277
www.sassymoosejacksonhole.com

All six rooms in the Sassy Moose have outstanding views of the Tetons, just part of the charm of this bed-and-breakfast located only minutes from the ski resort. And when you're done skiing, you can relax in the indoor hot tub surrounded by picture windows or hit the hay under the comfy down comforters. All rooms have cathedral ceilings, private baths, and bathrobes, and some have fireplaces, while an on-site spa and boutique offers massage and skin-care therapy. Rates at the Sassy Moose peak from June to Sept, while the low seasons—Apr and Nov—find prices nearly cut in half. There's no smoking at the inn, and additional adults are $15 per day. Children age 11 and younger stay free.

i Although Jackson is a busy place during winter, room rates are significantly cheaper than in summer. Even with three popular ski resorts nearby, visitor numbers in winter pale in comparison with summer tourists wanting to get a glimpse of Grand Teton and Yellowstone National Parks.

SPRING CREEK RANCH $$$$
1800 Spirit Dance Rd.
(307) 733-8833, (800) 443-6139
www.springcreekranch.com

A variety of lodging options—all with dynamite views of the Tetons—are available at this beautiful ranch, located a few miles outside and 1,000 feet above Jackson. Hotel-style rooms offer one king or two queen-size beds, wood-burning fireplace, balcony, coffeemaker, minifridge, cable TV, and full bath. Studios are one large room with a complete kitchen, sleeping area, fireplace, and sunken living room, with a queen-size wall bed and queen-size sofa bed. Sitting suites offer a living room and a bedroom with a connecting bath; suites with two bedrooms are also available. You can also rent condominiums,

which have one, two, or three bedrooms in a variety of configurations. All condos have fireplaces, full kitchens, and balconies. And if you need even more room, Spring Creek has several 4,500- to 6,000-square-foot executive homes for rent. The renowned Granary restaurant and the Rising Sage Cafe offer lots of dining options for guests, and golf and skiing are just two of the activities just outside your door.

TETON MOUNTAIN LODGE $$$$
Teton Village
(800) 801-6615
www.tetonlodge.com

This slopeside lodge is one of Teton Village's finest lodging options, with 129 lodge rooms and suites featuring unique rustic styling and a host of luxury services and amenities. Room options include the hotel-like Lodge Rooms, a variety of suites that sleep up to 12, and a large penthouse suite. Many rooms include kitchens and fireplaces, and the on-site Mountain Lodge Spa offers a pool, a hot tub, and a variety of treatments. The lodge's Cascade Grill House offers fine dining, a nice bar, and room service.

THE WILDFLOWER INN $$$$
3725 Teton Village Rd.
(307) 733-4710
www.jacksonholewildflower.com

The cozy log-cabin confines of the Wildflower Inn have won accolades from *Sunset*, *Bon Appétit*, and *Glamour* magazines and have placed the inn on numerous "best of" lists. Owners Sherrie and Ken Jern built the Wildflower in 1989 and have five elegant and tastefully decorated rooms for rent, each with handcrafted log beds, down comforters, pedestal sinks, private baths, and beautiful country views. Each room is decorated with its own unique style, and all but one feature a private balcony. The highlight of the inn may be the incredible solarium, complete with a big hot tub and massive hanging plants. Rates range from $280 to $380, depending on the season, and children are welcome.

Campgrounds & RV Parks

Price Code

$................. Less than $16
$$ .... $16 to $23
$$$ .... More than $23

GRAND TETON PARK RV RESORT
AND CABINS $$$$
1 mile east of Grand Teton National Park, Moran
(307) 543-2483, (800) 563-6469
www.yellowstonerv.com
This year-round resort offers 120 RV sites at its location a mile east of Moran, 36 miles from Jackson, just outside the east entrance of Grand Teton National Park. Full services, including a pool, recreation room, and laundry, are available. Sixty tent sites are offered during summer.

LAZY J CORRAL $$$
10755 South US 89
(307) 733-1554
You'll find this year-round 24-site RV park 13 miles south of Jackson on the road toward Hoback Junction. The park offers full services, including a recreation room and a pool, but doesn't have any tent sites.

SNAKE RIVER PARK KOA $$$$
US 89
(307) 733-7078, (800) 562-1878
www.srpkoa.com

This Kampgrounds Of America location is open from Apr 12 to Oct 6 and has 50 RV sites and 30 tent sites, as well as cabins and tepees. There are no pull-throughs, but you'll find all other services. Snake River Park is south of Jackson on US 89. The nearby Teton Village KOA, 5 miles west of Jackson on WY 22, offers 150 sites from the beginning of May to Oct 12. You can reach that KOA by calling (307) 733-5354.

*TETON VALLEY
CAMPGROUND $$$–$$$$
128 Idaho Hwy. 31, Victor, ID
(208) 787-2647, (877) 787-3036
www.tetonvalleycampground.com
Teton Valley has four cabins and 75 RV spaces at its location on the west side of Teton Pass, just south of Driggs and about an hour from Jackson. Pets are allowed here, and the campground has hookups, laundry, dump stations, showers, pull-through sites, playground, modem hookups, and a swimming pool. Tent sites are also available.

THE VIRGINIAN RV PARK $$$
750 West Broadway Ave.
(307) 733-7189, (800) 321-6982
www.virginianlodge.com
Adjacent to the Virginian Lodge hotel, this full-service RV resort features 104 sites with 50-amp hookups, 64 of which are pull-through spaces. RV guests are entitled to all of the amenities available to lodge guests, including the pool, hot tub, and laundry. The resort is open from May 1 to Oct 15, depending on weather, and there is a restaurant and saloon on the property.

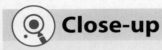 **Close-up**

A Big "Hole"

Is it Jackson or Jackson Hole? Well, the two are virtually interchangeable, but Jackson is the town and Jackson Hole is the valley. Why "hole"? Early fur traders referred to the high-country valleys of the West as holes and usually named them for trappers who discovered or frequented them. This one was named for mountain man David Jackson in 1829. Before that the valley belonged to American Indians. Tribes such as the Crow, Blackfoot, Gros Ventre, and Nez Perce hunted the valley's elk and bison during the warm months of the year.

In the early 1800s John Colter came to the area and began trading with the tribes at Fort Raymond, at the confluence of the Yellowstone and Bighorn Rivers. He stumbled into the Jackson Valley, and soon it was a major trapping spot for such famous mountain men as Jim Bridger, Jedediah Smith, and Jackson. The boom was short-lived, however, as beaver hats went out of fashion, and the fur trade died off by 1850. The valley would remain mostly deserted until government expeditions began mapping the area 20 years later.

The 1871 Hayden Expedition was one of the first through the area. William H. Jackson, a member of the expedition team, took the first known photos of the Teton Range, and it didn't take long for the images to appear all over the world. In 1879 painter Thomas Moran put the peaks on canvas and went on to have one of the most beautiful summits in the Tetons named for him. By the mid-1880s the first permanent settlers began arriving.

Some of the first families were the Wilsons, who founded the town at the bottom of the east side of Teton Pass, and the Driggs, who coined the town on the other side of the pass. Incidentally, that valley—now called Teton Valley or Basin—was originally called Pierre's Hole, named for Iroquois fur trader Pierre Tevanilagen. Other "holes" were Gardner's, Brown's, and Ogden's. Only Jackson still retains its link to the past.

RESTAURANTS

Price Code

Prices represent meals for two people, excluding beverages, tip, and tax.

$	Less than $20
$$	$20 to $27
$$$	$27 to $35
$$$$	More than $35

THE ACADIAN HOUSE $$
170 North Millward St.
(307) 739-1269

The Acadian dishes up authentic and reasonably priced Cajun cuisine for dinner seven days a week. The menu offers more than 30 selections, from steaks and seafood to catfish, crawfish, and gumbo. Catfish Acadian—blackened with a crawfish étouffée—is the most popular dish. Other recommendations include the snapper Louisane, the Creole chicken, the halibut Orleans, and the Louisiana alligator appetizer for those wanting something different. All entrees are served with your choice of a house salad or seafood gumbo, vegetable, and starch. Out of all the great items at the Acadian House, the last one you try may be its most famous. The Louisiana bread pudding is the only dessert offered, and it takes only one taste to see why. The Acadian House accepts reservations.

THE ALPENHOF $$–$$$$
Teton Village
(307) 733-3462
www.alpenhoflodge.com
The Alpenhof—at the base of Jackson Hole Mountain Resort—is actually two great restaurants under one roof. In the main dining room, called the Alpenrose, you'll find fantastic regional cuisine, while the bistro, (307) 733-3242, serves lighter gourmet fare. The dining room specializes in game dishes, such as venison and caribou for two, the caribou roulade, venison loin, and medallions of antelope. Vegetarians will love the Mediterranean timbale, and seafood lovers should try the bouillabaisse. Prices range from $17 to $30 per plate. In the bistro you'll find smoked duck rolls, grilled portobello mushrooms, salmon pasta, rainbow trout, and grilled honey-lime chicken. It's a popular après-ski spot to grab a drink and an appetizer, and it sports a sundeck for those bluebird days. Prices at the bistro top out at around $16, but most items are less. The dining room advises you to make reservations.

THE BACK DOOR DELI $
410 West Pearl St.
(307) 733-3354
Need a good sandwich? Well, the Back Door stocks more than 75 domestic and imported meats and cheeses and boasts a whopping 36 choices on the menu. No fast food here, though. Selections include corned beef, pastrami, turkey, prosciutto, mortadella, salami,

and more, served with such cheeses as Jarlsberg, Gruyère, and Muenster. If you don't care for the gourmet cheeses, the folks at the Back Door will be happy to whip up any combination you choose, and a full vegetarian menu is offered as well. For the little ones there's also peanut butter and jelly and kid-size ham and turkey sandwiches. The Back Door offers in-town delivery, too. Summer hours are 8 a.m. to 6 p.m. Mon through Fri and 9 a.m. to 5 p.m. on Sat. Winter hours are 9 a.m. to 7:30 p.m. Mon through Fri and 10 a.m. to 6 p.m. on Sat.

BAGEL JAX $
145 North Glenwood
(307) 733-9148
Choose from more than 15 varieties of bagels and seven different cream cheeses at Bagel Jax, where you can also get specialty sandwiches for lunch. Bagel choices include such delicious oddities as chocolate chip, apple streusel, and Asiago cheese, and you can top them off with such cream cheeses as honey maple pecan, tangerine almond, or strawberry. Sandwich selections include turkey avocado, Mediterranean, veggie, and honey-cured ham. A baker's dozen of bagels runs less than $7, and there isn't a sandwich over $4.

BETTY ROCK CAFE $
325 West Pearl St.
(307) 733-0747
www.bettyrock.com
Re-opened in 2009, the Betty Rock serves great breakfasts, lunches, and dinners Mon through Sat. Get bagels, coffee, omelets, pancakes, and more in the morning and salads, sandwiches, pizza, and paninis for lunch. The cafe also boasts homemade breads, soups, desserts, fruit smoothies, and a full

espresso bar. Thur is all-you-can-eat pizza night.

THE BLUE LION $$$
160 North Millward St.
(307) 733-3912
www.bluelionrestaurant.com
This quaint little restaurant is one of Jackson's more popular eateries, due to its casual, bistrolike atmosphere, outstanding continental cuisine, and summer patio dining. The menu offers something for everyone, including exquisite pastas, creative vegetarian, fresh seafood, and hearty beef and game dishes. The signature dish is the roast rack of New Zealand lamb, but don't hesitate to try the Thai shrimp linguine, Rocky Mountain trout filets, or the asparagus and sun-dried tomato risotto. In fact, it takes an extra-long time to decide what to eat here, as every item on the menu is tantalizing. Dinners come with a nice-size salad and delicious bread, but save room for dessert. Any one of the nightly specials is worth it. In summer the patio provides an outside meal away from the hustle and bustle of the town center, as the Blue Lion is located a few blocks north of busy Broadway Ave., Jackson's main street. An extensive, affordable wine list and a friendly staff ensure that the meal will leave a lasting impression. The Blue Lion has an early-bird special—20 percent off your bill from 6 to 6:30 p.m. with a coupon found each week in the *Jackson Hole Guide*. The Blue Lion serves dinner only and strongly recommends reservations.

BON APPETHAI $$
245 West Pearl St.
(307) 734-0245
www.bonappethai.com
This authentic Thai restaurant serves lunch and dinner daily at its downtown location. Traditional menu items like pad Thai, curries, and stir-fry dishes can also be prepared vegetarian or vegan, and beer, wine, and cocktails are available. Lunch is served 11 a.m. to 2:30 p.m., while dinner starts at 5 p.m.

BUBBA'S BAR-B-QUE $$
515 West Broadway Ave.
(307) 733-2288
Bubba's is Jackson's place for all things barbecue—chicken, ribs, turkey, and steak. Ribs are slow smoked over a hickory fire and then finished on the charbroiler with Bubba's secret sauce. Dinner plates are served barbecue-style, with garlic toast and your choice of two of the following: french fries, coleslaw, potato salad, corn on the cob, and beans. You get the same choices with your lunch, which features numerous reasonably priced specials, as well as a big bowl of beans and franks. If you're not in the mood for barbecue, choose from fish-and-chips, shrimp, and chili. Bubba's is also open for breakfast, beginning at 7 a.m. seven days a week.

THE BUNNERY $
130 North Cache St.
(307) 733-5474
www.bunnery.com
Breakfast at the Bunnery is a Jackson Hole tradition, and the secret has been let out. In the morning you'll often see a line extending out the door with people waiting to get a taste of fresh-baked breads and pastries, gourmet omelets, and whole-grain pancakes and waffles, which is just a sampling of the extensive menu. The wait is worth it, of course, and selections like the Bunnery Benedict, the Glory Bowl, and the Mother Earth will give you plenty of energy for a

Consider Autumn

Fall around the Jackson Hole Valley is quiet and peaceful and can be a more relaxing and less expensive time to visit. Most lodging is discounted during the shoulder seasons—the time between the end of one tourist season and the beginning of the next—and you can find well-appointed rooms at a reasonable rate. The streets and trails will also be less crowded, and chances are you'll get to see the first snow of the season dust the high peaks of the Tetons and surrounding mountains. If you visit in fall, remember that some park services close in early Oct. Call Grand Teton National Park, (307) 739-3399, for information.

day on the trail or the slopes. The croissants, sticky buns, and buttermilk coffee cakes make great grab-and-go meals, and fresh juices and espresso are also available. The Bunnery serves up creative sandwiches, burritos, and veggie specialties for lunch and is open for dinner in summer.

THE CADILLAC $$$
55 North Cache St.
(307) 733-3279
www.cadillac-grille.com
From the outside the Cadillac looks like an unassuming 1950s-era diner, with a lively atmosphere not fit for a typical fine-dining experience. And that's just the restaurant's point—you don't have to appear stuffy to serve renowned cuisine. Dining should be fun, and the Cadillac makes sure of it.

Selections include Black Angus blue cheese tournedos, hazelnut-crusted rack of lamb, pan-seared duck, and flame-kissed Atlantic salmon. The menu changes frequently, and the restaurant features an award-winning wine list. The Cadillac suggests reservations.

THE GUN BARREL STEAK AND
GAME HOUSE $$$$
862 West Broadway Ave.
(307) 733-3287
www.gunbarrel.com
This Jackson dining institution features a variety of steak and game dishes cooked over an open river-rock mesquite grill, served in an old-time hunting lodge atmosphere—complete with full trophy animal mounts from the old Wyoming Wildlife Museum and Taxidermy. Meat lovers can choose from venison, elk, beef, and bison steaks, as well as pork, chicken, and seafood dishes. Roosevelt's prime rib is a popular choice, and there is always a variety of homemade desserts to complete your meal. Beer, wine, and liquor served, and reservations are recommended.

JEDEDIAH'S HOUSE
OF SOURDOUGH $$$
135 East Broadway Ave.
(307) 733-5671
Jedediah's serves up great pioneer sourdough cookin' in a historic log cabin decorated with memorabilia and old photographs. You can start your morning in Jackson here, choosing from such selections as Teton taters and eggs, sourdough flapjacks, and a variety of omelets. The early-riser special, served from 7 to 9 a.m., is one of the best deals in the valley. You get two eggs, meat, home fries, and all the biscuits and gravy or flapjacks you can eat for $7.50. The lunch menu includes soups, salads, burgers,

and sandwiches—mostly served on sourdough bread. No beer or wine here, but the folks at Jedediah's will be happy to provide the glasses and a corkscrew if you bring your own.

KOSHU WINE BAR $$$
200 South Broadway
(406) 733-5283
www.koshuwinebar.com
Cocktail hour in Jackson got a little hipper when Koshu came to town in 2002. Chef Joel Holland serves Asian/Latin-influenced cuisine, paired with a small but well-selected wine list, making this the locals' hangout at the end of the day. It's a chichi way to unwind with a glass of wine and share "family-style" selections of unusual dishes, such as wok-fried green beans with hoisin and sesame or whole, fried Idaho catfish with a citrus dipping sauce. With its light but satisfying fare, Koshu offers an excellent way to sample everything on the menu with a group of friends for dinner. Reservations are not accepted. Enter through the Jackson Hole Wine Company.

i The world's only public auction of elk antlers takes place each year on the Jackson town square on the third Sat in May. The antlers are shed by elk on the National Elk Refuge and are collected by local Boy Scouts. The majority of the auction proceeds go back to the refuge for the next year's elk feeding program.

MASA SUSHI $$$
Inn at Jackson Hole, Teton Village
(307) 732-2962
Located on the second floor of the Inn at Jackson Hole in Teton Village, this restaurant flies in seafood several times a week to make the array of sushi rolls offered here. With specialty rolls ranging from sea eel to hot spicy salmon, you'll be pleasantly surprised by the exquisite combinations prepared by chef Masa Kitami. Open seven days a week from 5:30 to 9:30 p.m. in the winter and summer. Reservations are required.

MILLION DOLLAR COWBOY STEAKHOUSE $$$
25 North Cache St.
(307) 733-4790
www.milliondollarcowboybar.com
The Million Dollar Cowboy is one of Jackson's most recognizable establishments—a big, flashy sign and lots of Harleys parked out front. Inside, the bar stools are saddles and the atmosphere is western, right down to the Remington and Russell prints on the walls. The food here is western, too, with juicy hand-cut steaks, fresh seafood, and wild game. You can get just about any cut of steak you want and finish off your meal with a homemade dessert. The full bar also features more than two dozen single-malt scotches. Dinner reservations are recommended.

MOUNTAIN HIGH PIZZA PIE $
120 West Broadway Ave.
(307) 733-3646
Mountain High serves up some of Jackson's best pizza, available in traditional, whole wheat, and deep-dish crusts with a variety of fresh toppings. Choose from traditional, tomato-based pizzas or a number of specialty pies, including the Santa Fe, Thai pie, sunny chicken pesto, and barbecue chicken. You'll also find huge calzones, subs, salads, and appetizers. Mountain High is open daily until 10 p.m. in winter, 11 p.m. during summer. Beer, wine, and delivery are available.

If you're pitching a tent while staying in the area, the earliest campground to open is the Snake River KOA, around Apr 12. Outlying state and federal campgrounds generally open around June 15, but Colter Bay and Jenny Lake inside the park open a month earlier. Most every campground is closed by the end of Oct—right before the winter chill.

NANI'S GENUINE PASTA HOUSE $
242 North Glenwood
(307) 733-3888
www.nanis.com
Featuring different foods from one of Italy's 20 regions each month in addition to the classical menu, Nani's vows to take you on an authentic culinary tour. Favorites like veal Marsala and the spicy Pasta Pesce have kept Jacksonites coming into Nani's little house for more than 15 years. On Sun, Mon, and Tues nights, look for "family specials," perhaps spaghetti and meatballs or regional lasagna. Children are welcome, and child portions for kids age 12 and younger are available on the classic menu pastas. Reservations are appreciated; open nightly from 5 to 10 p.m.

OLD YELLOWSTONE GARAGE $$$
175 Center St.
(307) 734-6161
A move from the tiny neighboring town of Du Bois to Jackson's town square has brought more people in to linger over the food at the elegant Old Yellowstone Garage, but the food hasn't changed a bit. A self-proclaimed "Western Italian restaurant," the only thing western about OYG is its Wyoming location. Otherwise this food is straight from Italy. Owners Cincia and Daniel have

strong connections to Italy, and both their menu and wine list reflect this. In addition to 14 wood-oven pizzas, the menu features delectable fresh mussels in a broth perfect for soaking up the house-made bread and a slow-cooked lamb shank in a terra-cotta pot, along with the best tiramisu this side of the Mediterranean Sea. The menu changes seasonally and is offered for dinner only from 5:30 p.m. until closing.

PEARL STREET BAGELS $
145 West Pearl
(307) 739-1218
Pearl Street has two locations—the second is at Fish Creek Center, WY 22 in Wilson (307-739-1261)—to fix your early morning need for a good bagel. Both locations offer several varieties of bagels as well as sandwiches and coffee to go.

✳RENDEZVOUS BISTRO $$
380 South Broadway
(307) 730-1100
www.rendezvousbistro.net
Away from the town square, but not from the center of action, Rendezvous Bistro was founded by the former chef of the renowned Snake River Grill. The food is classic American gourmet, with daily specials ranging from whole Maine lobster to roast prime rib. A long list of appetizers and a raw bar serving oysters on the half shell and ceviche make this a hopping spot with the cocktail set. On the other hand, it's also an upscale family restaurant, with selections as approachable as meat loaf, roasted chicken, fish-and-chips, and sandwiches. Open nightly from 5:30 p.m. to closing. Closed Sun during the winter only.

THE SILVER DOLLAR BAR AND GRILLE $–$$
Broadway and Glenwood
(307) 732-3939
www.worthotel.com
Located on the first floor of the historic Wort Hotel, the Silver Dollar serves up big sandwiches and tasty appetizers in the bar and more elaborate fare in the main dining room. The bar is a popular spot to grab a reasonably priced meal, such as a burger, chicken sandwich, or wings or nachos. Dining-room entrees include prime rib, trout, elk chops, and chicken pesto primavera. Live entertainment is featured nightly in the bar, making the Silver Dollar a choice après-ski destination and a nightlife hot spot.

✳SNAKE RIVER BREWING CO. $$
265 South Millward St.
(307) 739-2337
www.snakeriverbrewing.com
If you like a good brew with your meal, there aren't many places better than the Snake River Brewery. Its award-winning English-style ales, porters, and stouts and European lagers are made on the premises and go perfectly with the variety of pastas, sandwiches, and pizzas served in the restaurant. The pizza, baked in a wood-fired oven, is the most popular and just the right size for one with a hearty appetite, or for two who don't want to stuff themselves. If you don't want to eat a full dinner, the brewery is a great place to hang out, munch on some appetizers, and sample the fine, handcrafted beers. A popular spot with many of the younger locals, the brewery is open daily until midnight.

SNAKE RIVER GRILL $$$$
84 East Broadway Ave.
(307) 733-0557
www.snakerivergrill.com

Make reservations if you want to eat at the Snake River Grill, one of Jackson's most popular and well-known restaurants. Located across from the town square, the restaurant features a variety of fresh fish, free-range veal and chicken, wood-fired pizza, and wild game. Selections you're apt to find on the menu include Chilean sea bass, grilled ahi tuna, venison chops, braised antelope, fresh Idaho trout, and fettuccine with grilled chicken. The wine list continues to be praised by *Wine Spectator* for its more than 200 selections, and outside dining is available in summer. The Snake River Grill serves dinner daily from 6 p.m., 5:30 p.m. in the summer.

WILD SAGE RESTAURANT $$$$
175 North Jackson St.
(307) 733-2000, (888) 739-1749
www.rustyparrot.com
The Wild Sage Restaurant at the Rusty Parrot Lodge and Spa is one of two restaurants in Wyoming and Montana to earn the prestigious AAA Four Diamond designation. The intimate, 26-seat restaurant offers exceptional regional cuisine as well as fresh seafood and game dishes served in a cozy atmosphere enhanced by a river-rock fireplace. Executive chef Rick Sordahl's focus is on organically grown products, local produce and meats, and sustainable fish and proteins. Some of Sordahl's creations include rosemary and green tea–smoked duck breast, a watercress and apple salad, and a tamari bacon stung Berkshire pork tenderloin. Reservations are strongly encouraged.

SHOPPING

Shopping is why many people come to Jackson. For a small town it has a remarkable number of galleries, boutiques, clothiers, and specialty shops. The list below includes a few of the more-well-known shops but contains only a fraction of Jackson's shopping options.

It doesn't include art galleries or clothing stores—you could write a book just on those—concentrating instead on specialty stores you may have trouble finding. Jackson is the kind of place where you really need to just start walking around downtown. There will be several neat shops around every corner you turn, and hard-core shoppers can spend a lot of time looking around.

BROADWAY BOTTLE
200 West Broadway Ave.
(307) 739-WINE
You can get beer, liquor, and wine at this shop on the corner of Millward and Broadway, 2 blocks from the town square. You'll find a large selection of regional microbrews and fine wines to choose from, as well as an array of spirits and liquors.

CAYUSE
255 North Glenwood St.
(307) 739-1940
www.cayusewa.com
If you're looking for Old West artifacts, Cayuse is your best bet. The shop specializes in antique western art and artifacts, early lodge furnishings, and national park memorabilia, as well as early Jackson and Yellowstone material. Cayuse also features the contemporary buckles of Clint Orms Silversmiths and Engravers.

D. D. CAMERA CORRAL
60 South Cache St.
(307) 733-3831
This Jackson shop has served locals and visitors for more than 40 years. You'll find all

major brands of film and equipment here, as well as two-hour photo finishing and five-minute color enlargements. Also, if you want a recorded memoir of your vacation, the Camera Corral offers camcorder and camera rentals.

FISH CREEK CENTER
WY 22, Wilson
Coming to Jackson you'll pass this little shopping center on the south side of the highway. You'll find **Pearl Street Bagels,** (307) 739-1261 (see listing under Restaurants earlier in this chapter), which offers coffee, bagels, and sandwiches, and **Wilson Backcountry Sports,** (307) 733-5228, which has everything you need for safe and effective travel in the outdoors. The center is also home to Prime Properties and Fish Creek Construction Services.

HOLE IN THE WALL SNOWBOARD SHOP
Teton Village
(307) 739-2689
One of Jackson's original snowboard shops, Hole in the Wall offers sales, demos, tuning, and clothing in its location at the base of the Bridger gondola at the Jackson Hole Mountain Resort. The shop is open from 8 a.m. to 6 p.m. daily and carries gear by Lib Tech, Salomon, Burton, K2, Roxy, Bonfire, DaKine, and more. If you want your ride back in a hurry, Hole in the Wall will tune or repair it overnight.

JACKSON HOLE CHAMBER OF COMMERCE
990 West Broadway Ave.
(307) 733-3316
www.jhchamber.com
Shopping at the chamber? Well, not exactly.

Ski Shops

Jackson Hole may just have the most ski shops per capita of anywhere in the world—too many to list in this guide. But to give you an insiders' peek, here's a few of the best:

Skinny Skis (65 West Delaney, 307-733-6094) is your cross-country and backcountry touring headquarters, offering top-of-the-line gear and accessories, as well as rentals and demos.

Wilson Backcountry Sports (1230 Ida Dr., 307-733-5228) offers sales and rentals of telemark, randonnée, cross-country, and snowshoe equipment, as well as advice and tips on where to go.

Hoback Sports (40 South Millward St., 307-733-5335) features demo and high-performance rentals, snowboards, clothing, and a repair shop, while **The Edge Sports** (490 West Broadway Ave., 307-734-3916) offers beginner to advanced ski sales; ski demos from Atomic, Stockli, and Dynastar; and a Wintersteiger-equipped tuning center.

In Teton Village, **Wildernest Sports,** (307) 733-4297, has one of the largest rental shops in the valley, including kids' and high-performance gear, as well as Burton snowboard rentals and an overnight repair service. **Teton Village Sports,** (307) 733-2181, also has a high-performance demo ski center, featuring equipment from Rossignol, Volkl, Salomon, Tecnica, Marker, and more.

And it's worth a drive to Driggs to stop in and say hello to the friendly staff at **Yöstmark Mountain Equipment,** 12 East Little Ave., (208) 354-2828, where Clair Yöst has been making and selling his legendary Mountain Noodle telemark ski since 1990. You'll find a huge selection of backcountry gear here, as well as snowboards and clothing, and a knowledgeable group of employees full of tips on favorite places to go.

But if you're looking for the sought-after posters from the past and present Old West Days and Fall Arts Festivals, this is the place. Stop in to see the selection of posters available.

JACKSON HOLE RESORT STORE
50 North Center St.
(307) 739-2767
If you don't ski or can't make it up to Teton Village, stop in at the downtown location of the Jackson Hole Resort Store, where you'll find a full selection of T-shirts, hats, clothing,

and gifts bearing the resort's trademark logo. You can also buy lift tickets at the store, located on the east side of the town square.

MOUNTUNES MUSIC AND ESPRESSO
265 West Broadway Ave.
(307) 733-4514, (800) 982-2241
www.mountunes.com
Mountunes is Jackson's only full-service store for CDs, cassettes, and accessories. You'll find music from rock and reggae to country and classical. There's also a large selection of regional and local artists, and Mountunes

sells concert tickets for upcoming shows around the valley. Mountunes also has an Internet and espresso cafe.

TOBACCO ROW
120 North Cache St.
(307) 733-4385
You'll find the largest selection of cigars, cigarettes, and pipe and rolling tobaccos in the area at Tobacco Row, which also features handmade humidors and smoking accessories. There is also a nice selection of fine, locally roasted coffee. Tobacco Row opens at 10 a.m. daily.

NIGHTLIFE

There's a lot to do after the sun sets in Jackson, and both summer and winter have vibrant nightlife scenes. A night on the town wouldn't be complete without a stop in at the legendary **Million Dollar Cowboy Bar,** (307) 733-4790, directly across from the town square. With saddle-shaped bar stools and Thursday-night swing-dance lessons—and a lot of cowboy hats—the Cowboy Bar is a true western experience.

The **Mangy Moose,** (307) 733-9779, located at the base of the ski resort in Teton Village, is the most popular bar for live music and features local and national acts. The walls and ceilings of the bar are covered in Jackson Hole memorabilia—looking is entertainment in itself—and the Mangy Moose is the ski resort's most celebrated après-ski spot. For live music in town, also check out the **Silver Dollar Bar,** (307) 732-3239, in the Wort Hotel; **Sidewinders,** (307) 734-5766; and the **Shady Lady Saloon** at Snow King Resort,

(307) 733-5200, which features live music on Wed. **Teton Pines,** (307) 733-1005, and the **Granary Lounge** at Spring Creek Ranch, (307) 733-8833, feature live pianists several nights a week. If you want to drive a little bit, the **Bull Moose Saloon,** (307) 654-7593, in Alpine, and **Dornan's,** (307) 733-2415, in Moose, feature local and national bands on a regular basis. The **Snake River Pub and Brewery,** (307) 739-2337, is a mellow hot spot for the younger crowd.

The **Performing Arts Company of Jackson Hole** puts on numerous productions throughout the year in the **Pink Garter Mainstage Theater,** (307) 733-9787. The **Jackson Hole Playhouse,** (307) 733-6994, does a dinner and theater combination in the tradition of the old western playhouse, which usually makes for a side-splitting evening of raucous entertainment. Also try the **Off Square Theater Company,** (307) 733-4900, which puts on several productions a year at the Jackson Hole Center for the Performing Arts.

Sports fans may want to check out the **Jackson Hole Moose,** a Senior-A hockey team that plays at the Snow King Center several times per month. Call (307) 733-5200 for information.

ℹ️ When you hear people refer to the Teton Village road or the Moose–Wilson road, they're talking about the road north from ID 22 near Wilson to Moose, inside the border of Grand Teton National Park. It's the main route to the ski area, but the stretch past Teton Village starting at the park boundary is closed in winter.

WEST YELLOWSTONE

West Yellowstone, or "West" as the locals call it, is a town that thrives on tourism associated with Yellowstone National Park. Perhaps more than any other gateway town, West depends on the influx of visitors during summer and winter to fuel its economy, and it's been this way for more than 100 years. Millions of tourists arrive in West every year, entering the park by car, snowcoach, or snowmobile. The town is still the starting point for many family vacations, and in summer and winter it is bustling seven days a week. With this many visitors, the town has grown to accommodate them. Numerous hotels, restaurants, shops, galleries, and attractions make it a great spot for people to stay and enjoy the wonders of the park and surrounding area.

Unless otherwise indicated, all listings in this chapter are located in West Yellowstone, Montana.

OVERVIEW

West Yellowstone sprang up in 1908 when Union Pacific's Oregon Short Line brought the first trainload of passengers into the area. The train came south from Ashton, Idaho, over Targhee Pass to the west entrance of the park, where visitors could enter the park on stagecoaches. Before that the only way down to the west entrance was by horse or foot from Bozeman or Virginia City—a trip only a few hearty travelers made each year.

The Oregon Short Line would serve West Yellowstone for 52 years, until the introduction of the automobile signaled the railroad's end. Cars were allowed into the park for the first time in 1915, when they shared the road with stagecoaches (although that didn't last long). The following year one of the largest stagecoach companies called it quits, and more and more private cars were driving on the park's roads. In fact, the traffic was so great that most of the park's infrastructure had to be rebuilt. Since the mid-1930s, when

the roads were paved, West Yellowstone has attracted tourists from around the world.

Not surprisingly, the local population is driven by the service industry. From snowmobile rental shops to pancake houses, gas stations to museums, and fly-fishing shops to rafting companies, chances are that if you live here you're associated with something that serves visitors. Just under 1,200 people call West home year-round and find it an exciting mix of commerce, recreation, and natural beauty. Centrally located between Bozeman and Jackson, West is great not only for tourists but also for locals who flock here to enjoy the millions of acres of national forests and hundreds of miles of trails and waterways. And when West quiets down during the shoulder seasons, it is a peaceful, beautiful place to call home.

The difference between summer and winter in West basically comes down to one thing: snowmobiles. Chances are you've never seen anything like it. Snowmobiles buzz around town on the snow-covered roads, hopping from motel to restaurant and into the park. Trails start in the middle of town and head into the woods, giving snowmobilers instant access to unmatched terrain, scenery, and fun.

Snowmobiling in West has changed. The Clinton administration and the National Park Service enacted a ban on snowmobiling in Yellowstone and Grand Teton National Parks that had been scheduled to take effect in the winter of 2003–04. This controversial issue divided the town. Some said the ban would cause businesses to close. After all, snowmobilers are a big part of the town's economy, and why would they come here if the park is off-limits? Others argued that numbers would drop only slightly and that West's other attractions would keep visitors coming—just as they always have. The controversy caused the Bush administration to lift the ban, instead enacting stricter rules on the snowmobile industry. Under the current winter-use plan, a limited number of snowmobiles and snowcoaches are allowed into the park, and visitors who tour the park on snowmobiles must have a guide and ride environmentally friendly four-stroke machines. This ongoing issue is again being scrutinized, with another legislation decision on the horizon that will take effect in the winter of 2011–12.

West is also one of the premier cross-country skiing destinations in the world. With 580 miles of snowmobile and ski trails around West Yellowstone, there is plenty of powder to go around.

Just outside West Yellowstone you'll find the communities of Ennis, Montana, and Island Park, Idaho, which will be included in this chapter. Refer to the Greater Yellowstone Area map at the beginning of the book for their locations.

ACCOMMODATIONS
Hotels
Price Code
Some rates are based on availability. The following codes indicate the average nightly rates for two adults. Accommodations accept all or most major credit cards, unless otherwise noted.

$. . . . . **Less than $70**
$$ . . . . **$70 to $90**
$$$ . . . . **$90 to $110**
$$$$ . . . . **More than $110**

ALPINE MOTEL   **$$**
120 Madison Ave.
(406) 646-7544
www.alpinemotelwestyellowstone.com
This highly rated small motel is run by Brian and Patty Watson, owners who pride themselves on taking care of their guests and helping them experience all that the area has to offer. There are standard rooms with one or two queen/double beds, as well as a two-room suite and a kitchen unit that sleeps up to six. The reasonably priced rooms are nonsmoking and include cable TV, wireless Internet, air-conditioning, refrigerator, and hair dryer, and there are hot beverages and a microwave in the lobby. For large groups, the kitchen unit and two-room suite can be combined to sleep 10 comfortably. The standard rooms are open May through Oct, while the larger rooms are open year-round.

BEST WESTERN DESERT INN   **$$$**
133 Canyon St.
(406) 646-7376, (800) 574-7054

There are four Best Westerns in West, but the 76-room Desert Inn is the largest and nicest. Each well-appointed room features high-speed Internet, cable TV, microwave, refrigerator, and coffeemaker, and an indoor heated swimming pool and hot tub are available for guests. A complimentary continental breakfast is offered, and pets are allowed. Children under 18 stay free with an adult.

THE BRANDIN' IRON INN $$$
201 Canyon St.
(406) 646-9411, (800) 217-4613
www.yellowstonevacations.com

Two blocks from the west entrance to Yellowstone, the Brandin' Iron offers 79 remodeled king-size and queen-size suites, a spacious lobby with a stone fireplace, oversize Jacuzzis, and a laundry facility. The rooms are big and tastefully decorated with oak furniture. The Brandin' Iron also offers bus tours of the park during summer and winter snowmobile rentals.

CITY CENTER MOTEL $
214 Madison Ave.
(406) 646-7337, (800) 742-0665
www.yellowstonevacations.com

This budget hotel offers 25 clean and comfortable rooms at a convenient location 2 blocks from Yellowstone's boundary. There's a nice hot-tub room, in-room coffeemakers, cable TV, and a health club. The City Center also offers summer bus tours and winter snowmobile packages and has undergone a renovation.

DAYS INN $$$$
801 Madison Ave.
(406) 646-7656, (800) 548-9551
www.allyellowstone.com

This 115-room hotel is worth mentioning because of the 100-foot waterslide that empties happy kids into the indoor pool. Standard hotel rooms include double queen-size beds and cable TV, although kitchenettes and suites with in-room spas are available. The attached restaurant—Trapper's Restaurant—has great food for families. The hotel is right across from All Yellowstone Motorsports and SnoVan Tours.

GRAY WOLF INN AND SUITES $$$$
250 South Canyon St.
(406) 646-0000, (800) 852-8602
www.visityellowstonepark.com

The Gray Wolf is one of West's newer hotels and offers 102 guest rooms, including 16 one- and two-bedroom apartment-size suites. All rooms have 25-inch TVs, pay-per-use Nintendo gaming systems and movies, clock radios, hair dryers, coffeemakers, speaker telephones with dataports, voice mail, two vanity areas with sinks and mirrors, full bath with tub/shower combination, and individually controlled heat and air-conditioning units. Suites include complete kitchens with microwaves, dishwashers, toasters, dishes, and utensils. Rooms have been recently remodeled and are nicely decorated with soft colors and oak woodwork. The three-story building also houses an indoor pool, a sauna, a hot tub, a coin-operated guest laundry, and an indoor heated parking garage. Continental breakfast is served in the lobby.

✳HIBERNATION STATION $$$$
212 Gray Wolf Ave.
(406) 646-4200, (800) 580-3557
www.hibernationstation.com

Stepping into the rustic log cabins of the Hibernation Station might give you the impression you're in a remote resort in the middle of Yellowstone, not 3 blocks from its entrance. Since 1994 guests have been staying in these elegantly appointed cabins, which offer king-size, queen-size, and double-bed combinations. Each impressive cabin has a different theme, named for regional rivers and streams. The Madison's handcrafted king-size bed, jetted tub, and fireplace will leave you warm and well rested. The Henry's Fork has three queen-size beds, a fireplace, full kitchenette, and a dining area for six people. Whichever cabin you choose, you'll get down comforters, extra-soft bath towels, and an overall luxurious and rustic atmosphere. When you're done gaping at the incredible log construction of the cabins and furniture, you can relax in the center courtyard's Jacuzzi room while marveling at the largest bronze sculpture in Montana. Winter packages are available.

KELLY INN $$$$
104 South Canyon St.
(406) 646-4544, (800) 635-3559
www.yellowstonekellyinn.com
The Kelly Inn is a large hotel located on West's main thoroughfare and features 78 large, nicely appointed rooms with one king-size or two queen-size beds. Standard rooms offer 25-inch TV, wireless Internet, pay-per-view movies, Nintendo, and electronic keyless entry. Specialty suites feature a wet bar, whirlpool, refrigerator, microwave, and hair dryer. There is an indoor heated pool, a Jacuzzi, and a sauna. Enjoy the daily continental breakfast in the lobby. The Kelly Inn is located on the south side of town across from the IMAX movie theater and the Grizzly Discovery Center. The parking lot is large enough to accommodate snowmobile trailers. Winter packages are available.

PONY EXPRESS MOTEL $
4 Firehole Ave.
(406) 646-7644, (800) 323-9708
www.yellowstonevacations.com
Nothing fancy here, just nice-size, clean rooms at a price that will leave you with plenty of cash left over for the area's numerous attractions. Rooms have a warm, knotty pine decor, and winter snowmobile packages are available. This single-story hotel is right across the street from the Yellowstone entrance.

STAGE COACH INN $$$
209 Madison Ave.
(406) 646-7381, (800) 842-2882
www.yellowstoneinn.com
You can't miss the Stage Coach, which looks like a grand Swiss ski chalet. With 91 rooms and an underground heated parking garage, the Stage Coach is one of West's largest full-service hotels. The new Montana Cattle Company restaurant is one of the town's more popular eating and partying places, specializing in mouthwatering steak dinners, and nightly live entertainment during winter can be heard in the Coachman Lounge, located downstairs.

**WEST YELLOWSTONE
  HOLIDAY INN** $$$$
315 Yellowstone Ave.
(406) 646-7365, (800) 646-7365
www.visityellowstonepark.com
This deluxe Holiday Inn is West's largest hotel, with 123 rooms, including deluxe executive suites with stone fireplaces, king rooms with jetted tubs, and two-room family units. All rooms have refrigerators, 32-inch TVs, coffeemakers, hair dryers, and microwaves. There's also an indoor pool, hot tub, sauna, exercise room, and conference center with 10,000

square feet and room for 500 guests. The popular Oregon Short Line restaurant serves up excellent grub, including bison kabobs, barbecue short ribs, and pan-fried trout. The Iron Horse Saloon offers video gambling and a large selection of Montana microbrews. If you have time, walk through the fully restored 1903 Oregon Short Line railcar, one of the best-preserved train cars of its type in the world. Winter and summer packages are available.

YELLOWSTONE COUNTRY INN $$
234 Firehole Ave.
(406) 646-7622, (800) 646-7622
This centrally located hotel, formerly called the Big Western Pine Lodge offers just about everything you will need during your stay. Forty-five rooms feature updated carpeting and furniture, cable TV, and tub/showers. The three-bedroom, two-bath cottage is great for large parties and snowmobilers and features a full kitchen, living room, laundry room, wood-burning stove, hardwood floors, and maid service. There is also a cabin that sleeps 20, with two kitchens, two baths, and two TVs. The outdoor heated pool is open only during summer, but a large hot tub and sauna is relaxing enough after a cold day of trail riding. The attached Rustler's Roost restaurant offers a wide variety of food, including a soup and salad bar, and specializes in wild game. You can get appetizers and pizza in the lounge, where you'll find a pool table and several video gambling machines. The hotel also serves as West Yellowstone's Greyhound depot, and pets are allowed.

YELLOWSTONE LODGE $$$$
250 Electric St.
(406) 646-0020, (877) 239-9298
www.yellowstonelodge.com

The deluxe Yellowstone Lodge features 80 rooms, with your choice of two queen-size beds or one king-size bed with a queen-size sofa sleeper. Suites that accommodate up to six people are available. Each room has a coffeemaker, 25-inch cable TV, telephone with dataport, two vanity areas with sinks, and full baths with a tub/shower combination. Approximately one-third of the rooms have small fridges. The three-story hotel also has an indoor heated pool, a hot tub, a coin-operated laundry, and ample parking for large vehicles.

Bed-and-Breakfasts, Lodges & Cabins

Price Code
$.................. Less than $85
$$ .... $85 to $115
$$$ .... $115 to $150
$$$$ .... More than $150

BAR N RANCH $$$$
890 Buttermilk Rd.
(406) 646-0030
www.bar-n-ranch.com
You'll get a complete Montana vacation at Mike and Gayle Gavagan's Bar N, located southwest of West Yellowstone and 5 miles from the park. The recently built main lodge is a breathtaking structure, with a three-sided fireplace and hand-hewn logs, and is full of family heirlooms and old-fashioned charm. You can listen to music from one of the 1890s pianos or watch the sunset from the hot tub on the wraparound porch. The Bar N's main lodge has seven rooms that accommodate two to six people and seven private cabins for groups up to eight. All the rooms, even in the main lodge, have a fireplace, and each cabin has a private hot tub. Anglers take note: The Bar N has 5 miles

of private access on the South Fork of the world-famous Madison River. Rates include a full, made-to-order breakfast each morning of your stay and all the Rocky Mountain scenery you can take in. The ranch is currently open May through Oct.

☀FIREHOLE RANCH $$$$
P.O. Box 686, West Yellowstone, MT 59758
(406) 646-7294
www.fireholeranch.com

Nestled between the shores of Hebgen Lake and Coffin Peak, the Firehole Ranch caters to anglers. The rustically elegant, Orvis-endorsed fishing lodge is consistently rated among the best in the West, and it provides a complete Montana vacation for both seasoned and novice anglers. The 10 cabins are tucked into the woods and are spaced far enough apart for privacy but are really made only for two people, with the exception of a few adjoining ones that can accommodate larger groups. However, the capacity of the ranch is limited to 20 guests.

Reminiscent of an old hunting camp, the main lodge houses a huge stone fireplace and numerous animal racks. Meals are included and are as much a visual feast as a tasteful one. The dining room offers expansive views of the lake and surrounding mountains. The ranch is surrounded by some of the best trout-fishing streams in the world, including the Madison, the Yellowstone, the Gallatin, the Henry's Fork of the Snake River, the Gibbon, and the Firehole. Head guide Scotty Hall leads a team of eight guides that will have you hooking the big ones in no time.

i Quake Lake, created by a massive earthquake in 1959 that took out an entire mountainside, is a short drive from West Yellowstone on US 287. The fatal quake dammed up the Madison River, creating this small lake just west of the larger Hebgen Lake. Stop in at the Forest Service's visitor center for the interpretive display that commemorates a violent and tragic day in Montana history.

PARADE REST RANCH $$$$
1279 Grayling Creek Rd.
(406) 646-7217, (800) 753-5934
www.paraderestranch.com

Have yourself a real western experience at the Parade Rest, which can be found by heading west on US 287 at the junction with US 191, 8 miles from West Yellowstone. The ranch offers rustic log cabins with full bathrooms that accommodate 2 to 10 people. The R & R Lodge is an activity center for all ages, and you can play horseshoes, volleyball, and basketball on the premises. In summer the ranch wrangler will guide novice horse riders on easy morning or afternoon rides, while advanced riders can take a challenging journey up to higher elevations. The price includes three meals, and the ranch will pack a lunch for you to take along when you leave to explore. You'll know when it's time to eat at the Parade Rest—just listen for the old-fashioned dinner bell. Rates are discounted 20 percent from mid-Sept to mid-June and include transportation to and from the West Yellowstone airport if needed.

THE PINES AT ISLAND PARK $$$$
3907 Philips Loop Rd., Island Park, ID
(208) 558-0192, (800) 455-9384
www.pinesislandpark.com

Each immaculate log cabin at this luxury resort boasts 1,500 square feet of space, three bedrooms, two bathrooms, loft, living and dining rooms, fireplace, laundry facilities, satellite TV, hot tub, and full kitchen. Leather and log furniture complete the western atmosphere. Snowmobiling and fishing opportunities await you just outside your door. The Pines is located 25 miles south of West Yellowstone.

Campgrounds & RV Parks

Price Code

$	Less than $10
$$	$10 to $20
$$$	$20 to $30
$$$$	More than $30

LA SIESTA RV PARK $$
510 Madison Ave.
(406) 646-7892

La Siesta's 12 sites make it one of the smallest RV parks in town, but its downtown location also makes it one of the most convenient. Open year-round, it offers cable TV, laundry, showers, electric hookups, flush toilets, drinking water, and plenty of shade trees for those hot summer days.

MADISON ARM RESORT CAMPGROUND AND MARINA $$$
South Shore of Hebgen Lake
(406) 646-9328
www.madisonarmresort.com

Summer is a busy time at Madison Arm, where the campgrounds and RV sites are nestled in a large stand of lodgepole pines and on the shore of scenic Hebgen Lake. Choose from 70 RV and 20 tent sites, and enjoy the lake by renting a boat, canoe, or kayak. Facilities include a general store, laundry, showers, electric hookups, dump stations, and a full-service marina, where you'll find a boat ramp, docks, and fuel. Madison Arm is open from mid-May to mid-Oct. To get there take US 191 north out of town for 3 miles, then take a left on Forest Service Road 291. The resort is 5.5 miles from the turnoff.

SUPER 8 MOTEL/LIONSHEAD RESORT $$$
1545 Targhee Pass Hwy.
(406) 646-7662
www.lionsheadrv.com

The year-round Lionshead, with 194 RV and 48 tent sites, is the area's largest RV park. It's located about 8 miles west of town on US 20, part of a large complex including a Super 8 and Alice's Restaurant. A favorite activity here is nightly square dancing in summer, and snowmobilers flock to the Lionshead for its proximity to the great riding near Targhee Pass and the Lionshead area. RV facilities include laundry, showers, drinking water, flush toilets, and electric hookups.

YELLOWSTONE GRIZZLY RV PARK AND CABINS $$$$
210 Electric Ave.
(406) 646-4466
www.grizzlyrv.com

This large RV park is located downtown and within walking distance of all services. Choose from 196 RV sites and 16 tent sites. The park offers a laundry, convenience store, gift shop, game room, showers, and restrooms. Each RV site is nicely landscaped with a grassy area and decorative rocks, paved patio, and picnic table. All tent sites have a barbecue grill and picnic table.

YELLOWSTONE HOLIDAY RV
CAMPGROUND & MARINA $$–$$$$
16990 Hebgen Lake Rd.
(877) 646-4242
www.yellowstoneholiday.com
Opened in 2000, Yellowstone Holiday is located outside town, only 13 highway miles from the west entrance to Yellowstone National Park. Sitting on the shores of Hebgen Lake, the campground and marina are open from mid-May to early Sept. Accommodations include 28 large, rig-friendly RV sites, 10 Elk Haven cabins, four Moose Cottage duplex cabins, and six Bear Necessity cabins. Cabins are not equipped with bedding, towels, soap, or kitchen utensils. All accommodations are within a short walking distance of the lakeshore. A modern facilities building provides a dataport desk, laundry, bathroom and shower facilities, and a small general store. The marina provides rental fishing boats, kayaks, canoes, and paddleboats; a launch ramp and boat slips; and fuel. The cabins sleep four to seven persons.

YELLOWSTONE PARK KOA $$$$
US 20
(406) 646-7606, (800) 562-7591
www.yellowstonekoa.com
Enjoy 360-degree mountain views from this KOA, located 6 miles west of town. Amenities include laundry, showers, Wi-Fi, dump station, indoor pool, and hot tub. Cabins and cottages are also available for rent, and the on-site Patio Restaurant offers pancake breakfasts and nightly BBQ dinners.

RESTAURANTS

Price Code
Prices represent meals for two people, excluding beverages, tip, and tax.

$.................. Less than $19
$$ .... $19 to $27
$$$ .... $27 to $35
$$$$ .... More than $35

BAR N RANCH $$$$
890 Buttermilk Rd.
(406) 646-0030
www.bar-n-ranch.com
The Bar N provides a fine-dining experience at a reasonable price with true western hospitality. The menu is traditionally western, with steak, game, and seafood selections, while the appetizer menu features delicious treats like gingered portobello mushrooms. There is a full bar and an extensive wine list, and the rustic yet elegant setting couldn't be more appropriate. The dining room is open to the public, with more limited hours during the winter.

BEARTOOTH BBQ $$$
111 North Canyon St.
(406) 646-0227
The Beartooth is one of the town's newest establishments but has quickly become one of the most popular, due to its excellent food, big portions, and decent prices. Choose from pulled pork, beef brisket, burgers, brats, ribs, and more, all with a variety of sauces to choose from. The casual decor is simple—a few TVs here and there with sparse decorations—but it's the food that keeps people coming back. You can't miss the building's red façade on Wes Yellowstone's main drag—it stands out among all the other businesses.

CANYON STREET GRILL $
22 Canyon St.
(406) 646-7548
The Canyon Street feels like a classic diner from years ago, right down to the shiny red

vinyl chairs and booths, huge chocolate malts, big burgers, and 1950s-era decorations. The walls are adorned with old advertising signs and pictures of hot rods. Food is standard American fare, including sandwiches, burgers, and fish-and-chips.

EINO'S $
8955 Gallatin Rd.
(406) 646-9344
You won't see a lot of fancy advertisements for Eino's, one of West's best word-of-mouth eating establishments. In fact, only a small neon sign on a satellite dish lets you know where it is—north of town near the junction of US 191 and US 287. You'll find the menu on the wall by the bar—steaks or burgers, cut to your liking, and priced by the ounce. When you order you'll be given a slab of meat and shown the grill, because you're the chef here. Season your meat the way you like it, and cook it over an open flame; then enjoy your meal with great views of Hebgen Lake. Eino's is a popular spot for snowmobilers, as you can eat and gas up.

i Need a good cup of coffee in the morning? Stop in at the Book Peddler or Mocha Mamma's for a quick fix. *The Book Peddler* (106 Canyon St., 406-646-9358) has a coffee bar in the back with fresh-baked goods and a good selection of tea as well. Mocha Mamma's is located in the Free Heel and Wheel shop (40 Yellowstone Ave., 406-646-7744) and also has baked goods, tea, and espresso.

ERNIE'S BAKERY AND DELI $
409 Firehole Ave.
(406) 646-9467
www.erniesbakery.com

This locals' favorite is a great place to grab a quick bagel or breakfast sandwich in the morning, as well as a box lunch for your day on the river. Choose from homemade bread and pastries, specialty sandwiches, sliced meat and cheese, salads, and an assortment of gourmet items. Party trays, beer, and wine are also available.

THE GUSHER PIZZA AND SANDWICH SHOPPE $
40 Dunraven Ave.
(406) 646-9050
www.gusherpizza.com
The Gusher is one of West's favorite places to grab a burger or a sandwich after a day in the park or on the trails. There are also steaks, shrimp, soups, salads, chili, and vegetarian dishes. The seven-ounce sirloin steak sandwich and the Gusher Special pizza—beef, sausage, pepperoni, Canadian bacon, mushrooms, olives, green peppers, and onions—are popular and tasty items. Everything on the menu is available for takeout and delivery. There's also a pub and game room with pool tables, video games, and Montana poker.

THE MONTANA CATTLE COMPANY $$
209 Madison Ave.
(406) 646-7381
Montana Cattle Company is located in the Stage Coach Inn. Chef Jack Cole serves up a diverse American menu in this new restaurant, formerly called the Coachman. Choose from steaks, fresh seafood, chops, and pasta, or try a delicious buffalo burger and enjoy your meal in the restaurant's casual atmosphere. Homemade desserts and a full wine list are available. The Cattle Company also serves breakfast from 7 to 11 a.m. and lunch from 11 a.m. to 2 p.m. and will box your

lunch so that you can take it with you. Dinner starts at 5:30 p.m.

PETE'S ROCKY MOUNTAIN PIZZA AND PASTA $
104 Canyon St.
(406) 646-7820

Pete's—a popular spot for locals and visitors alike—is known for its excellent and filling meals. You'll find traditional Italian dishes here, but the pizza ensures return customers. Choose from a variety of toppings—including sauerkraut and barbecue sauce—or try the Original Incredible Combination pizza. There are excellent salads, chicken, pasta, and homemade spaghetti. Pete's offers free delivery.

RUNNING BEAR PANCAKE HOUSE $
538 Madison Ave.
(406) 646-7703

The Running Bear serves up delicious breakfasts and lunch seven days a week from 7 a.m. until 2 p.m. It's no surprise that the house specialty is pancakes, but there are plenty of traditional breakfast favorites, homemade baked goods, and a full lunch menu, including burgers, sandwiches, soups, and salads. The Running Bear is closed during Nov and Apr.

*SYDNEY'S MOUNTAIN BISTRO $$$
38 Canyon St.
(406) 646-7660
www.sydneysbistro.com

This intimate bistro with a funky atmosphere serves eclectic dishes like veggie risotto, butternut squash ravioli, and chicken breast stuffed with Brie and mushrooms—a refreshing change from the typical West Yellowstone restaurant. The ingredients are fresh, and great care is taken in the preparation of every meal. Sydney's is a great place for a romantic dinner for two, but it also offers a kids' menu. Outdoor seating is available, making Sydney's a busy place during the summer, and a nice brunch is served on weekends.

TIMBERLINE CAFE $
135 Yellowstone Ave.
(406) 646-9349

The historic Timberline is only open during the summer season—early May through early Oct—but it packs in the crowds for its yummy all-American menu and friendly family atmosphere. Owners Tom and Dee Tipton pride themselves on good service, and the menu features everything from classic burgers and hot dogs to gourmet entrees like homemade lasagna, enchiladas, and the finest steaks and chicken. There is also a full soup, salad, and potato bar. The Timberline is open for breakfast, lunch, and dinner.

*WILD WEST PIZZA $
14 Madison Ave.
(406) 646-4400

Owner and West Yellowstone local Aaron Hecht has quickly turned the Wild West into one of West's most popular eateries. The pizza is delicious, and the newly remodeled space stands out among some of the town's more dated establishments. A good-sized dining room is great for families, while sandwiches, pasta, appetizers, and pizza can also be ordered in the adjacent saloon. Wild West has also become the best place to see live bands on the weekends in the summer and winter.

SHOPPING

*BOOK PEDDLER
106 Canyon St.
(406) 646-9358

This is West's oldest and best bookstore, and it specializes in books, maps, and related items of the West and Yellowstone National Park. There's a large selection of hiking, travel, tourism, and recreation books, as well as numerous titles by local and regional authors. Relax in the espresso bar with homemade baked goods and gourmet coffee and tea, or savor your treats at one of the outside tables during summer.

EAGLE'S STORE
3 Canyon St.
(406) 646-9300
www.eaglecompany.com

Open year-round, Eagle's has been West Yellowstone's one-stop shop and family business since 1908. You'll find a complete line of western wear from Stetson, Levi, Lee, Tony Lama, and Acme, as well as sportswear from Woolrich and Columbia. There's hiking and backpacking equipment and fishing tackle, and a gift section including American Indian arts and crafts, T-shirts, and souvenirs.

FLYING T TRADING POST
311 Canyon Ave.
(406) 646-7557

Looking for something old and western? Try the Flying T (open year-round), where you'll find a large selection of western trappings, old toys, antique firearms, American Indian artifacts and trade beads, dolls, china, and more. There is also a den of animal mounts and a gallery of western art.

MADISON CROSSING
121 Madison Ave.
(406) 646-7621
www.yellowstoneshop.com

This is West Yellowstone's newest year-round retail complex, consisting of nine stores. **The Gallery,** (406) 646-4300, features the latest western wildlife and landscape art. **Treetop Toys,** (406) 646-7621, has unique toys for all ages, including a large selection of stuffed animals. The **Yellowstone Apothecary,** (406) 646-7621, is a full-service pharmacy that carries gifts and cards. **Homeroom,** (406) 646-4338, has a variety of accessories, gifts, and home furnishings. You'll also find a one-hour photo store, a florist, a kitchen store, an activewear outlet, and an interior design shop.

NORTHERN BEAR TRADING POST
109 South Canyon
(406) 646-7150

Honoring the heritage of the American West, Northern Bear, open year-round, features Yellowstone gifts and garments reflecting nature and wildlife. You'll find Christmas ornaments, metal art, handmade pottery, American Indian artifacts, wood carvings, and T-shirts.

RARE EARTH STORE
111 Yellowstone Ave.
(406) 646-9337

You can mine for gold, garnets, Montana sapphires, and other gems at the Yellowstone Mining Company, a working sluice that is part of Rare Earth. In the store is a dazzling array of rocks, fossils, and minerals, including the largest amethyst geode in Montana. There are also postcards, souvenirs, apparel, and stuffed animals to choose from. Open year-round.

Looking

WOLF DEN GIFT GALLERY
29 Canyon St. #5
(406) 646-9760
At the Wolf Den you'll find animal-related items, including affordable wildlife art, contemporary art, and limited-edition prints. You can also get an authentic wolf-paw casting, leather art, and Christmas items. The Wolf Den is open year-round.

YELLOWSTONE T-SHIRT COMPANY
20 Canyon St.
(406) 646-7722
The Yellowstone T-shirt Company has a large selection of silk-screened T-shirts, sweatshirts, and hats. Custom designing and silk-screening is available for groups and activities, and the shop recently added a full line of gifts and curios reflecting the Yellowstone region.

NIGHTLIFE

The Coachroom Lounge (209 Madison Ave., 406-646-7381) is West's favorite seasonal bar, located in the Stage Coach Inn. It has a cozy feel, thanks to the large fireplace, and offers a big-screen TV, gambling machines, and licensed poker dealers. During winter and summer the Coachroom offers live entertainment several nights a week.

If you're snowmobiling around the West Yellowstone area, a stop in at **Eino's Tavern** (8955 Gallatin Rd., 406-646-9344) is a must. Near the end of the day, you'll start to see snow machines heading north along US 191 to Eino's, where the parking lot will slowly fill up. Inside, riders gather to talk about the trails that day and where they will go the next, then cook themselves up a burger or a steak on Eino's grill. It's a great atmosphere, and one of West Yellowstone's more interesting sights.

Grizzly Lounge (205 Yellowstone Ave., 406-646-7475), adjacent to the Three Bear Lodge, is a mellow place full of great old photos depicting Yellowstone's rich history. There is a big-screen TV and a casino for you to try your luck in. **Rustler's Roost** (234 Firehole Dr., 406-646-7622, 800-646-7622) is a casual and enjoyable lounge with a big-screen TV and electronic gambling machines. It's a favorite spot to go after a day of snowmobiling, where visitors and locals mix comfortably. There is an extensive wine list and plenty of beers to choose from.

Summer Shows

Looking for something to do at night? Go see a show at the **Playmill Theatre,** which has provided entertainment for summer visitors for more than 40 years. Shows are every night but Sun and usually include a rotating series of musicals, dramas, and comedies. The season typically runs from Memorial Day through Labor Day. Reservations are strongly encouraged and can be made by calling (406) 646-7757. Check out the theater's website at www.playmill.com for schedules and ticket information.

BOZEMAN

With a history of agriculture and a current economy that thrives on tourism, the scenic college town of Bozeman is one of the best examples of the inherent contrast present in Yellowstone Country. Like many other Montana cities, its residents grapple with the displacement of farmland by roads and infrastructure, while at the same time promoting the town's booming high-tech industry—all the while touting the open space that surrounds the community.

Unless otherwise indicated, all listings in this chapter are located in Bozeman, Montana.

OVERVIEW

Bozeman, elevation 4,795 feet, is located in the beautiful Gallatin Valley and is the county seat for Gallatin County. The city has a population of about 38,000, but the county's population of around 80,000 is a more accurate description of the number of people who live around the city. Many folks choose to live in one of the outlying towns—Belgrade, Three Forks, Manhattan, Big Sky, and even Livingston—and make the commute to work in Bozeman.

The city sits at the intersection of I-90 and US 191, offering two direct routes to Yellowstone National Park. Heading 90 miles south on US 191 will take you along the breathtaking Gallatin River, past Big Sky, and on to West Yellowstone. Heading east over Bozeman Pass will put you in Livingston, a mere 60 miles from the north entrance to the park on US 89. It is this reason that many visitors to the Yellowstone region make Bozeman the starting and/or ending point of their journey, as they have for more than 135 years.

The best thing about Bozeman is the contrast. **Historic Main Street** boasts acclaimed art galleries, renowned restaurants, and upscale shops, while at the same time offering typical Montana taverns, hardware stores, and fly-fishing shops. From sushi bars to T-shirt stores, Bozeman's Main Street is a place where you can spend the day just walking around and taking in the sights, sounds, and smells of one of Montana's finest cities.

While Main Street is still a hot spot for business, Bozeman is suffering the same symptoms of urban sprawl that many other Montana cities have already gone through. Wal-Mart and Target have set up shop on the north end of town, and North Nineteenth Ave. has seen its acres of farmland give way to housing developments, strip malls, shopping centers, and restaurants. This is a hot topic in Bozeman, and the city is doing its best to regulate business expansion while at the same time promoting the downtown district. So far it seems to be working out, as even Bozeman's East Main Street has seen the addition of restaurants and shops.

Bozeman is home to the nearly 15,000 students of **Montana State University,** which is located on College Street on the south side of Main Street. The beautiful campus is a great place to walk around, and the school contributes much to the city's thriving arts and cultural scene. Theater shows, art exhibits, and live music are continuously present on campus, and the competitive Division I sports teams are great fun to watch if you have the time. MSU is also home to the **Museum of the Rockies,** a world-famous museum that offers exhibits in paleontology, geology, contemporary art, and more, as well as the Taylor Planetarium and museum gift shop. Check the local newspapers for listings and exhibits.

Of course, Bozeman is rich in history. The Shoshone, Nez Perce, Blackfoot, Flathead, and Sioux tribes roamed here several hundred years ago. Lewis and Clark traveled through the area in 1805, arriving at the three forks of the Madison, Jefferson, and Gallatin Rivers, about 30 miles west of town. And it was 1863 when John Bozeman came through Wyoming over a pass from the east, dropped into what the Indians called "Valley of the Flowers," and settled in the town that would bear his name. With him and leading the wagon train was legendary frontiersman Jim Bridger, who now has a mountain range, canyon, and numerous trails named for him. It wasn't long before the rest of the world discovered the same beautiful spot.

Bozeman's weather is typical for a higher-elevation mountain town. Summers are often dry and hot but a little on the short side. June is hit or miss and can be either a cold, wet extension of spring or a warm, dry beginning to summer. Winters can be long and cold, with plenty of snow but lots of blue sky to go around. Typically winter runs from Thanksgiving to May, but it is not uncommon to have snow in Oct or July. For

Staying Caffeinated

If you're a coffee lover, you'll have plenty to choose from just on Main Street alone in downtown Bozeman, but one thing you won't find is a Starbuck's. All of the coffee shops downtown are independently owned, and each offers its own eclectic atmosphere.

Rockford Coffee (628 West Main St.) has a hip, modern feel, while the **Leaf and Bean** (35 West Main St.) is the town's oldest coffeehouse. **Wild Joe's** (18 West Main St.) and the **Home Page** (242 East Main St.) are two of the newest coffee shops, while **Rocky Mountain Roasting Company** (777 East Main St. and 701 West Main St.) has been roasting its own blends since 1992. All of these establishments offer free Wi-Fi service as well as fresh beans to go, and with this many coffee shops to choose from, you won't find it hard to stay caffeinated.

summer, July through Sept often brings the best weather, and snow lovers will want to be here Jan through Mar.

Look around Bozeman and you'll notice the geographical contrast. The lush, wide valley gives way to rugged, snowcapped peaks—the Madison and Gallatin Ranges to the south, the Tobacco Roots to the west, and the Bridgers to the northeast. On a clear day you can see far north up the valley into the Big Belt Mountains near Helena. It's no wonder they call Bozeman a mountain town. And because of this, it is an outdoor lover's dream.

From blue-ribbon trout streams and world-class skiing to white-water boating, rock climbing, and mountain biking, Bozeman offers something for every sport. Miles of hiking trails wind through the adjacent **Gallatin National Forest,** where even a novice hiker can summit a 10,000-foot peak. Championship golf courses abound, cross-country skiing trails are everywhere, and beautiful mountain lakes are close by, making Bozeman a hard place to leave.

In short, Bozeman is a mixture of Old West and New West, chic and country bumpkin, lively and livable. It's a great Montana city, one full of a vibrant past and an exciting future, and a place that residents take pride in. You may leave Bozeman but it will never leave you, and it isn't hard to see why many people fall in love with this charming town.

ACCOMMODATIONS

Hotels

Price Code

Some rates are based on availability. The following codes indicate the average nightly rates for two adults. Accommodations accept all or most major credit cards, unless otherwise noted.

$ .... Less than $65
$$ .... $65 to $99
$$$ .... $99 to $135
$$$$ .... More than $135

BLUE SKY MOTEL   **$$**
1010 East Main St.
(406) 587-2311, (800) 845-9032
www.bluesky-motel.com
The Blue Sky's view from the courtyard is a good selling point, as the peaks of the Bridger Range loom in front of the hotel's courtyard. There are 27 rooms here, all on the ground floor and with queen-size beds. Other amenities include an indoor Jacuzzi, microwaves and refrigerators, suites and family rooms, individually controlled heat and air-conditioning, free Wi-Fi, winter plug-ins, and free local calls. If you like to walk, the Blue Sky is a great choice. It is adjacent to Lindley Park, one of Bozeman's largest and prettiest parks, which connects to the Peets Hill trail system. The pet-friendly motel is also within walking distance of downtown shops and restaurants, and the Jackpot Casino and Grill is just across the street. You'll find the Blue Sky on East Main Street as you are heading out of town toward the interstate.

THE BOZEMAN INN   **$$$**
1235 North Seventh Ave.
(406) 587-3176, (800) 648-7515
www.bozemaninn.com
This busy hotel is located on one of Bozeman's main commercial thoroughfares and offers queen-size beds, free local calls, outdoor pool, hot tub, sauna, and a free continental breakfast. Attached to the hotel is Santa Fe Red's restaurant, lounge, and casino, which offers excellent Mexican and American food at reasonable prices.

✳C'MON INN   **$$$**
6139 East Valley Center Rd.
(406) 587-3555, (866) 782-2717
www.cmoninn.com
This is another new hotel on the city's northwest side, near the shopping centers that line North Nineteenth Avenue and I-90. In addition to well-done single and double hotel rooms, there are extended-stay kitchenette, Jacuzzi, and fireplace suites and two-room suites to choose from. The hotel has a large pool, a baby pool, and five hot tubs, in addition to an exercise room and a game

room. Free high-speed Internet and a complimentary continental breakfast are offered.

THE DAYS INN $$$
1321 North Seventh Ave.
(406) 587-5251, (800) 987-3297
www.daysinn.com
If you're traveling with a pet, the Days Inn accepts them with a deposit. The remodeled hotel offers courtesy airport shuttle, spa, sauna, fitness center, guest laundry, complimentary HBO, local phone calls, and a free, cooked-to-order breakfast every day. The Days Inn is located on the corner of Oak and North Seventh Ave., close to any service you may need. Within walking distance are the shops in the Bridger Peaks Town Center, which offers everything from grocery stores, restaurants and dry cleaning to such brand-name stores as Gap, Pier 1 Imports, and Old Navy.

GALLATIN RIVER LODGE $$$$
9105 Thorpe Rd.
(406) 388-0148, (888) 387-0148
www.grlodge.com
At the Gallatin River Lodge, you can fish, ride a horse, take a sleigh ride, and enjoy a fine-dining experience all without leaving the property. Situated on a small trout pond and near the East Gallatin River, the upscale lodge has an elegant, cozy feel. The lodge is especially suited for anglers, who can find world-class fishing just out the door. Owners Steve and Christy Gamble offer complete packages with meals, lodging, and guide services included. The outstanding restaurant offers creative American cuisine, from seafood to game dishes (the duck is excellent). Each rustic but elegant suite features a Jacuzzi tub, a fireplace, and an outstanding view of the mountains and rivers surrounding the lodge.

i If you are planning on being in Bozeman during the three-day Sweet Pea Festival of the Arts, held each year during the first full weekend in Aug, book your hotel room extra early. The city swells with visitors from around the region, and most plan far in advance.

THE HAMPTON INN $$$
75 Baxter Lane
(406) 522-8000, (800) 426-7866
The Hampton Inn is located in the hotel district just off of the North Seventh Ave. exit from I-90. The tastefully decorated rooms offer coffeemakers, hair dryers, and irons, and business travelers will appreciate the phones with dataports. On-site amenities include an indoor pool and spa, fitness facility, laundry, and winter automobile plug-ins. The Hampton also offers a free airport shuttle and a deluxe breakfast bar, served in a western-style eating area with views of the magnificent Spanish Peaks.

HILTON GARDEN
INN BOZEMAN $$$$
2023 Commerce Way
(406) 582-9900
This new hotel is conveniently located near I-90 and adjacent to much of the development on the city's North Nineteenth Ave. stretch, where big-box stores and local merchants coexist in a nicely done strip-mall setting. Plenty of shopping and restaurants are within walking distance or a short drive. The hotel features 123 guest rooms, each equipped with a work desk, high-speed Internet, and a flat-panel HDTV. Each room also includes a microwave, refrigerator, coffeemaker, iron and ironing board, and hair dryer. An indoor pool, whirlpool, and fitness

center are located within the hotel, plus a full-service restaurant and bar.

HOLIDAY INN $$$
5 Baxter Lane
(406) 587-4561, (800) 366-5101
www.hibozeman.com
This is Bozeman's largest full-service hotel, with 179 rooms furnished with queen- or king-size beds and free cable TV with a premium movie channel. A large indoor pool and Jacuzzi are offered, and Cantrell's Food and Spirits boasts a nightly happy hour with complimentary hors d'oeuvres and a locally famous Sunday champagne brunch that will leave you stuffed for around $10 per person. Free airport transfers are available.

MAGNUSON GRAND CITY CENTER $$$
507 West Main St.
(406) 587-3158
www.magnusonhotels.com
The 63-room City Center—formerly a Best Western—has one of the best locations in town, situated on Main Street a few blocks from the center of activity. Rooms are bigger than average, and the two-floor hotel has an indoor pool, a hot tub, and a workout gym. Attached to the hotel is the Black Angus Steakhouse and casino (406-587-0652), with good food and moderate prices for breakfast, lunch, and dinner. If you want a place where you can walk from, the City Center is a good choice.

RESIDENCE INN $$$$
6195 East Valley Center Rd.
(406) 522-1535
This is a new hotel on the city's northwest side that features rooms designed for extended stays, including studios and one- and two-bedroom suites with separate kitchen, living, and sleeping areas. The nicely appointed

rooms are fully equipped with a fridge, microwave, dishwasher, stove, and coffeemaker. Additional amenities include high-speed Internet, hotel shuttle, complimentary breakfast, indoor pool, and spa. The complimentary grocery shopping service is a nice touch, and the Residence accepts pets.

WINGATE INN $$$
2305 Catron
(406) 582-4995
www.wingatebozeman.com
Conveniently positioned on the North Nineteenth Avenue corridor, this business traveler's hotel is close to the airport and to the amenities of Bozeman and is one of the best values. Although the inn is at the I-90 and Nineteenth Avenue interchange, the rooms are quiet, clean, and comfortable. The hotel is a new-construction, mid-priced property catering to all types of travelers, but it focuses on businesspeople, with high-speed Internet access included in the price of the room. All 86 rooms have breathtaking views of the Bridger and Spanish Peaks mountain ranges, are oversize with separate work areas, and include a continental breakfast. There is also an exercise room with indoor pool and whirlpool on the property.

Bed-and-Breakfasts
Price Code
$.................. Less than $85
$$ .... $85 to $115
$$$ .... $115 to $150
$$$$ .... More than $150

FOX HOLLOW BED
AND BREAKFAST $$$
545 Mary Rd.
(406) 582-8440, (800) 431-5010
www.bozeman-mt.com

This newer bed-and-breakfast is located midway between Bozeman and Gallatin Field, near the town of Belgrade. Fox Hollow offers a country setting with spectacular views of the Bridgers and Tobacco Roots from its wraparound deck, which houses a hot tub for soothing soaks after your day of exploring the area. Guests can choose from five nonsmoking rooms, three of which are located in the main house and two in an adjacent building.

Each room offers a queen-size bed, private bath, and breathtaking views. A gourmet breakfast is served each morning, and guests can relax by the fire in the family room. Owners Nancy and Michael Dawson operated their own travel agency for 10 years and pride themselves on understanding the needs of travelers, so don't hesitate to inquire about what to do during your stay. Nancy's parents also own the Cason Gallery in Helena, and the walls at Fox Hollow are peppered with original, contemporary, and western art.

THE LEHRKIND MANSION $$$
719 North Wallace St.
(406) 585-6932, (800) 992-6932
www.bozemanbedandbreakfast.com
When Julius Lehrkind, owner of Bozeman Lager Beer, built this magnificent mansion in 1897, he had each brick soaked in large vats of beer before setting them, making it truly "the house that beer built." Situated in Bozeman's historic Brewery District, where classic Queen Annes mingle with gritty industrial buildings, the Lehrkind offers guests an elegant reminder of Montana's Victorian past. The Thoreau Room was the mansion's original nursery and features an antique brass bed; the Muir Room lets the sun in from a south-facing stained-glass window; the Leopold Room includes a private bath

and a high-back oak bed, writing desk, and reading chairs; and the plush Audubon Suite includes a private bath and a tower sitting room with a direct view of the Bridger Mountains. Guests can also choose from five rooms in the newly added Garden House, which are equally charming.

Rounding out the immaculate decor is the mansion's music parlor and library, complete with a rare, 7-foot-tall 1897 Regina music box and a large book collection highlighting the area's spectacular national parklands. A complimentary full breakfast and late afternoon tea are included. Incidentally, owners Jon Gerster Jr. and Christopher Nixon worked as rangers in Yellowstone and Grand Teton National Parks, so most questions won't go unanswered.

THE OLIVE BRANCH INN $$
201 Lindley Place
(406) 587-8403, (866) 587-8403
www.theolivebranchinn.com
This beautiful downtown bed-and-breakfast is in the Joseph M. Lindley House, built in 1889 by one of the city's first pioneers. Listed on the National Historic Register and just 2 blocks from Bozeman's historic downtown area, the completely renovated house features six guest rooms, each with its own private bath. The Olive Branch strives to pamper its guests, from plush terrycloth robes and down pillows to custom soaps and a dizzying selection of exotic teas. Antique furnishings abound, and an enclosed English garden is the highlight of the fully landscaped property.

SILVER FOREST INN $$–$$$
15325 Bridger Canyon Rd.
(406) 924-4222
www.silverforestinn.com

The inn is located just minutes away from the trails and beauty of the Gallatin National Forest, Bridger Bowl downhill ski area, and Bohart Ranch cross-country ski center. Listed on the National Register of Historic Places, this hand-hewn log bed-and-breakfast features six charming guest rooms. Individually decorated, each guest room is appointed with a mix of antiques and western-influenced handcrafted furnishings that are cozy. The inn was built in 1932 by Arthur L. McKinney as a private home and became a bed-and-breakfast in 1990. Tucked in the trees, the three-story log home is reminiscent of the Victorian era, and innkeepers Mike and Teresa are knowledgeable and eager to make your stay pleasant.

✳THE VOSS INN $$
319 South Willson Ave.
(406) 587-0982
www.bozeman-vossinn.com
Located on one of Bozeman's most historic and architecture-rich streets, the Voss Inn offers six Victorian-style rooms in an elegant, late-19th-century brick home. Proprietors Bruce and Frankee Muller have taken great pride in keeping the Voss Inn true to its Victorian roots. Each room has a private bath and its own decor, including the 9-foot brass headboard of the Chisholm Room and the private deck of Robert's Roost to the oversize claw-foot tub in the Pease Room and the private sitting area of the Elliott Room. The parlor on the first floor offers a quaint area for relaxation and socializing, and a full breakfast is prepared for guests to enjoy in the comfort of their own rooms or in the guest parlor. An afternoon tea is also served. Willson Avenue is full of Dickensian charm, and the Voss Inn is only a five-minute walk from downtown Bozeman.

Campgrounds & RV Parks

Price Code
$	Less than $9
$$	$9 to $16
$$$	$16 to $23
$$$$	More than $23

BEAR CANYON CAMPGROUND $$$
4000 Bozeman Trail Rd.
(406) 587-1575, (800) 438-1575
www.bearcanyoncampground.com
This campground and RV park is located 4 miles east of Bozeman, just off the Bear Canyon exit of I-90. There are spaces for tents and RVs, a heated pool, electrical outlets, dump sites, showers, restrooms, laundry, and a convenience store. Weekly, monthly, and group rates are available. The campground has picnic shelters and public phones and is close to hiking trails.

BOZEMAN KOA $$$–$$$$
81123 US 191
(406) 587-3030
www.koa.com
A campground with your own hot springs? Well, not quite, but Bozeman's KOA is located right next to Bozeman Hot Springs, where a few bucks will get you a good soak and full spa services are available. This KOA has more than 100 RV and tent sites and 15 one- and two-bedroom cabins. Cabins run about $55, and there are on-site showers and laundry facilities. The campground is located about 10 miles southeast of Bozeman, adjacent to the hot springs (406-586-6492).

FORT THREE FORKS MOTEL
AND RV PARK $$
10776 US 287, Three Forks
(406) 285-3233, (800) 477-5690
www.fortthreeforksmotel.com

This modern facility is located at the junction of I-90 and US 287 in Three Forks, about 30 miles west of Bozeman and 60 miles south of Helena. It's also the site of Fort Three Forks, also known as Old Fort Henry, one of the first trading posts between the Mississippi River and the Pacific Ocean. Established in 1810 by John Colter and Andrew and Pierre Menard at the headwaters of the Missouri River, the post was abandoned a year later due to the perilous nature of leaving the camp to do what the men set out to do: trap beaver. These days you'll find a large, full-service motel and an RV park with full hookups, pull-throughs, laundry facilities, showers, and playground equipment.

SUNRISE CAMPGROUND $$
31842 East Frontage Rd.
(406) 587-4797
This campground and RV park is east of Bozeman and is close to the interstate. It's open from Apr 15 through Nov 15 and offers water, electric and sewer hookups, restrooms, laundry, ice, and grills. Leashed pets are welcome.

RESTAURANTS

Price Code
Prices represent meals for two people, excluding beverages, tip, and tax.
$. . . . . Less than $19
$$ . . . . $19 to $27
$$$ . . . . $27 to $35
$$$$ . . . . More than $35

BAGELWORKS $
708 West Main St.
(406) 585-1727
www.bozemanbagelworks.com

If you're on the road early to the ski slopes or the river, a stop at Bozeman's only true bagel shop is mandatory, quick, and convenient. You can choose from about 15 varieties of fresh baked bagels and have them fixed to your liking. Especially tasty are the breakfast bagels prepared with an egg and your choice of meat or cheese. One of these and a coffee or juice won't even set you back five bucks and is filling enough to last until lunch. You can dine in or take it with you, and Bagelworks is open every day starting at 6:30 a.m.

THE BAY BAR AND GRILLE $–$$
2825 West Main St.
(406) 587-0484
www.thebaybarandgrille.com
The Bay has become a popular Bozeman restaurant because of its wide variety of options. From typical bar fare, burgers, salads, and sandwiches to incredible steak and seafood entrees, the Bay can be a great place for the family or a romantic spot for two. There's a large selection of appetizers (the shrimp wontons are excellent), and the sandwiches are some of the most creative in town. The restaurant also has a gaming room and occasional live music and is located in the Gallatin Valley Mall.

i During Sweet Pea Festival week (the first weekend in Aug), the 6 blocks of Main Street in downtown Bozeman are closed to traffic for a street party featuring dozens of vendors selling a variety of food for the "Bite of Bozeman." Tables set with white linen line the center of the street, music plays, and people dance and eat.

CAFÉ ZYDECO $
1520 West Main St.
(406) 994-0188
www.cafezydeco.com
Specializing in authentic Cajun food, chef Kevin Carlos whips up po'boys and spicy one-pot dishes daily to the tunes of Cajun music. Choose from indoor and outdoor seating. Don't miss the mouthwatering crawfish étouffée or the classic red beans and rice. Café Zydeco is open Sat and Sun mornings for the fresh beignets and excellent coffee. Otherwise, it's open for lunch and dinner Mon through Fri.

CATEYE CAFE $
23 North Tracy Ave.
(406) 587-8844
www.cateyecafe.com
One block off Main Street in downtown Bozeman, the Cateye has an eclectic menu heavy on comfort food. Serving the best breakfast burritos and huevos rancheros in town, it's a funky local hangout popular with skiers during the winter season. The fresh-baked breads, cinnamon rolls, and good strong coffee are enough to bring you back again and again. Open for breakfast and lunch seven days a week; open for dinner Thur through Sat.

THE DAILY COFFEE BAR $
1013 West College St.
(406) 585-8612
If you're over near the university or want a quick snack, the Daily serves up locally roasted, fair trade, and organic coffee and a variety of brownies, scones, croissants, and cookies. Interested in something other than coffee? Check out the juices, ice cream, and milk shakes. There's always local art on the walls and lively conversation going on inside.

Another location on Bozeman's north side opened in 2008, serving up great coffee in a refurbished industrial space on the corner of Oak Street and Rouse Avenue.

DAVE'S SUSHI $–$$
115 North Bozeman Ave.
(406) 556-1351
www.davessushi.com
Just 2 blocks from Bozeman's downtown Main Street, Dave's serves fresh, artful sushi. His little shop flies in seafood daily and offers preparations from nori and nigiri rolls to sashimi, as well as tempura, noodles, beer, wine, and sake. The seaweed salad is also excellent, and the prices are very reasonable.

Green Market

Held every Tuesday evening from June through September, the **Bogert Farmers' Market** is a true reflection of this community. You'll see local gardeners selling vegetables and flowers alongside vendors with handmade furniture and elegant wool sweaters, and also see kids playing violins. The market is held at the Bogert Park pavilion on South Church Street, rain or shine, from 5 to 8 p.m. The larger Bozeman Farmers' Market is similar and held at the Gallatin County Fairgrounds on Saturday from 9 a.m. to noon.

FERRAROS $$$
726 North Seventh Ave.
(406) 587-2555
www.ferrarosfineitalian.com

Ferraros offers fine Italian dining seven days a week. The restaurant boasts the largest Italian wine selection in Montana, so ask your server for a recommendation if you're unfamiliar with some of the names and regions of wines. A variety of pasta, chicken, and seafood selections is on the menu, as well as beef and lamb. Seafood fans will love the scallops served with linguine and the restaurant's trademark Pink Floyd sauce—a delicious combination of tomato and Alfredo sauces that will leave a lasting impression. Salads are served house style—one big bowl for everybody, a fitting example of an authentic Italian meal. The brick-oven pizza is also delicious. Dinner only.

*JOHN BOZEMAN'S BISTRO $$$$
125 West Main St.
(406) 587-4100
www.johnbozemansbistro.com

Named for the legendary pioneer who founded the city in 1864, this wonderful bistro is one of Bozeman's most popular fine-dining establishments. Although the food remains high end, the atmosphere is casual and lively. The ever-changing menu offers a hearty selection of seafood, wild game and pasta dishes, an extensive wine list, and Montana microbrews served on tap. If you can't shell out the bucks for dinner, the Bistro's lunches offer the same quality at lesser prices, about $10 per person. Either way, save room for the restaurant's signature homemade tiramisu; it's worth the price of the meal alone. The restaurant is closed Sun and Mon.

LA PARILLA $
1533 West Babcock St.
(406) 582-9511
www.wordofmouthconcepts.com

Absolutely Bozeman's best bang for the buck is this pint-size restaurant that makes some of the fattest wraps around. Choose from traditional fajita- and burrito-style Mexican wraps or the restaurant's signature wraps, including the Wrap of Khan (Thai spices), barbecue-smoked chicken, Caesar salad, jambalaya, blackened salmon, and fettuccine Alfredo wraps. La Parilla also offers tacos and kids' choices, dessert wraps, and outdoor patio dining in summer.

THE LEAF AND BEAN $
35 West Main St.
(406) 587-1580
www.leaf-bean.com

This eclectic coffee shop is a great way to begin your day of strolling around Bozeman's downtown shopping district with a hot cup of coffee or tea, or a great way to end the day by stopping in for a decadent dessert. The bright, cozy atmosphere is perfect for warming up on a chilly evening, listening to the live acoustic music playing several nights a week (the schedule is on a chalkboard in the back).

You can also look through a selection of gifts and whole-bean coffee to go. Try the homemade hot chocolate or the delicious milk shakes if you're not a coffee drinker, and if you're in a hurry for lunch, stop in and grab a premade sandwich or salad.

LOOIE'S DOWN UNDER $$$$
101 East Main St.
(406) 522-8814
www.looies-downunder.com

Looie's offers everything from gourmet beef tenderloin meat loaf (not your mom's) to delicious steak and seafood entrees. If you've never had bison, this is the place to try it, and the mashed potatoes are more than a side

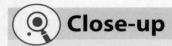 **Close-up**

The Bozeman Trail

People labeled **John Bozeman** as either foolhardy or brave when he set out in 1863 to find a better route to the Bannack and Virginia City gold mines from Fort Sedgwick, near the Nebraska-Colorado border. Bozeman, a native Georgian who moved west in search of gold in 1861, was living in Bannack (Montana's first territorial capital) at the time and set out in the spring with fellow pioneer John M. Jacobs and Jacobs's daughter, 11-year-old Emma. The three of them traveled to Three Forks, across the Gallatin Valley and over its eastern pass to the Yellowstone River, the same route William Clark took in 1806.

Bozeman ignored the fact that his route would violate a treaty and slice through land sacred to the Sioux, Crow, and Cheyenne Indians, figuring that conflict could be avoided. Although the party had a few run-ins, the three travelers arrived at the North Platte River near the Oregon Trail a few months later. They would regroup there and try to return to the mines with a wagon train.

The route Bozeman wanted to take back left the Oregon Trail near present-day Douglas, Wyoming, crossed the Powder and Tongue Rivers, and continued on the Bighorn and the Yellowstone Rivers to the pass he had come through a few months before. The planned route would cut more than 800 miles and six weeks off the Oregon Trail route up through Idaho to the Montana mines. In July 1863, 46 wagons and 89 people set out from the North Platte to try what was called the Bozeman-Jacobs cutoff.

They got as far as what is now Buffalo, Wyoming, before running into a large party of Sioux and Cheyennes, who wouldn't let them pass. After realizing they weren't going to get by, most of the wagon train returned to take the longer, safer Oregon Trail to the mines. But Bozeman and a few others were determined.

dish. Dinner is complemented by a terrific wine list and excellent, gourmet desserts. Looie's also has a great bar, perfect for enjoying a glass of wine or a cold beer with one of the many outstanding appetizers. Also featured at Looie's is Jadra's Sushi Bar (406-582-0393), as authentic as you'll ever find.

MACKENZIE RIVER PIZZA CO.   **$**
232 East Main St.
(406) 587-0055
www.mackenzieriverpizza.com
This is Bozeman's most popular lunch and dinner place for pizza, and its gourmet deep-dish pies are what people come here for. With signature items like the Flathead, the

Brandin' Iron, and the Bobcat, MacKenzie River offers gourmet pizza with traditional and nontraditional sauces and toppings. Smoked trout on a pizza? No problem. Want a pizza with Thai spices and a peanut sauce? Try the Thai pie. The pizzas are made with a choice of five fresh sauces (tomato, pesto, barbecue, Alfredo, and extra virgin olive oil), marinated and grilled meats, and chunky fresh vegetables, then topped off with a three-cheese blend. MacKenzie also offers great sandwiches and huge, mouthwatering salads (try the house dressing, a specialty) as well as wine and several beers on tap. The kids will love this place, as they can choose their own personal-size pizzas.

The men loaded up their horses and raced across Wind River Country and down the Clark's Fork of the Yellowstone, traveling at night, until they reached the pass into the Gallatin Valley—now dubbed Bozeman Pass—in early Aug. They arrived at the mines safely, but Bozeman deemed the attempt a failure since the wagon train didn't make it. Nonetheless, Bozeman and Jacobs knew that future trains could be successful, and they returned to the North Platte via Salt Lake City for another run at it.

Over the next three years, the trail was heavily used as settlers and miners moved west. It went by many names, including the Montana Road, the Bonanza Trail, the Big Horn Road, and the Powder River Road. But for most parties the Indians made sure it was a bloody excursion, thus the nickname: the Bloody Bozeman Trail.

The US Army established two forts along the popular trail—Fort Reno and Fort Phil Kearney—and fortified them at the same time government officials were in the field assuring the Sioux this was not taking place. Needless to say, this did not go over well. In 1866 William Fetterman and his party of 80 men ignored orders not to leave the trail and were ambushed by a band of Indians led by Red Cloud. Fetterman and his entire party were killed.

After the Fetterman Massacre, as it was called, use of the trail dwindled, and two years later the route was deemed unsafe and illegal by the Fort Laramie Treaty of 1868. Although Bozeman's trail was popular for only a few short years, it was indeed a faster route. And Boseman did manage to get a pass, a trail, and a town named for him (and eventually one of his namesake town's best restaurants). As for Bozeman himself, he was killed by Indians in 1867.

The actual route of the Bozeman Trail is not well marked and is on private land, but numerous monuments and informational signs are located where the trail intersects public roadways.

The restaurant has become a staple throughout Montana and has locations in several cities, including Belgrade, 8 miles west of Bozeman. Bozeman's was the first in 1992, and the restaurant's rustic, lodgepole pine interior is a great example of Montana-inspired architecture. MacKenzie River also delivers.

MAIN STREET OVER EASY $
9 East Main St.
(406) 587-3205
Serving the fastest breakfasts in town, Main Street Over Easy is open for breakfast and lunch Tues through Sun. Culinary Institute–trained Erik Carr traded five-star restaurant

experiences for this sunny, down-home cafe. Daily specials are something to look forward to—chili verde or eggs Benedict, it's all good. The restaurant is tucked back inside a downtown building, but look for the colorful sidewalk sign with a rooster on it and follow the buzz of conversation from the diners who fill this locals' hangout regularly.

✳MONTANA ALE WORKS $$
611 East Main St.
(406) 587-7700
www.montanaaleworks.com
This popular grill and pub in the old Montana Transportation depot has become one of Bozeman's dining and social hot spots.

The bar features more than 40 beers on tap, and the food ranges from casual fare like burgers and chicken sandwiches to more eclectic fare like buffalo potstickers, grilled mahi mahi fish tacos, and gorgonzola pasta. It's also a great place to go for appetizers—the pepper Parmesan fries are to die for—and a fun place for the after work and nightlife crowd.

i From June through Sept the Bozeman Gallery Association offers "Art Walks," receptions open to the public at downtown-area art galleries. The walks are a fun social and shopping event and take place on the first Fri of each month.

THE NAKED NOODLE $
27 South Willson Ave.
(406) 585-4501
www.wordofmouthconcepts.com
This hip lunch and dinner spot offers oodles of noodles prepared to order any way you like them. Italian, Asian, American—just choose the type of noodle and the toppings; the cooks will sauté it right in front of you on the range in the open kitchen. Whether you are craving pesto, lo mein, or good ol' mac 'n' cheese, you'll find it in this casual eatery, which also offers a variety of delicious and original salads.

OLD CHICAGO $
1940 North Nineteenth Ave.
(406) 587-9404
A hit with the college crowd as much as with families, this franchise offers a little something for everyone. Continuous broadcasts of sports programming on flat-screen TVs in every corner of the restaurant is one of the attractions. Serving 101 beers on tap is another angle.

But the food is genuinely good, and the portions are generous. Offering pizzas, salads, pasta, calzones, sandwiches, and burgers at fair prices with quick service that can't be beat, the restaurant is open daily and serves a full menu from 11 a.m. to 1 a.m.

THE PICKLE BARREL $
809 West College St.
(406) 587-2411
Big and cheap—that's what the sandwiches at Bozeman's oldest sandwich shop are. You can get a half or a whole, but don't be fooled: A half is about as big as other whole sandwiches and is plenty for one person. Local favorites include the Bobcat (named for the university's athletic mascot), Ken's Special, and the Mushroom Steak. The College Street store delivers and, of course, every sandwich includes a signature pickle—plucked right from the barrel. There is also a location in Belgrade in the IGA shopping center.

PLONK $$$
29 East Main St.
(406) 587-2170
www.plonkwine.com
Plonk (which is French for "swill") is essentially an urban wine bar. Swanky music pipes through the restaurant, where wine lovers and foodies flock to sip obscure French and Italian vintages as well as California wines. The tapas menu offers small dishes of tasty gourmet preparations, from duck breast to assorted farmstand cheeses. Beer and cocktails are also served, and Plonk also has a hip nightlife scene as well as outdoor seating.

SANTA FE RED'S $$
1235 North Seventh Ave.
(406) 587-3176
www.bozemaninn.com

Museum of the Rockies

A stay in Bozeman wouldn't be complete without a trip to the **Museum of the Rockies** (600 West Kagy, 406-994-3466), which boasts one of the finest paleontology collections in North America as well as strong collections in Western history, textiles, Native American artifacts, and photography. In fact, resident paleontologist and professor Jack Horner is one of the world's foremost dinosaur experts, and served as the technical advisor for the *Jurassic Park* films. Founded in 1957 by Dr. Caroline McGill and affiliated with Montana State University, the museum's permanent exhibitions, which tell the story of the development of the Northern Rockies over the past four billion years, are augmented by changing exhibits representing various facets of cultural and natural history. National touring art exhibitions also make stops here, and there is a fully operational 19th-century living-history farm on-site that helps preserve the state's agricultural traditions. The Taylor Planetarium presents educational and entertainment shows on a regular basis, and the Martin Discovery Room is an engaging children's space for those age 8 and under. Explore Yellowstone, a new children's space centered around Yellowstone National Park, opened in 2010. The museum is a great way to spend a day in Bozeman and is fun for the entire family. For more information, visit the museum's website at www.museumoftherockies.org.

Located in the Bozeman Inn, Santa Fe Red's is one of Bozeman's most popular Mexican restaurants. You'll find all of your favorite selections here, including chimichangas, enchiladas, tacos, burritos, and a large assortment of tasty appetizers. The margaritas are especially good, and the bar has an extensive tequila selection. There is a nice patio for outdoor dining, and a newly added sunroom gives the restaurant an airy feeling.

STARKY'S AUTHENTIC AMERICANA $
24 North Tracy Ave.
(406) 556-1111
www.starkysonline.com
This downtown deli has already become a staple in the diet of many Bozemanites and visitors alike in the few short years it

has been open. Starky's is open seven days a week at 10 a.m., and specializes in hearty sandwiches, soups, and salads made from scratch. Dinners feature American staples—think meatloaf, ribs, fish and chips, burgers—as well as eclectic fare like wild mushroom and asparagus polenta and pan seared salmon. The deli has a good selection of packaged goods for sale, and the large seating area can hold plenty of hungry diners.

TED'S MONTANA GRILL $$$
105 West Main St.
(406) 587-6000
www.tedsmontanagrill.com
Ironically, this national franchise owned by media mogul and part-time Montana resident Ted Turner didn't open a restaurant in

the state until 2008. Located downtown in the historic Baxter Hotel, Ted's offers an original take on American comfort foot with signature dishes like bison meat loaf, beer-can chicken, and cedar-plank salmon. Nearly 20 different burgers are on the menu—diners can choose between beef or bison—and there are almost as many chicken sandwiches available, too. Ted's also offers hand-cut steaks, salads, soups, and a large kids' menu. The chain is known for its turn-of-the-20th-century Montana grill atmosphere, and this location also features a nice outdoor patio.

THE WESTERN CAFE $
443 East Main St.
(406) 587-0436
If you gaze at the walls of the Western, you'll see magazine and newspaper articles highlighting the cafe's celebrity guests and longtime local patrons. Farm and ranch old-timers give the Western its namesake atmosphere. Nothing is fancy here, but the servings are hearty and the mood is relaxed. Breakfast is the main staple, where you'll often see college kids mingling with the regulars, and the Western is usually a busy place for lunch. If you're staying in Bozeman, a meal at the Western is a satisfying tradition that anyone can take part in.

THE WOK $$
319 North Seventh Ave.
(406) 585-1245
The Wok is one of Bozeman's better Chinese restaurants, and its selections are pretty much standard Chinese fare. The Mongolian Beef is especially good. You can also choose from a healthy number of seafood entrees. If you don't want the food delivered to your door, you can eat in the Wok's delightfully casual atmosphere.

SHOPPING

ALARA
42 West Main St.
(406) 522-8844
www.alarajewelry.com
Metalsmith Babs Noelle considers downtown Main Street the fashion hub of Bozeman. Featuring exclusive custom jewelry from European designers as well as Noelle's own one-of-a-kind pieces, the boutique is more of an art gallery than a store. Inventory ranges between $35 and $6,000, and the service is "hyper friendly." A 20-plus-year veteran of retail, Noelle specializes in creating original designs using platinum and other precious metals as well as gems. She travels regularly to Europe to select unique pieces to sell at Alara. Her passion, however, is making her own pieces for customers with personal requests. Noelle has created pieces for individuals as diverse as Elizabeth Taylor, Clint Black, and the members of ZZ Top. Open Mon through Sat from 10 a.m. to 6 p.m.

BRIDGER PEAKS TOWN CENTER NORTH
Nineteenth Avenue and Oak Street
This strip mall–type shopping center is an example of the development taking place on North Nineteenth Avenue near the interstate. It's a nice-looking structure that blends into the New West environment, and it offers an excellent variety of shops, services, and restaurants. Among these are Pier 1, Old Navy, Gap, Kentucky Fried Chicken/A&W, a dry cleaner, and a bank.

CACTUS RECORDS
29 West Main St.
(406) 587-0245

At Cactus you'll find a healthy selection of bluegrass, world, rock, folk, pop, local, and used CDs, as well as an eclectic selection of T-shirts, candles, cards, knickknacks, and novelty items. You can buy tickets here for local concerts, which are advertised on the chalkboard behind the counter. Cactus will let you listen to any album before you buy it.

✴COMMUNITY FOOD CO-OP
908 West Main St.
(406) 586-1023
www.bozo.coop
This is the place to go for organic produce, dairy products, meat, and groceries. The co-op is a popular Bozeman spot with reasonable prices and a selection that would satisfy most shoppers. The co-op carries beer and wine and has a large selection of bulk grains and other items. There's also a great deli that serves delicious soups, salads, and sandwiches for lunch.

COUNTRY BOOKSHELF
28 West Main St.
(406) 587-0166
Since 1973 the Country Bookshelf has been supporting regional authors by selling signed copies at this downtown location. Independent bookseller Mary Jane DiSanti has stayed the course with her appealing little store, hosting author readings and other literary events. The knowledgeable staff can direct you toward national best sellers, obscure fiction, fascinating nonfiction, and the most captivating children's books.

CROSSROADS
27 East Main St.
(406) 587-2702
Luxury kitchen and bath items are the main attraction at this longtime Bozeman boutique. But look a little closer and you'll see subtle nuances that are appropriate for every part of your home. High-end cooking utensils, cutlery, dishes, furniture, and bedding all have a primitive elegance here. You'll see it in the hand-painted Portuguese soup tureens or the French-country bed frame layered with luxurious Egyptian linens.

ELIZABETH & COMPANY
311 East Main St.
(406) 586-6525
From sultry to swank, this boutique offers sleek clothing for men and women. It is a nice departure from the usual cowboy chic style found on Main Street in popular western towns. Look for tasteful jewelry, handbags, and shoes to match apparel.

THE EMERSON CULTURAL CENTER
111 South Grand Ave.
(406) 587-9797
www.theemerson.org
The two-story Emerson, as you'll often hear it called, is a former school that has been converted into more than 40 art galleries, shops, and studios. There's often music, dance, or theater going on in the main auditorium, and there's an espresso bar as well the Emerson Grill restaurant on the first floor, which serves up delicious and fresh northern Italian cuisine. The Emerson is part of a nonprofit organization that offers art and related classes as well as exhibits, concerts, and films.

THE GALLATIN VALLEY MALL
2825 West Main St.
(406) 586-4565
This small shopping center is located on the west end of town near the Main and College intersection. Anchor stores include

the Macy's and JCPenney, and some of the other stores include Eddie Bauer, Bath and Body Works, Barnes and Noble, and Victoria's Secret. There's also a variety of restaurants, a game room, flower and framing shops, a post office, an eight-plex movie theater, and a bank—plenty to keep you busy on a rainy afternoon.

Bozeman Tragedy

Walking around downtown Bozeman, you might notice the half-block empty space and large hole in the ground on East Main Street. A natural gas explosion in 2009 blew apart three buildings, killing one person and devastating a city that prides itself on its historic downtown. Four businesses were lost—as well as the entire American Legion building—but most have relocated to other parts of downtown. The empty crater you can still see is a grim reminder of a chilling part of Bozeman's recent history.

MERIDIAN
101 East Main St.
(406) 585-0608
This is the shop where Bozeman women come to find elegant party dresses and cutting-edge casual wear. It's a store loaded with the latest high-fashion clothing for any occasion. Featuring such designer labels as Kate Spade and Kenneth Cole, the store is a downtown fashion anchor in Bozeman.

MONTANA GIFT CORRAL
237 East Main St.
(406) 585-8625
If you want to pick up something from your trip that says Montana, this is the place. From antler candleholders to moose-laden dishcloths and sweatshirts, Montana Gift Corral has a large selection of unique items for the home. There is also a Montana Gift Corral store in Big Sky.

MURDOCH'S RANCH AND HOME SUPPLY
2275 North Seventh Ave.
(406) 586-8466
Let's say you're staying in a cabin with a woodstove. You're outside chopping wood, and somehow you break the ax and rip your brand-new flannel shirt. After that you notice Fido's food is gone and the truck's low on oil. At Murdoch's you can replace your ax, grab a new flannel, pick up some dog food, and fill your truck up with oil all in one stop. There's a big selection of western wear, as well as designer clothes from Ralph Lauren, and plenty of pet supplies—and just about everything in between. It's a popular store that is spreading to different cities around the state.

NORTHERN LIGHTS TRADING COMPANY
1716 West Babcock St.
(406) 586-2225
www.northernlightstrading.com
This store is representative of Montana's active lifestyle. Here you'll find gear for backcountry skiing, rock and ice climbing, canoeing and kayaking, and more. Northern Lights has a great selection of casual wear, sweaters, shirts, pants, and shoes, and rents kayaks and canoes during summer and skis

and snowshoes in winter. There's also a large topographic map and book selection. For real bargains on designer overstocks and last year's gear, check out their outlet store—The Barn, West Huffine Lane, (406) 585-2090.

ODYSSEY
2 West Main St.
(406) 587-5521
Whimsical yet practical clothes and lavish silver jewelry are what you'll find at this corner boutique. Look for fashionable summer linens and unforgettable earth-tone sweaters for summer and fall, as well as graceful scarves for anytime. There is something spare yet rich about the clothing here. It's reasonably priced and versatile. You'll also find a large selection of New Age books, an important resource for modern goddesses.

PERSPECTIVES
37 South Willson St.
(406) 522-7125
Filled with clever gift items, stationery, and jewelry, this store is tucked around the corner from the Main Street entrance of the Blackwood Building, but it's worth seeking out. You can order custom stationery, pens, embossers, and journals here or choose from the tempting store inventory. It's easy to spend a lot of time browsing in the shop's artistic and urban atmosphere.

POOR RICHARD'S NEWS
33 West Main St.
(406) 586-9041
This classic downtown newsstand has just about any magazine you could want, as well as local and national newspapers and books of regional interest. Poor Richard's also sells cigars, pipe tobacco, and imported and specialty cigarettes. It closes at 9 p.m.

THE ROOT
36 West Main St.
(406) 582-0079
Fun and funky fashion for swingin' girls is what the Root brings to downtown Bozeman. From faux leather pants to platform shoes, this store is all about retro style. It's popular with the college and high school set and even the 30-something crowd who want to put a little zip into everyday clothes.

SCHNEE'S BOOTS AND SHOES
121 West Main St.
(406) 587-0981
www.schnees.com
After more than 20 years in Bozeman, this local shop is still the best place to find the perfect hiking, biking, running, or dress shoes in town. The high-quality products are half the attraction, but the honest and attentive service is what really makes shopping here a pleasure. Owner Steve Schnee carries a line of custom work boots, and his staff can recommend the best fit for your needs. If you get really hooked on a certain pair, order online or request a catalog.

VARGO'S JAZZ CITY AND BOOKS
6 West Main St.
(406) 587-5383
This downtown fixture has a great selection of new and used books and a large selection of jazz CDs and hard-to-find records. A large regional author section highlights some of Montana's more well-known writers, including David Quammen, William Kittredge, Rick Bass, Tim Cahill, Thomas McGuane, Annick Smith, Mary Clearman Blew, and more. Vargo's also has many rare and older books for sale.

NIGHTLIFE

BELGRADE LOUNGE AND KARAOKE CLUB
32 East Main St.
Belgrade, MT
(406) 388-6098

This popular spot is located in Belgrade, about 8 miles west of Bozeman on the Frontage Road. The Frontage Road becomes Belgrade's Main Street, and you'll find the lounge on the left as you come into town. Karaoke is entertaining here, and live country and rock music is featured on the weekends. Bill's Grill (406-388-8840), serving up good breakfasts, lunches, and dinners, is attached to the lounge.

THE CAT'S PAW
721 North Seventh Ave.
(406) 586-3542

This spacious bar has a large selection of tap beer and packaged liquor to go. There are plenty of gambling machines and a card room in the back for those feeling lucky.

THE CRYSTAL BAR
123 East Main St.
(406) 587-2888

This downtown fixture is a mix of locals and college students and is a classic Montana bar, complete with cowboy boots and the occasional scuffle. Don't let that discourage you, though, as the Crystal can be a great place to hang out, especially in summer, when the upstairs patio serves up great burgers, sandwiches, and drinks.

THE HAUFBRAU
22 South Eighth Ave.
(406) 587-4931

This is where old tables go to die. Walk in the Haufbrau, look up, and you'll see old wood tabletops nailed to the ceiling, full of initials, names, and phrases that people carved in long ago. There are a few booths and tables here, a pool table, and a small stage in the corner. The bar hosts an open mike or a local singer/songwriter every night of the week, with Tex Tucker being the one-man house band. Tex is a local icon, and he can belt out just about any tune you request. The Haufbrau also serves up a good—and cheap—lunch.

THE MINT BAR AND CAFE
27 East Main St., Belgrade
(406) 388-1100

Just across the street from the Belgrade Lounge (see above) you'll find the Mint, a great spot to soak in some real Montana atmosphere. You'll often find cowboys sipping martinis here, as the Mint offers more than 30 different styles, from classic to eccentric. The restaurant in the Mint offers excellent steaks and seafood, and there is usually live acoustic music once or twice during the week.

MIXERS NIGHTCLUB
515 West Aspen St.
(406) 587-1652

Mixers is a popular nightclub with the college crowd and features different styles of music throughout the week, either live or by DJs. The club, which also serves food, used to be called Little John's; it has undergone extensive remodeling.

MONTANA ALE WORKS
611 East Main St.
(406) 587-7700

This bar/restaurant is on the east end of town, which has seen a resurgence of building over the past few years. The large establishment is one of the most popular places in town from happy hour (4 to 6 p.m.) until closing. You can get food late, and there are hourly and coin-operated pool and snooker tables. The bar doesn't offer liquor but instead serves up its own brand of beer, specially brewed by Helena's Blackfoot River Brewing Company. But your choices aren't limited to that; you can choose from more than 40 tap and bottled beers as well as a good selection of wine. It's open until midnight Sun through Thur and to 1 a.m. on Sat and Sun.

THE ZEBRA COCKTAIL LOUNGE
321 East Main St.
(406) 585-8851
The cocktail lounge, located in the basement of the old Bozeman Hotel building, is one of two bars located in the same area. You'll find live music on weekends and DJs during the week (it can get quite loud), and right next door is the more quaint and quiet Colonel Black's lounge, where there are two pool tables and plenty of comfy chairs.

BIG SKY

This year-round resort community was founded in 1973 by late NBC newsman Chet Huntley and sits in a small valley between Bozeman and West Yellowstone, surrounded by the Gallatin National Forest and the Lee Metcalf Wilderness Area. Big Sky is a popular spot in summer and winter, when most visitors come to play in the shadow of Lone Mountain, a cone-shaped 11,166-foot peak that dominates the horizon. Big Sky truly is one of the prettiest places in Montana, and a place well worth visiting any time of year.

If you don't have a car or don't want to drive, the free Skyline bus service (406-995-6287) runs in the summer and winter with stops in the Meadow, the Mountain and the Canyon. The Skyline Link also connects Bozeman and Big Sky, offering free daily trips throughout the year. Stops in the Big Sky area are marked by a Skyline sign— similar to a city bus stop sign—in front of local businesses, condo complexes, and shops. The best way to find out schedules and routes is to visit www.skylinebus.com.

Unless otherwise indicated, all listings in this chapter are located in Big Sky, Montana.

OVERVIEW

Big Sky's location—about 20 miles from the Yellowstone National Park border and along the Gallatin River—makes it a tourism-driven place, and because of that there is plenty to do. Summer visitors to the park often spend time in Big Sky, taking advantage of horseback rides, hiking and biking trails, fly fishing, rock climbing, and white-water rafting just outside their doorstep. Big Sky is also home to rustic dude ranches, posh guest lodges, excellent restaurants, and world-class golf courses. The local guest ranches host BBQ dinners on a regular basis, and the Arts Council of Big Sky puts on classical, bluegrass, and country concerts at their outdoor pavilion. Past performers include Willie Nelson, Randy Travis, Del McCoury, Bonnie Raitt, and the Bozeman Symphony. Check the

organization's website, www.bigskyarts.org, for schedules.

Powder-hungry skiers and snowboarders from all over the world flock to **Big Sky Resort** in winter, hoping to catch some of the annual 400 inches of snow. The European-style ski area boasts more than 120 trails on three mountains, 3,600 acres, a high-speed lift system, and a total vertical drop of 4,350 feet, making it one of the premier destinations in the Rockies. Montana's newest ski area, **Moonlight Basin,** is another attraction for Alpine skiers and sits in the Jack Creek valley on the north side of Lone Mountain. **Lone Mountain Ranch** is a world-class Nordic resort, offering 75 kilometers of beautiful trails, professional instruction, gourmet cuisine, Yellowstone tours, lodging, and sleigh rides. The posh **Yellowstone Club**—a private ski area for the rich and famous—is also located here. Snowmobiling is the other popular winter activity, with hundreds of miles of trails accessible from the Big Sky area. For more on these activities, see the Winter Sports chapter.

Big Sky is different from other ski towns in that there is no quaint little village like Aspen, Telluride, or Park City, and since it is fairly new, development has been scattered around the mountain, dividing Big Sky into three distinct parts: the Canyon area, the Mountain Village, and the Meadow Village (including the new Town Center development).

The **Gallatin Canyon area** at the entrance to Big Sky refers to the shops and services located along the Gallatin River at the junction of US 191 and the Lone Mountain Trail (MT 64), which heads west toward Lone Mountain and the two ski resorts. The Canyon area has many shops, restaurants, hotels, and other services and is about 9 miles from the mountain.

After driving 2 miles west on MT 64, you'll come to the **Meadow Village.** This is really the center of town for the locals, and it's where you'll find grocery stores, galleries, banks, restaurants, shops, and a post office. You'll see plenty of condos along the Arnold Palmer–designed golf course and lots of new construction. Big Sky is a booming place, with multimillion-dollar homes, shopping centers, and condominiums sprouting up. You'll also hear people refer to the Town Center, which is the area on the south side of the road across from the golf course. The Town Center has restaurants, lodging, and shops and includes the **Westfork Meadows** area. You'll often hear people refer to all of these locations by their nicknames: Mountain, Meadow, Westfork, Town Center, etc.

Mountain Village refers to everything that is around the base of the ski resort. To get to the village, turn left off MT 64 at a well-marked sign. This will take you past Lake Levinski and numerous condo complexes. A turnaround loop is located at the main cluster of buildings, which include the Huntley Lodge, the Summit Hotel, and the Shoshone Condominium, and there is a pay parking lot for guests here. Summit Hotel guests have the option of underground valet parking, and other condos have their own parking. If you're just skiing for the day, a free skier parking lot is located a short walk from the Mountain Village. In the Mountain Village, you'll register for resort rooms and condos and find guest and skier services, shops, galleries, restaurants, and real estate offices.

Driving past the Mountain Village on MT 64 will take you toward **Moonlight Basin** resort, where you will find a recently constructed lodge and even more places to stay. There are chairlifts to Moonlight Basin, providing some of the many ski-in/ski-out lodging opportunities available at Big Sky. In 2003 Moonlight opened its smooth ski terrain to the public and has since become a major destination for visitors and locals.

HISTORY

Big Sky has an interesting and colorful history. Shoshone and Crow Indians inhabited the area before trappers arrived in the early 1800s and were followed by gold prospectors, who left their mark on nearby towns Virginia City and Nevada City. Early homesteaders lived off the land, which even today is full of wildlife and natural beauty. In the early 1900s numerous dude ranches sprang up in the remote Gallatin Canyon to give Big

Sky its first tourists. Many of these historic places, including the **320 Guest Ranch,** the **Covered Wagon Ranch,** and **Lone Mountain Ranch,** are still in full operation today—a testament to the way the area draws visitors in droves to experience a piece of true western history. The original **Crail Ranch house,** named for early pioneer and cattle rancher Frank Crail, can be seen by the golf course in the Meadow Village.

In 1969 well-known newscaster Chet Huntley teamed up with a group of investors to buy the old Crail Ranch and began his dream of putting a ski area in this once-remote, incredibly stunning setting. In 1973 Big Sky Resort opened its doors, but Huntley died of cancer shortly before his dream was realized. Boyne U.S.A., which owns several resorts around the country, bought Big Sky in 1976 and developed the area into a world-class summer and winter destination.

Today Big Sky really is a place where people come and create their own vacation. If you want to be pampered, Big Sky Resort and Moonlight Basin have everything you desire: spas, five-star restaurants, luxurious hotels, and guided recreation. This is the New West version of Big Sky. If you want the Old West, you can stay in a rustic cabin and hike back into a mountain lake, or take a horseback ride for the day and cook out over a campfire. And if you're the adventurous type, you'll be in paradise. Run the Gallatin in a raft or kayak, climb the Gallatin Tower, or mountain bike down from what seems like the top of the world. Big Sky is also a place that more and more locals are calling home, becoming a hodgepodge of ski bums, entrepreneurs, retired folks, and adventure seekers.

SEASONS

Obviously Big Sky is driven by the seasons. In summer and winter it can be a busy place, but quiet compared to most other resorts. In fact, most people come to Big Sky because of its laid-back, relaxing atmosphere and to get away from the crowded resorts of the East and West. Around 5,000 people make the busiest day on the slopes, and most days are half that. That's a far cry from the most popular destinations in Colorado, Utah, California, and Vermont, and it's also one of the reasons more and more people are discovering the area.

In spring and fall, typically referred to as shoulder seasons, the town can seem deserted. There are great deals on lodging and other activities during these times, making for an uninterrupted, peaceful vacation.

Traffic on the highway between Bozeman and West Yellowstone (and all the way to Jackson) can be heavy during summer and winter, and this is also a trucking route. Be especially alert on the often winding, narrow road, which can turn icy and snowy during winter.

Big Sky's summer doesn't get going until mid-June and typically is fairly dry and warm. The high mountains can sometimes trap clouds, leaving Big Sky socked in with rain, hail, and even snow. (Willie Nelson once played in a storm with driving, dime-size hail.) Temperatures drop considerably when the sun goes down, so bring warm clothes.

Some of the resort services close for a period during the off-season, so check closure dates before you plan your trip. Unless otherwise indicated, all listings in this chapter are located in Big Sky, Montana.

ACCOMMODATIONS
Hotels & Condominiums
Price Code
Some rates are based on availability. The following codes indicate the average nightly rates for two adults. Accommodations accept all or most major credit cards, unless otherwise noted.

$.................Less than $100
$$ ....$100 to $150
$$$ ....$150 to $200
$$$$ ....More than $200

BIG SKY RESORT $$–$$$
1 Lone Mountain Trail
(406) 995-5000, (800) 548-4486
www.bigskyresort.com
Besides offering rooms in the slopeside hotels (Summit, Huntley, and Shoshone), Big Sky Resort has everything from studio condominiums to ski-in/ski-out luxury log cabins. Units available include Black Eagle, Arrowhead, Snowcrest, Village Center I, Beaverhead, Powder Ridge, Saddle Ridge, Skycrest and Alpenglow, Big Horn, Stillwater, and Lone Moose. The resort also manages the Whitewater Inn, located in the Canyon area on US 191 a half-mile south of the turnoff to Big Sky. This standard hotel is one of Big Sky's best values and features an indoor pool with a 90-foot waterslide.

✳BUCK'S T-4 LODGE $$
P.O. Box 160279, Big Sky, MT 59716
(406) 995-4111, (800) 822-4484
www.buckst4.com
Buck and Helen Knight established Buck's T-4 in 1946 as a hunting camp, but it was converted to the present-day lounge bar four years later and became a popular spot for visitors heading down the canyon to

Yellowstone. Buck and Helen sold the establishment in 1972, and now Buck's is a full-service resort complex with a western feel. The hotel unit features 75 deluxe rooms, two outdoor hot tubs, and a complimentary hot breakfast buffet every morning. There is great food in the lounge and even better food in the renowned dining room, which has been featured in *Ski Magazine, Gourmet, Mountain Living,* and the *Chicago Tribune.* The wine list consistently wins awards, and entree selections include a long list of seafood and game dishes. Buck's is located 1 mile south of the Big Sky entrance on US 191.

CASTLE ROCK INN $
65840 Gallatin Rd., Gallatin Gateway
(406) 763-4243
Situated next to the Gallatin River and beneath the towering rock spires that line the Gallatin Canyon, the Castle Rock Inn is one of the few establishments on US 191 from Bozeman to Big Sky. You can choose from eight medium-size riverside cabins that sleep up to six people comfortably, and you'll find groceries, propane, gasoline, and camping supplies at the small store. There's also a family-style cafe and a 10-unit trailer court with full hookups and modern bathrooms.

THE CORRAL BAR, CAFE,
**   AND MOTEL** $
42895 Gallatin Rd., Gallatin Gateway
(406) 995-4249, (888) 995-4249
www.corralbar.com
This basic eight-unit log motel is located on US 191 about five minutes south of MT 64. It's one of the most affordable places to stay in the area, and rooms include phones and use of an outdoor hot tub. The grub at the popular cafe is legendary—big burgers,

great steaks, and a salad bar, as well as huge breakfasts to get your day started right.

*MOONLIGHT BASIN LODGE $–$$$$
East West Resorts, 1020 MT 64
(406) 993-6000, (800) 845-4428
www.moonlightbasin.com
Moonlight Basin is Big Sky's newest resort and ski area, and offers a variety of deluxe lodging opportunities. Choose from quaint slopeside log cabins to ski-in/ski-out condos, homes, and chalets. The penthouses are conveniently located in the heart of Moonlight Lodge and sell out quickly, so be sure to make reservations early. From any of these lodging options, guests can easily access the Timbers Restaurant and Bar, spa facilities, the outdoor heated pool, and ski/hiking trails.

i When people refer to the Big Sky entrance, they are talking about the junction of US 191 and MT 64. MT 64 heads west from the highway toward the ski resorts. Also, if you hear Gallatin Road mentioned, that means US 191.

THE SUMMIT HOTEL AT BIG SKY $$$$
P.O. Box 160001, Big Sky, MT 59716
(406) 995-5000, (800) 548-4486
www.bigskyresort.com
The impressive Summit is one of the most recent additions to the lodging at the base of the ski area, and its 10 stories tower over the Mountain Village. The 222-room structure is also one of the most luxurious in Big Sky, designed in an elegant Euro-western style with leather couches, finely crafted furniture, and mammoth rock fireplaces. You'll find restaurants, boutiques, a fitness center, a spa, underground valet parking, outdoor soaking pools, and hot tubs all within a few

hundred feet of the chairlifts. Rooms are designed so that they can be interchanged as studios and one-, two-, and three-bedroom units and feature kitchens, fireplaces, balconies, and hot tubs in many units.

Guest Ranches & Lodges
Price Code
$	Less than $85
$$	$85 to $115
$$$	$115 to $150
$$$$	More than $150

CINNAMON LODGE $–$$
37090 Gallatin Rd.
(406) 995-4253
The Cinnamon Lodge is located 11 miles south of MT 64 and features individual log cabins, some of which are on the Gallatin River and include full kitchens. The full-service bar and restaurant offer the area's best Mexican cuisine as well as Montana steaks, burgers, chicken, homemade desserts, and vegetarian dishes served daily in the summer and winter from 5 to 10 p.m. The Cinnamon Lodge also offers horseback rides and guide services, and nearby you'll find fishing, hunting, river rafting, hiking, biking, skiing, and snowmobiling.

COVERED WAGON RANCH $$$$
34035 Gallatin Rd., Gallatin Gateway
(406) 995-4237
www.coveredwagonranch.com
The Covered Wagon has provided mountain dude-ranch vacations since 1925 and prides itself on a true western experience without the glitz or glamour associated with many other resorts. At the CW you'll find comfortable one- and two-bedroom rustic log cabins with private baths and a spacious, stunning main lodge where you'll be fed

ranch-style meals three times a day. The ranch, which sits at 6,700 feet above sea level, is located about 18 miles south of Big Sky on US 191, 3 miles from Yellowstone National Park and adjacent to the Taylor's Fork of the Gallatin River. Nature is just out your door, and in summer you can partake in guided horseback rides and hikes, fly fishing, and mountain biking. Evenings are capped with a bonfire outside the main lodge. The CW is open from June 1 to Oct 15.

LONE MOUNTAIN RANCH $$$$
P.O. Box 160069, Big Sky, MT 59716
(406) 995-4670, (800) 514-4644
www.lmranch.com
Lone Mountain Ranch is a renowned destination resort for cross-country skiers, but even if you don't hit the 75 kilometers of groomed trails, there is plenty to do. There are two options for staying here: the individual, cozy guest cabins or the Ridgetop Lodge, an incredible six-bedroom guest lodge perfect for families or large groups. The cabins are warm and comfortable, and each has a private bath, wood-burning stove, or fireplace and electric heat. None of them have phones or a TV, making sure nothing distracts you from enjoying the area. The smaller cabins have one bedroom/living area and bath, and the larger cabins have a separate living room and two to three bedrooms. The main lodge is a breathtaking structure that exemplifies Montana-style architecture and features one of the best restaurants in Big Sky.

In summer activities include horseback riding, naturalist tours, fly fishing, guided Yellowstone Park trips, and programs for kids. During winter enjoy the snowshoe trails and sleigh rides, and Big Sky Resort is only 5 miles away. Lone Mountain Ranch is located about halfway between the Meadow and Mountain Villages on MT 64.

RAINBOW RANCH $$$$
Gallatin Canyon
(406) 995-4132, (800) 937-4132
www.rainbowranch.com
The Rainbow Ranch—which burned to the ground in 2008 and has since been rebuilt—has been voted one of the 25 best American lodges by *Travel & Leisure* magazine, and is located about 10 miles south of Big Sky on US 191. The ranch was first occupied by the Lemon family in 1919, when few people lived in the area. After realizing that cattle ranching on the land was too difficult, the family built the Halfway Inn (named for the inn's location halfway between Bozeman and the entrance to Yellowstone), offering meals and cabins for rent. The Lemons sold the ranch in 1946, and since then it has gone through different owners and names. The barn down by the river is the only building that remains from the Lemon family's days at the ranch.

These days the Rainbow Ranch is a year-round vacation spot that offers guests luxurious accommodations and gourmet dining. Guest rooms include lodgepole pine beds, fireplaces, whirlpool tubs, handcrafted duvet covers over stuffed comforters, and private decks overlooking the Gallatin River. The Rainbow offers horseback rides from its own stables and fly fishing right out your back door. The ranch's restaurant is one of Montana's finest. (See the Restaurants section of this chapter.)

✳RIVER ROCK LODGE $$$
3080 Pine Dr.
(406) 995-2295, (800) 995-9966
www.riverrocklodging.com

The small, luxurious River Rock Lodge provides European-style service in a relaxed, warm atmosphere that's walking distance to the new Big Sky Town Center. The lodge, located 3 miles from the MT 64 turnoff, features 29 secluded guest rooms and an executive suite, each with a stocked minibar, VCR, and designer bath, as well as such personal touches as natural toiletries, fresh-cut flowers, and comfy bathrobes. The rooms are decorated in typical western fashion, and the Vista Suite includes a fireplace, private balcony, and Jacuzzi tub. The River Rock has custom packages to suit your needs, and anglers will want to take advantage of the guided trips offered by 1997 Orvis Fly-Fishing Guide of the Year Gary Lewis.

✳320 GUEST RANCH $$$
205 Buffalo Horn Creek
(406) 995-4283, (800) 243-0320
www.320ranch.com
The 320 Guest Ranch has a rich history as one of the first guest ranches in the Big Sky area, beginning in 1898 when two homesteads were combined to total 320 acres. The ranch was purchased in 1936 by Dr. Caroline McGill, Montana's first female physician, and has been a working ranch and a favorite spot for visitors ever since. Accommodations range from cozy, one-bedroom cabins to large, three-bedroom guest homes. The 320 has several activities to keep you busy, including horseback riding, fly fishing (you can fish 2 miles of the Gallatin without leaving the property), snowmobiling, sleigh riding, and skiing. The Old West steakhouse at the 320 offers superb dining and is open to the public. The Monday night barbecues are popular with locals and visitors, and a great way to enjoy the ranch.

RESTAURANTS
Price Code
Prices represent meals for two people, excluding beverages, tip, and tax.

$	Less than $19
$$	$19 to $27
$$$	$27 to $35
$$$$	More than $35

ANDIAMO ITALIAN GRILLE $$$$
Village Center, Mountain Village
(406) 995-8041
This nicely adorned Tuscan-style restaurant is one of the newest and best restaurants in the slowly expanding Mountain Village area. The prices are a little high, but the food is excellent and the atmosphere is unlike anything else in Big Sky. Most of the pasta is handmade, and choices range from standard pasta and sauce options to wood-fired pizzas, seafood, and exotic salads. Before coming to Big Sky, chef Jody Koestler was named San Francisco and Napa Valley Chef of the Year and has medaled several times as the National Seafood Chef of the Year. A nice wine list is available, and choosing a dessert is a must at Andiamo.

BLUE MOON BAKERY $
3090 Pine Dr. #1
(406) 995-2305
Most people who stay in Big Sky will stop at the Blue Moon Bakery many times during their visit, either for a delicious breakfast bagel or fresh pastry in the morning, or a hefty sandwich or fresh-baked pizza later in the day. The bakery is a great spot for a quick coffee in the morning, and there is also a nice selection of homemade treats to tempt your sweet tooth.

BUCK'S T-4 LODGE $$$$
US 191
(406) 995-4111, (800) 822-4484
www.buckst4.com

The main restaurant at Buck's T-4 Lodge has been recognized as among the finest in Montana and the skiing community. Executive chef Scott Peterson's menus focus on wild game and continental cuisine, creating a unique combination of traditional local ingredients and classic culinary techniques. You'll usually find bison, venison, and elk on the menu, as well as a variety of clever seafood dishes. There is an extensive wine list to complement your meal, while the pub dining room serves up lower-priced fare such as burgers, sandwiches, and salads. Dinner in the main dining room is served from 6 p.m.

BUGABOO CAFE AND SPIRITS $
47995 Gallatin Rd.
(406) 995-3350

The Bugaboo Cafe is located in the Big Horn Center, a large log structure just north of the Big Sky entrance that houses other shops as well. The atmosphere at the Bugaboo is a subtle combination of rustic and contemporary decor. Eye-catching photos capture the heart of American spirit and adventure and are meant to express the traditional American style of food here. That means fresh ingredients, uncomplicated recipes, and good flavor. Take the barbecue ribs, with fall-off-the-bone tenderness; they're cooked for hours in a smoky sauce made by the chefs Paul and Kim Cameron. Or savor the unique flavors in the chicken Marguerite and the classic burger. Breakfast is a popular time here, with original creations and old standbys. Bugaboo Cafe is open for breakfast, lunch, and dinner every day but Mon.

BY WORD OF MOUTH $$
Meadow Village
(406) 995-2992
www.bigskycatering.com

This quaint bistro serves delicious food in a fun, festive atmosphere. With a varied menu that features Montana beef and local produce, By Word of Mouth offers one of the best dining experiences in Big Sky. The restaurant features a full bar but is best known for its wine list, which has received the acclaimed *Wine Spectator* Award of Excellence. By Word of Mouth is open nightly at 4 p.m. Reservations are recommended; call for shuttle information from the Mountain Village.

CABIN BAR AND GRILL $$$$
Mountain Village
(406) 995-4244
www.cabinbarandgrill.com

This excellent restaurant, which was formerly called First Place and located in the Meadow Village, now operates on the third floor of the Arrowhead Mall at Big Sky Resort. Served in a rustic, elegant atmosphere reminiscent of a log cabin, the dinner menu offers steak, wild game, seafood, and pasta dishes as well as a long list of appetizers and salads. The Cabin is one of the best lunch values at the resort, where most choices are under $10—including the incredible bison and elk burger with Cajun mayo, and the tasty Cabin chili with beef and bison. The Cabin is open for lunch and dinner seven days a week during winter and for dinner five nights a week during summer.

CHOPPER'S PUB AND GRUB $$
77 Lone Peak Dr.
(406) 995-3830

Chopper's Grub and Pub is one of the newest additions to the Big Sky dining scene and is located in the Town Center area. It's a big, good-looking building with plenty of seating (indoor and outdoor) along with a terrific bar and a separate casino/gaming room. There's a great burger menu and plenty of other choices, including salads, steaks, sandwiches, and pasta. For sports lovers, 12 flat-screen TVs dot the walls, and real motorcycles are placed throughout the restaurant. Open for lunch and dinner.

CINNAMON LODGE   **$$$**
37090 Gallatin Rd.
(406) 995-4253

The Cinnamon Lodge has become a dining tradition for Big Sky locals and visitors alike, mainly for its delicious and filling Mexican meals, which include huge chimichangas and burritos and entrees like chile rellenos and steak with enchiladas. If Mexican isn't your thing, don't worry, because the Cinnamon also cooks up Montana-style steaks, sandwiches, and burgers. All of the food is served in a recently built log cabin with a big stone fireplace, which takes the place of the original structure that burned down a few years ago. The Cinnamon is located 11 miles south of the Big Sky entrance on US 191.

i If you are an advanced skier and can't find suitable skis at the resort's rental shop, try one of the local ski shops on the mountain or in the canyon. You can pick from a variety of advanced equipment and rent it for the duration of your stay.

CORRAL BAR, CAFE,
** AND MOTEL**   **$–$$**
42895 Gallatin Rd., Gallatin Gateway
(406) 995-4249, (888) 995-4249
www.corralbar.com

If you're staying in Big Sky and don't make the short drive down US 191 for a meal at the Corral, you'll be missing out on some of the best grub from Bozeman to Jackson. Breakfasts here are legendary—big, greasy omelets, chicken-fried steak, and homemade biscuits and gravy—and a favorite of early-morning skiers, snowmobilers, and hikers. A burger at the Corral for lunch or after a day of skiing is a delicious and filling local tradition. For dinner the restaurant is famous for its monster mouthwatering steaks, but the menu also offers seafood, sandwich, and pasta selections. There's an all-you-can-eat salad bar, and the chili will have you shedding layers in no time.

LA LUNA   **$$**
Meadow Village
(406) 995-3280
www.lalunabigsky.com

La Luna is primarily known for its good Mexican food, but chef Eric Ross's menu also features Thai, Japanese, and Italian cuisine. In addition to traditional dishes like flautas, enchiladas, and chimichangas, you'll find steaks, burgers, salads, and wraps. The menu also features several kids' choices. The delicious margaritas are among the best in town, and the homemade desserts are the perfect way to top off your meal.

✳LONE PEAK BREWERY   **$**
48 Market Place
(406) 995-3939

Award-winning brewmaster Steve Nordahl crafts delicious handcrafted ales in this new building located in the Meadow Village Center adjacent to the Country Market grocery store. Porters, stouts, pale ales, blondes, and more are featured on the ever-changing beer menu, while hearty sandwiches and

Dining Out—Literally

Everyone likes to eat out, but how about eating outside? In the middle of winter, a few miles back in the woods? Well, in Big Sky it can be done, as many restaurants and outfitters offer sleigh ride, horseback, or snowcat dinners and lunches. It's a romantic and family favorite for locals and visitors alike.

Montana Backcountry Adventures (406-995-3880, www.skimba.com) offers moonlight dinners, where guests are transported to MBA's backcountry dining lodge by snowcat, then invited to feast on a delicious dinner prepared on the spot. After dinner, guests enjoy live music until it's time to go back—which always seems to come too soon. Rates (including tax and gratuity) are $79 for adults and $65 for children.

Sleigh Ride Dinners at the Lone Mountain Ranch (see Accommodations section, this chapter) are extremely popular and offer a true western experience not found in many places. Horse-drawn sleighs take diners out to the ranch's remote North Fork cabin, where a prime rib dinner is cooked on an old-fashioned woodstove and served by the light of the lantern. Western guitar music and songs by area musicians round out the evening. Dinner is available six nights a week (the other day is reserved for ranch guests) and cost $85 per person for adults and $70 per person for children ages 4 to 12 for the 2010–11 season. Holiday rates are slightly higher. Call (406) 995-2783 for reservations, which are strongly encouraged.

At the **320 Guest Ranch** (see Accommodations section, this chapter), beautiful Percheron draft horses pull an old-fashioned sleigh along the Gallatin River every winter evening to a campsite where guests can warm themselves by the crackling fire, enjoy cowboy chili and hot beverages, and listen to stories of the ranch and the western lifestyle. Rides begin at 5:30 and 7 p.m. and cost $32 per adult, $18 per person ages 3 to 12, and free for children under age 3. Reservations are required.

appetizers will satisfy your hunger for lunch or dinner. Open daily.

✳THE LOTUS PAD $$
3090 Pine Dr. #2
(406) 995-2728
www.lotuspadbigsky.com
Owners Alex and Scott Hoeksema serve up delicious Thai cuisine at the Lotus Pad, which has become one of Big Sky's most popular eateries since opening in 2007. Located in the Westfork Plaza next to the Blue Moon Bakery, the Lotus Pad is a cozy place with an eclectic atmosphere. On the menu are traditional Thai dishes like shrimp pad thai, along with a variety of curries and popular appetizers such as lettuce wraps and spring rolls. Beer and wine are available, and a small upstairs bar offers unique cocktails in a hip setting. Hours vary depending on season, it's best to call to find out when it's open.

MILKIE'S PIZZA AND PUB $
Westfork Meadows
(406) 995-2900

This lively local hangout has great food at reasonable prices served in a pub-style atmosphere. The pizza here is top notch and a big hit with hungry skiers after a day on the mountain. Other fare includes standard selections of burgers, salads, appetizers, and sandwiches. Milkie's is a popular nightlife spot.

M. R. HUMMERS $$-$$$$
Mountain Mall
(406) 995-4543

This popular Mountain Village establishment has served up old-fashioned lunches and dinners since 1983. If you stop in for lunch, try the hot pastrami sandwich or Joe's Famous Chili, and steak lovers should make it a point to head here for supper. You can get a filet mignon, sirloin, New York strip, prime rib, or T-bone steak any way you like it. Hummers also has crab, lobster, and surf-and-turf specials and is open for lunch 11 a.m. to 3:30 p.m. and dinner from 5:30 p.m.

> **i** When you're parking in the free skier parking lot during winter, a skier shuttle—a big Ford truck pulling an even bigger trailer with benches—will come around every five minutes or so and take you up to the resort and back to the parking lot. It's not a far walk, but the convenience is nice, especially after a tiring day on the slopes.

PEAKS $-$$$
Mountain Village
(406) 995-8076

Beautifully decorated in Euro-western fashion—lots of dark wood, black, and chrome—and with a great view of Lone Mountain out the windows, Peaks is a great place to come for an après-ski appetizer or a romantic dinner. The homemade, big-enough-for-two pizza is made with a whole wheat crust and is a great choice for lunch. If it's a warm day, enjoy your food or drink out on the patio, which is only about 50 yards from the slopes. Peaks recommends making reservations for dinner; the restaurant is located in the Summit Hotel.

RAINBOW RANCH $$$$
Gallatin Canyon
(406) 995-4132, (800) 937-4132
www.rainbowranch.com

The public restaurant in this well-known lodge (see the Guest Ranches and Lodges section) has been featured in *Bon Appétit* and *Outside* magazines. Combining local, regional, and international cuisine to create a unique and imaginative menu, the restaurant features wild game, fresh fish, and vegetarian items. Sample entrees include black quinoa tabouleh with leek and carrot–wrapped enoki mushrooms, caramelized spaghetti squash, and a Haitian pepper sauce; pan-seared Chilean sea bass with Thai sticky rice, grilled fingerling potatoes, and a saffron and vanilla bean sauce; and New Zealand rack of lamb crusted with tobacco mushrooms with a pomegranate mustard glaze, chestnut–lima bean succotash, and buffalo mozzarella. The wine list boasts more than 500 selections and is consistently recognized for excellence by *Wine Spectator* magazine. The ranch recommends reservations.

TIMBERS RESTAURANT, BAR, AND DELI $-$$$$
Moonlight Basin Lodge
(406) 995-7777
www.moonlightbasin.com

The Moonlight Basin Lodge is situated at the base of the Powder River ski run and the Iron Horse chairlift on the north side of Lone Mountain. It is a magnificent structure, with huge picture windows, massive pine pillars, leather furniture in the lobby, and a 37-foot stone fireplace. The bar at Timbers serves fresh soups, blue-cheese burgers, and excellent chicken sandwiches for lunch and dinner, and the spicy fries are delicious. Chef Scott Méchura runs the Timbers restaurant, which specializes in American classics with a metropolitan accent, including beef tender-loin topped with a wild mushroom tomato confit, herb and juniper–crusted lamb loin, oven-steamed salmon, grilled yellowtail tuna, and venison. The restaurant serves lunch and dinner.

The deli at Timbers serves lighter fare for breakfast, lunch, and dinner, including sandwiches, soups, salads, and cheeses, and it carries a few grocery staples as well. A big south-facing patio is perfect for sunny, warm days when taking a break from skiing at the lodge. If you are driving to the lodge, continue on MT 64 past the entrance to the ski resort and follow the signs to the Moonlight Lodge, about 2 miles.

i The Big Sky Town Center is the hub of the lower village activities in the summer. The quaint area has restaurants, shops, and services, as well as the Big Sky Farmers' Market every Wed and the Arts Council of Big Sky's Music in the Mountains free concert series every Thur. The new Town Center Park features a new outdoor amphitheatre, as well as a full-size ice rink in the winter. For more information visit www.bigskytowncenter.com.

WHISKEY JACK'S $$
Mountain Village
(406) 995-5786
The slopeside Whiskey Jack's features decent bar food with a southwestern flair. The large saloon is a popular spot for lunch and après-ski. Open for dinner seven nights a week, Whiskey Jack's has live music on the weekends and hosts larger concerts a few times during the winter.

THE WRAP SHACK $
Meadow Village
(406) 995-3099
www.werollemfat.com
The Wrap Shack has become one of Big Sky's most popular eateries since it opened in 2004 in the Westfork Meadows Plaza. The lively restaurant serves up huge burritos and tacos for lunch and dinner, including such favorites as the Smokin' Gringo, the Buddha, and the Big Kahuna. You can also build your own and add your own toppings, all of which are made from scratch. The frozen margaritas are extremely popular. Beer and a variety of other beverages are also available.

SHOPPING

BIG SKY BOARDROOM SNOWBOARD SHOP
Mountain Mall
(406) 995-5840
Located in the lower level of the Mountain Mall at the base of the ski area, this is Big Sky's only true snowboard shop. You'll find equipment and apparel from Burton, Sims, K2, and Salomon, and a full-service repair shop will put your board in top condition. The shop is also a Burton test center, and demos are available. It's open daily from 9 a.m. to 6 p.m.

THE COUNTRY MARKET
Meadow Village Center
(406) 995-4636
The Country Market is Big Sky's largest grocery store and has been since 1983. It's not what you'd really call a supermarket, but it has everything you need. There's fresh produce, a bakery, and a deli, as well as a large selection of beer and wine. You'll also find Montana-made gifts and souvenirs. The Country Market offers a winter delivery service, too, and is open from 8 a.m. to 8 p.m. daily.

GALLATIN ALPINE SPORTS
Westfork Meadows
(406) 995-2313
www.gallatinalpinesports.com
Gallatin Alpine Sports is a full-service ski and snowboard shop that sells other outdoor equipment, including shoes, climbing gear, backpacks, and outerwear. Owner Tom Owen has the largest cross-country selection (classic and skate) in town, and he rents cross-country and Alpine skis and snowboards as well.

GRIZZLY OUTFITTERS
Meadow Village
(406) 995-2939
www.grizzlyoutfitters.com
With a new location in the Town Center, Grizzly Outfitters offers equipment for downhill skiing, touring, ski mountaineering, snowboarding, telemarking, snowshoeing, backpacking, climbing, and mountain biking. You can also rent downhill and cross-country skis, snowshoes, mountain bikes, and camping gear, and a repair shop offers complete ski, snowboard, and bike tune-ups.

HORSE OF A DIFFERENT COLOR
Meadow Village
(406) 995-3133
This quaint shop offers everything from cards and unique gifts to furniture and western art. Located across from the Big Sky post office, Horse of a Different Color has become a popular shop for locals and visitors alike.

✴HUNGRY MOOSE
Market Town Center
(406) 995-3045
www.hungrymoose.com
Owners Mark and Jackie Robin moved to a new location in 2005, and they now offer even more selections of grocery and deli items. Hungry Moose specializes in gourmet and hard-to-find items, but it has just about anything you may need during your visit to Big Sky. The deli offers breakfast and lunch sandwiches, sliced meats and cheeses, and an espresso bar, and there is a large beer and wine section. The market is open from 6:30 a.m. to 10 p.m. nearly every day of the year and also delivers grocery orders.

J. P. WOOLIES
Mountain Mall
(406) 995-4542
The hand-knit wool ski hats at J. P. Woolies have been keeping Big Sky skiers warm for two decades. You'll also find a big kids' selection, jewelry, gifts, candles, bath supplies, home furnishings, clothing, and toys. Many items are handcrafted by artists from around the Northwest.

LONE MOUNTAIN RANCH OUTDOOR SHOP
P.O. Box 160069, Big Sky, MT 59716
(406) 995-4734

New Year's in Big Sky

Big Sky is a blast on New Year's Eve, but plan extra early and find out what's going on before you book your trip. Most bars and restaurants have special dinners early and then reopen with entertainment later in the evening. Most sell prepaid tickets, so plan ahead. At midnight everyone streams out into the center of the Mountain Village to watch the spectacular fireworks display light up Lone Mountain and then returns to the bar to finish the night off. Of course, the night doesn't have to be about partying—the fireworks can be seen from many condominium windows and from just about anywhere in town.

Located in the historic Lone Mountain Ranch (see the Guest Ranches and Lodges section), this shop (open daily 8 a.m. to 7 p.m.) has a full selection of cross-country equipment, accessories, and apparel, as well as Montana-made gifts and unique American Indian jewelry. You can rent cross-country skis and snowshoes and get your dinged skinny skis repaired.

LONE MOUNTAIN SPORTS
Arrowhead Mall
(406) 995-4471
This full-service Mountain Village ski shop has a retail area upstairs and a rental and repair shop downstairs, specializing in performance-shaped skis. You can rent skis or snowboards by the day or week, and the

friendly staff will set you up with the proper equipment for the conditions. A full selection of clothing, equipment, and accessories is available in the retail shop. This shop is open from 8 a.m. to 6 p.m. daily during winter.

THE LONE SPUR
Shoshone Lobby
(406) 995-3980
www.lonespur.com
If you want to pick up some real western wear during your stay, stop in at the Lone Spur and get done up the cowboy way. Pick out a nice hat and a pair of boots, and choose from leather and traditional apparel. There's also stuff for kids and a unique selection of gifts.

PAPARAZZI FUR AND LEATHER
Huntley Lodge and Mountain Mall
(406) 995-4705, (406) 995-4605
This upscale furrier has been selling designer furs, wearable art, leather fashions, and accessories since 1985. Prices start at $100 for certain headwear, but this stuff is not cheap. Fur coats from Zuki and other famous designers run from $2,500 to $80,000. Paparazzi specializes in the latest, trendy fashions, or what co-owner Craig Swick calls "fun furs." These are often found in magazines such as *Vogue* and appeal to much of the high-dollar crowd at Big Sky. Stopping in just to look is OK.

PLUM LOGO
Mountain Mall
(406) 995-4141, (406) 995-2155
If you're looking for something that says Big Sky, this is the place. At Plum Logo you'll find fleeces, sweatshirts, hats, mugs, key chains, and stickers, all with the Big Sky logo on

them. You'll also find a great selection of other clothing, jewelry, gifts, and plenty of stuff for the kids.

WILLOW BOUTIQUE
Meadow Village Center
(406) 995-4557

You'll find designer clothing, jewelry, gifts, furniture, and accessories for the home at this quaint shop, located in the Meadow Village next to the post office. There is a large selection of western-style knit sweaters and hats to choose from to complete the Big Sky look.

WILSON'S VIDEO
Westfork Meadows
(406) 995-4046

Want to chill out with a movie after a rough day of skiing? Wilson's is Big Sky's only video store and offers a wide selection of new releases and kids' videos. You can also grab some popcorn, candy, ice cream, and soda to complete your viewing experience. Open daily all year.

NIGHTLIFE

Big Sky is not really known for its nightlife, but as the area grows, more and more spots are popping up. Most après-ski places are in the Mountain Village and become more mellow the later it gets. There are a few genuine party bars, but you may have to head down into the Meadow or Canyon to find that atmosphere.

THE BLACK BEAR BAR AND GRILL
Mountain Village
(406) 995-2845

This loud and lively bar is located a half-mile from the Mountain Village and is popular with the under-30 crowd. The atmosphere

can range from quiet to rowdy—mostly the latter—and is where many of the ski-resort employees hang out after work. The lounge serves decent appetizers and sandwiches and has pool and foosball tables, as well as occasional live music.

THE CARABINER
Mountain Village
(406) 995-8078

This newer lounge is on the terrace level of the 10-story Summit Hotel and is a great spot to end your day on the slopes. A fireplace keeps the small space toasty, and the chairs and couches are extra comfy. You can order from a nice selection of appetizers, and there are plenty of liquor, beer, and wine choices. Après-ski entertainment usually consists of acoustic music performed by a local tunesmith.

THE CAVE
Town Center
(406) 995-4343

This is Big Sky's only full-service liquor store, located in the Town Center in the Marketplace Building. The Cave features an extensive wine selection and a variety of local and imported beers, as well as a large selection of uniquely Montana gifts and trinkets.

CHET'S
Huntley Lodge
(406) 995-4253

Chet's is a mellow place named for Big Sky's founder, Chet Huntley. It is a popular après-ski spot, and there is regularly scheduled live music, usually a solo guitar player or duet, in the evening. A menu of hearty appetizers should satisfy most appetites after a day of playing around the area.

HALF MOON SALOON
45130 Gallatin Rd.
(406) 995-2928

This authentic Montana roadhouse has live music on the weekends while serving up delicious barbecue fare in the attached restaurant. Located on the banks of the Gallatin River a few miles south of Big Sky, the Half Moon is famous for its outdoor summer barbecues and parties on the bar's big deck overlooking the river. It also has sand volleyball courts and horseshoe pits.

MILKIE'S PIZZA AND PUB
Westfork Meadows
(406) 995-2900

This is the Meadow's little hot spot, although it depends on the night. Some nights you'll find a real party crowd here, full of locals celebrating a powder day, and other nights the bar will be better suited for quiet conversations. Either way, Milkie's is a hoot, with a pool table, a few dart boards, and great food served late.

SCISSORBILLS
Mountain Village
(406) 995-4933
www.scissorbillssaloon.com

This Mountain Village bar and grill is mostly an après-ski spot, but occasionally folks stay well into the night. It's a small place with tasteful decor, tables, and booths under exposed beams and lots of windows. The popular bar has live music or karaoke several times a week.

WHISKEY JACK'S
Mountain Mall
(406) 995-5786

Whiskey Jack's is a happening place on the weekends, when live music is often heard until the bar closes at 2 a.m. The crowd is a mix of tourists and locals, and the big, barnlike structure can hold plenty of people. You'll usually find a solo performer during the après-ski scene, generally from about 3:30 until 6 p.m.

LIVINGSTON

If there is such a thing as a "new Montana," Livingston is it. Here writers, artists, and Hollywood movie stars mingle with ranchers, railroad workers, and miners. With a population of 7,500, the town is a little bit blue collar, a little nouveau riche, a little outdoorsy, a little glitzy, a little Old West.

Livingston is a community where old and new generations coexist and intermingle and thrive in their own unique ways. A stroll down historic Main Street reveals the melding of the town's diverse interests. In the 6 blocks of the neatly restored downtown, you will find art galleries, cowboy-boot makers, fly-fishing shops, interior designers, and hardware stores next door to one another. This is authentic small-town USA, where a handwritten sign on the door of any retail shop reading GONE FISHING OR BACK IN 10 MINUTES seems perfectly acceptable in the context of good business.

Unless otherwise indicated, all listings in this chapter are located in Livingston, Montana.

OVERVIEW

One thing that both old and new residents share is a pride in Livingston's heritage. Just ask the 1,500 citizens who made national headlines when the US Postal Service tried to move the historic Livingston post office from downtown—it took just four days for them to compile a petition, contact their congressman, and stop the move. Residents have also worked hard to meticulously restore the Livingston Depot Center, a tribute to the town's original 1882 railroad roots. This community's spirit is evident in so many places, from the Carnegie Library to the artfully designed Sacajawea Park, with its fishing bridge, lagoon, and river path.

Livingston's location makes it seem like paradise. Sitting on the big bend of the legendary Yellowstone River and surrounded by three mountain ranges—the Absaroka, Crazy, and Gallatin—Livingston is just 55 miles from Yellowstone National Park's northern entrance. The quality of life also makes this an appealing community. Living here means embracing the wondrous natural beauty and appreciating a lifestyle that is removed from the fray of a large metropolis. Visiting here means adjusting to the easygoing pace and taking things as they come.

i Livingstonites refer to Paradise Valley, located south of town on your way to Yellowstone, as "the Valley." Since there are quite a few valleys around, it can be confusing if you're new to the area.

Like many other Montana towns today, Livingston struggles with a changing economy that has moved from dependence on the railroad and natural-resource industries to tourism and high technology. Although most residents would never call their town a bedroom community to Bozeman, nearly 35 percent of the population commutes to jobs in the "big city," just 23 miles to the west on I-90. The Livingston Rebuild Center—a longtime headquarters for repairing locomotive engines—is still a major employer, as is Montana Rail Link.

Although the actual population of Livingston has remained steady for the past 20 years, it is not undiscovered. Robert Redford's film *The Horse Whisperer* and local resident Dennis Quaid's TNT movie *Everything That Rises,* as well as parts of *A River Runs Through It* were filmed here. Singer Jimmy Buffett also wrote the hit song "Livingston Saturday Night" about this town's raucous nightlife. And judging by the number of bars, saloons, and casinos within a 3-block radius—more than a dozen in all—you can see why. You could do your own kind of pub crawl, moving from the old-timer's cowboy clique at the Stockman, to the rowdy biker sanctum of the Hyatt House, or to the sound of blues at the Murray. On a weekend night during summer, don't be surprised if you find folks sipping wine at gallery walks or two-stepping in the streets for the annual Fourth of July celebration.

ACCOMMODATIONS
Hotels & Motels

Price Code

Some rates are based on availability. The following codes indicate the average nightly rates for two adults. Accommodations accept all or most major credit cards, unless otherwise noted.

$ . . . . Less than $49
$$ . . . . $49 to $75
$$$ . . . . $75 to $100
$$$$ . . . . More than $100

BEST WESTERN
YELLOWSTONE INN **$$$$**
1515 West Park St.
(406) 222-6110, (800) 826-1214
www.bestwesternmontana.com
This 100-room modern hotel is for the business traveler. Focusing on attracting conferences and large events, its service is the key to keeping guests happy. The Yellowstone's staff will readily arrange activities for visitors to the area with advance notice. Each well-appointed room features free Internet access, cable TV, coffeemaker, and king beds; refrigerators, microwaves, and sofas are available in select rooms. The hotel also provides shuttles to Bozeman airport and Bridger Bowl ski area. An on-site restaurant and lounge can keep you happy, but if you'd like to enjoy other areas of Livingston, you might want to drive or call a taxi.

✳CHICO HOT SPRINGS LODGE
AND DAY SPA **$$–$$$$**
1 Old Chico Rd., Pray
(406) 333-4933, (800) HOT WADA
www.chicohotsprings.com
Not far from the river, just south of Livingston and 30 miles north of Yellowstone National Park, is Chico Hot Springs Lodge, an oasis in the rough. Rooted in history, the resort has been a secret getaway spot since its opening in 1900. Most people come to soak in the natural hot springs, but it's the true rustic charm and unpretentious glamour that draw visitors again and again. Without the modern distractions of telephones or TVs in the rooms, this destination resort

provides sheer relaxation. Guests can explore the wonders of Yellowstone on a day trip; enjoy hiking, mountain biking, or horseback riding; or choose the simple luxury of doing nothing at all.

Although the many locals who frequent Chico would like to keep the place their little secret, the turn-of-the-20th-century Victorian-style inn attracts visitors from around the world. Choose from accommodations ranging from the cozy antique rooms in the main lodge, private cabins on the hillside, a room in the comfortable motel addition, or the option of beautifully decorated new rooms in the lower lodge. Wherever you lay your head, Chico's amenities will win you over.

ℹ️ The Livingston Farmers' Market is held every Wed June through Sept from 4 to 7 p.m. at Sacajawea Park along the Yellowstone River. You'll find locally grown beef and lamb, home-baked pastries and breads, crafts, and gorgeous wildflowers.

THE MURRAY HOTEL $$$
201 West Park St.
(406) 222-1350
www.murrayhotel.com
According to a *New York Times* article, "The historic Murray Hotel appeals to celebrities and to a certain Western disorder." It is true that the hundred-year-old hotel rented a permanent room to the late director Sam Peckinpah—the room is still decorated with some of his lamps and pictures. Located in the historic district, within walking distance of museums, restaurants, and fishing, the 30 comfortable rooms are inspired by the western tradition. The elegant lobby, with Victorian and art deco decor, invites you to

lounge with a good book and hot cup of tea. A rooftop spa has views of all three mountain ranges, and the Murray Bar downstairs features live music throughout the week.

RAINBOW MOTEL $$
5574 US 89 South
(406) 222-3780
Just a stroll from the Yellowstone River, the Rainbow is an old motel without a lot of frills, except a quaint 1950s swank style that can't be replicated. The single-story units wrap around a courtyard and a gravel parking lot. It's just on the eastern edge of Livingston, so not too convenient for walking to downtown or restaurants, but it's a tidy, locally owned place that is close to fishing and a great value.

Bed-and-Breakfasts & Guest Ranches

Price Code
$ . . . . Less than $85
$$ . . . . $85 to $115
$$$ . . . . $115 to $150
$$$$ . . . . More than $150

MOUNTAIN SKY GUEST RANCH $$$$
480 Big Creek Road, Pray, MT 59065
(406) 587-1244, (800) 548-3392
www.mtnsky.com
Driving up the rocky Forest Service road will make you feel as if you were in the backcountry, but the truth is that guests of Mountain Sky do not rough it. All the details from food to fun are taken care of here. Tucked into the Gallatin Range, south of Livingston, this dude ranch combines luxury with simple western style. The charming rustic cabins are tucked into groves of lodgepole pines and are secluded, though they are only a short walk from the main lodge.

Dining at Mountain Sky is an event on its own. Whether it's a poolside barbecue featuring steaks and chicken or seafood or an inside meal of gourmet continental cuisine, you won't want to miss it. Breakfasts range from light to hearty, depending on your preference. Lunch, served outside buffet-style after the morning ride, may include homemade soups, deli sandwiches, pasta salads, stir-fries, or other specialties. Don't worry, you won't go hungry here.

Hiking and horseback riding, designed for any fitness level, are the ranch's main activities. The children's program is educational and very active, catering to all ages so that the folks can get some guilt-free adult time. Tennis courts, a pool, sauna, volleyball, horseshoe pits, and table tennis should keep you busy if simply relaxing becomes tiresome.

YELLOWSTONE RIVER INN CABINS $$$
4950 US 89 South
(406) 222-2429, (888) 669-6993
www.yellowstoneriverinn.com
Sitting on the edge of the Yellowstone River, just 4 miles south of Livingston, this little inn looks up to the Absaroka mountain range. Dee Dee Van Zyl and her family share this exquisite spot by renting two cabins and a restored sheep wagon on their property. The Victorian-era house resembles homesteads of old and feels like a step back in time. Both cabins have been refinished with western influences, hardwood floors, and covered porches overlooking the river. Each has a kitchenette and requires a three-night minimum stay. Just a stone's throw from the river, you are minutes from hot fishing spots and cool shady spots to wade in on a warm summer day. Weekly rates are available.

ℹ️ Make your reservations a year in advance if you plan to visit Livingston on Independence Day. Fourth of July is bigger than Christmas in Livingston. The whole town kicks off a three-day celebration with a downtown parade and the first night of the Livingston Roundup Rodeo. The rodeo is held July 2, 3, and 4, ending with fireworks every night.

YELLOWSTONE VALLEY LODGE $$$$
3840 US 89 South
(406) 333-4787, (800) 626-3526
www.yellowstonevalleylodge.com
More of a fishing lodge than a B&B, the cabins here are perched on a cliff just above the Yellowstone River in Paradise Valley. If you are fly fisher, you can stroll down the path to the river to be the first one on the water at dawn. No matter what you are doing, this location provides unbeatable views of the Absaroka and Gallatin mountain ranges. Hearty breakfasts are served starting at 7 a.m. and dinner begins at 6 p.m. in the Paradise Valley Grill and outside on the terrace. Dinner is more luxurious, offering appetizers and a cocktail hour before you settle into a four-course meal featuring organic and local produce, handcrafted sauces, and elegant preparations of fresh-flown fish or local meat. The dining room is open to the public and accepts reservations for small groups of four to six people. Rates vary, but for anglers the Montana Sampler begins at $1,595 per person for a three-night stay, based on double occupancy. The all-inclusive package includes daily fishing guide service, airport shuttle from Bozeman, meals, lodging, and two private rod fees.

Campgrounds & RV Parks

Price Code

$.................	Less than $10
$$	$10 to $16
$$$	$16 to $23
$$$$	More than $23

MALLARDS REST $
US 89 South
(406) 222-1892
Though this campground is alongside a major thoroughfare into Yellowstone National Park, its location on the Yellowstone River makes it seem a world away from the flow of traffic. Just a handful of campsites are located here, and they fill up quickly almost any time of year. It's a great stopover between Livingston and Yellowstone, located about 8 miles south of Livingston. The area is popular with anglers as a drop-off point to float down the river. Tall cottonwoods shade most of the sites, and the sound of the river is audible from every spot. Bald eagles perch in the trees across the river and are easy to watch hunting or soaring in the early mornings and evenings. The grade of the road is short but steep, so large RVs cannot make the turn or the climb back up the hill. This is a campground for small trailers and tents. Although running water and bathrooms are available, the amenities are otherwise a bit rustic. It's a great spot to enjoy the river, even if the area is a bit isolated.

PARADISE VALLEY/LIVINGSTON
  KOA $$
163 Pine Creek Rd.
(406) 222-0992, (800) 562-2805
There may not be a better-located campground than this one along the shady banks of the Yellowstone River. A heated indoor pool, ice-cream socials, outdoor pancake breakfasts, and Sun evening chapel are only half of why this place has been running for three decades. Experienced guides and support staff make it seem as if you were an old friend, and they will make you want to come back year after year. Accommodations include cabins with riverfront porches, RV hookups, and tent sites. Bike and raft rentals are available here as well. Reservations are a must, however, and it's a good idea to book at least six months in advance.

PINE CREEK CAMPGROUND $$
Off East River Road
(406) 222-1892
Just 12 miles south of Livingston, this popular local campground is convenient, clean, and picturesque. Tucked into the shadows of high lodgepole pines, the 20 campsites here accommodate large RVs and small tents. Each site features fire pits, chopped firewood, picnic tables, and conveniently located toilets with potable water nearby. There's access to the astoundingly clear Pine Creek and a short creekside trail, as well as popular hikes to Pine Creek Falls or the longer Pine Creek Lake. It's a special campground that you won't want to leave. To top it off, on the drive up you can stop at a lookout point that offers a supreme view of Paradise Valley.

YELLOWSTONE'S EDGE RV PARK $$
3502 US 89 South
(406) 333-4036, (800) 865-7322
www.mtrv.com
Located 18 miles south of Livingston on US 89 heading toward Yellowstone National Park, this RV park is much more than a roadside crash pad. The views are better here than at any other hotel or lodge in the

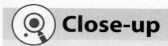

Close-up

Iron Horse Revolution

Like so many towns in the American West, Livingston was bolstered by the historic race between the Burlington Northern and the Northern Pacific Railway companies to complete a transcontinental railroad in the late 1800s.

In this little burg along the Yellowstone River, the Northern Pacific Railway won. The town was founded in 1882 and was originally named Clark City because it was a stopover for Captain Clark's Corps of Discovery. By 1889 (the same year Montana was declared a state), a sizable locomotive repair shop and established downtown with electric lights anchored the town; it was renamed for Crawford Livingston, an influential railroad executive.

By that time the Northern Pacific had secured contracts with the federal government to bring travelers into the northern entrance to Yellowstone National Park. The railroad company built a 60-mile spur line that transported eastern tourists to "Wonderland" via the Cinnabar Station and later Gardiner. From there they traveled by wagon to the Mammoth Hotel and on to Old Faithful; it was the original "grand tour" of Yellowstone.

Livingston was a hub for curious adventure seekers and hearty entrepreneurs in its early days. At one point in the late 1880s, the town boasted six general stores, two drugstores, two hotels, one hardware store, two restaurants, two watchmakers, three blacksmiths, two wholesale liquor dealers, two meat markets, and 30 saloons. An ornate train depot was constructed to greet railroad passengers; its iconic yin and yang symbols of the Northern Pacific Railway are still visible today.

The depot has been restored and is on the National Register of Historic Places. It is still a central landmark in this small town and houses a railroad museum during the summer months.

area, on the banks of the Yellowstone River and looking toward the incredible Absa-roka Range. Offering water, electricity, sewer, shower, laundry, and store, this RV park with 3,000 feet of Yellowstone River frontage has 81 RV hookups and 13 tent sites. Because of the busy highway traffic, Yellowstone's Edge is more suited to RV travelers than tent campers.

RESTAURANTS

Price Code

Prices represent meals for two people, excluding beverages, tip, and tax.

$	Less than $20
$$	$20 to $27
$$$	$27 to $35
$$$$	More than $35

CHADZ   **$**
104 North Main St.
(406) 222-2247

This eclectic coffeehouse and Wi-Fi hot spot serves breakfast and lunch until 2:30 p.m. Mon through Sat, featuring delicious espressos and drinks along with a creative menu and fresh-baked goodies. Children are welcome; there's a playroom in the back. Lingering is encouraged, as evidenced by the seating options from classic table and chairs to slouchy couches and a tea table in the window with floor pillows.

**CHICO HOT SPRINGS LODGE
AND DAY SPA** $$$$
1 Old Chico Rd., Pray
(406) 333-4933
www.chicohotsprings.com

People began raving about the restaurant at Chico Hot Springs Lodge 100-plus years ago. It started with a bowl of strawberries during the height of the Montana gold rush. A young couple named Bill and Percie Knowles opened a modest boardinghouse near a natural hot springs and catered to fortune-seeking miners weary of campfire meals and washing their clothes in the creek. They promised a slice of luxury amidst a rugged way of life. What they offered was a clean bed, a hot bath, and fresh strawberries with every meal. What they learned is that folks will travel far for a good soak and a fine meal. That's still true today, as Chico has been written up in *Bon Appétit, Gourmet,* and the *New York Times.* The restaurant has received *Wine Spectator's* Award of Excellence for its well-rounded wine list numerous times.

Over the decades the melding of culinary styles has improved upon those comfort-food roots. Chef Jack Hall and his crew still rely on fresh ingredients from the year-round greenhouse and garden, as well as on the local offerings of the area—Montana beef, farm-raised fowl, wild game, and regional trout. Signature dishes on the menu reflect the traditional hearty tastes: rosemary rack of lamb, beef Wellington, Grand Marnier roasted duckling, and smoked trout. But there is also an element of refinement that has been integrated to bring out the richness of those basic foods: a pork loin chop stuffed with sun-dried cherry, walnut, and cornbread stuffing; grilled venison served with a merlot vin rouge; pine nut–crusted halibut finished with a fresh fruit salsa and port wine butter sauce; baked Brie served over lingonberry and hollandaise sauces. The result is a menu that is uniquely Montana—as appealing to a local rancher or a Hollywood celebrity as it is to the bon vivant.

COFFEE CROSSING $
104 North Second St.
(406) 222-1200

Located across from the post office and next to the movie theater, this funky coffee shop is a great people-watching spot. Owner John Rawlins and staff serve up the espresso drinks with friendly smiles and wry humor. To pass the time the guys who work here think up witticisms to paste on the paper take-out cups. "Wherever you joe, there you are" and "Don't joe there!" are some of the favorites, but they change weekly.

CRAZY COYOTE $$
206 South Eleventh St.
(406) 222-1548

Situated on an unlikely corner, this family-run Mexican restaurant is the real thing. Homemade salsa—from spicy chipotle to tangy tomatillo—is a highlight of the menu. Don't be put off by the plain atmosphere of the place. It's clean and efficient, and the food is excellent. Try the chile verde. If you are lucky, you'll be in the one or two days a year when a batch of fresh tamales is offered.

✳**LIVINGSTON RIB & CHOP HOUSE** $$
305 East Park St.
(406) 222-9200
www.ribandchophouse.com

Voted Livingston's favorite restaurant, the Chop House, as locals call it, serves the best baby back ribs with a secret homemade barbecue sauce. It is known for the fast, friendly, and lively atmosphere at the small bar and throughout the restaurant; it's rare that this place isn't hopping with customers. Owners Burke and Melissa pride themselves on their southern hospitality (Louisiana), and Montana-style portions bring customers back again and again. From steak to seafood, there isn't much on the menu that won't tempt your taste buds. Adjacent to the chamber of commerce, the Chop House is open seven days a week from 11 a.m. to 2 p.m. and 5:30 to 10 p.m. This Montana and Wyoming chain also has locations in Billings, Miles City, Cody, and Sheridan.

MARK'S IN AND OUT $
801 West Park St.
(406) 222-7744

The opening of Mark's In and Out every Mar (it's open from Mar 1 to Nov 1) is a sure sign that spring is coming in Livingston. The neon lights go on, the open sign goes up, and a life-size cutout of Marilyn Monroe beckons you to slurp up a malt with her. There are no car hops to serve the shakes, burgers, and fries as there were when this cute drive-up opened in 1954, but otherwise not a lot has changed. Home of the Super Cheese—two patties with two slices of cheese and your choice of toppings for less than $2—it's hard to beat the nostalgia served up here. If there ever is a perfect time to have dinner on the hood of your car, it would be in July when Mark's sponsors the Old Car Show. American flags line the streets to guide a parade of several hundred vintage cars. It's a step back in time that is a must-see.

NORTHERN PACIFIC BEANERY $$
108 West Park St.
(406) 222-7288
www.thenpbeanery.com

Formerly Martin's Cafe, the Beanery recently had a complete kitchen overhaul and dining room remodel. Gone are the Formica tables, homely hunter green window trim, and dated train memorabilia. In their place is a warm and inviting dining room with a country style. Serving classic breakfast and lunch items seven days a week, the restaurant is located just off the historic Livingston Depot and borders the very active railroad tracks. Train memorabilia or not, the real thing rails right out the front door, rattling the windows when it does, and that alone is a reminder of the significant railroad history in this little town.

THE PICKLE BARREL $
131 South Main St.
(406) 222-5469

This place has the biggest sandwiches in town. This corner restaurant is casual and clean, serving hot and cold subs as well as locally made Wilcoxson's ice cream. The food is consistent, quick, and filling. Their signature is that you will never feel like you need to ask for a second helping of anything. Founded in the early 1970s by a local ski bum in Bozeman, the Pickle Barrel is a long-time success. It is the ideal spot for the entire family to grab a good lunch or quick dinner to stay or eat on the go.

✳PINE CREEK CAFÉ $$
2496 East River Rd.
(406) 222-3628
www.pinecreeklodgemontana.com

Look for the neon arrow that points to this neighborhood hangout in the cul-de-sac community of Pine Creek on East River Road in Paradise Valley. Serving an offbeat mix of southwestern-influenced western food, the menu is reasonably priced, savory, and somehow the perfect finish to a day spent outdoors—hiking or boating in summer or cross-country skiing in winter. Try the smoked trout tacos or the pear quesadilla. The locally brewed beer on tap isn't bad either. On Sat during the summer, Pine Creek has a following of locals who come for the small outdoor concerts and barbecue served under the white tent out back. The music varies from bluegrass to classic rock, but it's always a fun scene.

i If you are heading to Yellowstone from Livingston, take East River Road off US 89 for a meandering scenic drive along the Yellowstone River. This route is about 10 miles longer but could actually be a shortcut in summer because of heavy tourist traffic on the main highway.

PINKY'S $
109½ South Main St.
(406) 222-0668
Take a seat at the counter for an espresso and a chance to catch up on all the local scuttlebutt. A traditional Butte Pasty isn't the only thing that's juicy; Livingston is a lively community that shows in the hot gossip that abounds. Pinky is an old-time local guy who bakes delectable pastries and cheesecakes. The diner-inspired restaurant is a haven for eclectic art and inspirational sandwiches. Open for breakfast and lunch Mon through Fri 7 a.m. to 2 p.m.; Sat 7 a.m. to 1 p.m.; closed Sun.

2ND STREET BISTRO $$
123 North Second St.
(406) 222-9463
www.secondstreetbistro.com
Adjacent to Livingston's historic Murray Hotel, 2nd Street Bistro offers a menu anchored by chef Scott Samson's French cooking techniques mixed with Mediterranean flavors and Montana flair. Partners Brian Menges, chef Samson, and John McNaughton wanted to create a bistro in the true European tradition—a neighborhood restaurant where you feel comfortable having a pizza and a beer after getting off the river or getting dressed up and having a night on the town. The trio also owns the Murray Bar, a town fixture; they plan to maintain it as the same good old Montana bar that Jimmy Buffet sings about in his song "Livingston Saturday Night." Since opening in 2004, 2nd Street Bistro has had a stream of regular customers who enjoy their varied menu and wine list. The energetic menu ranges from gourmet pizzas to meat loaf to seafood specials. The seafood stew features the freshest ingredients, flown in from the coast three times a week. Pizzas are available in the bar, where lunch is offered from noon daily. The bistro is open seven days a week from 5 p.m. until "late," and reservations are recommended.

THE SPORT $$
114 South Main St.
(406) 222-3533
The walls of this ca. 1909 western bar and restaurant have stories to tell about fortunes won and lost in all-night poker games, barroom brawls, hard luck, hard work, and hard-earned money spent on rounds of drinks. But this once rowdy saloon is pretty tame these days; the last brawl here was a staged scene for a TNT movie in 1997 directed by

Dennis Quaid. He and fellow celebrities Robert Redford and Peter Fonda belly up to the bar every now and then.

Renovated to showcase original pressed-tin ceilings and an oak bar, the space was originally dubbed the Beer Hall in the late 1800s. The walls give glimpses of history from photos of Livingston's unpaved Main Street to cowboy memorabilia. The original molded-tin ceilings and richly painted walls retain that turn-of-the-20th-century charm. The menu offers a reasonably priced array of classic western grilled burgers and steaks, as well as Tex-Mex dishes. There are rumors that the famous Sport Burger is as good as it gets. They proudly serve local meat for lunch and dinner. There is something for everyone here, and families are welcome.

THE STOCKMAN BAR $$
118 North Main St.
(406) 222-8455
For 50-plus years this old-timer's bar and restaurant has been serving unforgettable burgers. It's the place to go to for a slice of Americana Old West–style with french fries on top. Sure, the salads are strictly iceberg lettuce and the tablecloths are red-checked vinyl, but folks don't come here for the greens or the atmosphere. There's nothing fancy about this restaurant, but it is a Livingston mainstay. Its greatest strength is consistency—whether it's the rib eye or the New York steak, you can count on the quality. The food is simple and the service is fast. This is a fine family restaurant. On weekend nights there may be a 30- to 45-minute wait, so plan ahead and come hungry. They do not accept reservations.

Z BAR AND GRILL $
Neptune's Brew Pub
119 North L Street
(406) 222-7837
www.zbarandgrill.com
Tucked into a little out-of-the-way side street, Z Bar and Grill is the site of locally brewed Neptune ale that boasts a lively local atmosphere. Master brewer Bill Taylor keeps the taps flowing with his newest batches of microbrews. Neptune's Pale Ale can be found in Yellowstone National Park restaurants and other regional establishments. Z Bar is open every day from 11 a.m. to 2 a.m.

SHOPPING

BOOKS & MUSIC, ETC.
106 South Main St.
(406) 222-7767
Offering everything from autobiographies to science fiction and Sinatra to the Shins, this is a shop with something for everyone. You'll find comfy chairs tucked away throughout the store to promote browsing. Owner Tim Gable is very knowledgeable on a broad number of topics, and his shop contains a notable travel section.

For anglers who are hitting the Yellowstone River without a guide, there are several businesses that offer river shuttles to take the logistics hassle out of your day. Good options include River Source Outfitters (406-223-5134) and B & G River Shuttles (406-222-3174).

OBSIDIAN COLLECTION
107 South Main St.
(406) 222-2022
www.obsidiancollection.com

One of Livingston's oldest women's clothing stores, Obsidian is known for its sales staff. With so many regular local customers, the staff here makes personal calls when the new season's fashions arrive in the store. A large variety of gifts, from bath and body care to baby toys, is available upstairs.

SAPHIRE
108 West Callendar St.
(406) 222-1301

A vibrant women's boutique with feminine, urban fashion in mind, Saphire is a fun, affordable store. Most of the women under 60 buy their clothes here if they are shopping in town. From sultry shoes to slinky dresses and everything in between, this boutique is a great complement to this western town.

✳SAX AND FRYER COMPANY
109 West Callendar St.
(406) 222-1421

This quaint bookstore opened in 1883 and is Livingston's oldest business. Inside, not a lot has changed, although there are more magazines to choose from now. Owned by John Fryer, who took on the shop from his father, who'd worked it with his own father, this is a great source for books written by local and western authors, Fryer's specialty. Here you'll find signed copies from local novelist Tom McGuane, Missoula author James Welch, and international adventure writer Tim Cahill, who also lives in town.

TIMBER TRAILS
309 West Park St.
(406) 222-9550

It's hard to miss this hip outdoor shop at the edge of the historic district—there is a bicycle mounted on the rooftop. Though the retail space is small, the selection is vast. The shop sells clothing and equipment for rock climbing, Alpine and cross-country skiing, cycling, mountaineering, snowshoeing, and backpacking. Owner Dale Sexton is a do-everything kind of outdoorsman, and his store reflects that. He has made the shop a priceless resource for equipment rental and advice on local recreation spots.

> **i** Famous for its artist-colony community, Livingston attracts painters, sculptors, writers, and filmmakers. See them all during one of the summer Art Walks. Downtown touts 15 galleries and hosts openings monthly from June through Sept. Go to www.livingstongalleries.com for a schedule, or look for ads in the *Livingston Enterprise* and the *Montana Pioneer.*

WILD WEST CUSTOM CLOTHING
116 East Callendar St.
(406) 222-8716

This corner boutique offers sassy women's and children's clothes. You'll find the outfit that's just right for a summer barbecue or your victory ride through the arena as Rodeo Queen. The clothing isn't something you'd find at a large western chain store; it is uncommon finery. Alterations and custom fitting are also offered here.

WILSON BOOT COMPANY
1014 West Park St.
(406) 222-3842
www.wilsonboots.com

The only problem with a pair of cowboy boots from this landmark boot maker is that they will never wear out. Established in the 1950s, Sterling and Dixie Bowman have seen their business grow from the local cobbler's shop into a booming international product. They do custom fitting in their Livingston shop, but the major factory is in San Antonio, Texas.

NIGHTLIFE

THE MINT BAR AND THEATER
102 North Main St.
(406) 222-0361
www.mintbarandtheater.com
The well-known Mint has been various things since it was built at the turn of the 20th century—including a mercantile, hotel, and even a speakeasy during Prohibition. It was granted Montana's first liquor license in 1933 when it was turned into a legal, full-fledged bar, and has been a Livingston staple ever since. The Mint was purchased by the Moss family in 2008, completely renovated in 2009, and reopened in 2010 to great fanfare as one of the town's finest watering holes. Historical photographs adorn the walls, and the theater in back often shows movies and hosts local and national bands.

THE MURRAY BAR
201 West Park St.
(406) 222-6433
www.themurraybar.com
The Murray has been Livingston's go-to bar for more than 100 years, whether it's for a quick drink after work or for one of the many local and regional country bands that perform on the weekends. The Murray draws a healthy mix of locals, travelers, and celebrities, and has an authentic, down-home atmosphere. It should be a definite stop if you're passing through Livingston.

THE OWL LOUNGE
110 North 2nd St.
(406) 222-1322
You never know who you might recognize at the Owl, a legendary place where various members of the national literary and film scene have been known to belly up. With a classic lounge atmosphere and occasional live music, the Owl is another staple of the Livingston bar scene and is well worth a stop in for a cold one.

GARDINER

No other town has boasting rights that include the words "located right across from Yellowstone National Park." Gardiner, however, has had this distinguished honor since its founding days in 1880. It sits only paces away from Yellowstone's northern entrance, the park's first official entrance and only gate open year-round to vehicles.

What is most genuine about Gardiner is that you won't find any paved streets gussied up for the tourists or any promotional stunts to make you stay a little longer. It makes a great base as you explore Yellowstone. This town offers a quiet, homey perch above the river to refuel, relax, and maybe even rethink your tightly scheduled trip. If you do this you might hear the quiet whisper that says, "If you like what you see, stay awhile."

Unless otherwise indicated, all listings in the chapter are located in Gardiner, Montana.

OVERVIEW

Ever the service town, the little burg of Gardiner originally cropped up to feed and shelter miners searching for gold in nearby Jardine. Later it catered to soldiers when the US Army managed the National Park Service from Mammoth's Fort Yellowstone. It boomed as a tourist town in 1883 when the Northern Pacific Railroad routed its Park Branch Line as far as Cinnabar; reportedly there were six restaurants, two dance halls, four houses of ill-repute, one milkman, and 21 saloons all catering to the thousands of visitors who came to see the wilds of Yellowstone at that time. In 1903 Gardiner hosted President Theodore Roosevelt when he dedicated the Roosevelt Arch, officially marking the gateway to "America's gem."

Since those beginnings the town's 200 year-round residents have cultivated their love-hate relationship with the park. Just 5 miles from Mammoth, where park employees reside all year, Gardiner shares its public school but borrows Mammoth's medical clinic. It is home to the warehouses of Xanterra Parks and Resorts, Yellowstone's largest concessionaire. Gardiner is still the supply town, with an economy reliant upon tourism, mining, and Yellowstone employee needs.

Encircled by the Absaroka-Beartooth Wilderness, Gallatin National Forest, and national park land, there isn't a lot of potential for Gardiner to grow. It is arguably one of the most scenic locations in North America, with the Yellowstone River running through the center of town, but also. the most limited. People either love it or leave it for this reason.

Its beauty is double edged, because as gorgeous as it is here, it can't ever really be much more than a quiet stopover for workers or tourists or wanderers. As a result, the folks who do call this cul-de-sac home are hearty, dedicated, and real. It is a tight community that looks out for its neighbors and relies on them in times of need. Everyone here truly knows everyone else's business, although ties loosen up in summer when the number of "parkies"—Yellowstone employees—doubles the town's population. Many of the residents claim their heritage of old mining families, their experiences in Yellowstone, and their love of nature as the reasons they remain in Gardiner. They are stickers, and if you want to live here, you'll have to show 'em you're a sticker, too.

ACCOMMODATIONS
Hotels

Price Code

Some rates are based on availability. The following codes indicate the average nightly rate for two adults. Accommodations accept all or most major credit cards, unless otherwise noted.

$.................. Less than $50
$$ .... $50 to $75
$$$ .... $75 to $100
$$$$ .... More than $100

∗ABSAROKA LODGE   **$$$$**
310 Scott St.
(406) 848-7414, (800) 755-7414
www.yellowstonemotel.com

With a balcony overlooking the Yellowstone River and Yellowstone National Park on every room, it is hard to beat the Absarokee's location. Owners Dick and Irene Herriford keep their lodge clean, comfortable, and cozy, considering the place bustles year-round. Each room offers all the modern conveniences you could imagine with a friendly crew to back it all up. In addition to rooms with a view, the hotel has picnic tables on a

nice lawn along the banks of the river. Rates are almost cut in half during the shoulder seasons and in winter.

BEST WESTERN BY MAMMOTH
    HOT SPRINGS   **$$$**
US 89
(406) 848-7311, (800) 828-9080

Ask the locals where to get in a good steak, a little dancing, and a slick room, and they'll tell you it's at the Best Western. The hotel houses the Yellowstone Mine Restaurant and the Rusty Nail Lounge to make everything simple for its guests. Sitting on the banks of the Yellowstone River, this local Best Western combines modern amenities with rustic influences. All 85 rooms offer the usual modern conveniences, along with a laundry facility just off the lobby. The hotel has been renovated, and it has a large indoor pool for the kids to romp in after a long drive through the park.

YELLOWSTONE SUPER 8   **$$$**
702 Scott St. West (US 89)
(406) 848-7401
www.yellowstonesuper8.com

This basic hotel gets good reviews for its friendly staff and modest accommodations close to the park. Restaurants and shops are within walking distance, and there are both smoking and nonsmoking rooms, as well as an indoor pool. The rooms on the west side have a nice view of the park, and the hotel accepts pets.

Bed-and-Breakfasts
& Guest Ranches

Price Code

$.................. Less than $86
$$ .... $86 to $115
$$$ .... $115 to $150
$$$$ .... More than $150

GARDINER

DOME MOUNTAIN RANCH $$$
2017 US 89, Emigrant
(406) 333-4361, (800) 313-4868
www.domemountainranch.com
Maybe you have already toured through
Yellowstone Park and now want to find out
what the western pace of life is really like.
Dome Mountain Ranch is the place to experience the quiet of life in Big Sky country,
from feeding the cattle in winter to hiking
wildflower-covered trails in summer. Tucked
in the Absaroka Range on 5,000 private acres
with more than 4 miles of Yellowstone River
frontage, Dome Mountain Ranch is a million
miles away from any urban distractions.

From family reunions to corporate
retreats, this dude ranch has a little something for everyone. Accommodations range
from a bed-and-breakfast-style house to rustic cabins, modern houses to wilderness
camps. The options are limitless here, and
the staff will happily arrange horse-pack
trips into the park and floats on the river, or
point you in the right direction for finding
the secret spots in Yellowstone on your own.
Just 20 minutes from the park's northern
entrance, staying here gives you the opportunity to day trip into Yellowstone and at
the same time enjoy a really unusual place
to stay.

GARDINER GUEST HOUSE $$
112 East Main St.
(406) 848-9414
www.gardinerguesthouse.com
Operated by Parks Fly Shop owners Richard
and Nancy Parks, this quaint stone house
was built in 1903 and is an angler's home
away from home. The three precious main
rooms are uniquely decorated in the period
of this historic house and outfitted with

comfortable beds, private baths, and many
other amenities. A small cabin behind the
house is also available. A home-cooked
breakfast is served daily, and snacks are
always on hand at the kitchen pass-through.
Families and pets are welcome to stay for
short or long periods; the house is within
walking distance to all of Gardiner.

NORTH YELLOWSTONE BED AND
   BREAKFAST $$$
172 Jardine Rd.
(406) 848-7651
www.northyellowstone.com
Located 2 miles outside of Gardiner on Jar-
dine Road, this feels more like a dude ranch
or a summer camp than a B&B. You are
sure to have a piece of Montana wilderness
nearly to yourself here, with only two log
cabins on the property. Owners Peggy and
Bill Hoppe will make you feel like it's your
little piece of paradise. A fifth-generation
Montanan, Bill might even tell you some
stories about his ancestors—he claims that
his great-grandfather was "the first white
child born in Montana Territory ca. 1864." He
has lived and guided in Yellowstone for more
than 25 years and offers a wealth of knowl-
edge on the area. Ask about extended-stay
discounted rates. Other meals, including pic-
nics, can be arranged.

i It's common to see elk or bison
lazing or grazing on the front
lawns of Gardiner residences, particu-
larly in winter. The herds loll across
park borders in search of the town's
lower elevation and warmer tempera-
tures.

YELLOWSTONE SUITES BED AND BREAKFAST $$
506 Fourth St.
(406) 848-7937, (800) 948-7937
www.yellowstonesuites.com

The white picket fence around this charming sandstone house tells the whole story of this bed-and-breakfast: home sweet home. Built in 1904 by famous Yellowstone architect Robert Reamer, the house is located in a peaceful residential neighborhood. The four bedrooms are decorated in a nonfussy Victorian style, with antiques and good taste. A private veranda and garden make for pleasant dining in the mornings, while the library is ideal to curl up with a book. The bed-and-breakfast is open year-round.

Campgrounds & RV Parks

Price Code
$....................Less than $9
$$ ....$9 to $16
$$$ .... $16 to $23
$$$$ .... More than $23

CANYON CAMPGROUND $
US 89 South
(406) 848-7375

Halfway through Yankee Jim Canyon, just 18 miles north of Gardiner, this tiny campground's 12 units are separated by massive boulders. Located at the base of the canyon wall, across the highway from the Yellowstone River and traces of the first toll road into Yellowstone National Park, this campground has two toilets but no other facilities. The old railroad bed and the Yellowstone Trail, the first automobile route into the park, are on the far side of the river as well. The campground is open year-round and is on a first-come, first-served basis. RVs are limited to 48 feet.

EAGLE CREEK CAMPGROUND $
Jardine Road
(406) 848-7375

It's tough to find a bad campsite in this loosely formed campground, but cruise through the entire area from top to bottom before you choose your spot. At the top you'll find designated tent spaces tucked into the trees. At the bottom there are open spaces with mowed grass. To the east is the corral, and there's plenty of room to pull through with a fifth-wheeler. Don't be alarmed if you end up sharing your morning coffee with a couple of resident elk or deer. They like this spot because of the fine grazing, the sweet creek, and the fact that it is a little off the beaten path. To find it, head straight for the camp sign of the Rocky Mountain RV Camp, but don't turn in. Bear left past the entrance instead and drive east approximately 1.5 miles until you see a Forest Service sign for the campground on the left. The services are limited here: There are two toilets, one that is wheelchair accessible. But bring your own water and pack out your garbage.

ROCKY MOUNTAIN RV CAMP $$$
14 Jardine Rd.
(406) 848-7251
www.rockymountaincampground.com

Overlooking Gardiner and Yellowstone National Park, Rocky Mountain RV Camp has one of the lower 48 states' most breathtaking views. Follow the neon camp sign to this communal oasis after touring the hot, dusty roads of the West. This campground offers 87 RV sites and 21 tent spaces with grass. For the wayward camper, whether RVing it or roughing it, this is an ideal spot to rest or use as a base to sightsee in the park. With public showers, coin-operated laundry, RV dump station, wireless Internet, and garbage drop

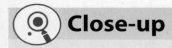

Close-up

Yellowstone's Bison Controversy

If having the first official entrance to Yellowstone National Park wasn't enough to put Gardiner, Montana, on the map, the controversy of Yellowstone's bison is.

A government-sanctioned killing of the park's bison in 1996 brought national attention to Gardiner. The clashing politics of the National Park Service, environmental groups, Montana Department of Livestock officials, and even former president Clinton were put to the test over how to manage the nation's last free-roaming bison herd. It was an issue that landed protesters in prison and sparked a nationwide debate that continues today.

In the winter of 1996–97, heavy snows and limited food supplies drove Yellowstone's bison over park borders (primarily to areas north and west of the park in Montana) onto public and private lands where domestic cattle graze in spring and summer. Fearing the transmission of brucellosis from the buffalo to their cattle, livestock producers objected.

Brucellosis is an organism transmitted through birth material left from bison on land where cattle later graze. It can cause cows to abort their calves. Montana has been a brucellosis-free state since 1985, which means the state's ranchers do not have to test their herds for the disease before selling them out of state.

Although there is no documented case of Yellowstone bison transmitting brucellosis to cattle, wildlife biologists estimate that nearly half the park's herd carries the disease. There is no vaccine to prevent the transmission of brucellosis. Montana ranchers felt the risk was too great to be ignored and demanded that the bison not be allowed to roam freely beyond the borders of Yellowstone.

As a result, during the winter of 1996–97, 1,100 bison were shot or sent to slaughter after exiting the park. Another 300 to 400 animals died naturally due to harsh

(just toss it into the back of the 1948 dump truck parked by the office), this is your one-stop shop. If you roll in during the wee hours of darkness, there is an after-hours registration for your convenience by the office door. The campground is open Apr 15 to Oct 15.

✳TIMBER CREEK CAMPGROUND $
Jardine Road
(406) 848-7375

Spring rains and winter snow will seem dreamy in this open meadow encircled by a wonderfully isolating stand of Douglas fir and lodgepole pines. But summer brings a spread of wildflowers with every color imaginable. With the small creek gurgling by your tent, camping will never seem better. Open from June 15 through Oct 31, Timber Creek Campground is about 5 miles north of Gardiner and 4 miles north of Jardine. Bring your own water, as there is none here. RVs are limited to 48 feet, and the campground is on a first-come, first-served basis.

> **i** Locals refer to Gardiner's Park Street as Front Street, since it was the first avenue built in town and faces the entrance to the park.

winter conditions, bringing the herd numbers down to 2,400. American Indian tribes, animal-rights activists, and environmentalists were in an uproar. And though government officials listened to protests, the interim-management solution of eliminating the bison to protect cattle continued.

Bison management in Yellowstone has been an issue since the park's inception, when national herd numbers had dwindled down to just 1,000 animals from the former population of 65 million in North America. Market hunting and poaching nearly eliminated the majestic creatures, prompting the National Park Service to restore their numbers in 1902 with the instigation of the "Buffalo Ranch" in the Lamar Valley. Buffalo were raised like domestic cattle until the 1930s, when the herd finally grew to a healthy number. The government saved America's last free-roaming bison herd, but with that intervention began the ongoing question of what is the best method to manage them: as wildlife or livestock?

After much debate, in 2000 the government released a Final Environmental Impact Statement regarding the Yellowstone bison. Under this plan the NPS is to maintain the overall herd population at 3,000. If bison leave the park, officials will test for brucellosis. Those testing positive will be sent to slaughter and those testing negative will be moved back into park boundaries. The plan is still denounced by many conservation groups; it is one of compromise for all parties involved. In the winter of 2004 the government-sanctioned public lottery bison hunt was reinstated, and it continues under strong public and media scrutiny.

The issue tests the very principles upon which Yellowstone was founded in the congressional act of 1872, when it was designated as both a place to "preserve all natural wonders and curiosities within" and a place for "the benefit and enjoyment of the people."

RESTAURANTS

Price Code

Prices represent meals for two people, excluding beverages, tip, and tax.

$ . . . . Less than $20
$$ . . . . $20 to $27
$$$ . . . . $27 to $35
$$$$ . . . . More than $35

✳HELEN'S CORRAL DRIVE INN $
711 Scott St.
(406) 848-7627
Owner and local character Helen Gould has been serving up her legendary buffalo burgers for more than 40 years. This is a Gardiner staple and a greasy spoon that shouldn't be passed up. Regular beef burgers are also served, half-pounders that come sizzling from the grill to the table with a basket of hand-cut french fries. The burgers are famous and Helen is notorious for offering straightforward, gruff, unsolicited advice. Any time of year is a good time for a Helen burger, but summer offers a pleasant spot out on the patio. The rest of the year it's indoor dining at a handful of tables. No credit cards are accepted.

GARDINER

K-BAR AND CAFE $$
202 Main St.
(406) 848-9995

It's hard to beat the thick-crust pizza here. Inspired by Chicago-style pies, the ingredients offered may be basic, but they're all good. With the kitchen located just to the left of the actual dining room, the staff makes your order right in front of you. This is the kind of bar that has that "it's a small world feeling," the kind of place where you'd run into an old friend whom you haven't seen in years. The pool table and jukebox see a lot of action, particularly during long winter months. It's a big Monday-night football spot in town.

SAWTOOTH DELI
AND RESTAURANT $
220 Park St.
(406) 848-7600

This small eatery with a western atmosphere is a good value for breakfast, lunch, and dinner. Breakfast is especially good, including the breakfast burritos and huevos rancheros. The sandwiches are fresh, and dinner choices include steaks, seafood, wood-fired pizza, and pasta. Beer and wine are available, and the Sawtooth is open from Tues to Sat from 8 a.m. to 9:30 p.m.

SHOPPING

FLYING PIG CAMP STORE
511 Scott St.
(406) 848-7510
www.flyingpigrafting.com

Snow in July, 10 days of rain in June, stifling heat in Nov during your trip to Yellowstone? Layering your clothes is the way to prepare for the temperamental weather flashes this area is notorious for, and this store has the perfect clothing for all conditions. It's a kind of everything outdoor store, selling cameras, equipment, knives, and even jewelry. It's a gear store and place to book rafting, horseback riding, or guided trips. There's also a computer with Internet access if you feel you need to get back in touch with the outside world or if you must check your e-mail. For an inspiration, ask a clerk to tell you the story behind the store's name. Five percent of all profits are donated to nonprofit groups.

Yellow Parade

Every year on June 1 and 2, Gardiner marks the beginning of the summer tourist season as the townsfolk gather on Front Street to welcome the return of the "yellow buses" as they drive through Roosevelt Arch. These 1930s-style retro vehicles are replicas of the buses that transported passengers along Yellowstone's Grand Loop before it was open to private car travel; today they run on biodiesel fuel and are available as shuttles throughout Yellowstone National Park.

KELLEM'S MONTANA SADDLERY
214 Park Ave.
(406) 848-7776

The glitzy, red-fringed leather riding gloves and platter-size belt buckles may be the bait that lures customers into this western shop, but it's Les Kellem's artistry that keeps them coming back. Though you can buy your cowboy duds here, the selection of western wear is limited. Saddles are the specialty of the house, as customers as far away as

Europe will attest. As an artisan, Kellem makes his custom saddles to last a horse's lifetime and then some, with prices ranging from $1,700 to $10,000. His wife, Carol, makes beautiful chaps (pronounced "shaps"). They have owned the store for more than a decade and have built such a following that they don't even need to advertise.

PARKS' FLY SHOP
202 South Second St.
(406) 848-7314
www.parksflyshop.com
Owner Richard Parks grew up in Gardiner and has been guiding in the Yellowstone area all his life. He has plenty of opinions on park management policies and isn't afraid to express them with gentle conviction. Open since 1953, the shop itself is simple compared to others, but the basics are here. Parks' offers a wealth of knowledge to the curious angler, custom-tied flies, and expert guide service.

COOKE CITY

Perched high in a crook of the rugged Beartooth Mountains, Cooke City is surrounded by four national forests, two wilderness areas, and Yellowstone National Park.

The friendly locals are less guarded to tourist traffic than any other place in the state. A stronghold for ski bums, recreationists, and lifetime Yellowstone Park devotees, Cooke City has a culture unto itself. The town's 90 hearty year-round residents welcome winter visitors who snowmobile, backcountry ski, or snowboard. During summer months the population swells to about 300 people who join tourists in a love for hiking, backpacking, fishing, hunting, and hiding out in summer getaway cabins. Instead of a dead end, you can see it as a starting point for exploring the outdoors or a simpler lifestyle.

Unless otherwise indicated, all listings in this chapter are located in Cooke City, Montana.

OVERVIEW

The 8 "blocks" of this mountain village are small and quaint reminders of bygone days when gold miners staked their claims in the 1800s. What this translates to is that, though the area is gorgeous, only people with ulterior motives (striking it rich, in this case) would dream of settling here.

Today's residents live here for a different kind of treasure: high mountain trails, abundant wildlife, pristine wilderness, and silence. The mountains rise up just beyond the edge of the road, seemingly close enough to reach out and touch. Sitting at 7,651 feet, you don't fight the lights of a city to see the stars or watch the moon rise over Mount Republic. And you don't have to worry about traffic jams.

Things are simple up here. Life is quiet and probably a little quirky when the cabin fever kicks in sometime during the long, dark winter nights. This is literally the end of the road come Oct when they stop plowing the Beartooth Scenic Highway (US 212) to Red Lodge, Montana. In Nov, Wyoming highway crews stop plowing the Chief Joseph Scenic Byway to Cody. Cooke is snowbound until Apr and can be accessed only via Yellowstone National Park to the southwest.

With the founding of the New World Mine, Shoo Fly changed its name to Cooke City in honor of Jay Cooke Jr. in 1883. Cooke planned to promote the area's development and bring a branch line of the Northern Pacific Railroad to town, but he ran into financial difficulties and never made good on his promises. As a result the area remained relatively isolated, preserving the region's beauty.

In Silver Gate, just 3 miles down the road from Cooke, it's evident that the founding fathers had big plans for the area. Meant to be an Old West attraction, it was platted in the 1930s with covenants that dictated rustic architecture and log construction. The notion never really took, although today Silver Gate services many summer and winter visitors with lodging and meals.

Cooke City is best known as a stopover en route to Yellowstone National Park (the northeast entrance is only 4 miles away) or to Red Lodge along the Beartooth Pass. But the mid-1990s saw the community recognized as a hotbed of political controversy when the Noranda Mine Company proposed an open-pit gold mine in hopes of tapping the largest gold deposit known in North America. The act threatened to change the face of Cooke City and Yellowstone Park forever. In an unprecedented move, President Clinton stopped the development and persuaded Congress to buy out shareholders' mining rights.

Rather than returning to its mining roots, today's economy is reliant on tourism. One clue to this is the 15 lodging facilities between here and Silver Gate. But don't let this fool you; Cooke City is no tourist trap. It's a genuine alpine hamlet just trying to make a living.

ACCOMMODATIONS
Motels, Lodges & Cabins

Price Code
Some rates are based on availability. The following codes indicate the average nightly rate for two adults. Accommodations accept all or most major credit cards, unless otherwise noted.

$................. Less than $50
$$ .... $50 to $75
$$$ .... $75 to $100
$$$$ .... More than $100

ALPINE MOTEL $$$
112 East Main St.
(406) 838-2262, (888) 838-1190
www.cookecityalpine.com
It's a good idea to make your reservations as early as possible at this popular, 25-unit, high-country motel. Located right in the middle of town, it's an easy walk from one end of Main Street to the other. The Alpine has sparkling clean rooms ranging from singles to suites with kitchens. Most of the rooms, though, have single or double beds. You'll find newer rooms in a two-story complex built in 1993. The Alpine is open year-round.

ANTLERS LODGE $$$
311 East Main St.
(406) 838-2432, (866) 738-2432
www.cookecityantlerslodge.com
Within walking distance of Cooke City's restaurants and bars, Antlers Lodge offers 20 rustic cabins that accommodate two to seven The Absaroka-Beartooth Wilderness is home to a greater concentration of high-altitude alpine lakes than anywhere else in the world. Nestled in the shade of lodgepole pine forest, the cabins all feature private bathrooms and are nonsmoking. Some have kitchenettes and loft sleeping areas. Hiking trails in summer and snowshoeing paths in winter can be accessed from your doorstep. Antlers Lodge is open year-round. Free Wi-Fi is available in the main lodge.

COOKE CITY SINCLAIR & CABINS $$$
115 Main St.
(406) 838-2000
www.cookecitysinclair.com
Cooke City Sinclair & Cabins offers two cozy and clean cabins with queen and full log beds, new TVs with satellite, and private

bathrooms. Complimentary coffee is available at the Sinclair. The log cabins are non-smoking, and no pets are allowed. Owners Steve and Lisa Schluter sold everything they owned to purchase the little Sinclair. They moved from Baltimore and now live in Cooke year-round. Ask about extended rates for five days or more.

HIGH COUNTRY MOTEL $$
200 Main St.
(406) 838-2272
www.cookecityhighcountry.com
Winter and summer, the High Country offers cabins and motel rooms to weary travelers and wayward snowmobilers. In summer High Country's 15 units fill fast, often months in advance between mid-June and mid-Aug, so be sure to call ahead. You'll find an assortment of carpeted, wood-paneled rooms with either one queen-size or two double beds. Montanans love to come here, and Christmas, New Year's, and Presidents' Day weekend are booked almost a year in advance.

✳SODA BUTTE LODGE $$
209 US 212
(406) 838-2251, (800) 527-6462
www.cookecity.com
Soda Butte Lodge is the closest thing to a resort that you will find in Cooke City. Open all year, the lodge has everything you might need during your stay, including an indoor pool and spa, laundry, fax, and snowmobile rentals. The lodge's 32 rooms range from those with one double bed to king suites.

Built in 1962, Soda Butte Lodge is simple and functional. Locals and tourists gather here for Monday Night Football and happy hour in the Ore House Saloon. An on-site restaurant, the Prospector, complete with a picture window overlooking a creek, serves three square meals a day. Soda Butte Lodge is a hopping place throughout the year. Call for details on snowmobile packages.

Campgrounds & RV Parks

Price Code
$....................Less than $9
$$ ....$9 to $16
$$$ ....$16 to $23
$$$$ .... More than $23

CHIEF JOSEPH CAMPGROUND $
US 212
(406) 848-7375
With access to two outstanding trails, this six-unit campground is a find. The trailheads for Kersey Lake and Clarks Fork Trail begin here and lead you along difficult but rewarding hikes. With just a small number of campsites available, this campground is often occupied by large groups traveling together. It's a favorite spot for family reunions and group vacations because of its proximity to Cooke City (4 miles to the west) and, of course, the Beartooth Highway. But if you're lucky you might be able to get a site in here. The campground is open July through Sept.

COLTER CAMPGROUND $
US 212
(406) 848-7375
Just 1.5 miles east of Cooke City, this campground offers a rare scenic view over 8,000-foot Colter Pass. Burned in the Yellowstone fires of 1988, this campground was cleared and now has a thick growth of new young trees. While those little trees don't do much in the way of providing a barrier between you and other campers, you will find campsites are far apart. From here you have easy access to hiking up Lulu Pass Road (a mile

to the east), which leads to Grasshopper Glacier. Open from mid-July to mid-Sept, Colter Campground is a popular spot for Yellowstone visitors. Campsites fill quickly each morning with campers who were unable to find room at park campgrounds. The grounds include several toilets, drinking water, and trash cans. The RV length limit is 48 feet.

i With an average of 500 inches of snow annually, Cooke City is a winter haven for backcountry skiing and snowboarding. For a small fee Bill Blackford, owner of the Cooke City Bike Shack, offers snowmobile rides to popular Daisy Pass, 7 miles east of town, where you can ski all day. But after the first run, you do have to hike back up— or ski all the way back down to town.

CRAZY CREEK CAMPGROUND $$
US 212
(307) 754-7207
Just inside the Wyoming border, this campsite is a surprise of lush green grass and purple lupines within the Shoshone National Forest. It's about 6 miles off the US 212 junction and worth the short detour from the main route. Tucked into a stand of lodgepole pines, you'll find 19 campsites with water and restrooms available. A short trail begins at the campground and leads to Crazy Creek's small waterfall. RVs are limited to 32 feet. All-terrain vehicles are a popular way to see some of the area's backcountry. Several roads in town lead up to deserted turn-of-the-20th-century mining camps and outstanding mountain views.

HUNTER PEAK CAMPGROUND $
WY 296
(307) 754-7207
WY 296, also known as the Chief Joseph Scenic Byway or the Chief Joseph Highway, offers several camping possibilities, including this small Forest Service campground. It is secluded, well shaded in heavy timber, and an ideal stopover between Cody, Wyoming, and Cooke City, Montana. This quiet resting place lies next to the Clarks Fork River, where the fishing should be fine. Since grizzlies frequent the river, you should be on the watch for bears and store your food appropriately. There are only nine campsites. If you are traveling during peak tourist season, plan to get here early. You'll find full-service amenities here, including water and garbage pickup.

*ISLAND LAKE RECREATION AREA $$
US 212
(307) 754-7207
This might be as close as you can get to camping on top of the world (at least from your car). Sitting at 9,600 feet, Island Lake Recreation Area is in the Clarks Fork District of the Shoshone National Forest. Sites in this beautiful and well-used campground are scattered among big round boulders, behind conifers, below and above the winding road, and back in the trees. Adjacent to the campground you'll find a boat launch leading into the icy waters of Island Lake, a popular float-tubing lake full of pan-size brook trout. Trail #620 will lead you to alpine meadows brimming with wildflowers and numerous lakes in the Absaroka-Beartooth Wilderness. Island Lake has 20 campsites. Depending on snow conditions, this campground is open from June 1 until Sept 15. Prepare to see snow and ice in Sept and possibly during summer months when you're up this high.

SODA BUTTE CAMPGROUND $
US 212
(406) 848-7375

This is the first campground to fill up with overflow campers from Yellowstone National Park's northeast entrance. The campground is a good staging spot for wolf watching in Yellowstone's Lamar Valley, if you can get up that early. Set under the heavy cover of forest, dawn comes late here and night falls quickly. That means it stays cool most of the time and it's hard to roust yourself from that cozy sleeping bag on a cold morning. Don't be surprised to be eating watermelon in the snow on Fourth of July, as snow is not unusual during any month of the year at this campground. You'll find water and trash pickup here. There are 27 campsites. RVs are limited to 48 feet.

RESTAURANTS

Price Code
Prices represent meals for two people, excluding beverages, tip, and tax.

$ . . . . Less than $20
$$ . . . . $20 to $27
$$$ . . . . $27 to $35
$$$$ . . . . More than $35

✳BEARTOOTH CAFE $$
East Main Street
(406) 838-2475
www.beartoothcafe.com

From this cafe's deck, view 9,000-foot snow-capped mountains. You'll feel like you are dining in the Swiss Alps. The menu is sophisticated enough to be in Switzerland, too, with gourmet dishes featuring pastas, meat, and seafood. Winter recreationists pack into this log building after a day of backcountry skiing, snowboarding, or snowmobiling to slurp down a couple of the trendiest micro-brewed beers. During summer months the outdoor seating gives you the best view of Cooke City's main street.

BUNS N BEDS DELI AND CABIN $
201 Main St.
(406) 838-2030

This classic sandwich shop for hearty eaters (though they do have salads if you are so inclined) is located in Cooke City's oldest log structure. The deli offers cold sandwiches in half or whole portions with cowboy-inspired names, such as the Roper with roast beef, jack cheese, and horseradish sauce; or the Bull Rider with ham, turkey, pepperoni, jack and Swiss cheeses, and 9 Fingers mustard sauce. Best of all, try anything from the grill, whether it is the footlong hot dog or the daily barbecue plate.

PROSPECTOR RESTAURANT $–$$
209 US 212
(406) 838-2251
www.cookecity.com

Located inside the Soda Butte Lodge, this is where you can experience "fine sit-down dining." Featuring Montana-style steaks (read: big) and nightly specials that range from chicken to pasta, the Prospector is a local's favorite. Open nightly throughout the year, the restaurant is decorated with mining memorabilia in honor of the town's beginnings as a gold cache site.

SHOPPING

BLAIN GALLERY
211 East Main St.
(406) 838-2474

The Blain features work from local artists: watercolors, oils, pastels, pencil drawings, limited-edition prints, Ilfochrome photographs, baskets, beaded purses, jewelry, and Montana sapphires. The gallery is open daily 9 a.m. to 7 p.m. (closing at 5 p.m. on Sun).

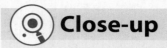 **Close-up**

Beartooth Mountains

Encircling Cooke City, Montana, and tipping the northeastern edge of Yellowstone National Park, the Beartooths are renowned for their pristine moonscape beauty. Some of the world's oldest rocks, dating from 2.5 to 3 billion years ago, were found in the Beartooth mountain range, a discovery that solidified a reverence for this craggy, jagged formation that its admirers have felt for decades.

There are a number of different theories on how these skyscraping peaks formed. However, geologists generally agree that the range emerged when a giant block of Precambrian volcanic rock was uplifted 25,000 feet through the course of 70 million years, then carved by glaciers and streams.

Today, driving along the heralded Beartooth Scenic Highway, you'll witness a series of plateaus averaging about 10,000 feet high, glaciated spires, and layers of sedimentary rock indicative of an ancient sea that once covered the region. The Beartooths make up the highest continuous region in the United States and are home to the highest point in Montana, 12,799-foot Granite Peak. At 10,947 feet, the striking Beartooth Pass is encased in snow for most of the year, but from June through Oct thousands of visitors traverse it by car, bike, and motorcycle.

Although the horn-shaped Pilot and Index Peaks were used as landmarks by early travelers to the Yellowstone region, few people actually penetrated the Beartooths before the 19th century. Even today the 600,000 acres of alpine terrain are home to unexplored lakes, basins, and waterfalls. Even without knowing their geological history, to see the peaks jutting up from the prairie on the eastern side is to see them as magnificent, vast, and ancient.

COOKE CITY BIKE SHACK/GRANITE PEAK ESPRESSO & ICE CREAM

200 US 212

(406) 838-2412

Since 1992 the Bike Shack has been Cooke's source for outdoor gear, bike repair, clothing, maps, and backcountry accessories. The espresso and delectable snacks are just a bonus. They serve Montana-made Wilcoxson's ice cream and Montana Coffee Traders coffees and other goodies, but the White Chocolate Mocha is the signature drinks. Look for daily specials. Open daily 7 a.m. to 6 p.m. Owners Bill and Tami Blackford also operate the Yellowstone Yurt Hostel.

NIGHTLIFE

MINER'S SALOON

208 Main St.

(406) 838-2214

Sooner or later everyone in Cooke City ends up at the Miner's Saloon. In the center of town, it's practically the only place that is open after 10 p.m. It's the gathering place for drinks, billiards, video poker, and friends, and also serves burgers, pizza, and sandwiches. Because the town is so small, it's not unusual to see families hanging out here. You might have to share a pool table with a group of 10-year-old kids, but it's still the happenin' spot in town.

RED LODGE

Nestled at the base of the Beartooth Mountains, Red Lodge's historic main street is what remains of the raucous little settlement that once housed outlaws, miners, Wild West legends, gamblers, and prostitutes in its heyday.

Named for the red dirt painted on tepees, Red Lodge was originally considered Crow Indian country until massive coal deposits were discovered here in 1866. The mines brought hundreds of Finnish, Scottish, Irish, Italian, Slavic, and Scandinavian immigrants and their families, adding to the town's colorful heritage.

Founded in 1888, most of the brick buildings on Broadway—the town's main thoroughfare—proudly speak of a time when this was a thriving community from the influx of coal-mining money. Most of the downtown buildings, which are listed on the National Register of Historic Places, have been nicely restored to showcase their intricate turn-of-the-20th-century architectural details. During the summer months Yellowstone National Park visitors flood the streets of Red Lodge, but during the long winters this is largely a weekend ski playground for residents of Billings and Cody.

Unless otherwise indicated, all listings in this chapter are located in Red Lodge, Montana.

OVERVIEW

You won't find big-box retail outlets or a strip of fast-food chains anywhere in Red Lodge. This little mountain town is as close to undiscovered as the West can be these days. It is easily the most breathtaking gateway to Yellowstone via the 11,000-foot view from the Beartooth Scenic Highway (US 212); the late journalist Charles Kuralt called it America's most beautiful drive. Given its location bordering thousands of miles of spectacular wilderness, proximity to Yellowstone National Park, excellent skiing, and access to a well-serviced airport (an hour away in Billings), it's hard to believe that Red Lodge hasn't blossomed into a chichi resort community akin to Aspen or Vail, Colorado. Despite national magazine articles that dubbed this quiet burg "America's Last Great Place" and "the West's next great boomtown," Red Lodge has stayed small. Although population numbers have jumped a bit countywide with newcomers buying up agricultural acreage for second homes, the town itself has maintained a population of about 2,500 people.

Still, Red Lodge has its legitimate struggles with growth and the ever-expanding shift from a natural resource economy to one based predominantly on tourism. High-paying jobs are scarce here (the median household income is $55,990), which is most likely what keeps the population numbers down. The community is almost evenly divided between families and business owners who work hard to preserve Red Lodge's

Smith Mine Disaster

Just 8 miles east of Red Lodge, you'll see the long-abandoned buildings of Smith Mine right before you drive into the tiny settlement of Belfry. The remarkably preserved skeleton of the mine stands as an eerie memorial to the largest disaster in Montana's mining history. In 1943 the coal mine exploded and killed 74 men. A commemorative plaque marks the site and details the tragic event that brought an end to coal mining in the area.

small-town integrity and the transient recreationist residents who come here to labor through a season of skiing or mountain biking. Teetering on the edge of whether to keep this great spot a secret or to shout the area's attributes from the top of Beartooth Pass, Red Lodge folks are keenly aware of how good life is here.

ACCOMMODATIONS
Hotels, Lodges & Cabins

Price Code

Some rates are based on availability. The following codes represent the average nightly rates for two adults. Accommodations accept all or most major credit cards, unless otherwise noted.

$.................... $50 to $75
$$ .... $75 to $100
$$$ .... $100 to $300
$$$$ .... More than $300

LONE PINE LODGING　　　$$$
715 Holly Valley Lane
(406) 446-1867, (866) 446-1867
www.lonepinelodging.com
Situated on rushing Rock Creek, Lone Pine Lodging is a collection of cabins and suites. The main lodge captures a Ralph Lauren style of luxurious western living. Room sizes vary and can accommodate 4 to 10 people. The complex is popular with wedding parties and family reunions. A short walk from town, this location is the best of both worlds.

LUPINE INN　　　$$$
702 South Hauser St.
(406) 446-1321, (888) 567-1321
www.lupineinn.com
This good-value hotel, formerly a Best Western, is located off the main drag and features large rooms with king and queen beds, wireless Internet, and air-conditioning, while other amenities include a fitness room, pool, spa, and sauna. Rooms are basic and clean, and a free continental breakfast is offered. Pets are allowed, too, and all rooms are nonsmoking.

✳THE POLLARD HOTEL　　　$$$
2 North Broadway
(406) 446-0001
www.pollardhotel.com
From the outside, this three-story brick building on the corner is unassuming. But as you step through the double-glass doors into the lobby of the Pollard Hotel, you experience the elegance of a bygone era. Decked out with classic oak-paneled walls, jewel-colored floral carpets, and plush furniture, the lobby is only the beginning of the tasteful restoration. Built in 1893, this was the first brick building in Red Lodge, at a time when the town was on a steady roll

as a result of mining in the area. The hotel serviced regular folk as well as the famous and infamous. Everyone from salesmen and ranchers to Buffalo Bill Cody, Calamity Jane, Liver Eatin' Johnston, and William Jennings Bryan signed the guest register. The Pollard was known for its gambling, billiards, and fine accommodations and cuisine. In its heyday it was the place to see and be seen in Red Lodge.

Though today's Pollard has been pared down a bit—catering more to skiers and Yellowstone visitors than to the famous—the focus is still on quality and service. There was a major renovation of the entire facility in 1994, restoring the historic integrity and beauty of the place. You'll notice the *Wall Street Journal* and the *New York Times* are available every morning in the History Room, just off the lobby. Each of the 50 hotel rooms is decorated with modern but classic furnishings inspired by Victorian period decor. You can choose from rooms with two queen-size beds and a mountain view or a suite with a Jacuzzi tub and an interior balcony overlooking a sitting area and soothing fireplace. All the rooms are tastefully finished, and the hotel's location makes it possible to walk all over town to restaurants and shops.

You don't even need to leave the premises for food. The hotel has a formal dining room with excellent service and food. Lavish breakfasts, lunches, and dinners are served daily.

✳ROCK CREEK RESORT   **$$$**
US 212
(406) 446-1111, (800) 667-1119
www.rockcreekresort.com
When Olympic skier Pepi Gramshammer (of Colorado's famed Beaver Creek Ghast Haus Gramshammer) bought Rock Creek Resort in the 1970s, it was anything but a resort. First he fixed up the property's existing Grizzly Condos to be used as lodging for students participating in his summer ski clinic on the west side of the Beartooth Pass. Next he put an addition on the historic Old Piney Dell restaurant (it was once a fur trapper's cabin), and things snowballed from there. Today it is an 88-room complex with accommodations ranging from the unbelievably romantic Stoney Honeymoon Cabin (it has a fireplace in the bedroom and a private Jacuzzi next to the creek) to vaulted-ceiling condos and small ski chalet–inspired rooms with decks overlooking the stream. Since there are countless configurations connecting rooms both upstairs and down, the resort has become popular for large family reunions, weddings, and conventions.

The property sits along the banks of Rock Creek and features two restaurants, a massive convention facility, health club, indoor swimming pool, kids' trout fishing pond and playground, a soccer field, tennis courts, and hiking trails. The lobby of the Beartooth Lodge, with its river-rock fireplace, antler chandeliers, and comfortable chairs, invites you to lounge with a good book. The Old Piney Dell, well known for its fine dining and select wine list, serves breakfast and lunch in the Kiva Dining Room. The only things that might lure you away from this all-purpose vacation spot are Red Lodge Mountain's skiing and the shopping in Red Lodge (just 5 miles away). Although with the on-site Twin Elk Fine Collections boutique, you may even forgo that trip to town. En route to the Beartooth Scenic Highway, Rock Creek is popular with Yellowstone visitors and makes a great base for exploring the area.

Take a self-guided walking tour of Red Lodge's historic buildings, most of which are on the National Register of Historic Places. Brochures for the tour are available at the Red Lodge Area Chamber of Commerce and Carbon County Historical Museum.

THE YODELER MOTEL $$
601 South Broadway
(406) 446-1435, (886) 446-1435
www.yodelermotel.com

This funky chalet-inspired motel reflects some of Red Lodge's early influences from German, Swiss, and Austrian immigrants who came to the area to work in nearby coal mines. Sitting at the south edge of Red Lodge's main street, the no-frills motel offers you an easy walk to downtown restaurants and shops. Across the street is a picnic area along the banks of Rock Creek, and skiing at Red Lodge Mountain is only a short drive away. The Yodeler prides itself on the very clean rooms and sincere hospitality. They also advertise in-room dataport phones for business travelers and high-quality mattresses for guaranteed comfort. Ground-floor rooms are spacious with front and back doors. The main-level rooms are half-basement units with large daylight windows.

Bed-and-Breakfasts

Price Code
$................. Less than $85
$$ .... $85 to $115
$$$ .... $115 to $150
$$$$ .... More than $150

BLUE SKY CABINS $$$$
32 Blue Sky Lane
(406) 446-0186
www.blueskycabins.com

These four luxurious cabins cater to the romantic traveler or to families with kids over age 16. Located 19 miles from Red Lodge and closer to the town of Roscoe, this is a place to put all your cares aside. Situated in the pretty fields in the shadow of the mighty Beartooth Range, this B&B is as quiet as it gets without a hike into the backcountry. Blue Sky requires a two-night minimum stay. Each cabin includes the ingredients for a hearty breakfast—fresh eggs, juices, gourmet coffees and teas, pancake mixes, cereals, and oatmeal. For other meals you'll have to bring your own food, drive into Red Lodge, or drive 6 miles into Roscoe to the famous Grizzly Bar and Steakhouse.

WILLOWS INN $
224 South Platt Ave.
(406) 446-3913
www.bbhost.com/willowsinn

Owned by Kerry and Carolyn Boggio, this is a classic Victorian cottage restored to all its painted lady glory. The ca. 1909 house has five guest rooms with private baths and a white picket fence out front. A delicious home-baked breakfast is served each morning between 8 and 10 in the quaint dining room. Behind the inn, a charming two-story cottage has two bedrooms, a fully equipped kitchen, adjacent laundry room, color TV, gas fireplace stove, and authentic country antiques. The natural fir floors and country style make it easy to relax here with a good book.

Campgrounds & RV Parks

Price Code
$.................Less than $9
$$ ....$9 to $16
$$$ .... $16 to $23
$$$$ .... More than $23

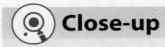 **Close-up**

Kevin Red Star

In the art world the mention of Red Lodge, Montana, is synonymous with premier American Indian artist **Kevin Red Star.** Through his dynamic, soulful depictions of the proud and powerful Crow Indians, it's as if he is asserting the original Crow Indian ties to the land surrounding Red Lodge. He has gained praise and acclaim all over the world as an artist preserving a rare culture. On exhibit at galleries across the West, his work demands respect and admiration.

Museums holding Kevin Red Star originals in their permanent collections include the Smithsonian Institution; Institute of American Indian Art in Santa Fe; Denver Art Museum; the Heard Museum in Phoenix; the Pierre Cardin Collection in Paris; the Eiteljorg Museum of American Indian and Western Art in Indianapolis; the Whitney Museum of Western Art in Cody; and museums in Belgium, China, Germany, and Japan.

Born in Lodge Grass, Montana, on the Crow Indian Reservation, Red Star now lives just outside Red Lodge in the small town of Roberts. The artist calls himself a "romantic" because his bold portraits of Crow warriors and dancers, mystical animals, tepees, and proud women are realistic but also exaggerated. Brilliant colors jump from his oil canvases and speak of bravery, sadness, war, joy, and wisdom. Red Star uses his heritage for inspiration as he records the Crow Nation's culture.

While Red Lodge, Montana, seems an unlikely place to find such an acclaimed painter, Red Star is responsible for inspiring an unprecedented art movement in the community. He returned to his home state after spending years in the competitive art scenes of Santa Fe and San Francisco. Back in Montana, he found the place that feeds his creativity.

Though Red Star does not consider himself a political artist, his work does make a statement that commands you to realize he is recording a vanishing culture. His paintings preserve the powwows, the magnificent dress and physical features of his ethnicity, and a people who impacted western history. Check his website at www.kevinredstar.com.

BASIN CAMPGROUND $
US 212
(406) 446-2103, (800) 280-CAMP
Drive 1 mile south of Red Lodge and you'll see a brown forest service sign marking a campground. From there head west for 7 miles on Forest Road 71 to Basin Campground. This pretty campground has 28 tent and camper sites, picnic tables, public toilets, and fire pits. A hand pump provides water, and there is a Dumpster for trash. Remember that this area is bear country, so store food

properly. Campsites are tucked into a heavily forested area, but if you take the nearby Basin trailhead you can hike to incredible views of the Beartooth Mountains. This can be reserved through the National Recreation Reservation Service at www.recreation.gov.

M-K CAMPGROUND FREE
US 212
(406) 446-2103
About 7 miles south of Red Lodge you'll find one of the few free camping facilities in

the region, the M-K Campground. A brown Forest Service sign marks the turnoff for this campsite. Originally a field camp during the construction of the Beartooth Highway in the 1930s, this secluded spot offers incredible views of the mountains above and the Rock Creek Valley below. Although both picnic and camping sites are available here, the area is considered a "reduced-services" site—meaning that you will need to pack out your trash and provide your own water. Though the amenities are spare, the M-K is a wonderful spot to experience the feeling of camping in the backcountry while only paces from the convenience of your vehicle. Campsites are first come, first served.

PARKSIDE CAMPGROUND $
Rock Creek Road #421
(406) 446-2103
On the west side of US 212, about 12 miles south of Red Lodge, Parkside Campground is the largest of three Forest Service campgrounds clustered within a mile of one another. All part of the Red Lodge Ranger District of Custer National Forest, sites here are easily accessible for travel on the journey along the Beartooth Highway. (The elevation is 7,200 feet.) At Parkside you'll find conifers, grass, wildflowers, and cool mornings along the banks of Rock Creek. The access roads are paved, and sites have back-in spurs. The RV limit is 40 feet. Of the 26 sites, 15 can be reserved through the National Recreation Reservation Service: www.recreation.gov.

PERRY'S RV PARK AND
CAMPGROUNDS $$
7262 US 212
(406) 446-2722
www.perrysrv.us

The only sounds you'll hear at Perry's are the creek, the shivering of aspen leaves, and the muffled voices of content campers. This location 2 miles south of Red Lodge is cozy, comfortable, and packed with amenities. Situated along the banks of little, roaring Rock Creek, you'll find plenty of aspens and cottonwood trees for shade at your campsite. You'll also find showers, electrical and water hookups, laundry facilities, a convenience store, and a dump station at Perry's. Guests can take advantage of the picnic area's barbecue grills. Perry's has 20 RV units and space for 10 tent camps.

RED LODGE KOA $$$$
7464 US 212
(406) 446-2364, (800) 562-7540
An oasis of a campground, the Red Lodge KOA is just 4 miles north of Red Lodge heading toward Beartooth Pass. Many treed sites on Rock Creek make for pleasant camping in either a tent or RV. Featuring a heated pool, gift shop, bike rental shop, snack bar, miniature golf course, game room, and Internet access, this is a deluxe campground. Add to that a laundry facility, hot showers for tenters, and long pull-throughs for RVs, as well as pet walking areas, and this will seem like a home away from home. The campground is open from mid-May to late Sept.

RESTAURANTS

Price Code
Prices represent meals for two people, excluding beverages, tip, and tax.
$.................. Less than $20
$$ .... $20 to $27
$$$ .... $27 to $35
$$$$ .... More than $35

BEAR CREEK SALOON AND
STEAKHOUSE $
Highway 308, Bear Creek
(406) 446-3481
www.redlodge.com/bearcreek
Also known as Bear Creek Downs, this could very well be the only place in the world where you can have dinner while watching the pig races. Round and round the track the little piglets go, cheered on by spectators grazing on thick steaks and hefty burgers. (Thankfully, there are no pork items on the menu.) While you wait for your dinner to be served, you can place a bet on the pig of your choice—part of the winnings go to a local education fund. Just a short drive 6 miles east of Red Lodge, this tiny saloon in the middle of nowhere once serviced the coal miners from the nearby Smith Mine. Well-worn, wide-plank pine floors and walls give the Bear Creek an Old West atmosphere. Old black-and-white photos and countless magazine clippings about the famous swine hang on the walls. During summer months the races are held outside on a larger track. This spot is open Fri, Sat, and Sun from Memorial Day to Labor Day and Christmas to Easter.

i   Take a tour of historic Red Lodge from an old-fashioned seat. During summer months a horse-drawn wagon picks up guests at local hotels every evening from 7 to 9 for a free 30-minute ride through town.

BOGART'S $$
11 South Broadway
(406) 446-1784
Established in 1975, Bogart's claim to fame is the margaritas. In fact, the margaritas are so popular that when the doors open at 11:30 a.m., Bogart's staff is ready with a 15-gallon batch of margarita mix. Owners Tom Leatherberry and Judy and Jody Christensen won't tell you what the secret ingredient is, but after years of taste tests they know what they've made is the good stuff. The menu at Bogart's is a mishmash of Mexican and Italian dishes, hand-tossed pizzas, and sandwiches. We recommend sticking to the south-of-the-border theme and going with anything Mexican at Bogart's—if you're not counting calories, definitely try the sour cream enchiladas. There is a comfortable, fun atmosphere here, complete with Humphrey Bogart posters and lots of plants. Bogart's is popular with the after-work crowd, who order pitchers of the oh-so-drinkable margaritas.

*BRIDGE CREEK BACKCOUNTRY
KITCHEN AND WINE BAR $$$
116 South Broadway
(406) 446-9900
www.eatfooddrinkwine.com
Owners Anne and Peter Christ knew just what the Red Lodge restaurant scene was lacking when he opened the Bridge Creek Backcountry Kitchen in 2000. The restaurant is casual and elegant at the same time, with an inviting atmosphere. As you enter, a small bar beckons you to sit down for a pre-dinner glass of wine. You can keep yourself busy looking at regional topographic maps of the nearby wilderness (remember the word "backcountry" in the restaurant's name). Since the Christs are respected wine enthusiasts, the restaurant's extensive list includes rare finds from his "private collection." A wine storage area divides the wine bar from the formal dining area in the center of the restaurant.

Bridge Creek puts a casual spin on upscale gourmet cuisine and features steak, seafood, and pasta entrees. After an exhausting day of skiing, you might want to sit in front of the fireplace with a Montana microbrew and indulge with something from the large appetizer list—we recommend the spicy beef quesadilla. The menu changes seasonally and utilizes fresh local ingredients as much as possible. Look for the organic beef provided by a local distributor, the Lazy E-L Ranch. But save room for dessert—they serve a crème brûlée of the day, a decadently smooth custard that may be infused with the tasty flavors of rosemary, coffee, or huckleberries. Don't worry if this doesn't interest the kids—the kids' menu features a variety of options. During summer months enjoy the outdoor dining on the sidewalk.

CARBON COUNTY STEAK HOUSE $$
121 South Broadway
(406) 446-4025
www.carboncountysteakhouse.com
Locals vote this restaurant the best place to eat for the certified Angus beef served here. Bring a hearty Montana-style appetite for the lean sirloin or the perfectly roasted prime rib. The menu also offers a wide selection of seafood, from mussels to Alaskan salmon and king crab legs. Known for excellent food as well as service, the Carbon County Steak House is a must-dine kind of place. Call for hours of operation.

COFFEE FACTORY ROASTERS $
6½ South Broadway
(406) 446-3200
www.coffeefactoryroasters.com
With a light, airy atmosphere and a big window looking out on Red Lodge's main street, the Coffee Factory is an easy spot to while away the morning watching the town come to life. A wall-size chalkboard lists the selection of pastries, bagels, juices, smoothies, and sandwiches. Large jute bags of coffee beans are piled against the far wall, and the actual roasting is done in-house—take home some of the Beartooth Blend. Kids are welcome at this cafe, as clearly evidenced by the overflowing basket of toys and small shelf of children's books. If you need more reasons to stay, there is a computer with Internet access for checking e-mail or surfing the web, if you really must on your vacation.

THE DINING ROOM AT
THE POLLARD $$$$
2 North Broadway
(406) 446-0001
www.pollardhotel.com
This Victorian-style dining room feels much the way it did a century ago, when the likes of Buffalo Bill Cody and William Jennings Bryan dined here. The atmosphere is sheer old-fashioned luxury, with crisp white linen and fresh flower arrangements on the tables. Plush drapes filter light through ceiling-high windows that look out to Red Lodge's historic district. Along with ambience and an impressive seasonal menu, the staff here offers exquisite service with knowledgeable suggestions about the restaurant's award-winning wine list. The restaurant was opened in the historic Pollard Hotel after it was rigorously restored to its former glory. Ever-changing gourmet cuisine helped put the place back on the map as a Red Lodge landmark. You'll find a European influence added to wild-game items. Signature dishes include huckleberry duck breasts and elk medallions with a port wine butter sauce. Reservations are recommended here, summer or winter. Breakfast, lunch, and dinner

are served daily. Don't pass up the outstanding Sunday brunch.

THE RED BOX CAR $
1300 South Broadway
(406) 446-2152
On your way out of town and up the Beartooth Highway, don't miss your chance to get the best malt or milk shake in Carbon County. The Red Box Car is an authentic hundred-year-old boxcar, renovated as Red Lodge's oldest fast-food restaurant. Since 1972 people have enjoyed the tasty grilled burgers, onion rings, or the signature Indian taco. But it's the ice-cream treats that make it most worth stopping. Situated along Rock Creek, it's a unique restaurant in a fun location. The Box Car is open during summers only.

RED LODGE ALES BREWING CO. $
417 North Broadway
(406) 446-4607
www.redlodgeales.com
Master brewer Sam Hoffmann prides himself of making beer from the pure water of the Beartooth Mountains. Sample his fine local microbrews here in the new taproom just north of town, which also features great bar food and a very cool outdoor beer garden. Also look for his brews on tap and in the bottle around Red Lodge, in Yellowstone National Park, and throughout the Yellowstone region. Sam's taproom and eatery is open 11 a.m. to 10 p.m. in the summer, with variable hours in winter.

RED LODGE PIZZA COMPANY $
222 Broadway
(406) 446-3333
Although this downtown establishment offers everything from burgers and steaks to salads and calzones, it's the pizza that keeps folks coming back. The hand-tossed crust is baked in stone-lined ovens, and you can add just about any topping you can think of. For pizza flavor in something a little different, try a "Montana Roll," where pizza crust is baked with cheese and rolled up with selected ingredients. There is also a large beer selection, small game room, and a large back area for groups and parties.

SHOPPING

In the past decade there has been a visible shift from a downtown that catered to locals to one that has focused on snagging tourist dollars. The grocery, hardware, and lumber stores all moved off Broadway to be replaced by high-end shops peddling espresso drinks, expensive knickknacks, and western art. Everything from Harley-Davidson motorcycles to handmade quilts can be found in the local shops. With everything clustered downtown, it's easy walking to the little shops bustling with people during summer and winter.

KIBLER AND KIRCH
101 North Broadway
(406) 446-2226
www.kiblerandkirch.com
Part old-world European aesthetic and New West panache, this home and design store will keep you daydreaming long after you've walked out the door. Featuring high-end furnishings and household accents, it's an anchor store in downtown Red Lodge.

MAGPIE TOYMAKERS
115 North Broadway
(406) 446-3044
You won't find the latest selection of PlayStation games or anything battery operated

here. Magpie Toymakers is an old-fashioned shop that carries toys powered by your imagination—Lincoln Logs, boomerangs, hula hoops, dominoes, jack-in-the-boxes, and children's books. You'll find Betty Boop dolls and Curious George lunch boxes tucked alongside collectible hand-carved wooden toys and yo-yos. Owner Wayne McClane, a toy aficionado, can tell you who invented the Slinky and which wooden tray puzzle is developmentally appropriate for a toddler. He is the resident toymaker, crafting one-of-a-kind works from wood that are more for whimsical adults than for playful children. (Some cost several thousand dollars.) Whatever your fancy, this is the place where you'll encounter some favorite old toy that brings back memories of childhood.

MONTANA CANDY EMPORIUM
7 South Broadway
(406) 446-1119
Even if you don't have a sweet tooth, the volume of confections in Montana's oldest and biggest candy store will dazzle you. At the Montana Candy Emporium, in addition to 22 kinds of fudge made while you watch, they carry 2,300 kinds of candy. Bushel baskets line the walls of this turn-of-the-20th-century shop, each one filled with mouthwatering caramels, taffy, mints, chocolates, and every kind of hard candy imaginable, from basic to extravagant. One of the biggest sellers is the huckleberry bark, but the fudge is a close second. This main-street shop is a picture right out of Willie Wonka's Chocolate Factory, only better because it's real.

TWIN ELK AT ROCK CREEK RESORT
US 212
(406) 446-3121, (877) TWINELK

Cutting-edge fashion for women, high-end skiwear, and winter apparel are signatures of Twin Elk. Gifts and jewelry are easy to find in this abundant store located on the premises of Rock Creek Resort. You will also find unusual home furnishings influenced by rustic designs of the West. It's worth the 5-mile drive south of town to browse or buy here. Call for hours of operation.

WHISPERING PINES
12 South Broadway
(406) 446-1470
With two floors of wonderfully tactile housewares, antiques, garden accessories, linens, and Montana-made products, it's impossible to leave this store without purchasing something. The list of inventory may sound like a jumble, but Whispering Pines is a store with beautiful design and tempting items for the home. It is open seven days a week from 10 a.m. to 6 p.m.

NIGHTLIFE

THE ROMAN THEATER
110 South Broadway
(406) 446-1942
Films at this historic movie house seem better somehow. It could be because there is more legroom between aisles than at most modern multiplex theaters or that the once-exclusive recital hall still holds a certain elegance. It could be that in addition to the regular buttery popcorn, you can buy freshly made caramel corn. It could definitely be that you can sit and watch the movie on a sofa (one of four, in fact), slouch down, put your feet up on the coffee table, slurp your drink, and enjoy the big screen. It's better than renting a video at home. The Roman has a niche as a funky hometown theater where you can get comfortable. They don't

charge an arm and a leg for refreshments either.

THE ROUND BARN
US 212
(406) 446-1197
You'd never know this homey, old, round brick building was once a dairy barn built in 1941 by the Kent family. Current owner Marcee Farrar has fixed it up as a restaurant and dinner theater. Dinner is served buffet-style with four entrees (a range of meats and fish), homemade mashed potatoes, a fresh vegetable such as steamed snow peas, and dessert. A 15-foot salad bar features fresh salads, homemade soups, and bread just out of the oven. You don't have to eat to get into the theater upstairs in the hayloft, but we recommend it. From June through Sept, Farrar books professional actors, singers, musicians, and comedians to perform in her "theater in the round." The schedule changes depending on the season, so call ahead. The Round Barn is closed in Jan and Feb.

i If you want to do some backcountry camping with a lighter load, try renting a llama to carry your backpack and gear. The animals are easy to handle and make great company. Call High Prairie Llamas at (406) 445-2057.

SILVER STRIKE
609 North Broadway
(406) 446-3131
With advertising that touts "Tons of TV," the Silver Strike is primarily a bowling alley. But you can also enjoy the sports bar, a game of billiards, and a video poker casino. Local bowling leagues are competitive and meet here every Tues and Thur. You might have to sign up on a waiting list to get a slot on a team. (Obviously, the winters are long in Red Lodge.)

✳SNOW CREEK SALOON
124 Broadway
(406) 446-1100
www.snowcreeksaloon.com
There is nothing historic or nostalgic about the Snow Creek Saloon, but you can catch live music here every weekend. It is the place to be when you say you're going to have a night out on the town in Red Lodge. Eventually everyone ends up here before 2 a.m. on a weekend night. The bar welcomes you with a party atmosphere—neon beer signs, shot glasses, and patron names carved into wooden tables. It's dark and a little seedy. The band plays in the back of the house just a little above a dirty, well-scuffed dance floor. Usually you can count on good old rock and roll, sometimes a little country, maybe some rhythm and blues. The Snow Creek is everything a small-town watering hole should be.

CODY

William Frederick "Buffalo Bill" Cody left an indelible mark on western history, and nowhere is it more alive than in his namesake town of Cody. In this historic western community, Buffalo Bill is the beginning, middle, and end. He played every role from visionary, fund-raiser, negotiator, and marketer to celebrity in order to put "Cody City" on the map in 1896.

In his day, while traveling with his Wild West Show, Buffalo Bill was an authentic western hero. He was famous as a Pony Express rider, a scout, a hunter, and an entrepreneur, and he was a showman who became a friend to presidents and kings, senators and governors, and many of the country's most influential businessmen. With his connections he was included in economic developments that would later shape the West. It was no mistake that the Burlington Northern Railroad led to Cody in 1901 or that Yellowstone National Park's east entrance was opened around that time as well. When the world's first national park was founded in 1872, Buffalo Bill smelled the potential fortune in an area he came to know during his youth. As a result he built his own lodge, Pahaska Tepee, just yards from Yellowstone's eastern boundary—a place that still bustles with tourist traffic both summer and winter. In anticipation of the visitors who would come on the railroad, W. F. Cody built the now-historic Irma Hotel, with a restaurant and saloon to cater to all his guests' needs.

Unless otherwise indicated, all listings in this chapter are located in Cody, Wyoming.

OVERVIEW

Buffalo Bill had an image, and he was never too shy to use it to further himself. He made investments throughout the West, but none were quite as successful as the town of Cody. His influence often overshadows the sweat equity that fellow Cody citizens put into making the town a success. There were others, of course, who built the lively town, which was once uncharted territory—the streets of downtown Cody bear their names and echo through the city's foundation. But it was Buffalo Bill who truly saw the potential and shaped this corner of the western frontier into a thriving place to live and work.

Today's Cody still upholds and reaps the benefits of Buffalo Bill's legacy, using his name, his image, and his business savvy to market itself to tourists. Located only 50 miles from Yellowstone, the town has much to sell, with its rivers, mountains, wildlands, and history. One million visitors annually flood the streets and mountains and establishments of this town that has a regular population of around 8,000 residents. Folks here put on nightly rodeos and shoot-outs for entertainment, and the community proudly builds upon the unprecedented collection of art and artifacts at the Buffalo Bill Historical

CODY

Center. In summer Cody is alive with festivals, gatherings, and attractions that fill up the nights and days. Winter is much sleepier here, although there is no shortage of recreationists who come to enjoy Yellowstone and the Shoshone National Forest trails. But in town it's more a time to rest and regroup for the next season of tourists.

i In and around the city of Cody you'll find a series of trails for walking, in-line skating, or jogging. Some of the paths are wheelchair accessible, and most are geared toward recreationists of any ability.

If Cody lacks in any way, it is because it has perhaps sold itself too much and catered too often to the needs of visitors rather than its bona fide citizens. Some of that is changing, however, as more voices in the community speak this sentiment. In 2000 the **Victor J. Riley Arena and Community Events Center** was constructed to serve as a community gathering place for both locals and visitors. Doubling as an ice-skating arena, the 25,000-foot facility is available for conventions and events from Apr through mid-Oct after the ice-skating and hockey seasons finish. For more information contact P.O. Box 1902, Cody, WY 82414; (307) 587-1681.

As a retail, medical, and entertainment hub for the entire Bighorn Basin, Cody has witnessed drastic changes to the face of its historic town, with major retail chains popping up on the west end. Commonly referred to as the West Strip, this part of Cody was never zoned with historical integrity in mind. Several major national hotel chains and various gas stations dominate the landscape here on the highway that leads to

Yellowstone's east entrance. Although the Cody Nite Rodeo grounds and Old Trail Town are located at this end of town, there have been community disputes about whether the type of growth seen on the west side is a positive addition. Regardless, major national businesses have boosted the local economy by attracting many outlying residents for shopping, though partially at the expense of the mom-and-pop stores that were once the backbone of the town.

It is the classic struggle that faces many American communities. Cody struggles with finding a way to grow a healthy, diverse economy, but so far it's doing pretty well. With the oil and gas industry continuing to be Wyoming's greatest industry, Cody is not entirely reliant on tourism dollars. The town has been an area of strong traditional values, never a place for rabble-rousing or dissent. A community approach that says a handshake is still enough to seal a deal and that most people are just plain honest folk is what largely governs the mentality of the body politic here. In turn, Cody is a nice place to raise a family, a fine location in which to retire, and a great spot to plant your roots.

ACCOMMODATIONS
Hotels, Lodges & Cabins

Price Code

Some rates are based on availability. The following codes represent the average nightly rates for two adults. Accommodations accept all or most major credit cards, unless otherwise noted.

$ .... Less than $100
$$ .... $100 to $200
$$$ .... $200 to $300
$$$$ .... More than $300

AMERICINN LODGE & SUITES $$

508 Yellowstone Ave.
(307) 587-7716, (800) 396-5007
www.americinn.com

Located a short distance from the center of town, but worth the trip, this modern log-and-stone lodge is just west of the Buffalo Bill Historical Center and about a 15-minute stroll to the Cody Nite Rodeo grounds. The warm, welcoming lobby with its large river-rock fireplace and cozy, oversize furniture is the hotel's best attribute. A practical breakfast area is tucked into a corner near the staircase for the morning's continental breakfast. All 65 rooms—decorated in a subtle western motif—feature lodgepole pine beds and all the modern amenities. An indoor pool, Jacuzzi, and sauna are pleasant extras. Additionally, the staff members go out of their way to offer directions and extra hospitality.

BUFFALO BILL VILLAGE $$

1701 Sheridan Ave.
(307) 587-5544, (800) 527-5544
www.blairhotels.com

Built in 1914 as housing for crews that were building the town of Cody, Buffalo Bill Village has a classic western flair. The historic wooden exterior has been maintained, while the interior has been modernized. The Village consists of 83 individual cabins, varying from single units with king-size beds to family suites featuring two bedrooms, all with private baths. Within walking distance to downtown, you can take advantage of all Cody has to offer. The Holiday Inn and Comfort Inn in Cody are also part of the same company. Buffalo Bill Village is closed Jan through Apr.

✳CHAMBERLIN INN $$–$$$

1032 Twelfth St.
(307) 587-0202, (888) 587-0202
www.chamberlininn.com

This 22-room boutique hotel is just footsteps from downtown Cody's shops and restaurants, and is the town's finest overnight stay. The concept of this quiet, genteel location is a pleasant departure from the corporate hotel chains that dominate town. A newly restored 1903 building that combines historic boardinghouse, office building, and the original county courthouse still has stylish old-fashioned touches without sacrificing luxury. The walled garden behind the inn is ideal for small weddings or family reunions. At the Chamberlin Inn, expect exceptional service and personal attention that will keep you thinking about Cody, Wyoming, long after you've gone home.

CODY COWBOY VILLAGE $$$

203 West Yellowstone Hwy.
(307) 587-7555
www.codycowboyvillage.com

Though it is located in the ever-expanding West End strip, this new complex of cabins and suites is memorable for one very important reason: the beds. Really, they are fantastically comfortable, featuring high-end linens for the best night's sleep at incredibly reasonable rates. Open May through Oct, the log cabins are clean, simple, tastefully accented with cowboy decor, and equipped with flat-screen TVs. A generous continental breakfast is included in the stay, and the heated outdoor pool and hot tub are nice additional amenities. Don't be put off by the address; it is just at the edge of town and still accessible to all local attractions.

Connecting Cody's Past and Present with Old-time Trolley Tours

The one-hour, 22-mile trolley tour presents local history, area attractions, geology, wildlife, and outstanding scenery while telling the compelling story of Buffalo Bill Cody. Tickets cost $24 for adults, $22 for seniors, and $12 for kids 6 to 17, and are available at the Irma Hotel. The tours run from June through Sept; call (307) 527-7043 for reservations or go to www.codytrolleytours.com.

CODY LODGING COMPANY $$-$$$$
1302 Beck Ave., Suite B
(307) 587-6000, (800) 587-6560
www.codylodgingcompany.com
If you want to test-drive how it feels to live in a Cody neighborhood, stay at one of the Cody Lodging Company's guest houses. You can rent just one room or a whole house in one of the cottages, duplex suites, and homes in Cody's historic residential neighborhood or mountain lodges. Rates for Cody Lodging Company properties are competitive with hotels and range from $150 nightly for two people or $150 to $450 for four to six guests. Destination wedding, conference, and family-reunion facilities are available.

ELEPHANT HEAD LODGE $$
1170 Yellowstone Hwy., Wapiti
(307) 587-3980
www.elephantheadlodge.com
These cabins are so comfy that you may not want to venture the whole 11 miles down the road to Yellowstone National Park. Cozy,

kitschy, and cool in a quaint way, all 12 historic cabins are modern but true to that Old West charm. While each cabin is decorated differently, they all come with a heavy, old-fashioned quilt and the luxury of pastoral peace. Most of the cabins are smaller, but one sleeps nine and a few have kitchenettes. The lodge, restaurant, and "Honeymoon" cabin were built in 1910 by Buffalo Bill Cody's niece, Josephine Thurston, and her husband.

While most guests use Elephant Head Lodge as a base for exploring Yellowstone and Cody, technically you don't ever have to venture beyond the lodge's property. Everything you need is right here, from horseback riding, hiking, rock climbing, and biking to children's activities. In the evenings you can even catch a movie in the old lodge living room or enjoy a family card game in the lounge. Hearty breakfasts, lunches, and dinners are served family-style every day. You won't be able to resist the aroma of fresh-baked bread and homemade pies wafting over from the main lodge, only 100 yards or so from your cabin. You can savor the tastes of grilled steaks and potato salad at one of five tables covered with red gingham tablecloths.

While overnight guests are welcome, most folks stay from three to five days to relax and enjoy the area. A European plan, in which guests pay a flat rate for their cabin and extra for meals and activities, is the best alternative unless you plan to do quite a bit of riding. The American plan includes lodging, three meals a day, and up to four hours of riding daily.

THE IRMA HOTEL $$
1192 Sheridan Ave.
(307) 587-4221, (800) 745-4762
www.irmahotel.com

When Buffalo Bill Cody was certain the railroad was coming to town, he built a luxury hotel to receive the wealthy visitors who would travel so far to see Yellowstone National Park. The Irma Hotel, named for his youngest daughter, went up in 1902 and became what some referred to as the last outpost of civilization. With its steam heat, gas lighting, and telephones in every room, the Irma was mighty fancy. Catering to a guest's every need, the hotel had an elegant bar, billiards, a telegraph office, a barber shop, and baths. In the dining room, weary eastern travelers enjoyed fresh produce and meat from the hotel's farm. A livery stable chartered every kind of rig and horse possible for forays into Yellowstone Park.

Today's Irma is still a landmark but not so much a luxury hotel. On the National Register of Historic Places, it commands attention and still stands as a cornerstone gathering place in the community. After so many years and so many visitors, the Irma is a little worse for wear, but a stay here is worth the experience. As you enter the hotel, a dozen mounted deer, elk, and bighorn sheep—reminders of Buffalo Bill, the great hunter—stand watch in the main hallway. A wide staircase leads upstairs, where most of the rooms are located. Accommodations range from simple to elegant, with a number of different sleeping combinations. All rooms have private baths and telephones. Specify whether you'd prefer the historic or motel section of the hotel.

PAHASKA TEPEE RESORT $-$$$$
183 Yellowstone Hwy.
(307) 527-7701, (800) 628-7791
www.pahaska.com
Buffalo Bill Cody built his hunting lodge on this spot at the turn of the 20th century, when big-game hunting was allowed in Yellowstone National Park. When automobiles became the popular mode of travel into the park during the mid-1920s, Pahaska became a hub with its enticing Tepee Tavern for cocktails and the Lodgepole restaurant for hearty western fare. Today, situated on the edge of Yellowstone's eastern entrance on US 14/16/20, Pahaska Tepee remains a bustling center for tourists looking to refuel, buy souvenirs, or grab a bite before continuing their drive.

There is, of course, Buffalo Bill's historic lodge, which has scarcely changed since 1904. The stone fireplace spans up to high vaulted ceilings and draws guests to circle around on cool evenings. There is also endless opportunity for horseback riding and the appeal of that Old West atmosphere. But what Pahaska is best known for is its cross-country skiing. Winter recreationists have access to 110 miles of groomed roads in the park, which run all the way to West Yellowstone, Montana. Large groups can stay in one of 48 older A-frame houses. This is the perfect spot for a family vacation or large family reunion. Additional fees are required for all activities. At this time, Pahaska is closed in the winter and has no restaurant, bar, or ski rentals available. A few cabins can still be rented during the winter, however.

Bed-and-Breakfasts

Price Code
$ . . . . $85 to $115
$$ . . . . $115 to $150

ANGEL'S KEEP $
1241 Wyoming St.
(307) 587-6205, (877) 320-2800
www.angelskeep.com

CODY

Owners Robert and Barbara Kelly purchased this former church in 2001 and have been hosting guests in its hallowed chambers ever since. There are three rooms, each decorated in a different style, and all rooms include air-conditioning, cable TV, and VCR. In addition to the scrumptious breakfast, complimentary beverages and snacks are always available, and homemade cookies are baked fresh every day. The on-site gift shop features Barbara's one-of-a-kind treasures created from an eclectic mix of antiques, vintage and collectible linens, and other recycled items.

MAYOR'S INN BED AND BREAKFAST $$
1413 Rumsey Ave.
(307) 587-0887, (888) 217-3001
www.mayorsinn.com

This large, turn-of-the-20th-century home built in 1905 by Frank L. Houx, the town's first elected mayor, offers five different rooms. Located in the heart of Cody's historic residential area, the Mayor's Inn is just removed enough from the bustle of town to be relaxing yet convenient. All the neatly decorated rooms have private baths. A lavish breakfast and lunch are available upon request in the dining room. Management can also help arrange activities in the area. All the rooms are nonsmoking, and children are welcome.

i If you've got a hankerin' to taste-test buffalo, the Wyoming Buffalo Company in downtown Cody will tempt you with a morsel of bison jerky. After that you might move on to another one of their numerous buffalo-meat concoctions.

Campgrounds & RV Parks

Price Code
$..................Less than $9
$$ ....$9 to $16
$$$ .... $16 to $23
$$$$ .... More than $23

ABSAROKA BAY RV PARK $$$$
US 14/16/20
(307) 527-7440, (800) 557-7440
www.cody-wy.com

Located neatly on the outskirts of Cody and near Beck Lake Park, the main problem with Absaroka Bay is that the resident ducks may be loud and the deer come to visit in the morning. Otherwise this clean and well-organized RV park offers all the amenities of home. Choose from 99 sites, and tents are welcome, too. Special amenities to note are the tidy paved roads, laundry, and sites for rigs up to 65 feet long. You are minutes away from the Buffalo Bill Historical Center, downtown Cody, and the rodeo grounds. Special weekly and monthly rates are available; the park is open year-round.

CODY KOA $$$
5561 Greybull Hwy.
(307) 587-2369

Staying at the Cody KOA feels more like staying at a dude ranch than a campground. The daily pancake breakfasts and nightly chuck wagon dinners make up for this campground's distance from town. Take the free shuttle to the Cody Nite Rodeo, and the campground is a pickup point for Powder River Tours. With 200 RV hookups and 100 tent sites, this KOA begins to feel like a village during peak season. Enjoy the swimming pool, playground, hot tub, laundry, and showers. The campground is open May through Sept.

GATEWAY CAMPGROUND $$
203 Yellowstone Ave.
(307) 587-2561
Staying at the Gateway Campground puts you in the perfect position to enjoy three of Cody's best things. You're just an easy stroll away from the Cody Nite Rodeo and old Trail Town (see the Attractions chapter) and across the street from Cassie's Supper Club. This campground, a mile west of downtown, is surrounded by a broad sweeping lawn and mature trees, making it feel like a little spot in the country. Next to the campground, owner Lura Showman's father offers horseback riding along the river. The quiet lawn behind the motel accommodates 30 tent spots, along with 41 RV sites. You'll find a laundry, clean restrooms with showers, a pay phone, and free coffee in the mornings. The Gateway is open from May through Sept.

NEWTON CREEK CAMPGROUND $
US 14/16/20
(307) 527-6241
This USDA Forest Service campground along the North Fork of the Shoshone River comes complete with bear boxes—containers provided on-site to make it simple for you to lock up your food. The Shoshone National Forest is in the thick of bear country, and the Wapiti Ranger District works hard to avoid bear-human confrontations. This campground closes each spring when the bears come out of hibernation and wander the riverbanks in search of food. The 31 campsites offer running water and a pleasant place to picnic about 31 miles west of Cody.

PONDEROSA CAMPGROUND $$$
1815 Eighth St.
(307) 587-9203
www.codyponderosa.com
At this massive in-town facility there truly is something for everyone. Try one of the six charming, hand-painted tepees instead of the luxury of your RV or convenience of your tent; you'll still be able to use the laundry facility and visit with neighbors in any one of the 140 RV, tent, cabin, and tepee sites. The great thing about the Ponderosa is the utter convenience to the scene in Cody; everything is within walking distance. Open May through Oct.

THREE MILE CAMPGROUND $
US 14/16/20
(307) 527-6241
Because this is a grizzly bear corridor into Yellowstone National Park, only hard-sided campers are allowed here. Most of the 33 sites are equipped with user-friendly bear boxes for food storage—use them, as this area is known as a favorite spot for grizzlies during the night, particularly in spring and fall. Four sites are situated along the North Fork of the Shoshone River and are for day-use only. Because this campground is 3 miles from the east entrance of Yellowstone, it's is a popular overnight spot for park visitors. Campsites are available on a first-come basis.

RESTAURANTS

Price Code
Prices represent meals for two people, excluding beverages, tip, and tax.

$	Less than $20
$$	$20 to $27
$$$	$27 to $35
$$$$	More than $35

THE IRMA HOTEL $$
1192 Sheridan Ave.
(307) 587-4221
www.irmahotel.com

CODY

You can't come to Cody without dining at
the Irma. Built at the turn of the 20th century
by Buffalo Bill himself and named for his
youngest daughter, the restaurant and bar
draw the locals. Still a cornerstone of the
downtown area, it exudes a nostalgic western charm. Standing at the long, intricately
carved cherrywood bar (a gift to Bill Cody
from the queen of England), listening to the
steady din of voices from people sitting at
the round tables scattered throughout the
room, looking up at the high pressed-tin
ceilings, and seeing the saloon doors swing
open, you're almost transported into another
era. Most people come for the prime rib dinners, but the menu also features barbecued
ribs, chicken-fried steak, trout, shrimp, and
chicken dishes. Serving breakfast, lunch, and
dinner, the Irma accepts reservations only
in winter.

MAXWELL'S RESTAURANT $$$
937 Sheridan Ave.
(307) 527-7749
Maxwell's is open for lunch and dinner, where
you can try the unforgettable meatball sand-
wich or indulge in the steak formaggio—
a six-ounce tenderloin pressed in cracked
peppercorns, grilled, and then topped with
Gorgonzola cheese and a cream sauce. An
old Victorian home (moved to this spot from
the outskirts of town) at the end of Cody's
historic downtown houses this comfort-
able and airy eatery. Maxwell's—a favorite
with locals and tourists alike—is known
for the wonderful array of fresh-baked spe-
cialty breads and pastries that accompany a
mouthwatering menu of dishes. Best of all is
savoring the fine food with a glass of wine at
an outdoor table in summertime.

Every Fri night in July and Aug,
musical performers from string
quartets to bluegrass bands play at the
City Park Bandshell at 6 p.m. Get there
early, and bring a picnic and some lawn
chairs.

MAYOR'S INN DINNER HOUSE $$
1413 Rumsey Ave.
(307) 587-0887, (888) 217-3001
www.mayorsinndinnerhouse.com
Often called the town's first true "mansion,"
this quaint Victorian home was built for Frank
L. Houx, Cody's first elected mayor, in 1905.
Moved here in 1997 and carefully restored
to its early 20th-century charm, it is now the
Mayor's Inn Bed and Breakfast, upholding
Cody's rich historic roots. On Thur, Fri and Sat
evenings, the dining room is open to the public as well as to guests. Pink linen tablecloths
and napkins appropriately accent the numerous antiques and collectibles in the house.
You might find wild sockeye salmon filet with
fresh dill sauce or succulent lamb chops with
a bright mint sauce for entrees; but the Scottish sticky toffee pudding and homemade
Peanut Brittle Persuasion ice cream are the
house specialties and shouldn't be passed up.
Seating begins at 5 p.m. Reservations are limited and highly recommended. The restaurant
is open May to Oct.

Fine dining in Yellowstone Country doesn't mean you have to
dress to the nines. Casual dress is
accepted almost everywhere.

THE PROUD CUT SALOON $$
1227 Sheridan Ave.
(307) 527-6905
With a long list of juicy steaks, including a
22-ounce porterhouse and 14-ounce prime

rib, the Proud Cut also serves Rocky Mountain Oysters (breaded bull-calf testicles). Either way you won't leave hungry. The restaurant is full of old local characters, and the walls are lined with cowboy memorabilia as well as black-and-white photos. If you think "Proud Cut" refers to the steaks, you are mistaken. Filled with the supposed machismo of the West, the proprietors will tell you the name refers to castrated stallions that can't quit acting like studs because the procedure was botched. Let's just say that just enough of the male equipment remains to make the stallion think he's still a stud. Those parties with kids must eat in a separate back room or out on the patio. During the height of tourist season, reservations are suggested for both lunch and dinner.

✳THE TERRACE RESTAURANT
AND BAR $$$$
525 West Yellowstone Ave.
(307) 587-5868
Situated next to the Cody Nite Rodeo, the Terrace has a more urban feel than the town's other restaurants and bars. The menu features old favorites like steak, burgers, and salads, but also features more eclectic dishes like almond crusted halibut, red pepper pesto crushed chicken, and hazelnut shrimp pasta. The Terrace is a great place to grab appetizers and drinks, and has a familiar bistro-like atmosphere that can occasionally get loud. All in all, it's one of Cody's better dining options for those who want excellent food at a reasonable price.

✳WYOMING'S RIB AND
CHOP HOUSE $$
1367 Sheridan Ave.
(307) 527-7731
www.ribandchophouse.com

Part of a small chain of popular restaurants in Montana and Wyoming, the Rib and Chop House offers a large variety of food with excellent service. Steaks and ribs are the signature items—try the hand-cut rib eye or the "baseball cut" sirloin—but there is also seafood, sandwiches, pasta, and salads on the menu. Entrees are served with a salad or soup and choice of one side, including baked beans, squash casserole, and garlic mashers. The pasta jambalaya and gumbo are also recommended for Cajun lovers, and the 27-ounce margaritas are a house specialty. Open Mon through Sat from 11 a.m. to 9 p.m., and Sun from 4 p.m. to 9 p.m.

SHOPPING

True to its pioneer heritage, most of the stores in downtown Cody offer different angles to western wear and American Indian sundries. The other influence that shapes the retail scene here is, of course, the outdoors. You'll find shops specializing in every mountain sport imaginable.

CODY NEWSSTAND
1121 Thirteenth St.
(307) 587-2843
Open since 1988, the Cody Newsstand features an entire wall of magazines—4,000 titles, to be exact. The store carries 20,000 book titles and showcases a wonderful collection of children's books. You can also buy a fine cigar to accompany your *Wall Street Journal*.

MUSEUM SELECTIONS, BUFFALO BILL
HISTORICAL CENTER
720 Sheridan Ave.
(307) 587-3243, (800) 533-3838
Authors frequently make appearances for book signings at the Buffalo Bill Historical

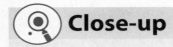 **Close-up**

Heart Mountain's Sad Legacy

Just west of Cody, the remains of a chimney spire and a few lonely buildings at the base of Heart Mountain are reminders of a tragic moment in American history.

On February 19, 1942, President Franklin D. Roosevelt signed an executive order approving the evacuation of more than 100,000 Japanese Americans from the West Coast to 10 relocation centers throughout the United States. **Heart Mountain Relocation Camp** was one of those centers.

People were forcibly removed from their homes, schools, and communities and placed in a desolate camp encircled by barbed wire and guarded with armed military personnel. The camp included 468 barracks, two mess halls, two laundry-toilet buildings, and two auxiliary buildings, as well as a fire station, water and sewage treatment plants, a power station, a hospital, and several administrative buildings. Internees were restricted from leaving the camp. At its peak nearly 11,000 Japanese Americans were contained here, making it the third-largest community in Wyoming.

During its three-year existence, Heart Mountain Camp saw the birth of 552 babies and 185 deaths. Despite the unjust confinement, the camp's residents organized themselves and established a school system, newspaper, and internal government. Life went on here as the world was at war. Many internees resorted to low-paying jobs as agricultural hands and kept the camp self-sufficient, as ordained by the federal government. The camp gave the communities of Cody and Powell an economic boost during wartime hardships.

Finally, in 1945 President Roosevelt proclaimed the internees could go free. Each person was given $25 and a train ticket to the destination of his or her choice on the West Coast. In theory this was good news, but in practice it left thousands of Japanese

Center. The store has a small collection of titles on art and western history. You'll also find posters and reproductions of paintings featured in the museum's collection, gifts, and a coffee bar.

NEW WEST FURNITURE
2811 Big Horn Ave.
(800) 653-2391
www.newwest.com
This is a store for collectors and fans of western and artfully crafted furnishings. There is a history of design that begins with the famous Molesworth furniture of the 1940s and continues today, as this retailer and interior design firm supports local craftspeople

and the culture of the American West through home style. The store and its design firm have been featured in several leading home magazines, including *Architectural Digest*. New West's custom western furniture has won multiple national awards for excellence; the classic Anti-Gravity Table is part of the permanent decorative arts collection at the Buffalo Bill Historical Center.

THE PLUSH PONY
1350 Sheridan Ave.
(307) 587-4677
The Plush Pony brings a feeling of urban chic to women's clothing with a slight western twist. It's a pricey little boutique, but

178

Americans homeless. During the internment most had their homes foreclosed and lost all their possessions. They didn't know where to go, and the government offered no further assistance. While the rest of the nation celebrated America's victory, Japanese Americans suffered their own defeat.

The order that created Heart Mountain Relocation Camp was signed under the guise that it was for the "protection" of the internees, but later it was verified that the establishment of these camps was an act of paranoia and prejudice, resulting in a gross violation of human rights. Although many of the camp internees were American citizens, all were suspected of being disloyal to America based on their race. In the mid-1980s Congress conceded this shameful fact, granting compensation to internees and their families who lost property as a result of their internment. Later a memorial plaque was placed at the site, which is now on the National Register of Historic Places. It reads: "May the injustice of the removal and incarceration of 120,000 persons of Japanese ancestry during World War II, two-thirds of whom were American citizens, never be repeated."

Visible from most any point in town, Heart Mountain is a foreboding sentinel of a sad moment in history. Although the camp's activities are finished, the affront to loyal American citizens has not been forgotten. In 2000 Wyoming senator Mike Enzi helped push legislation through the US Senate to approve a $500,000 federal economic development grant to be used toward the Heart Mountain Interpretive Learning center, which opened in 2004.

Heart Mountain is located 15 miles west of Cody. Take US 14A to Road 19 and continue 0.5 mile to the small memorial sign. Call the Heart Mountain Foundation at (307) 754-2272 or visit www.heartmountain.org.

with care you can make some great buys. And you might just toss your budget right out the window when you check out new designs from Liz Palacios, Brighton, and Patricia Wolf.

PRAIRIE ROSE NORTHERN PLAINS INDIAN GALLERY
1356 Sheridan Ave.
(307) 587-8181
The intricately beaded clothing that adorns this shop's walls are true works of art. Each seed bead has been hand stitched onto feather-soft leather in designs that have been passed down through generations of Northern Plains Indians. In here you'll find

peculiar utilitarian objects that American Indians use to make these beaded masterpieces, including seed beads, eye beads, trade beads, coyote and wolf knuckles, bear claws, Indian porcupine quills, elk hide, moose hair, and feathers. Prairie Rose also carries American Indian music, jewelry, and books.

SIERRA TRADING POST OUTLET
1402 Eighth St.
(307) 578-5802
www.sierratradingpost.com
An outlet for the famous catalog wholesaler, this popular store features deep discounts on a wide variety of name brand outdoor

gear. Everything from tents and backpacks to shoes and outerwear can be found here, and the helpful staff is knowledgeable about the products they sell.

SUNLIGHT SPORTS
1251 Sheridan Ave.
(307) 587-9517
www.sunlightsports.com
After three decades of serving Cody residents and their outdoor addictions, Sunlight Sports is still on top. Inside you'll find gear for backpacking, climbing, skiing, snowboarding, snowshoeing, rock and ice climbing, and all the right apparel to go with your recreational pursuits. Sunlight's ample stock suits all ages and levels of expertise. During winter months the ski shop offers rentals and beefs up its cold-weather clothes to get through the long season. This hometown sporting-goods store is also the place to go for tips on great local trails and climbing spots.

TIMBER CREEK INTERIORS FURNITURE AND DESIGN
1371 Sheridan Ave.
(307) 587-4246
There's so much to ooh and aah over in this richly furnished store. Overstuffed couches and heavy hand-hewn harvest tables invite you to have a seat, but you wouldn't dare. This high-end furniture store exudes the new upscale western motif. With rooms arranged like a house, Timber Creek welcomes you to imagine your own home so tastefully done. Antler chandeliers and sophisticated household accessories conjure up the possibilities of redecorating to the hilt. Let the store's expert designers advise you on how to bring a little bit of the West into your house without overdoing it.

TRADITIONS WEST
1131 Sheridan Ave.
(307) 587-7434
From dainty lace antique hankies to century-old steamer trunks, if it's western, you are likely to find it among the treasures in this antiques mall. Beautifully worn armoires, charming children's wagons, porcelain wash-basins, and vintage clothes—there is so much to look through in this large shop that you are sure to walk away with at least a little purchase. Many of the items at Traditions West are large pieces of stately furniture, both unique and common. Should you find furniture you can't live without, the store ships anywhere in the United States.

NIGHTLIFE

Cody and most of Yellowstone Country are known for quiet pastoral evenings. Beyond the raucous saloon experience or the peace of viewing the Milky Way, things are pretty sleepy. But here are a few things that might keep you busy once the sun goes down.

✳CASSIE'S SUPPER CLUB $$$
214 Yellowstone Ave.
(307) 527-5500
www.cassies.com
You don't need line-dancing lessons to enjoy the foot stompin' country-and-western music that pipes out of Cassie's dance hall. Owner Steve Singer, a Cody native, played music on the road for 20 years before he returned home to liven up the town's music scene. He plays music seven nights a week during summer months and Wed through Sat in the winter. Cassie's, owned in the 1920s by Cassie Waters, the renowned madam of Cody's other former nightlife attraction, has always been the place to go for fun and dancing. Singer grew up down the street from the

place; as a boy he played piano for the bar regulars. Since then he's become an avid collector of Cassie memorabilia. Look for her fur lap robe displayed in the entryway and the parrots above the bar. Singer has made a name for Cassie's as the place to go for dinner and dancing. The menu consists of steak and seafood items. Lunch is also served, and reservations are recommended.

CODY NITE RODEO
519 West Yellowstone Ave.
(307) 587-5155
www.codystampederodeo.com
The folks in Cody know what you came looking for in the West: cowboys. The old- time legend is alive and well here with bull riders, rodeo clowns, and barrel racers showing off their skills. The rodeo runs from June 1 to Aug 31 and starts at 8:30 p.m. It has become the town's No. 1 nighttime activity and attracts around 90,000 spectators each summer. Originally started in 1938 as a gimmick to lure Yellowstone tourists into Cody to stay the night, it still works. But the Cody Nite Rodeo is no tourist trap. It's the real thing, with the cowboys and stock putting their hearts into every performance.

DAN MILLER'S COWBOY MUSIC REVUE
1110 Beck Ave.
(307) 272-7855
www.cowboymusicrevue.com
This fast-paced family show features a night of cowboy comedy, poetry, and traditional songs of the American West. Shows begin at 8 nightly from May through Sept. This is truly a performance that's unique to this part of the world and well worth the $15 admission fee. Box office opens nightly at 7 p.m.

ATTRACTIONS

It goes without saying that in the Greater Yellowstone region, most people who visit come for the two main attractions: Yellowstone and Grand Teton National Parks. And while these certainly live up to their name, a closer look at the surrounding area reveals numerous events and activities that deserve mention. From museums and rodeos to state parks and scenic drives, there is much to see that is off the beaten path. Sometimes these can be the best part of a trip, an unexpected pleasure that will leave a lasting impression.

Attractions in Yellowstone and Grand Teton are listed first, followed by attractions in the surrounding towns in the same order as the main town chapters of the book.

YELLOWSTONE NATIONAL PARK

Yellowstone National Park is an attraction in and of itself. But the world's first national park is a complex place. At a glance you will see its astounding beauty, its vast wildness. Scrutinize it and you will notice flaws; examine it closely and you will recognize nature's intricate links to past, present, and future. Yellowstone is truly like no other place on earth. And to offer up a handful of highlights labeled "the best" or "the most interesting" or "the most dynamic" does not do the place justice. It is a place you must return to again and again to grasp its significance and to realize its importance and rarity. For some people it is worth moving here just to be near this natural wonder and to experience it on a regular basis. For others it's a one-time whirlwind tour that will linger in memory. This chapter highlights just a few of the places you must see if you will come here only once and a couple others that might lure you back for a return visit.

Grand Canyon of the Yellowstone

Renowned painter Thomas Moran may have been the first to fall in love with the Grand Canyon of the Yellowstone. He accompanied the 1871 Hayden Expedition, and his paintings helped convince Congress to create the world's first national park. In particular, his depiction of the canyon's richly layered colors from his perch at what is now called Artist's Point captured the area's uncommon grandeur and unparalleled beauty. Today you can still see it through his eyes from this same spot on the canyon's southern rim. You can also view the Lower Falls, which is the highest waterfall in Yellowstone (308 feet) from the North Rim Drive. At sunset Inspiration Point sets off a wild display of pinks in the canyon's rock layers. Walking and cross-country ski trails also wind along both rims of the canyon.

No matter where you stand, this canyon—24 miles long and 4,000 feet wide in some places—will leave you speechless. Its walls are colored in hues of red, brown, white, and orange layers where the Yellowstone River has over centuries cut through rock down to 800 or 1,200 feet below.

Yellowstone Lake

Whether it is from the perch of your canoe, a lakeside trail, the comfy seat in your campsite, or the elegant veranda of Lake Yellowstone Hotel, there isn't a bad view of Yellowstone Lake. Its pure, icy waters stretch 20 miles long and 14 miles wide across the cradle of the Yellowstone Plateau at 7,333 feet. On stormy days the water churns in oceanlike waves and looks foreboding. This is the largest high-altitude lake in North America, and you will find more than 110 miles of shoreline where you can sit and peer into the deep, frigid blue. But unless you have a dry suit, don't think about swimming in here—the average temperature is 41 degrees!

Fishing is encouraged, however. Yellowstone Lake is home to the largest inland population of wild cutthroat trout in North America. Unfortunately it also contains a growing population of lake trout, a non-native species that preys upon cutthroat and has depleted their numbers significantly since 1994.

During summer months the pristine blue waters span out into a crystalline plain. From the shore you can watch small sailboats, tour boats, and fishing rigs in designated areas or take a cruise around the lake yourself. At Bay Bridge Marina regularly scheduled scenic cruises depart throughout the day from June through Sept. You can also rent outboard motorboats and canoes, or charter a guided fishing trip. A favorite landlubber ride is the Sunset Tour on a historic replica of a 1937 white touring bus. The bus leaves from Lake Hotel and Fishing Bridge RV Park and motors through scenery around the lake to the breathtaking views at Lake Butte Overlook. On a clear day you can see snowcapped mountains ringing the surrounding plateau. By walking along one of the many designated hiking trails you can also get a closer look at geysers and fumaroles and hot springs that seep and steam into the lake's chilly water. Ask at the visitor center for details.

Even below the surface, Yellowstone Lake offers another intriguing world, but most of us don't get to experience it. Since 1999 researchers have been exploring the mysterious lake bottom and have unearthed a whole other system of geothermal features. Thirty- to 40-foot-high spires have been found, sprouting from the bottom of the lake like an underwater forest. Scientists discovered that the formation contains the same minerals found in the geyser basins, dating back 12,000 years. Look for new discoveries about Yellowstone Lake when you visit, and keep an eye out for research ships equipped with scuba-diving scientists.

Lamar Valley

In one morning it is feasible to see bears, wolves, foxes, coyotes, bison, and elk in Yellowstone's Lamar Valley. Located in the northeastern corner of the park, this is the wildlife-watching mother lode if you are patient enough to wait with your binoculars or a spotting scope. Called the Serengeti of North America, Lamar is a grassy, broad-sweeping drainage that provides ideal habitat for most of the animal species found in Yellowstone. It is probably best known as the stage for the 1995 reintroduction of the gray wolves, which were initially released here.

Since then the wolf packs have grown and claimed other territories, but it is still possible to glimpse these elusive creatures (early mornings in spring or fall are the best times).

Lamar Valley is historically known as the home of the Buffalo Ranch. By 1902 Yellowstone's bison were nearly extinct due to early market hunting by settlers and later poachers within park boundaries. The US government was moved to action and saved the last free-roaming bison herd by raising bison like domestic cattle until the 1930s, when the herd finally grew to a healthy number. Today Buffalo Ranch is the headquarters for the Yellowstone Institute, a nonprofit educational group that conducts field courses on topics ranging from park ecology to plein air painting.

Even without the wildlife or the history, Lamar is beautiful. Its vast landscape is captivating in a gentler, subtler way than some of the more dynamic attractions in Yellowstone. You can enjoy it from nearby Cooke City, Montana (3 miles past the northeastern gate), or from Slough Creek and Pebble Creek Campgrounds.

*Mount Washburn

From the summit of Mount Washburn you will see the Grand Canyon of the Yellowstone River to the east; to the south it's Hayden Valley and Yellowstone Lake. On a clear day you will also get a look at the Tetons, Absarokas, and the Gallatin Range. With a view like this, there's no question why this is Yellowstone's best-known mountain. Rising 10,243 feet above the west edge of Yellowstone's Grand Canyon, this mountain was named after Gen. Henry Dana Washburn, who led the 1870 expedition to the area. Since the park's creation, the mountain has been a popular hiking spot; historic photos even show early

travelers stepping out of stagecoaches at the summit (this should be your first clue that the hike is a moderate one).

Walking the 3 miles to the top, you will gain 1,500 feet in elevation and perhaps a friend's admiration should you decide to call from the pay phone at the summit. If you're lucky, you might also catch a glimpse of a few bighorn sheep. But regardless of which of the three trails you take, the walk is paved with wildflowers of every color. There is also a fire lookout at the summit where you can take shelter in bad weather.

Specimen Ridge

Near Tower Junction, Specimen Ridge holds the remnants of one of Yellowstone's greatest mysteries. Here scientists have discovered as many as 27 separate petrified forests, one on top of the other. Some of the trees are still standing and indicate that at one time the climate was much warmer. Among the identified species are redwood, pine, magnolia, dogwood, oak, maple, hickory, and walnut. The best way to see Specimen Ridge is through a tour led by one of the park's ranger-naturalists. Check at any visitor center to find out when you can catch one of these tours.

The Big Burn

The fires of 1988 were the greatest natural event to happen in the Greater Yellowstone Area since the massive caldera-forming volcanic eruption more than 600,000 years ago. We are still seeing the effects of the flames that covered 793,880 acres (35 percent) of the park. Though to many people the fires seemed like a tragic loss, biologists and ecologists saw the burn as a natural function of a healthy ecosystem. As new trees grow and forest underbrush replenishes the burnt areas, researchers are gaining new information on how a forest recovers from an event like this.

You can learn more about the long-term results of the Yellowstone fires, too. It's worth a walk and talk from a park ranger, who will take you on a "Fire Hike" through burnt area to see how the forest has regenerated two decades after the fires. A scheduled two-hour hike leaves from the Lake Overlook Trailhead in the West Thumb Geyser Basin parking lot afternoons in July and Aug. You must make a reservation to participate; call (307) 242-2650.

Geothermal Features

The eerie spouting, steaming, sulfurous areas of the Yellowstone region were unlike anything the early explorers had ever seen. The sight inspired the creation of Yellowstone National Park, but it wasn't easy to convince people of this natural curiosity. In 1807, when John Colter returned home with accounts of the area's geothermal activity, people laughed at him. In fact, until the Hayden Expedition of 1871 returned with photographs and paintings of Yellowstone's geysers and mud pots, people doubted their existence.

Yellowstone's geothermal features still enthrall visitors today. Geysers that shoot up hundreds of feet from the depths of the earth and pools that boil at temperatures beyond 450 degrees Fahrenheit have the power to remind us that we are part of a planet that is alive and ever changing. They are fascinating and strange and magical. With seven geyser basins accessible by car, it's possible to see some of the most spectacular specimens.

There are more hot spots in Yellowstone's backcountry. It's not possible to list them all, but here are a few. We haven't given specific directions to these locations because they are clearly marked on the map you'll get when you enter the park and on road signs.

Firehole Lake Drive

This level, one-way paved road begins from Old Faithful–Madison Road 8 miles north of Old Faithful and takes you through much of the Lower Geyser Basin. Active, ever-changing mud pots, constant geysers, and hissing fumaroles make it a worthwhile stop. There are also a number of colorful, bubbling hot springs to see just off the road if you are willing to stroll a little. As this is the largest basin in Yellowstone National Park, you'll find a dozen geyser groups here.

The most interesting group are the Fountain Paint Pots, with bubbling, creamy mud that resembles latex paint. Among this group is the Great Fountain Geyser, which was the first geyser seen by the Folsom-Cook-Peterson Expedition (see the History chapter to learn more about these explorers). This group is the largest in the Lower Basin, and the activity here increased dramatically after the 1959 earthquake. Great Fountain Geyser, one of Yellowstone's most spectacular, erupts about every 11 hours. It will overflow for about 70 minutes prior to erupting, so if the crater is full and you see water seeping out, definitely wait to see the eruption. Just beyond that is White Dome Geyser with its very large and impressive geyserite cone. White Dome erupts fairly frequently—about every 30 to 60 minutes.

Beyond White Dome you continue to pass thermal features, such as Pink Cone Geyser, which erupts infrequently, and

Firehole Lake, which deserves an exploration along its boardwalks. The Firehole Lake area is surrounded by large meadows where you might spot coyotes, bison, or sandhill cranes, particularly in the early morning.

Mammoth Hot Springs

You could come back to the cascading terraces of Mammoth Hot Springs and never see the same thing twice. The unusual travertine limestone terraces are a living sculpture, growing and changing minute by minute. These springs, with their source in a hillside above park headquarters, discharge about 500 gallons of hot water per minute. Almost two tons of travertine (calcium carbonate) are deposited every day. But these cascades of minerals don't just flow and grow, they also show off bright colors and ornate formations. There is no other formation like it anywhere else in the park.

A walking trail through the Lower Terraces and a one-way drive through the Upper Terraces offer views of these fascinating formations.

Mud Volcano

Discover turbulent and explosive mud pots, including Mud Volcano and Dragon's Mouth. View—and smell—Sulfur Caldron from the overlook just north of the Mud Volcano area. It is located on the road between Lake and Canyon, 6 miles north of Fishing Bridge Junction.

Old Faithful

The world's largest concentration of geysers (300 in all) is located here in the Upper Geyser Basin, with Old Faithful among its most famous. But there is much more to explore in this area. Several miles of trail begin at the visitor center, winding past geysers and hot springs too numerous to count. Names such as Beehive Grotto, Castle, Spasmodic, Grand, Giant, Riverside, and Morning Glory only hint at the wonders you will see. Stop at the visitor center for orientation and geyser information.

After a walk along nearby nature trails, we encourage you to check out the Old Faithful Inn. Completed in 1904, this massive building is still the largest log structure in the world. Beyond the sheer size of it, however, is the attention architect Robert Reamer placed on the aesthetics of the place. As you walk into the 80-foot-high lobby, knotty-pine balconies perch above. Notice the wrought-iron detail on door handles, hinges, room numerals, and the one-of-a-kind tower clock that clings to the huge stone fireplace. In its day Old Faithful was the height of luxury. Regular guided tours are available to the public every half hour; check at the front desk.

Steamboat Geyser

For a geyser that has had decadeslong dormant periods, Steamboat has been especially active in the 21st century. The world's tallest geyser erupted seven times between May 2000 and May 2005, roaring up to 400 feet in the air and spewing steam and debris for several hundred yards, but has not erupted since. It has a history of this—when it first became active in 1878, it hurled huge rocks into the air with such force that it killed nearby trees and plants with its burning mud. Still, an eruption from this legendary geyser happens so infrequently that word of its blowing draws park employees and geyser enthusiasts from 30 miles away. But you could get lucky—who knows when this geyser will go off again. In the 1980s Steamboat erupted 23 times in one summer.

Steamboat is only one of many geysers you can check out in Norris Geyser Basin, which is the home of the hottest geothermal features in the park. An elaborate trail system starts at the Geyser Basin Museum and winds around to Porcelain Basin. This ever-changing group of geysers sits in open terrain with hundreds of densely packed geothermal features. The features in the Back Basin are more scattered and isolated.

West Thumb Geyser Basin

Take a stroll down one of the prettiest boardwalk trails found anywhere in the park through West Thumb Geyser Basin (named for a thumb-shaped bay on the southwestern end of Yellowstone Lake). Situated on the shore of Yellowstone Lake, the boiling springs in this basin, including the famous Fishing Cone, discharge their waters into the icy lake. This odd-looking gray mound used to erupt regularly to heights of up to 40 feet. Nearby you'll find the jewel-colored greens of Abyss Pool and Black Pool. With the Absaroka mountains as a backdrop to the east, you won't forget this view.

GRAND TETON NATIONAL PARK

Menors Ferry Historic District

Located off Teton Park Road a half-mile north of Moose, this historic area offers a glimpse at what pioneer life was like in Jackson Hole. The site is the former home of William D. Menor, who came to the area in 1894 and set up a homestead here along the Snake River. He constructed a ferryboat that became a vital crossing for the early settlers of valley, charging 50 cents for a wagon team and 25 cents for a horse and rider. Menor operated the ferry until he sold it in 1918, and then a steel bridge was built in 1927. Today,

a replica of the ferry carries tourists across the river (depending on water levels), and visitors can see Bill Menor's original cabin and country store. The nearby Chapel of the Transfiguration is a popular spot, a beautiful place where the altar window frames the Teton peaks.

Yellowstone's Small, Small World

Walking along the park's boardwalks lets you observe the marvelous thermal features without disturbing the delicate microbial communities that color Yellowstone's hot springs, pools, lakes, and streams. You can learn more about the park's tiniest organisms by reading *Seen and Unseen: Discovering the Microbes of Yellowstone* (Falcon, 2005). The book takes you on a tour of microbial habitats in the park and explains the key roles microbes play in Yellowstone's ecosystem.

Snake River Overlook

This overlook on the northeast route between Moran and Moose Junctions is widely considered the best spot to see the panorama of the majestic Teton Range. Framed by the slow-moving water of the Snake River, the overlook is a popular wildlife-watching spot. Look for moose, beavers, river otters, and birds. It's also a lesson in history. The willow thickets that flank the river and its tributaries were home to the beaver that attracted the first fur traders to the Jackson Hole Valley. Farther up the road past the

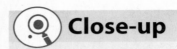 **Close-up**

Hoofing It in Yellowstone National Park

Retracing the footsteps of American Indians and mountain men who marked these trails two centuries ago, we set out on our 12-mile ride to Soldier's Corral camp in Gardner's Hole. Loaded with our supplies and gear, we—8 guests, 4 guides, 12 horses, and 8 pack mules—are on our third day of a five-day horse-pack trip in the northwestern corner of Yellowstone National Park.

On our way up to 10,000-foot Electric Pass, the narrow trail is steep and rocky. Our surefooted horses groan and huff as we climb up above tree line, gaining 2,000 feet of elevation in two hours.

"Imagine that you are an Indian from the Nez Perce tribe in Idaho or the Flathead from Missoula," says Dick Kendall, our guide from Diamond K Outfitters in Big Sky, Montana. "You would traverse this same route to get to Obsidian Cliff to gather material for toolmaking." As we crest the pass, we do imagine this. Perched on a saddle between two towering peaks—10,999-foot Electric and 10,102-foot Joseph Peaks—Yellowstone National Park unfurls into an oceanlike expanse of land with 150-mile vistas. We see the entire Absaroka-Beartooth Range and the high-water marks of its peaks above 12,000 feet. We can see Montana's Spanish Peaks and the Gallatins. Yellowstone's western plateau, all the way to Wyoming's east entrance outside Cody, is in front of us. Behind us is the bowl of Sportsman Lake, where we camped last night.

Looking across the most remote region in the lower 48 states, it is overwhelming and redeeming to know there is this much wild country left virtually untouched. We are hushed by the beauty of this place. Half of us are neophytes to horses and to Yellowstone National Park's backcountry. All eight of us hail from hectic lives in bustling towns or cities from California to Montana, from Oklahoma to New York.

We began at the Fawn Pass trailhead off US 191 west in Montana. Just 20 horse steps onto the trail and the rumbling sound of speeding semitrucks was muted. One mile in and the steady hum of summer traffic was still audible. After 2 or 3 miles farther down, the swoosh of vehicles was lost to a wash of wind in the pines. But 4 miles into that 14-mile horseback ride there was only the slow tromp of horse hooves and saddles squeaking, the intermittent chatter of small talk among strangers, and the trickle of Fan Creek's midday amble through sagebrush and willow.

"This is God's country for riding," said wrangler and camp cook Kip Saile.

We traveled along a dusty path and marked time by the change of landscape. We rode through sweeping grasslands into high, dense timber and moose-laden marshland and then into a forest graveyard of burnt trees left from the 1988 fires. Two, then three and four hours passed as we rode quietly, the only people on the trail. For us it seemed we were the only people in the park.

By that fourth hour there were grumblings of aching knees from the long ride and private whines of, "How much longer?" But just when we'd reached our greenhorn's limit, our horses broke into a happy trot, carrying us out of the burnt timber into a meadow carpeted with thick, green grass.

They knew we had reached our first camp before we did. To the south was tiny Sportsman Lake, a haven for native cutthroat trout. Towering above us were Electric and Joseph Peaks, framing the northwestern edge of this mountain cirque that is barely more than a mile wide.

That evening we pitched our tents and the outfitter crew built a core camp with cookstoves, a picnic table and stools, and hot water in tin bowls for guests to use to wash up. Kendall and his crew emphasize strict backcountry regulations when it comes to setting up camp. Sleeping tents are at least 100 yards from the food area, precautions are taken for waste and food storage to keep bears away, and most of the horses are set out to range freely to prevent overgrazing. Kendall believes in low-impact camping. A fifth-generation Montanan with 20 years as an outfitter in Yellowstone, he has a unique respect for protected wilderness and wildlife.

At 8,500 feet the Sportsman Lake camp is one of 302 backcountry sites, 104 of which are designated for horses and mules, in Yellowstone. Open from only July to Sept, the lake is an angler's jewel among the 1,200 miles of backcountry trails crowning the park.

"Between outfitters, llama trips, and hikers," said Kendall, "fewer than 100 people visit this lake each year." Although some sites are more popular, for the most part Yellowstone's sparse backcountry trail system sees a relatively small amount of use.

According to the National Park Service's backcountry office, only 12 percent of the three million people who visit Yellowstone annually ever go more than 1 mile off a road. That equates to an average of 45,000 people each year who experience Yellowstone's backcountry. Most of them book a trip with one of the region's 50 outfitters. With 95 percent of the park's 2.2 million acres considered wilderness, there's a lot to see, and riding in on horseback is an easy way to cover the miles.

We are far from city streets, but the aromas wafting through camp from the pots and pans in Saile's makeshift kitchen are straight from an upscale gourmet restaurant. Under the light of lanterns he asked us how we liked our steak cooked and then served up perfectly prepared beef tenderloin and lobster tails with drawn butter. Kendall cracked open bottles of fine wine; for dessert we had lemon meringue pie.

By the end of the next day's ride, we expect the luxury awaiting us at camp. We are spoiled. Tired and thirsty, we hardly notice the beauty cupped in this honey spot of a valley called Gardner's Hole.

Tiny purple asters and Queen Anne's lace sprout up through lush knee-high grass. The Gardner River snakes through the center of this historic spot, discovered by raucous mountain man Johnson Gardner in 1831. Trappers once held rendezvous here, and when the US Army was called to restore order in Yellowstone, the soldiers pastured several hundred horses here from 1892 to 1918. Weathered remnants of wood that were once the soldier's corral lay in recognizable shapes near our tents.

On a good day Kendall and the other wranglers claim this pocket of Yellowstone yields a wildlife display of Discovery Channel proportions. We don't believe them. But within 24 hours we spot two bull moose grazing near camp at dawn and bighorn sheep on the face of Electric Peak, spook a grizzly from his nap on a day ride, witness the Swan Lake wolf pack chasing a herd of 20 bull elk, hear the haunting call of sandhill cranes as they land near us, and watch a hawk hunt as it hovers 8 inches above the grass. We also see a meteor shower and enough stars in the seamless night sky to make up our own constellations. We know what it's like to have a good day in Gardner's Hole.

Moran Junction is the Oxbow Bend Turnout, where you can catch equally impressive views of towering Mount Moran.

Jenny Lake

Probably the most popular lake in the park, Jenny Lake looms beneath the three Tetons and Mount Owen, making it a great spot for photos or a lunch break. An easy, flat, 7.7-mile hike starts at the Jenny Lake turnout or the South Jenny Lake trailhead and circles the lake, making for one of the park's favorite routes. You can also take ranger-led trips across the lake to Inspiration Point. These depart from the Jenny Lake boat dock every summer morning at 8:30. A shuttle will also take you across the lake for $9 round-trip, where you can access the Cascade Canyon Trail and numerous other trails that lead into the Teton backcountry.

Laurance S. Rockefeller Preserve Center

Opened in 2008, this interpretive center is the first platinum LEED-certified building in the National Park System. Situated on a beautiful 1,106-acre parcel within the park boundary, there are eight miles of year-round woodland trails that provide views of the Tetons and Phelps Lake. The 7,500-square-foot building is situated to capture views of the Teton Range, and features a series of visual, auditory, and tactile displays to make visitors more aware of natural elements found on the Preserve. There are also resource and soundscape rooms, and a relaxing fireplace to sit around to enjoy the surroundings.

Grand View Point

This appropriately named spot produces one of the most dramatic views in the park.

To get to the beginning of the 1.1-mile trail, make the first turn on the east side of US 89 north past Jackson Lake Lodge. The road is fairly rough, so low-clearance vehicles may need to park at one of the turnouts on the dirt road. The trailhead isn't far, less than 1 mile from the turnoff.

The trail to the point starts out flat, but soon you'll come to a steep hill. Don't fret, the climb will be short and you'll be at Grand View Point—elevation 7,586 feet—when you reach the top. And once you get there, you'll get a fantastic look at Mount Moran and the rest of the mighty Tetons, as well as a sweeping vista of Two Ocean Lake and the Teton Wilderness. Round-trip is 2.2 miles, and it's downhill all the way from the top.

JACKSON, WYOMING

GRASSY LAKE ROAD
Flagg Ranch, WY, to Ashton, ID

If you are driving from Jackson to West Yellowstone (or vice versa) and don't want to go through Yellowstone National Park, the scenic Grassy Lake Road is a great option. From Jackson head north through Grand Teton National Park, along the John D. Rockefeller Jr. Memorial Parkway to Flagg Ranch, a few miles from the south entrance to Yellowstone. Turn left at the ranch and follow the signs for the Grassy Lake Road.

The 50-mile stretch of dirt road passes through numerous lowland meadows and the charred remains of 2000's Flagg Ranch Fire. Keep your eye out for deer, elk, and moose in the creek-filled meadows. You'll come to the huge Grassy Lake Reservoir and continue on a one-lane section of the road toward Ashton. A short side trip can be made to the Lake of the Woods, appropriately named for its timbered shores deep in the heart of the Targhee National Forest.

On the way out you'll pass Indian Lake and a trumpeter swan refuge, and you'll see great views of the Tetons. One of the best times to drive this road is in the fall, when plentiful stands of aspens turn bright gold, highlighting the contrast between the green pines, blue skies, and white-capped peaks of the Tetons.

As the dirt road turns to pavement, you'll drive through the rolling potato fields of eastern Idaho into Ashton. Turn right onto US 20 toward West Yellowstone. The road closes for the winter months and is not recommended for large trailers or RVs. Call Grand Teton National Park at (307) 739-3399 for road information.

✳JACKSON HOLE AERIAL TRAM
Jackson Hole Mountain Resort, Teton Village
You can ride the tram at the ski resort 2.4 miles up to the 10,450-foot summit of Rendezvous Mountain for one of the most spectacular views in North America. Bring your sweatshirt and jacket, as the wind can blow quite hard and the temperature can dip into the 20s. While at the top, walk around and soak in the views of the Tetons to the north and the mountains of Wyoming and Idaho in every other direction. You can also access trails in Grand Teton National Park and the Bridger-Teton National Forest from the top and grab a snack or a souvenir in the cafe. Rides cost $20 for adults, kids 5 and under free. Keep your eye out for the black bears and other wildlife that roam the mountain on the way up. The original tram has been replaced with a new, 100-passenger tram that opened in the winter of 2009. Grand Targhee Ski and Summer Resort and Snow King also offer scenic rides to the top of their respective summits.

NATIONAL ELK REFUGE
(307) 733-9212
You'll pass this 23,754-acre refuge as you head toward Grand Teton from Jackson. The territory serves as the annual winter range for as many as 10,000 elk, which migrate to the feeding grounds of the refuge as winter encroaches on the Yellowstone ecosystem. At the end of the winter season, local Boy Scout troops gather and auction the elk antlers that are naturally shed every spring, donating 80 percent of the profits to buy supplemental winter feed for the elk. Many buyers come from Asia, where antlers are considered to have medicinal value. In winter stop in at the interpretive center located in the National Museum of Wildlife Art.

NATIONAL MUSEUM OF WILDLIFE ART
2820 Rungius Rd.
(307) 733-5771
www.wildlifeart.org
The 51,000-square-foot National Museum of Wildlife Art houses more than 2,000 works of art, including pieces by American explorer artists, landscape artists, contemporary wildlife artists, and sculptors. Media include oil, bronze, stone, acrylic, watercolor, gouache, pastel, pencil, lithography, photography, and charcoal. Since it opened in 1987, the nonprofit museum has become an important educational center and meeting place for the Jackson Hole region. The new building, completed in 1994 at a cost of $10 million, sits perched on a hill across from the National Elk Refuge on US 89, 2 miles north of Jackson. The museum houses the interpretive center for the refuge during winter months. Interesting exhibits include the second-largest public collection of work by Carl Rungius, which features the only two bronzes he completed, and the American

ATTRACTIONS

Bison Collection, more than 100 images that portray the bison's relationship with humans and nature. Other artists represented include John J. Audubon, John Clymer, Karl Bodmer, Eugène Delacroix, and Charles Russell.

Museum facilities include 12 galleries, a 200-seat auditorium, two classrooms, a conference room, a gift shop, and a cafe. Hours are daily 9 a.m. to 5 p.m. Mon through Sat and 1 to 5 p.m. on Sun. Admission is $10 for adults, $9 for seniors, and free for those age 18 and under accompanied by an adult.

REXBURG & DRIGGS, IDAHO

SPUD DRIVE-IN THEATRE
231 South Idaho Hwy. 33, Driggs
(208) 354-2727
www.spuddrivein.com
Built in 1953, the historic Spud Drive-In Theatre is an old-fashioned drive-in where you can watch a movie in the shadow of the Teton Mountains. Enjoy a Famous Gladys Burger while watching Hollywood's latest attraction in the comfort of your own car. Shows start at 6:30 p.m. during summer only; admission is $5 per vehicle. The Spud also hosts concerts from big-name acts during the summer.

TETON AVIATION CENTER AND WARBIRDS CAFE
Driggs-Reed Memorial Airport, Driggs
(208) 354-3100, (800) 472-6382
www.tetonaviation.com
You don't have to charter a private jet or eat a meal here to check out the dazzling collection of fighter planes on display. Immaculately restored, the planes are kept in a hangar off the side of the restaurant where you can get a peak at a World War II–era N3N and modern fighters such as the MiG 15 and the T2-B Buckeye. Admission is free.

YELLOWSTONE BEAR WORLD
6010 South 4300 West, Rexburg
(208) 359-9688
www.yellowstonebearworld.com
This drive-through wildlife park has plenty of animals to see, including elk, reindeer, fallow deer, mule deer, bison, white-tailed deer, wild turkeys, wolves, pheasants, grizzly bears, and black bears. Look up and you're likely to see ducks, geese, and swans. Bear World accommodates all vehicles, even travel trailers, motor homes, and tour buses. If you're on a motorcycle, you can tour the park in a loaner car. At the Photo Den you can have your picture taken with a bear, wolf, or bull elk, and the Hungry Bear Cafe has cold drinks, burgers, ice cream, and more. There's also a petting zoo, where kids can feed the ducks and fish from the overlook deck. Admission is $16.95 for adults, $15.95 for seniors, $12.95 for children ages 3 to 10, and free for kids under age 3. Yellowstone Bear World is located just off US 20, about halfway between Idaho Falls and Ashton.

WEST YELLOWSTONE, MONTANA

✳GRIZZLY AND WOLF DISCOVERY CENTER
201 South Canyon St.
(406) 646-7001, (800) 257-2570
www.grizzlydiscoveryctr.com
If you want to get a firsthand view of real, live grizzly bears and wolves, this is the place. You'll see numerous big bears and gray wolves living in a natural setting and receive firsthand knowledge of their social and playful behaviors. The center presents interactive and educational exhibits, films, and presentations, and kids and adults will love the gift shop with a wildlife theme. The center is a nonprofit bear and wolf preserve

and is open year-round from 8:30 a.m. until 8:30 p.m. Admission is $10.50 for adults, $9.75 for seniors, and $5.50 for kids 5 to 12; children under age 5 are admitted free.

PLAYMILL THEATRE
29 Madison Ave.
(406) 646-7757
www.playmill.com
The Playmill has been West Yellowstone's only live theater for four decades, producing high-quality comedies, dramas, and musicals each summer season from Memorial Day to Labor Day. Shows are at 6 p.m. and 8:30 p.m. every day but Sun and typically feature three revolving productions, so you could actually see all three within the span of a week. Past productions include *Joseph and the Amazing Technicolor Dreamcoat*, *Fiddler on the Roof*, and *Annie Get Your Gun*. Call the theater or visit the website for current shows and prices. Reservations are recommended.

Nevada City Music Hall

Located an hour west of West Yellowstone, Nevada City is an excellent example of what an old Western town would have looked like 100 years ago. Today there are more than 90 historic buildings, one of them being this incredible music hall, which houses the largest public collection of automated music machines in North America. Many of these vintage gems are still in working order, while others are still being restored. It's an impressive and fun detour that kids and adults will love.

QUAKE LAKE VISITOR CENTER
US 287
(406) 646-7369
On August 17, 1959, one of the biggest earthquakes in North America struck the Yellowstone region with a magnitude of 7.5 on the Richter scale. In a span of 30 seconds, the massive quake left 28 people dead, a path of destruction, and a new lake. Twenty-foot waves caused by the quake swelled up over Hebgen Dam and swept down the Madison Canyon, destroying everything in its path. The walls of the canyon were made of strong, vertical layers of dolomite that supported loose, unstable schist underneath. The shock waves fractured the dolomite, and a million tons of rock, timber, and debris came crashing down. It was as though an entire side of a mountain fell off. This debris from the slide stopped the surging water and created Quake Lake. At the visitor center along the highway, you'll find lots of incredible photos from the earthquake and a detailed description of the tragic events that took place.

YELLOWSTONE IMAX THEATRE
101 South Canyon St.
(406) 646-4100, (888) 854-5862
www.yellowstoneimax.com
See the splendors of Yellowstone on a six-story screen with digital surround sound. This IMAX specializes in nature films, with *Yellowstone* and *Wolves* being two of the more popular films often showing here. *Yellowstone* is a great introduction to the history, wildlife, and geo thermal features of the park, allowing you to view some of its most famous features up close. Each movie lasts about 45 minutes, and there are shows every hour on the hour starting in the morning. Call or stop in for current IMAX movies

and showtimes. Admission is $9 for adults and $6.50 for kids; group rates are available.

BOZEMAN, MONTANA

GALLATIN COUNTY PIONEER MUSEUM
317 West Main St.
(406) 522-8122
www.pioneermuseum.org
This free museum is housed in the old Gallatin County Jail and is listed on the National Register of Historic Places. Inside you'll find a railroad photo display, a display on Bozeman's Chinese community from the 19th and 20th centuries, American Indian leather and beadwork, a cowgirl photo exhibit, and the historic Big Horn Gun. The Solveig Sales Memorial Library is open to the public and contains books, papers, and genealogical records of the county, and the photo archive contains more than 10,000 images from the past. The bookstore sells current history books, hard-to-find pamphlets, and maps relating to the Gallatin Valley and Montana. Summer hours are 10 a.m. to 5 p.m. Mon through Sat. Winter hours are 11 a.m. to 4 p.m. Tues through Sat. Donations are appreciated.

LEWIS AND CLARK CAVERNS
STATE PARK
MT 2
(406) 287-3541
Located about halfway between Three Forks and Whitehall on the scenic Jefferson River, this underground cave was Montana's first state park. Although in 1908 President Theodore Roosevelt named these caverns in honor of famous explorers Lewis and Clark, they never actually saw the caverns. In fact, whites only discovered the hole in the ground in the late 1800s, while American Indians knew about its existence for centuries.

The caverns are accessible by taking a two-hour tour that begins and ends at the park's visitor center. The tour starts with a 0.75-mile walk to the mouth of the cave and then descends 326 feet into the earth. The path is lighted and features 600 steps down into 12 different rooms filled with magnificent stalactite and stalagmite formations. Outside the caverns the park has 3,000 surface acres to explore. There's a campground with showers and flush toilets, RV dump sites, three camping cabins for rent, and plenty of nature trails. The fishing and floating on the nearby Jefferson is great, too. The park is open Memorial Day through Labor Day. To get here, exit I-90 at Three Forks and follow MT 2 and the signs to the caverns, approximately 19 miles.

THE "M" TRAIL
Bridger Canyon Road
It doesn't take much driving around Montana to notice the large, white letters that appear on various hillsides. Usually associated with the nearest town, the letters can be seen from miles away and often have trails leading up to them. In Bozeman's case, the gigantic letter "M" sits on a steep hill on the north side of the road leading into Bridger Canyon. It's the most popular trail in town, a spot where locals, dogs, and tourists climb to the top for tremendous views of the Gallatin Valley and the surrounding mountains. From the trailhead there are two routes to the top. One goes straight up and is recommended for hikers who are in good shape. The other is suitable for anyone, as it slowly meanders its way up in the span of about 2 miles. If you're still feeling good at the top, the trail continues as far as you want to take it and, in fact, traverses the entire length of the ridge of Bridger Mountains.

There are benches at the top where you can sit and watch the sun set over the Tobacco Root Mountains to the west. There will often be other people enjoying the view with you, many of them Bozemanites getting exercise after a hard day at the office. To find the "M" take North Rouse Avenue out of town. This will become Bridger Canyon Road, and the trailhead will be about 3 miles on your left, across from the fish hatchery. You can't miss it—there are often many cars parked there.

i Early summer and late fall are when ranchers outside the parks move their cattle herds to and from seasonal pastures. So don't be surprised if you get stuck behind a slow-moving cattle drive along one of Montana's or Wyoming's back roads—the West's version of a traffic jam.

⁕MUSEUM OF THE ROCKIES
600 West Kagy Blvd.
(406) 994-2251
www.museumoftherockies.org
A walk around the Montana State University–affiliated Museum of the Rockies is a journey through the 4.5-billion-year-old history of the Northern Rocky Mountains. The museum has permanent exhibits detailing the geology, archaeology, history, and paleontology of the region, as well as revolving displays of contemporary and historic regional artwork. The Taylor Planetarium, also housed in the museum, shows interpretive programs, such as "Native American Skies" and "Winter Skies." The planetarium also specializes in laser shows for kids and adults. In summer the Living History Farm gives visitors a glimpse of a working farm of the past, and a cafe serves lunch on the museum's terrace. In honor of the bicentennial of the Corps of Discovery,

the Lewis and Clark Challenge Course is an interactive exhibit that depicts an authentic period campsite.

Summer hours are 8 a.m. to 8 p.m. daily; winter hours are 9 a.m. to 5 p.m. Mon to Sat and 12:30 to 5 p.m. Sun. Museum admission is $13 for adults, $9 for students ages 5 to 18, and $12 for seniors. Kids age 4 and younger are admitted free. Your admission sticker is valid for two consecutive days. Call the museum for current shows and exhibits.

PALISADE FALLS
Hyalite Canyon
This is an easy, short hike that anybody can take to an impressive 120-foot waterfall cascading off the rocky cliffs of the Hyalite Canyon area. The quarter-mile trail is actually paved and wheelchair accessible and winds through tall timber stands to the base of the falls. Experienced hikers can make the short but steep climb to the top of the falls, producing great views of the Gallatin and Hyalite mountain ranges. To get to the Hyalite area, take South Nineteenth Avenue out of Bozeman until you see the Hyalite Canyon turnoff. Turn left here and take the road back to and around Hyalite Reservoir (popular for boating and swimming) and follow the signs to the falls. The road turns to dirt just before the reservoir but is in excellent condition.

LIVINGSTON, MONTANA

FARMERS' MARKET
Sacajawea Park on River Drive
(406) 222-0850
Homemade breads, magnificent wildflowers, fresh vegetables, crafts, and pottery are just a few of the wonderful local items you'll find at this quaint market along the main thoroughfare in town. The vendors and wares sold here change every week as the growing

season ebbs and flows. One week you'll find five different kinds of heirloom tomatoes, and the next the hot item will be brilliant purple delphiniums. The market is held on the banks of the Yellowstone River, weather permitting, on Wed from 5 to 7 p.m. June through Sept.

LIVINGSTON DEPOT CENTER
200 West Park St.
(406) 222-2300
www.livingstonmuseums.org/depot

Livingston was founded in 1882 as a base for Northern Pacific Railroad workers who ran railways and maintained repair shops in the region. Later the town became a jumping-off point for Yellowstone travelers. To accommodate them the railroad built a three-building brick complex for its depot. The Italianate architectural design of the building even showcases tiny red-and-black Northern Pacific Railroad logos throughout the ornate decorative exterior. Today it has been restored and is the home of the Livingston Depot Center, a combination museum, meeting hall, and convention and cultural center. On permanent display is Rails Across the Rockies, an extensive exhibit on railroading. The depot is a destination for the Montana Rockies Railroad, which originates in Sandpoint, Idaho, stays the night in Livingston, and buses guests to Yellowstone National Park for the day before continuing on to Billings. While the depot is an interesting stop for tourists, it is also a community gathering place that hosts an annual Christmas tree lighting, craft fairs, and parties. Admission is free and the museum is open Memorial Day through Labor Day. The Christmas festival is held the second weekend of Dec; call (406) 222-2300 for a schedule.

YELLOWSTONE GATEWAY MUSEUM
118 West Chinook St.
(406) 222-4184
www.livingstonmuseums.org/pcm

The 100-plus-year-old Northern Pacific Railroad caboose on the front lawn of the Park County Museum is just the beginning of the journey through the past offered here. Located in the historic Northside School, this little museum offers three floors of exhibits featuring memorabilia from life on Montana's frontier and the early railroad days. One exhibit is devoted to Calamity Jane, a western character who left her mark in Livingston. The museum is open from Memorial Day to Labor Day from 10 a.m. to 5 p.m.

GARDINER, MONTANA

ROOSEVELT ARCH
Park Street

Today the Roosevelt Arch stands in stark contrast to the quiet sloping land around it. But it was once the focal point of the Gardiner train depot, where it stood welcoming visitors to Yellowstone National Park. Standing 50 feet high with 12-foot-high walls at its edges, it curved around a beautifully landscaped pond and garden. The stately arch was the idea of Capt. Hiram M. Chittenden of the US Army Corps of Engineers (he and his troops managed the park and subsequent road improvements until 1916), who thought Yellowstone needed a "proper" entrance to dazzle visitors about to embark on a "grand tour of Wonderland." Chittenden and architect Robert Reamer came up with the plans to construct the arch out of local columnar basalt. President Theodore Roosevelt dedicated the majestic arch marking the official entrance into Yellowstone National Park on April 24, 1903. In his speech he said that Yellowstone was set aside "for the benefit and enjoyment of the people." These words are inscribed on the top of the arch's face.

RED LODGE, MONTANA

BEARTOOTH NATURE CENTER
615 Second St. East
(406) 446-1133
http://beartoothnaturecenter.org
The Beartooth Nature Center in Red Lodge offers an alternative for countless animals that are displaced by human activity, injured, or abandoned as babies and are not able to return to the wild. This nonprofit organization cares for black bears, moose, mountain lions, foxes, bobcats, sandhill cranes, and wolves. The kind staff fills in a gap that often cannot be fulfilled by the US Fish and Wildlife Department. It provides educational experiences with the resident animals, offering the public a chance to see them up close and learn about habitat, history, and lifestyle. Each spring staff members also raise a number of young animals and return them to the wild. If you're lucky you might get a glimpse of these babies before they are released. The kids will enjoy meeting domestic animals in the on-site petting zoo, where they'll find goats, sheep, and a miniature horse. The best time to see the animals is in the morning when the staff feeds them.

Located at the north entrance of town, the center is open 10 a.m. to 2 p.m. Oct through Apr; May through Sept, hours are 10 a.m. to 5 p.m. Admission is $6 for adults, $5 for seniors, and $2.50 for children ages 2 to 15.

✳BEARTOOTH SCENIC HIGHWAY
US 212
Along the Beartooth Highway out of Red Lodge, you will gain more than 5,000 feet of elevation to the highest drivable points in both Montana and Wyoming. The spectacular 65-mile drive is an extremely scenic route into Yellowstone National Park through the northeast entrance near Silver Gate, Montana. Charles Kuralt dubbed this the most beautiful drive in America, and the hundreds of motorcyclists who travel the narrow winding road to the Top of the World summit of 10,942 feet will agree.

Opened in 1936, this road seems to switchback up to impossible heights. From many points along the drive you can pull over to see broad, sweeping mountain meadows and endless peaks. Allow for at least three hours to enjoy the ride, or longer if you intend to set out on a hike on one of several difficult trails that begin up here. The snow never melts up top, as you'll notice driving through a mini-canyon of bluish drifts along the roadside toward the summit. Because of this, hardcore snowboarders and skiers pack their boards and hike up the snowy headwalls of the Beartooth Pass and bomb down the slopes to celebrate Fourth of July.

At the summit you will find the Top of the World Store, open only in summer. The owners, former schoolteachers, return each June to dig their store out of the snow. Depending on the time and amount of snowfall, this road is open from mid-May to mid-Oct. It can snow any month of the year here.

CARBON COUNTY HISTORICAL MUSEUM
224 North Broadway
(406) 446-3667
www.carboncountyhistory.com
Red Lodge has seen the booms and busts of trapping, coal mining, railroads, and

prohibition. The town has been a stronghold for celebrities, outlaws, and immigrants. It has ridden the highs and lows of wars, the Great Depression, and development. At the Carbon County Historical Museum, you can experience and learn about these rich beginnings. Inside the restored 1909 Labor Temple brick building, the Carbon County Historical Society has assembled a variety of exhibits that offer glimpses of Red Lodge's history. Most interesting is a simulated coal mine you can walk through to see a collection of old mining tools and photographs. You'll also find a collection of cowboy and rodeo memorabilia from the local Greenough family, who became world-renowned rodeo riders; a restored 1890s Yellowstone National Park stagecoach; and, oddly, an electroshock therapy machine from the more recent past. Traveling exhibits and classes are also scheduled each year. Contact the Red Lodge Chamber of Commerce for a current schedule (see the Resources chapter).

The Carbon County Historical Museum is open daily throughout the year. Admission is $5 for adults; $3 for children ages 6 to 17; it is free to historical society members and children under age 5. There is a family price of $12.

CODY, WYOMING

BUFFALO BILL DAM VISITOR CENTER
3638 South Fork Rd.
(307) 527-6076
www.bbdvc.org
The Buffalo Bill Dam transformed the geography of the Bighorn Basin. By blocking the conjunction of the South and North Forks of the Shoshone River, it gave new life to the dry lands and changed the area into a fertile valley for agricultural practices that continue to thrive. One of the first three major dams built by the newly formed Bureau of Reclamation, the Buffalo Bill Dam was the highest in the world (328 feet) when it was completed in 1910. It was raised to 353 feet in 1992. About 6 miles west of Cody, the little visitor center/rest area depicts the story of the dam's construction. Standing on the walkway above the dam, you get the spectacular views of the canyon and lake and a sense of how dramatically the dam changed the river. This visitor center is open May through Sept from 8 a.m. to 8 p.m. daily. There is no admission charge.

✳BUFFALO BILL HISTORICAL CENTER
720 Sheridan Ave.
(307) 587-4771
www.bbhc.org
The West may be wild, but it is not uncivilized. You'll find proof of this in the 290,000-square-foot Buffalo Bill Historical Center filled with art, artifacts, and interactive history exhibits. Within these museum walls you can experience the inspiration of Yellowstone as seen through the eyes (and paintbrush) of famous Hayden Expedition artist Thomas Moran. You can glimpse Buffalo Bill Cody's visionary presence in the history of the American West or experience the inside of a Hidasta Plains Indian lodge.

Founded in 1917 and dubbed the Smithsonian of the West, the BBHC is famous for an artful retelling of the American West through its collection of original paintings by western artists in the Whitney Gallery; the Cody Firearms Museum (the world's largest collection of American firearms); the Buffalo Bill Museum, which, of course, chronicles this legendary figure in one of our country's most exciting periods of growth; and the Plains Indian Museum, with its exhibits of the rich cultural objects and spiritual practices of the many American Indian tribes who inhabited this land before the 19th century. Inside this massive museum you will feel the formality of that characteristic look-don't-touch aura, but there is something else here. The BBHC is also an interpretive center, where you can experience the West through the eyes and ears of a Pony Express rider or a Sioux warrior. This place is alive with culture clashes, hardships, and triumphs of the West.

The recently built Draper Museum addition brings a unique approach to natural history, focusing on the influence of nature on humans and humans' effect on the environment by means of interactive exhibits. You won't be able to overlook its larger-than-life statues of a bison herd in front of the main center. Geared toward all ages, the Draper Museum teaches about the ecology, geology, and biology of the American West along with contemporary influences such as logging, oil development, ranching, and the reintroduction of wolves. But don't mistake this as just another bunch of old things behind glass—when you walk through the doors, you'll embark on a virtual expedition through the four ecosystems of the western environment, from the alpine tundra to the sweeping plains.

You'll want to spend at least a couple days at the center, as a quick run-through doesn't do it justice. Your museum ticket is good for two consecutive days and costs $15 for adults, $13 for seniors, and $6 for kids; children under age 4 are admitted free. A family ticket costs $40. The museum is open year-round but hours vary throughout the year.

CODY MURALS VISITOR CENTER
1719 Wyoming Ave. and Eighteenth
Street
(307) 587-3290
www.codymural.com

When you walk into the Cody Murals Visitor Center, you will get a history lesson of a different kind. The Cody Murals depict the first 70 years of the Latter-day Saints' colonization of Wyoming's Big Horn Basin, beginning with the great immigration of settlers from the East Coast to this region of the West. The early Latter-day Saints overcame hardships on the difficult trip westward in hopes of finding a new life and home to build upon with their faith. Their story is all here in the 18-foot-high mural, which spans the 36-foot-wide dome of Cody's Church of Jesus Christ of Latter-day Saints. Viewing the Cody Murals is free, and the visitor center is open from June 1 to Sept 1.

CODY NITE RODEO
519 West Yellowstone Ave.
(307) 587-5155
www.codystampederodeo.com
Every summer night in Cody is rodeo night. Since a rodeo is a reason to have a party in this part of the country, the town has its own kind of constant festive atmosphere. It's been that way since 1938, when the community rallied together in hopes of luring Yellowstone National Park visitors (and their wallets) to town. The idea stuck, and today that means you get to see a rodeo with true cowboys and rough stock that twist, twirl, buck, and spin. The Cody Nite Rodeo is one big attraction that runs daily from June 1 through Aug 31 at 8 p.m. Grandstand seating costs $18 for adults and $8 for kids. For more information see the Annual Events chapter.

**TRAIL TOWN MUSEUM OF THE
  OLD WEST**
1831 DeMaris Dr., west of Cody
(307) 587-5302
www.museumoftheoldwest.org

Just outside Cody the Old West is alive and well. Trail Town gives you a glimpse into frontier life as you walk along the boardwalks where outlaws Butch Cassidy and the Sundance Kid strolled, where Buffalo Bill strutted, where Jeremiah "Liver Eatin'" Johnston bellied up to the bar. Imagine when times were simpler in these parts, when there were good guys and bad guys, when people didn't have the modern conveniences of electricity, indoor plumbing, or cars. This cluster of 200-plus-year-old buildings stands as a monument to the frontier era. Walking through the dusty main street, you'll feel like you were almost there.

Owner Bob Edgar began collecting historic buildings and relics of the West in the 1960s, when he realized that if these remnants of western settlement deteriorated, so did an important piece of history. The project began as a labor of love for Edgar, who is an archaeologist and western historian. He and his wife, Terry, gathered homestead cabins, livery stables, general stores, and homes with the help of local ranchers and historians. Gradually his collection began to take the shape of a town on a piece of property where the original Cody City had been platted by Buffalo Bill Cody in 1895.

Today Trail Town consists of 26 buildings dating from 1879 to 1901. With more than 100 horse-drawn vehicles and frontier memorabilia, it is the largest collection of its kind in Wyoming. Trail Town is open daily from mid-May until mid-Sept. Admission is $8 for adults, $7 for seniors, $4 for children age 6 to 12 and kids under 6 are free.

PINEDALE, WYOMING

THE MUSEUM OF THE MOUNTAIN MAN
700 East Hennick
P.O. Box 909, Pinedale, WY 82941
(307) 367-4101, (877) 686-6266
www.museumofthemountainman.com
Learn about the romantic and rugged life of the mountain man through an interpretive and visual experience that details the era of the western fur trade. Pinedale and the surrounding Green River Valley were the hub of the Rocky Mountain rendezvous system, where fur traders in the early 1800s gathered once a year to sell their wares to wagon trains going back east. The 15,000-square-foot museum—part of the Sublette County Historical Society—houses exhibits on the fur trade, western exploration, and early settlement of western Wyoming. You can also take a look at famed mountain man Jim Bridger's rifle, watch living-history demonstrations, and listen to lectures. The museum is open daily from May 1 to Sept 30, and is open weekdays only through Oct. Admission is $5 for adults, $4 for senior citizens, and $3 for children ages 6 through 12.

ANNUAL EVENTS

The Yellowstone region is chock-full of all kinds of annual events and activities. Many of them celebrate the area's rich and colorful history, in some cases with live re-creations of life back in the days of the Old West. Still others celebrate the area's vibrant arts and cultural scene or the outdoor recreation opportunities that bring visitors here. As you get to know our area, you'll realize that just about every town has something going on every weekend. And although you may be staying in one of the larger gateway communities, by visiting the smaller, outlying towns you can get a great slice of our life here in Yellowstone Country.

This is just a partial listing, and dates for many events change within a few days every year. Contact local chambers of commerce for more information.

JANUARY

INTERNATIONAL ROCKY MOUNTAIN STAGE STOP SLED DOG RACE
Jackson, WY
(307) 733-3316
www.wyomingstagestop.org
If you've never seen a sled-dog race up close, this is the one to see. The race starts in Jackson and ends in Park City, Utah. Unlike a marathon race where dogs pull for extended periods of time, the stage stop is run in stages like cycling's Tour de France. Spectators are encouraged. The race is gaining in popularity and is drawing top mushers from around the world, who hope to snag a share of the $160,000 purse. If watching the race gives you the urge to mush, several Jackson companies offer sled-dog tours. The opening banquet and closing awards ceremony are also open to the public, but reservations are required.

FEBRUARY

BUFFALO BILL BIRTHDAY BALL
Cody Auditorium, Cody, WY
(307) 587-2777
www.bbhc.org
Of course they celebrate Buffalo Bill's birthday in Cody—he's the fuel for this town's engine. So if you happen to be in town on the Sat before Buffalo Bill's February 26 birthday, it's a great reason to get gussied up to go out and kick up the dust in honor of the western legend. Contact the Cody Chamber of Commerce for the exact date. The only thing you need to get into this annual bash is a turn-of-the-20th-century costume, since you wouldn't want to break tradition. The gala attracts almost 500 people for dinner and dancing. In years past the event has raised more than $70,000 for new exhibits and educational programs at the museum.

RED LODGE WINTER CARNIVAL
Red Lodge Mountain, Red Lodge, MT
(800) 444-8977
www.redlodgemountain.com

Enduring seven or eight months of winter in Red Lodge isn't a bad thing. Most folks just equate it to more time spent skiing and the best time for the annual Winter Carnival. For more than two decades, most of the town has come up to Red Lodge Mountain to watch at least some of the goofy competitions held here. The two-day event has a different theme each year, and everything from the snow sculpture contest to the races is based on the theme. In past years some of the themes were "Under the Sea," "Under the Big Top," "Back to the Future," and "Wild Wild West." The main event is the Cardboard Classic—contestants have to build a vehicle out of cardboard boxes and race down a ski slope to see who crosses the finish line first—optimally the "vehicle" cruises downhill fast enough that the cardboard doesn't have time to get soggy. Some contestants spend weeks designing and assembling their entries only to see them blown to pieces as soon as they hit the snow. Other events take place throughout town, but don't miss your chance to be crowned the carnival's King or Queen at the Snow Ball, where you can dance the night away with your very own royal court of Snowflakes.

MARCH

CLEAN SNOWMOBILE CHALLENGE
Jackson, WY
(307) 733-3316

Check out the future of snowmobiles at the annual Clean Snowmobile Challenge, where students from American and Canadian universities participate in an engineering-design competition aimed at solving the problem of noise and air pollution from snowmobiles in environmentally sensitive areas. Engineering students bring their teams' modified sleds to Jackson and compete against one another in a variety of events, including noise, emissions, acceleration, hill climb, fuel economy, design, and cold start. This event has attracted national recognition since the issue of snowmobiling in the national parks became front-page news in regional newspapers.

NATIONAL FINALS SKI-JORING
Red Lodge Rodeo Grounds,
Red Lodge, MT
(406) 446-1718
www.redlodge.com/ski-joring

Long winters cause some folks to resort to strange ways to pass the time. Skijoring is a case in point. The zany sport requires a strong, fast horse harnessed to pull a skier through an obstacle course of gates and jumps. It's not a pretty sport, but it does entail a certain amount of skill and horse training to ensure that the teams finish the 250-yard course in record time. Just to place in the event, competitors must land upright with at least one ski touching the ground when crossing the finish line. Sounds simple, unless the pony is a wild one. Racing against the clock, teams compete for purses of up to $7,000. This annual competition draws more than 100 teams from across the country (yes, there are that many people who do this) to the Red Lodge Rodeo Grounds. Admission is about $3.

RENDEZVOUS SKI RACE
West Yellowstone, MT
(406) 646-7701
www.rendezvousrace.com

The Rendezvous has been the region's premier cross-country ski event for more than 20-some years. More than 600 skiers compete in courses ranging from 5 to 50 kilometers. It's not just for hard-core racers; anybody can join in on the fun. Registration fees include the race, T-shirt, feed stations, and an awards ceremony. Prizes are awarded in both gender and age categories. The event has a real festival atmosphere and is great if you just want to watch.

TARGHEE TELEMARK FESTIVAL
Grand Targhee, Resort Alta, WY
(800) 227-2054
www.grandtarghee.com
This is a national gathering with an all-star cast of free-heel skiers and clinicians who come together for three days of workshops, guided tours, demos, and evening entertainment. It includes two days of telemark workshops/instruction, a two-day lift ticket, breakfasts, a banquet dinner, evening activities, free equipment demos, and a T-shirt. For expert skiers, an optional backcountry day is available, which includes breakfast and a guide for an additional $65.

WORLD CHAMPIONSHIP
SNOWMOBILE HILL CLIMB
Snow King Resort, Jackson, WY
(307) 734-9653
www.snowdevils.org
It sounds crazy, but people have been doing it for more than 25 years. Thrill-seeking snowmobile riders charge up a 1,500-foot hill at the Snow King ski area, all in the name of competition. The event draws crowds of 10,000 or more each year. Inclines are as steep as 45 degrees and, you guessed it, some of the contestants peter out and don't make it all the way to the top. Winners are

crowned King and Queen of the Hill. The event is held on the fourth weekend in Mar and is sponsored by the Jackson Hole Snow Devils.

WORLD SNOWMOBILE EXPOSITION
West Yellowstone, MT
(406) 646-4383, (800) 736-5276
www.snowmobileexpo.com
This is an event that die-hard snowmobilers wouldn't want to miss, held on the third weekend in Mar. Vendors let you check out all the latest equipment, but the highlight is the adrenaline-pumping SnoWest Snocross Challenge. Competitors race around a tight track with banked turns, jumps, and moguls. This event certainly is not for novices, but it is extremely exciting for sideline sledders. More than 10,000 spectators watch the climb each year.

APRIL

COWBOY SONGS AND RANGE
BALLADS
Buffalo Bill Historical Center, Cody, WY
(307) 578-4028
www.bbhc.org
For more than 20 years cowboy poets and musicians have been gathering in Cody to compete and share their original ballads and music of the Plains and mountain experiences. From fifth-generation ranchers to the new generation of western citizens, this is a gathering of authentic cowboys, young and old. Children's activities are a big part of the festival, held at the Buffalo Bill Historical Center.

POLE-PEDDLE-PADDLE
Jackson, WY
(307) 733-6433
www.polepedalpaddle.com

For more than 25 years this has been an original Jackson event, where individuals and teams race on Alpine and cross-country skis, bicycles, and boats. Hardworking athletes show up every year to test their endurance, and so does the local flavor: Many don hilarious costumes and run the river in less-than-seaworthy contraptions, making the event popular with spectators. It's also a fund-raiser for the Jackson Hole Ski and Snowboard Club's local youth skiing and racing programs.

Cycle Only Days

If you enjoy cycling, plan a trip to West Yellowstone and Yellowstone National Park between Apr 1 and 20 for **Cycle Only Days.** The park is closed to snowmobiles, cars, and buses, so riders have the roads to themselves and there is no entrance fee. From West Yellowstone, you can bike to Madison Junction, Canyon, or Mammoth, but the road between Madison and Old Faithful is closed. Side trips to Hebgen and Quake Lakes west of the park are encouraged, too. It's a great time to take in the splendor of the wildlife and scenery without any other noise—except your own breathing. Call (406) 646-7701 for more information.

✳**POND SKIM**
Big Sky Resort, Big Sky, MT
(406) 995-5000
www.bigskyresort.com

Thousands of spectators gather on closing weekend at Big Sky to watch skiers and snowboarders test their water-skimming ability. Contestants line up on the Ambush ski slope, then take aim at a 100-foot man-made pool of water at the bottom. Those who make it across stay dry, and those who sink typically elicit cheers from the crowd while getting a chilly dunk in the water. The event is followed by live music and a big party in the resort's plaza.

SWEET CORN SKI FESTIVAL
Daisy Pass, Cooke City, MT
(406) 838-2412
For the past decade Cooke City has hosted this spring underground event that takes place in a popular backcountry spot. The event used to draw only the heartiest of local powder hounds. Today it draws spring breakers from all over the state in search of the sweetest snow away from the high-speed trams and crowds at most resorts. Held at Daisy Pass, just 5 miles west of town, snowmobiles shuttle skiers and boarders to the top of the run. More than anything, though, Sweet Corn Festival is a great excuse for a spring party. Call Cooke City Bike Shack at the number above, and speak to Bill Blackford, who organizes the event.

MAY

OLD WEST DAYS
Jackson, WY
(307) 733-3316
www.jacksonholechamber.com
For a taste of the real Wild West of the 1800s, the place to be on Memorial Day weekend is Jackson, where thousands of visitors join the locals for the area's annual Old West Days celebration. The long weekend of activities includes a parade, a chuck-wagon dinner

and concert, bed races, the Mountain Man Rendezvous, a rodeo, and daily events on the town square and Glenwood Street. Cowboy hats and boots, black-powder guns, and Indian trade beads reign during this whooping western weekend.

Although events start Fri morning, the real kickoff is the first "shoot-out," which is held in the town square on Sat. Gunslingers give a western reenactment that pits the good guys against the bad, giving onlookers a taste of frontier justice. Old West Days include the first regular rodeo of the season on Sat night, live country music throughout the weekend, and historic walking tours of Jackson. At the Mountain Man Rendezvous you'll find a historically authentic camp, from tepees to campfire-cooked grub. The event concludes on Sun with the often-hilarious bed races, a local favorite.

i If it's your first time in Jackson, you must check out the Shoot-Out Gang, a live reenactment of cowboy gunfighters held every Sat from Memorial Day through Labor Day in the town square. It's been a tradition since 1957—the longest-running shoot-out in the country—and the gunslingin' gets under way at 6:15 p.m. Reservations are not required, and it's free.

JUNE

ANNUAL BEARTOOTH RUN AND RIDE
Beartooth Highway, Red Lodge, MT
(406) 446-1718
www.beartoothevents.com
When the snow finally melts off America's most beautiful highway, you know it's time for the Annual Beartooth Run. An unofficial celebration of the highway's yearly opening, this 8.2-mile race begins 14 miles south of

Red Lodge at 7,000 feet and switchbacks up US 212 to the finish line at 9,000 feet. A true test of mind and body, the course covers some of the most scenic (and breathtaking) high-altitude terrain in the region. Runners are congratulated with a picnic and awards ceremony at the finish line.

CODY GUNSLINGERS
The Irma Hotel, Cody, WY
(307) 587-4221
You'll see them slink out from the shadows of the building, their spurs jingling, their eyes slanted, hands ready to pull out the six-shooters. Every summer the Cody gunslingers transform the modern streets of town into a Wild West standoff. The fastest shots in the West, they get a lot of practice every evening except Sun from Memorial Day to Labor Day on the steps of Buffalo Bill Cody's historic Irma Hotel. The show is surprisingly realistic; the 13 actors research and represent authentic Wild West characters such as Bill Hickok, Flatnose George, and Calamity Jane. There's no admission fee.

✳CODY NITE RODEO
Stampede Park Rodeo Grounds, Cody, WY
(307) 587-2992
www.codystampederodeo.com
Every summer for more than 70 years, Jim and Cathy Ivory have been giving people what they want: a rodeo with cowboys and rough stock that twist, twirl, buck, and spin. Fans sit on the edge of their seats until the buzzer sounds and the judges' scores are announced—and not just for one night, but every night from June 1 until Aug 31. Though this rodeo is geared toward tourists (the guy driving up and down Sheridan Avenue with a blow horn advertising the night's event is your first clue to this), that

Picking Up Some Slack

In rodeo the majority of contestants compete in the "slack" events, held after, before, and between the scheduled rodeo. Every rodeo producer wants to keep the regular show short and engaging, so only a handful of cowboys compete in front of packed stands. Watching the slack competition can be just as intense and interesting as the main rodeo and can get you closer to the cowboys.

If you can't make it to one of the larger rodeos, stop in at Jackson's J. H. Rodeo, held at the rodeo grounds on Snow King Avenue every Wed and Sat at 8 p.m. throughout the summer. It features all seven main events, reserved grandstand seating, and plenty of up-close views along the arena fence. Any family can get in for $40, and there's free parking. Call (307) 733-2805 or visit www .jhrodeo.com for advance tickets and information.

doesn't mean it's just a show. The Ivorys raise calves, bulls, and broncs renowned for their feisty character; many of them are destined for the pro rodeo circuit. But more than that, the cowboys at this rodeo are the real thing. Sure, some of them are tired old-timers, but their heart and soul are into the sport. Other competitors here are in training for professional careers in rodeo.

The Ivorys make the Cody Nite Rodeo very accessible; a rodeo bus will pick you up at your campground or motel. Grandstand

seating is $18 for adults, $8 for children. Tickets for the 8 p.m. show can be purchased at the gate after 7 p.m., at the ticket-booth wagon in City Park, at many Cody businesses, at the chamber of commerce office, and at the website.

PLAINS INDIAN POWWOW
Robbie Powwow Garden,
Buffalo Bill Historical Center, Cody, WY
(406) 587-4771
www.bbhc.org
Beads, feathers, buckskin, and leather move to the rhythm of the Northern Plains Indian powwow drums each June in Cody. Sponsored by the Buffalo Bill Historical Society, the Plains Indian Powwow celebrated its 25th anniversary in 2007. American Indian performers from the Crow, Shoshone, Sioux, and Bannock Nations compete in dance and musical contests. The atmosphere is a festive and enthralling celebration of many different cultures all at once. Adults and children alike will be mesmerized by the movement and color of the dancers' traditional garb as they compete for prize money.

JULY

BEARTOOTH RALLY
Red Lodge Rodeo Grounds,
Red Lodge, MT
(406) 446-1718, (406) 664-3241
www.beartoothrally.com
Every summer hundreds of Harley-Davidson motorcycle enthusiasts pass through Red Lodge to tour the scenic Beartooth Highway. But during the third week in July the town resounds with the distinct rumble of countless bikes for the Beartooth Rally. The weekend is highlighted by the Highway 212 Poker Run, a 120-mile race that begins in Red Lodge and continues to Cooke City

and then over the Chief Joseph Highway and comes roaring down to Belfry at the Bearcreek Downs (home of the famous pig races). The purse for the event is $2,000 and attracts racers from all over the country. Next is the Iron Horse Rodeo (held at the Home of Champions Rodeo Grounds), where riders compete in barrel racing, obstacle courses, and other events. But you don't even need to own a "hog" to take in the live music and festive atmosphere in local bars and businesses—everyone is welcome.

CODY STAMPEDE RODEO
Stampede Park Rodeo Grounds,
Cody, WY
(406) 587-5155
www.codystampederodeo.com
If you don't believe that Cody is the Rodeo Capital of the World, then you haven't been to the Stampede. The excitement starts with a wild-horse race, where a team of cowboys chases down a wild horse and tries to saddle it. And if that doesn't impress you, then consider the fact that this is the richest rodeo a cowboy can win on July Fourth. Each year the rodeo's purse is $300,000, which is important in a sport where the cowboy with the most winnings qualifies for the National Finals Rodeo Championship at the end of the year. This kind of money draws the best players to the table. Most of the top hands on the national circuit show up here over the Fourth of July for at least one event before they fly off in a private jet to take in another competition in Red Lodge or Livingston. Even with more than 700 contestants, the Stampede is a fast-moving, top-notch rodeo with world-class stock. Admission ranges from $13 to $21, and the slack events are free.

ENNIS RODEO
Ennis, MT
(406) 682-4700
This annual rodeo is one of the most exciting and challenging rodeos in the state and is sanctioned by the Northern Rodeo Association. It includes standard events and attracts top cowboys and cowgirls from around the region. The fact that it takes place on Fourth of July weekend gives the two-day event a party atmosphere, and there are many other activities going on in town as well. Rodeo hours are 8 to 11 p.m. Sat and 2 to 5 p.m. Sun.

GALLATIN COUNTY FAIR
Gallatin County Fairgrounds,
Bozeman, MT
(406) 582-3270
www.gallatin.mt.gov
This weeklong event is fun for all ages and is representative of small-town Montana life. No beauty contest here, but ranchers love the livestock competitions and shows. Most of the fair centers around the area's rich history of agriculture, and there are numerous animal displays, commercial exhibits, arts and crafts, and music activities. There is also a four-wheel-drive mud bog, auto racing, theater, dancing, and storytelling. Youngsters love the wild carnival rides, too. Fair hours are Wed through Sat 10 a.m. to 10 p.m. and Sun 10 a.m. to 5 p.m. To get to the fairgrounds, head east on Tamarack Street from North Seventh Avenue. The grounds will be on your left; you can't miss them.

✳GRAND TETON MUSIC FESTIVAL
Jackson, WY
(307) 733-1128
www.gtmf.org
This world-renowned music festival has been bringing contemporary and classical music

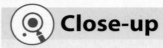 Close-up

Small-Town Shakespeare

Ahhh, the joys of summer. Floating and fishing on the river, lying in the sun, backpacking and . . . Shakespeare?

Well, we folks in Yellowstone Country are lucky enough to have **Montana Shakespeare in the Parks,** a professional Montana State University–based troupe that brings the Bard's plays to towns around the region. Even Birney—a small town in southeastern Montana with a population of 17—gets into the act.

The Shakespeare Festival is a summer tradition for many of us. Grab a picnic dinner, a blanket, and a bottle of wine and enjoy an evening of outdoor theater at its best. When the sun sets behind the stage on a beautiful Yellowstone evening, there aren't many better places to be, and it reminds us how lucky we are to live here.

Artistic Director Joel Jahnke has been with the touring company for most of the company's three decades in operation, and the Bard's works never lose their excitement. "Every time I do one, I gain more admiration for his work as a playwright," he says. "Working with gifted actors and designers, unlocking the magic there, his genius folds out for me anew." Jahnke picks two plays a year and hires actors from as far away as Seattle and Chicago. Many return each year, citing the incredible experience of bringing theater to small towns that don't exactly have many cultural activities. Up to 30,000 people see the shows each year.

Performances begin in Bozeman at the university around mid-June, and then travel from town to town through Montana, Wyoming, North Dakota, and Idaho. All performances are free, with the exception of the shows at Bozeman's Sweet Pea Festival of the Arts in early Aug.

For information on summer shows and schedules, call (406) 994-3310 or check out www2.montana.edu/shakespeare.

to Jackson for more than 30 years. Most of the 42 concerts take place in the Walk Festival Hall in Teton Village. The music lasts eight weeks from July through Aug, with at least two festival orchestras and two chamber music recitals per week, plus a 200-member resident company of players from all over the country. The festival includes numerous open rehearsals and children's programs.

GREEN RIVER RENDEZVOUS PAGEANT
Pinedale, WY
(307) 367-2242
www.meetmeonthegreen.com

This annual event on the second full weekend in July celebrates the region's rich fur-trade history and attracts modern-day mountain men and women from all over the country. The pageant is a colorful re-creation of the fur-trade rendezvous of the 19th century, when trappers would meet the supply wagons from back east to trade the fruits of a year's worth of work in the wilderness. There's also a rodeo each night at 7 p.m. The site of the celebration is only a few miles from the original rendezvous site on the Green River. Pinedale is about 88 miles south of Jackson on US 191.

HOME OF CHAMPIONS RODEO
Red Lodge Rodeo Grounds, Red
Lodge, MT
(406) 446-1718
www.redlodgerodeo.com

Red Lodge is the small town with the big rodeo. After more than 70 years, the Home of Champions Rodeo boasts some of Montana's most notable rodeo heroes and heroines, including the well-known Greenoughs and the Lindermans. Sisters Alice and Marge Greenough, raised on a ranch outside Red Lodge, were champion bronc riders who went all the way to Madison Square Garden in New York. Their brother, Turk, and Alice rode into fame from the 1920s clear into the 1950s. Held July 2, 3, and 4, Home of Champions is a Professional Rodeo Cowboys Association event and is part of what competitors refer to as the "Cowboy Christmas" circuit—there are so many professional rodeo events during this three-day period that it's considered better than Christmas. If you watch carefully you'll see cowboys arriving by private plane on the runway adjacent to the arena. They show up just in time to compete in their individual events before flying off to another rodeo. Few other places take their rodeo so seriously; in Red Lodge that means it's a great party. Admission ranges from $15 to $20.

LIVINGSTON ROUNDUP RODEO
Park County Fair Grounds,
Livingston, MT
(406) 222-0850

In 1883 the town of Livingston was the first in Montana Territory to hold an Independence Day celebration with a parade and rodeo. The party was a hit, and the Livingston Roundup Rodeo, which takes place on July 2, 3, and 4, is still around. Events kick off on the first day with a quaint hometown parade through historic downtown, and then at 8 p.m. the Professional Rodeo Cowboy Association events begin. You'll see some of the best in the business compete in bareback, saddle bronc, calf roping, steer wrestling, bull riding, team roping, and barrel racing. The Livingston Roundup is one of three Gateway Rodeos held over the Fourth of July weekend and offers cowboys the opportunity to make more prize money at one time than at any other time of the year. Competitors travel between Livingston, Cody, and Red Lodge, chartering private planes in order to squeeze in as many events as possible. Prize money for the Livingston Roundup alone is more than $60,000. Every evening begins with skydivers swooping into the arena and ends with an impressive blast of fireworks. Admission is $12 for reserved seats, $8 for general admission, and $4 for children ages 6 to 12.

i On Wednesday from mid-July through the beginning of September, look for "Lunch on the Lawn" in Bozeman at the Emerson Cultural Center, 111 South Grand Ave. Just a block from historic downtown, you'll find a gathering of families, businesspeople on lunch break, and plenty of others enjoying live music from local bands. Admission is free, and food, beverages, and ice cream are available. Music starts at 11 a.m. and plays until 1 p.m.

MUSIC IN THE MOUNTAINS
Big Sky, MT
(406) 995-2742
www.bigskyarts.org

The nonprofit Arts Council of Big Sky puts on great summer concerts at their outdoor pavilion in the Town Center Park. There are free concerts at 7 p.m. every Thur in July and Aug, as well as other performances and at least one headlining national act each summer. These concerts are a great way to see world-class performers in an intimate, beautiful setting, with majestic Lone Mountain as the backdrop. Performances cover a variety of genres, and you can bring in anything you want to the concert, except glass. Grab a cooler and a picnic lunch and enjoy music in the mountains under the big sky. The organization also helps sponsor Big Sky's Community Celebration Day on July Fourth, with live music and fireworks in a spectacular mountain setting.

RENDEZVOUS AT RED LODGE
US 212, north of Red Lodge, MT
(406) 446-1718
www.redlodge.com/rendezvous
Walk into the 1800s fur-trading era at the Mountain Man Rendezvous near Red Lodge. Held the first week of July, the event is a modern-day reenactment of the Rocky Mountain gatherings that brought trappers, American Indians, buffalo hunters, whiskey runners, and horse traders together for trading and festivities. This 10-day event attracts more than 1,000 people who come to relive a tradition that was once so integral to life in the 19th century. Mountain-man enthusiasts come to sell their wares—buckskin clothes, blankets, knives, beads, buffalo robes, quilts, and artwork. Black-powder gun clubs come together for shooting competitions, and others come to read cowboy poetry and play music. Admission is free but donations are accepted.

TARGHEE FEST
Grand Targhee Ski and Summer Resort,
Alta, WY
(800) 827-4433
www.grandtarghee.com
This three-day music festival typically takes place on the second or third week in July and celebrates acoustic-based Americana, folk, blues, and roots music. Great food, vendors, games, and on-site activities are all a part of the festival. Tent camping at Grand Targhee is available during the festival weekend in addition to resort lodging options.

TETON VALLEY BALLOON FEST
Teton Valley, ID
(208) 354-2500
Three towns—Driggs, Victor, and Tetonia—make up the Teton Valley, which you'll find at the west end of Teton Pass going from Jackson into Idaho. The Balloon Fest takes place at the Teton County Fairgrounds, where balloonists from around the country converge to float giant, magnificently colored hot-air balloons over the valley, with the striking Tetons as their backdrop. The event occurs in the first week of July and coincides with Victor's annual Old Time Fiddler's Contest in Victor and the Mountain Arts Celebration.

AUGUST

BARK IN THE PARK
Sacajawea Park Band Shell,
Livingston, MT
(406) 222-2111
Dog lovers converge on this quaint park on the banks of the Yellowstone River with live music, food vendors, a crafts fair, and children's activities. A fund-raising benefit for the private, nonprofit Stafford Animal Shelter, the event is kicked off by a 5-kilometer walkathon. The highlight of the party features

lighthearted canine contests showcasing Best Tail Wag, Best Bark, and Best Smile. Bring your own pooch for some fun, and support the local animal shelter.

BIG SKY FESTIVAL OF THE ARTS AND COUNTRY FAIR
Town Center Park, Big Sky, MT
(406) 995-3000
www.bigskychamber.com
Typically held on the first weekend in Aug, this family-friendly event features more than 100 artisans displaying their wares, live music, and kids activities. A parade and 5K race kick off the morning, and the event lasts until 5 p.m. There is always a variety of food vendors to keep you satiated during the day.

BUFFALO DAYS
Downtown Gardiner, MT
(406) 848-7971
This event is like an old, small-town block party, with dinner and dancing on Main Street. The music starts at noon and so do the vittles—barbecue, coleslaw, potato salad, and all the other good stuff. The whole town dances until the wee hours and takes part in a host of kids' activities, such as the potato sack races and a dunking booth where local celebrities get drenched again and again. A combination end-of-the-season celebration and fund-raiser for the Gardiner Ambulance Service, the event is weather dependent. If all goes well the fun begins the Sat of Labor Day weekend. Admission fees vary.

FESTIVAL OF NATIONS
Lion's Park, Red Lodge, MT
(406) 446-1718
www.festivalofnations.us
Don't miss the chance to find cannoli, lederhosen, Guinness beer, and cloggers all together at Red Lodge's Festival of Nations in Aug. This remote mountain town is an unlikely place to encounter such an array of cultural diversity, but its heritage stems from Scandinavian, Finnish, Italian, Slavic, German, Swiss, Austrian, and Scottish ancestors. Brought to the area in the 1800s with coal-mining and railroad jobs, these immigrants were initially at odds with one another. Neighborhoods in town were segregated into their own Little Italy, Finn section, and the High Bug District for more affluent Brits. Cultural barriers were scarcely crossed until the early 1930s, when the Festival of Nations was conceived to encourage some friendly intermingling. Because it was started during the Great Depression, it seemed that Red Lodgians knew they needed to rely on their neighbors, regardless of their nationality. The idea stuck. Currently the three-day event is packed with parades, dancing, music, and food. There is no admission fee.

✳SWEET PEA FESTIVAL OF THE ARTS
Lindley Park, Bozeman, MT
(406) 586-4003
www.sweetpeafestival.org
The first Sweet Pea Carnival was held on August 11, 1906, as a way to publicize Bozeman and the Gallatin Valley. The sweet pea flower was chosen as a symbol for its beauty, fragrance, and availability, and locals now compete for the best-looking one. More than 100 years later, the annual event has evolved into one of the biggest festivals in Montana, drawing upward of 18,000 people each day.

Held during the first full weekend of Aug, the Sweet Pea Festival of the Arts now spans three days and is a showcase for local and national artists, musicians, and thespians. The festival kicks off with the annual

Sweet Pea Run on Fri morning (participants must register ahead). After the parade on Sat, the action moves to East Main Street's Lindley Park. More than 100 artisans show their wares, while numerous stages present programs for kids and adults. Things get going around 10 a.m. Sat and Sun, with headlining national bands performing in the Bowl during the evening. There's tons of food, lots of kids, and an overall family atmosphere. You need a Sweet Pea button to get in, and you can purchase one at various locations around town or at the door. Admission is $15, good for all three days. Motel rooms fill up early this weekend, so plan ahead.

TARGHEE BLUEGRASS FESTIVAL
Grand Targhee Ski and Summer Resort, Alta, WY
(800) 827-4433
www.grandtarghee.com
This popular three-day music festival is fast becoming one of the premier bluegrass festivals in the country and is a yearly weekend journey for many of the region's bluegrass and folk lovers. Fri night typically features a regional band in one of the bars at the base of the ski resort, while Sat and Sun the music goes all day and into the evening. Part of the allure of the festival is the backdrop—beautiful alpine meadows and the peaks of the Tetons. Grand Targhee is located about 42 miles west of Jackson over the pass.

WEST YELLOWSTONE ROD RUN
West Yellowstone, MT
(800) 426-3148
This event marked its 40th anniversary in 2010, making it the oldest Rod Run in the Northwest. Street rods, custom cars, and special-interest vehicles cram the streets of West Yellowstone for four days. Participate in poker runs, tours, games, and other events that lead up to the big car show on the final day.

WILD WEST BALLOON FEST
Mentock Park, Cody, WY
(307) 527-7120, (307) 587-6122
Seeing 25 hot-air balloons tethered together at dusk in Cody's Mentock Park during early Aug, you will wonder if there has ever been a more beautiful sunset. The colorful silk balloons hover over town and cast a festive glow in anticipation of the two-day Wild West Balloon Fest. For a decade balloonists have come from throughout the region to participate in races and other fun competitions, but mostly just to show off their rigs. You can watch the crews inflate and launch their balloons and then track their skyway path across town. The best part, however, is when you get to take a ride and see Cody from up high. Balloon rides are available for a fee.

SEPTEMBER

FLY FISHING FESTIVAL
Wild Rose Park, Ennis, MT
www.madisonriverfoundation.org
Barbecues, banquets, and musical entertainment are all part of this fall festival, but people who attend don't lose track of their passion for fly fishing. Fly-tying clinics, casting competitions, gear shows, and good old-fashioned camaraderie are the backbone of the annual gathering. Come Sept Ennis's fishing season is hardly winding down; in fact, it stays in high gear until it gets too cold to cast your fly into the Madison River.

JACKSON HOLE FALL ARTS FESTIVAL
Jackson, WY
(307) 733-3316

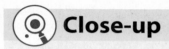 **Close-up**

Bozeman's Sweet Pea Festival

It was not so long ago that southwestern Montana's Gallatin Valley was known as the sweet pea capital of the nation.

At the turn of the 20th century, a variety of edible sweet peas grew so prolifically here that 17,000 acres were planted with crops that produced both seed peas and canning peas. Local farmers grew the crops and sold them to the Bozeman Canning Company, which later processed peas for the government to feed US troops during World War I. In the end, 16,334 cases rolled off the production line during that period.

Capitalizing on the prolific agricultural product, local businessmen in Bozeman hatched the idea of a Sweet Pea Carnival to celebrate the area's prosperity and to encourage visitors. The nonedible but fragrant and colorful sweet pea flower became the symbol of the festival.

In 1906 an unpaved Main Street was the thoroughfare for some 200 floats decorated with thousands of sweet pea blossoms in the city's first parade. Trumpets heralded the start of the parade, followed with floats pulled by showy white horses, marching bands, and, as a finale—the Sweet Pea Queen in her carriage.

"Amongst all the flowers which grow in such perfection and profusion here, there is one flower which seems as though nature herself has designed it to be grown at this particular spot where it has reached a perfection of growth, of form and color never before attained. That flower is the sweet pea, which has been selected as emblematic of the productiveness of the valley and the beauty of the city of Bozeman," said Lord High Chancellor J. A. Luce in an opening speech at that first Sweet Pea Carnival.

By the second year of the Sweet Pea Carnival, local merchants welcomed 10,000 visitors and their pocketbooks to town. To advertise the summer's carnival, boxes of the fragrant flowers were sent to neighboring communities. In town, well-dressed young women passed out bouquets of sweet peas to female passengers on trains coming through town, a tradition that lasted long after the carnival.

But by 1914 the annual event lost its gusto when blight wiped out the sweet pea crop. Townspeople complained that they were tired of the dusty Main Street and that it did not impress visitors, and enthusiasm for a summer carnival faded. Two years later the 1916 Sweet Pea Queen was crowned for a long reign at the last festival.

It wasn't until 1977 that the perfumed sweet pea was honored again in a revival of the celebration. The first Sweet Pea Festival was organized by local artists seeking a voice in the community. Since then the weeklong event has added dancing, painting, theater performances, competitions, parades, and food throughout the town. When 2,500 people showed up for the event, it was considered a success. Today Bozeman doesn't need to advertise the festivities outside town, since it draws more than 20,000 patrons each year. The series of lively shows and activities are now organized by an army of people who work throughout the year on an entirely volunteer basis. The Sweet Pea Festival has become an event that celebrates not only the arts but also the spirit of community.

This much-anticipated event shows off the top 100 entries of the national Arts for the Parks competition, along with shows, programs, workshops, and cultural events. The festival lasts 10 days, beginning in mid-Sept. This popular festival, which was started in 1985 as a way to showcase Jackson Hole's world-class art scene, also includes a silent auction, music, and chances to meet the artist who designed the annual poster you'll see hanging around town.

PATRON'S BALL
Buffalo Bill Historical Center, Cody, WY
(307) 587-2777
www.bbhc.org
You never know who you might see at this gala event: Ted Turner and Peter Fonda have both attended in past years. The grand black-tie affair includes dinner and dancing inside the BBHC and draws more than 600 guests. This elegant finale to the weeklong Rendez-vous Royale is a fund-raiser for the museum.

RENDEZVOUS ROYALE
Buffalo Bill Historical Center, Cody, WY
(307) 587-2777
www.rendezvousroyale.org
This weeklong event includes the well-known Buffalo Bill art show and sale, and is a fund-raiser for the Buffalo Bill Historical Center. The show features local and regional artists. Other events include Cody High Style, live and quick draw auctions, and the Patrons Ball gala—one of the premier social events in the Rockies.

OCTOBER

BRIDGER RAPTOR FESTIVAL
Bridger Bowl Ski Area, Bozeman, MT
(406) 582-0526
www.bridgerraptorfest.org

This is not your average festival. There are no carnival rides, cotton candy, or parades here, just the peace and tranquility of trying to spot some of the 17 different species of birds of prey that make their home in the northern Bridger Range. Witness the largest known migration of golden eagles in North America soaring over the range's knife-edge ridge as they head south. Festival activities include slide shows on raptor identification, kids' programs, and a birds-of-prey presentation with ambassador eagles, owls, and hawks from Big Sky Wildcare Raptor Center. There's also a 2-mile hiking trail with prime viewing locations. This event is held during the first week of Oct; be sure to call ahead for specific dates.

YELLOWSTONE NATIONAL PARK/OLD FAITHFUL FALL CYCLE TOUR
West Yellowstone, MT
(406) 646-7701
www.cycleyellowstone.com
When the tourist traffic thins and the aspens line the winding roads with a golden hue, 350 cyclists roll through Yellowstone. The bike ride begins in West Yellowstone and ends at the Old Faithful Inn. This easy cruise covers about 60 miles to the inn and back. Sag wagons carry water and medical support. Riders should bring their own sack lunch and snacks. The fee is $25, and proceeds benefit the Yellowstone Park Foundation.

NOVEMBER

TOWN SQUARE LIGHTING CELEBRATION
Downtown Jackson, WY
(307) 733-3316
Jackson's famous town square—you know, the one with the antlers—comes alive in winter as snow blankets the ground and the

lights go up. On the first Fri after Thanksgiving, townsfolk gather in the square to celebrate the season with refreshments, caroling, and plenty of western holiday cheer.

YELLOWSTONE SKI FESTIVAL
West Yellowtone, MT
www.yellowstoneskifestival.com
For more than 30 years, cross-country skiers from across North America and around the world have traveled here to begin their Nordic season at the world-class Rendezvous trail system. There are races, clinics, gear demonstrations, and more during the event, which takes place around Thanksgiving week each year.

DECEMBER

CHRISTMAS STROLL
Main Street, Bozeman, MT
(406) 586-4008
www.downtownbozeman.org
No matter how cold it is or how much snow is on the ground, Bozeman residents take to the streets in droves for this popular event, usually held the first Sat in Dec from 4:30 to 7:30 p.m. The city closes Main Street's downtown section, and vendors and artisans line the streets. Shops stay open into the evening, hoping to lure buyers in to purchase Christmas gifts. More than anything, this is one of Bozeman's premier social events, as it is a great way to run into people, wish them holiday cheer, and warm up with a cup of hot chocolate.

SANTA ON THE SQUARE
Town Square, Jackson, WY
(307) 733-3316
Visiting Santa on the Jackson town square has become a tradition for many local families and holiday visitors. Santa listens to holiday wishes at the Stage Stop building near the elk antler arches and the main entrance to the town square. You can visit Santa Dec 15 through 24 from 5 to 7 p.m.

KIDSTUFF

When Yellowstone National Park was first opened to the public at large, it was dubbed "Wonderland." Back in the 1800s the area's geysers, mountains, and animal life were unimaginable. Well, all the wonder of the place is still here. And today with the wide-open spaces, wildlife, Wild West shows, and wilderness to experience, there couldn't be a better vacation spot for kids. Out here, folks know that visiting Yellowstone and Grand Teton National Parks is a family affair. There are countless activities, celebrations, and contests to keep the kids having fun and enjoying this place as much as their parents. The following suggestions are listed in alphabetical order rather than geographical, but most communities are extremely kid friendly and will happily refer you to additional activities.

A IS FOR ART & ACTING

Every Aug in downtown Bozeman, Montana, kids cover the sidewalks with drawings for the annual **"Chalk on the Walk"** as part of the Sweet Pea Festival. Also in Bozeman check out **Beall Park Art Center and the Emerson Cultural Center,** 111 South Grand Ave., (406) 587-9797, where kids (ages 6 and older) can learn to sculpt, paint, or make their own paper in summer art workshops.

You'll have to learn to think on your feet at **Bozeman's Equinox Theatre Camp,** 2304 North Seventh Ave., (406) 587-0737, a summer program for kids ages 8 and older where instructors use improvisational acting to encourage self-expression and general silliness. At the **Livingston Art Center,** 119 South Main St., (406) 222-5222, children ages 4 and older can practice painting, writing, drawing, and craft skills throughout the year.

Check out the Young at Art program at **Jackson's National Museum of Wildlife Art,** 2820 Rungius Rd., (307) 732-5437. Jan through Mar they offer art classes for toddlers ages 5 and under, accompanied by their caregiver, focusing on the simple art concepts of color, shape, texture, and line. Children will learn about art and animals by looking at works in the museum galleries and doing fun, hands-on activities.

B IS FOR BEARS

If you aren't lucky enough to see the native grizzly or brown bear in the wild, try the **West Yellowstone Grizzly and Wolf Discovery Center,** 201 South Canyon St., (406) 646-7001 or (800) 257-2570. Here you'll see eight grizzlies searching for food and playing in a somewhat natural habitat of the 1.8-acre area. Across from the bears is a one-acre wolf exhibit, where these other elusive creatures live all year. Most of the animals in captivity were abandoned as babies or would otherwise have been destroyed. A wildlife biologist is on hand to answer questions. A visit to the Grizzly Discovery Center helps preserve grizzlies in the wild through the nonprofit international Grizzly Fund.

In Red Lodge the **Beartooth Nature Center,** (406) 446-1133, provides educational experiences with black bears in captivity. You will also see moose, mountain lions, foxes, bobcats, and wolves here; most of the animals are unable to return to the wild because of injury or human-related problems. You might even have the opportunity to pet some of the orphaned native animals in the petting zoo. The best time to see the animals is in the morning when the staff feeds them. Check out the Attractions chapter for additional information.

C IS FOR CLIMBING

. . . rocks and trees, walls, and mountains. During the regular school year, Cody, Wyoming, kids hurry to the **Cody Rock Gym,** 1314 Sheridan Ave., (307) 587-5222, to try out the challenging indoor climbing walls. In summer the gym is not very busy, but it makes for a great rainy-day activity and a safe environment to learn the sport.

The indoor wall at **Teton Rock Gym,** 1116 Maple Way, Jackson Hole, Wyoming, (307) 733-0707, can accommodate more than a dozen climbers at a time, with artificial holds and vertical and overhung walls. Climbing holds are arranged differently every few weeks. Lessons and equipment rental are available afternoons and evenings throughout the year.

There is also an excellent indoor climbing facility in Bozeman, the **Spire Climbing Center,** (406) 586-0706. Spire features summer camps and youth programs, including after-school climbing camps.

D IS FOR DINOSAURS

Some of the world's largest dinosaur fossil deposits have been unearthed in Montana and Wyoming. To view a life-size skeleton of a T. rex, go to the **Museum of the Rockies** in Bozeman, Montana, 600 West Kagy Blvd., (406) 994-2251. There you will find a fun and educational interactive exhibit that teaches children about these prehistoric creatures. Short videos, presentations, and lifelike dinosaurs will keep them fascinated.

E IS FOR ELK HABITAT

The Greater Yellowstone Area is home to about 40 percent of North America's majestic ungulates. (That's how wildlife biologists refer to them because their hooves are split.) Approximately 900,000 elk living between the United States and Canada prefer higher elevations in summer and move to mountain meadows when the snows drive them down to the lowland. You can see about 12,000 Rocky Mountain elk at the **Jackson Hole National Elk Refuge** from Oct through Apr. The state of Wyoming feeds the animals due to harsh winters and because prime grazing land has been developed for towns or agriculture.

For a closer look at the herds, take a sleigh ride. Rides leave three or four times per hour from the **Jackson Hole and Greater Yellowstone Visitor Center,** US 26/89/191, (307) 733-9212, in Jackson, Wyoming. There are other sanctioned feeding areas throughout the Jackson area and also one just north of Gardiner, Montana, where it is common for elk to walk down any street in the tiny town or to lie on the front lawn of the high school.

F IS FOR FISHING

Whether fishing to you means dropping a worm on a hook into a lake or learning the entomology of the Yellowstone River, you'll find plenty of places to cast your line on your vacation. The bridge in Livingston's **Sacaja-wea Park** is a favorite fishing hole for local kids. You are almost guaranteed to catch something since the pond is stocked with rainbow and brown trout each Aug for the Livingston Kids Trout Derby; call the Livingston Chamber of Commerce, (406) 222-0850, for registration details. If you throw your line into the **Bozeman Ponds** on the west end of town next to the Gallatin Valley Mall, 2825 West Main St., chances are good that you'll hook a rainbow, brook, or brown trout.

Teton Valley, Idaho, and Jackson, Wyoming, both have kids-only fishing spots. In Jackson it's **Flat Creek,** which meanders quietly across town and is reserved just for kids within city limits. In Teton Valley, it's the **Trail Creek Pond** at the base of Teton Pass, fenced safely away from ID 33, surrounded by blooming yellow mules' ears and bright-green picnic tables. Wherever you are, call a local fishing shop for recommendations.

In **Yellowstone National Park** the Park Service, (307) 344-7381, offers a ranger-led "Fly Fishing for Families" course in the summer; it's a great way to learn about aquatic ecosystems, trout, and the importance of catch-and-release fishing.

i In Yellowstone National Park fishing permits are required for kids age 11 and older.

G IS FOR GOLF

. . . miniature golf, that is. In Cody, Wyoming, the lush **Cody Mini Golf Course,** (307)

Yellowstone for Families

Yellowstone for Families is a program designed in cooperation with the Yellowstone Institute to introduce kids ages 8 to 12 to the wonders of Yellowstone through adventure-based programs. Families learn together about tracking animals, watching wildlife, taking photographs, or capturing scenery with paint. The learning-and-lodging package is available from July to mid-Aug. In summer 2010 a four-day, five-night session cost $639 plus tax per adult, based on double occupancy; $385 for children ages 8 to 12. For information and reservations call (866) 439-7375 or, or go to www.yellowstoneassociation.org.

587-3685, is right across from the chamber of commerce on Sheridan Avenue. Owned by the city, this golf course is open from Memorial Day until Labor Day. In summertime in Jackson, Wyoming, you can play miniature golf at the base of **Snow King Mountain;** call (307) 733-5200.

H IS FOR HOT SPRINGS

Summer or winter, the hot water is soothing and fun to play in. Look for cool pools, too, at public swimming facilities throughout the region. But the hot spots are unique, ranging from commercial pools to natural "hot pots" within Yellowstone's boundaries.

Inside Yellowstone National Park you'll be thrilled by the chance to soak in the

Boiling River, about 10 miles past Mammoth Hot Springs. After a short mile-long stroll on a flat path, you'll see steam rising on your left and a thermal stream that flows into the Gardner River. In the natural pools you can feel the freezing currents of the river blend with the scalding thermal flow to equal a just-right temperature for soaking. Jump into the **Firehole River Swimming Hole** in Yellowstone. Pack a picnic and steer your parents toward Firehole Canyon Drive (you'll see it on the Yellowstone National Park map they give you at the entrance gate). The road is just south of Madison Junction on the west side of the Madison–Old Faithful Road. Keep on going until you come to the Firehole River Swimming Hole. The only way you'll miss it is if your eyes are shut.

Just 30 miles north of Gardiner, Montana, is **Chico Hot Springs Lodge,** (406) 333-4933, where two naturally heated pools glisten in the cool mountain air, waiting for you to enjoy a game of volleyball or tag. Between Bozeman and Big Sky, Montana, you'll find **Bozeman Hot Springs,** (406) 586-6492, which houses seven pools of different temperatures under one roof. While you romp in the water, Mom and Dad can enjoy a spa treatment at this elaborate facility. In Idaho, just 35 miles southeast of Pocatello, you must find **Lava Hot Springs,** (800) 423-8597. Enjoy the Olympic-size pool in the summer for lap swimming and several different temperatures of hot pools. The Lava Hot Springs resort is open year-round.

I IS FOR ICE SKATING

Sharpen up your blades and skate your way through Yellowstone Country. In Bozeman, Montana, there are three free ice-skating rinks. At **Southside Park** on West College Street and South Seventh Avenue, you can play a pickup game of hockey or just skate. **Beall Park** at Villard and Black Streets offers broom ball on certain days of the week and recreational skating the rest of the time. If you are serious about hockey, head for **Bogert Park** at 325 South Church Ave. or Haynes Pavilion at the Gallatin County Fairgrounds.

In Livingston, Montana, you can get a taste for the way ice skating used to be—the beautiful but ungroomed pond in **Sacajawea Park** is a lively gathering place for kids after school. West Yellowstone, Montana, makes a skating rink each winter on **Electric Street,** and there is also a neat skating rink at **Mammoth Hotel** in Yellowstone National Park. You can rent skates for the whole family at Mammoth.

In Jackson, Wyoming, you pay a few bucks to skate at the indoor **Snow King Center Ice Rink** at 100 East Snow King Ave., (307) 733-5200. The rink is open from Aug to mid-Apr. And if you don't feel like skiing (or tennis), try out the skating area at **Grand Targhee** in Alta, Wyoming (the ski area floods the tennis courts and maintains the ice). Call Grand Targhee at (800) 827-4433, or drive up on Ski Hill Road out of Driggs, Idaho.

In Big Sky, an ice rink recently opened at the Fire Pit Park in the Town Center area. It's small, but the bonfire is always going, and the atmosphere can't be beat. Plans are underway for a larger rink to open in 2011 in the adjacent Town Center Park.

i Fish hatcheries are great places to learn more about trout. Some hatcheries also have feeding ponds where you can purchase a handful of fish food and attract trout as long as your arm. For Montana locations, visit www.fwp.mt.gov. For Wyoming locations, visit http://gf.state.wy.us.

J IS FOR JIGSAW PUZZLES

When the sun goes down in Yellowstone Country, things get awfully quiet around here. Many hotels in and around Yellowstone National Park have no phones or TVs in the rooms; that's all part of the charm. So in the quiet of the evening, why not revive a forgotten tradition? At **Chico Hot Springs Lodge,** 1 Old Chico Rd., Pray, (406) 333-4933, you will find a large selection of puzzles in the lobby area. It's common to see families sitting together at one of the tables piecing the puzzles together. Get back to the basics on your trip and check out the puzzles at **Old Faithful and Roosevelt Lodges,** too, (307) 344-7311.

The Ultimate Playground

Beautiful Sacajawea Park in Livingston, Montana, is home to **Pompey's Playground,** arguably one of the best places to romp in Greater Yellowstone. You can climb high into castle towers and storm across bridges, play a round of hide-and-seek, or shoot down a winding slide. There is also a designated area just for the little ones: the "tot lot," an enclosed area away from romping bigger kids. The elaborate playground was built during one weekend— an army of volunteers joined forces, using all private funds and donated materials.

K IS FOR KITES

You can fly a kite anywhere there is wind, of course, but in Livingston, Montana (supposedly the third-windiest town in America), they even hold an annual **Wind Festival,** (406) 222-0580, to celebrate gale-force gusts in the area. Every Oct the community sponsors a contest for the best "wind catcher." The competition brings out school kids with handmade kites and many local artists who create elaborate sculptures that blow with the direction of the wind like weather vanes. The community comes out for an afternoon of kite flying (wind and weather permitting) and contest.

L IS FOR LICKING ICE CREAM

On a hot day there is nothing better than the cool, sweet flavor of homemade ice cream. In these parts you can find special flavors like Huckleberry, Chocolate Moose, and Rocky Mountain Road. Look in any general store throughout Yellowstone National Park for **Wilcoxson's Ice Cream,** made in Livingston, Montana, at 314 South Main St., (406) 222-3270. This old-fashioned creamy ice cream comes in 50 flavors and has been made here since 1912. Try the Peanut Butter Chip, Cookies and Cream, or Praline Pecan. Look for Wilcoxson's outside the park, too, in West Yellowstone and other Montana towns.

Teton Valley may be the huckleberry shake capital of the world, so make sure you stop at the **Victor Emporium** for an old-fashioned treat made with hand-picked huckleberries and lots of smooth, rich ice cream. Victor Emporium is at 45 North Main St., Victor, Idaho, (208) 787-2221. Around Ashton you can get a fine milk shake served by a classic carhop. It'll be a blast from the past for Mom and Dad, so be sure you make them stop at the **Frostop Drive-in,** 26 North US 20, Ashton, Idaho.

M IS FOR MINING

Montana isn't known as the Treasure State for nothing: The 1860s kicked off the gold rush near Virginia City. From there the state's mining industry grew to include copper, coal, and the famous Yogo sapphires. In West Yellowstone, Montana, you can mine for gold and gems like the old-timers at **Yellowstone Mining Company** inside the Rare Earth Store, 111 Yellowstone Ave., (406) 646-9337. They will show you how a real working sluice operates and dazzle you with Montana's largest amethyst geode, as well as displays of rocks, fossils, and minerals.

You can also search for treasure during Bozeman's annual **Gem and Mineral Show** at the Gallatin County Fairgrounds, 901 North Black Ave.; call (406) 388-4152 for dates and details. Rockhounds from all over the state gather here to show off giant geodes and magnificent minerals. One vendor sells cups of rock and sand for a few bucks so that you can sift through them to find gemstones. You're guaranteed to find some pretty colored stones and learn a thing or two about where they come from.

N IS FOR NATURE WALKS

You are surrounded by more than two million acres of wilderness and Forest Service land out here. To learn about wildflowers, wildlife, and environmental issues, try one of many different field courses that get kids outside, seeing, smelling, touching, and hearing, including **Montana Outdoor Science School** (MOSS) in Bozeman. Call (406) 582-0526 or visit www.outdoorscience.org.

Just 8 miles east of Mammoth Hot Springs you'll find the **Northern Yellowstone Trail,** where you can race your kid brother the half-mile distance along the boardwalk. But take it easy on the way back to the car, and read some of the signs at trailside exhibits, which talk about wildlife habitat and fire ecology after the massive burn of 1988.

Both the **Teton Science School** and the **Yellowstone Institute** offer classes for kids, mostly in summer. (Teton Science School also has great winter programs for area schools and school groups.) Teton Science School, within Grand Teton National Park, is all about nature—lucky students spend as much as six weeks learning hands-on about ecology and the natural world while they live in cabins within the park. Nonresidential programs are also available for kids and adults. Call (307) 733-4765 or see the Education section of the Relocation chapter.

i If parents want to spend an adults-only evening out or try a particularly strenuous hike, ask about child care at the front desk of your hotel. Many resorts and guest ranches keep a list of reliable babysitters whom they call regularly to watch kids on the premises, or they may be able to suggest a local day-care center.

Yellowstone and Grand Teton National Parks are home to ranger-naturalist programs that can teach you about elk, bears, bison, geysers, forest fires, and mountain formation. In Yellowstone Park, check the *Yellowstone Today* newspaper that the ranger will give you at the entrance gate. Grand Teton's newspaper, available at all visitor centers and park entrances, is called *Teewinot.* Both publications provide descriptions of programs. You can also check the bulletin board at your campground for a schedule of evening campfire talks. Often the evening programs are geared toward children and adults.

O IS FOR OLD WEST

This is where the legends of mountain men, cowboys, and even outlaws were born. Half a million settlers crossed through this region on their migration to the West Coast. Signs of the Old West's booms and busts have been left throughout Montana, Wyoming, and Idaho—wagon ruts, abandoned mines, homestead cabins, and most of today's towns.

You can talk to mountain men and Pony Express riders during Jackson, Wyoming's **Old West Days,** (307) 733-3316, a celebration of 1800s life and legends in the area. Each May in the town square, locals reenact the legendary Mountain Man Rendezvous, made famous by such characters as John Colter, Jim Bridger, and Davey Jackson. Wander through a village of authentic wagons circled around campfires and tepees where you can taste traditional fry bread. You'll see gunslinger shoot-outs and rodeos and maybe even learn to promenade with your mom and dad during a street dance.

Get a glimpse of life on the frontier at **Trail Town Museum of the Old West,** 1831 DeMaris Dr., Cody, Wyoming, (307) 587-5302. Wagon ruts, abandoned mines, homestead cabins, and tombstones are the remnants of legendary mountain men, cowboys, and even outlaws of the West. The tales of the people who migrated through this area still remain in the form of this collection of historic western buildings at Trail Town. (The Attractions chapter can give you more details.)

P IS FOR PARADES

You could be the one spinning cartwheels down Main Street and tossing candy into the crowd. Or if you need moral support, dress your dog up as a clown, put him in a little red wagon, and walk the walk. Yellowstone Country is loaded with parades, some exclusively for kids.

Each year for July 4, Cody, Wyoming, kicks off its famous **Stampede Rodeo** with a kids-only parade on July 2. Bozeman and Livingston, Montana, both have kids-only parades in early Dec, when the towns welcome the holiday season with annual Christmas strolls. We suggest you contact the local chambers of commerce to learn about exact times and starting points for these parades. Cody Country Chamber of Commerce, 836 Sheridan Ave., (307) 587-2777; Bozeman Chamber of Commerce, 2000 Commerce Way, (800) 228-4224; Livingston Chamber of Commerce, 303 East Park St., (406) 222-0850.

Q IS FOR QUAKES

Did you know that the greater Yellowstone ecosystem sits on one of the largest fault lines in North America? At **Quake Lake Visitor Center,** located 8 miles north of West Yellowstone, Montana, you will see the proof. On August 17, 1959, an earthquake that rated 7.5 on the Richter scale was felt all the way to the Pacific Ocean and took the lives of 28 people. The visitor center sits above the location of a major landslide that put half a mountain into the Madison River. Quake Lake is the scar left from that day; you'll see trees growing from its depths and houses left in their watery grave. At the visitor center you can learn more about seismic activity in the area and the details of the 1959 earthquake. It is located in the Hebgen

Lake area on US 287, (406) 646-7369. (Check out the Attractions chapter for more details.)

R IS FOR RODEOS

Nearly all area rodeos offer kids' events. Sometimes it's mutton busting, where contestants try to ride sheep. Sometimes it's calf riding. Sheep bolt and calves buck, so it's hard to say which is more fun to watch or more difficult to do. You usually have to sign up in advance to participate, but in Cody, Wyoming, the **Cody Nite Rodeo** announcer invites kids out of the stands to join in the rodeo fun. In the calf scramble, a calf with dollar bills stuck to it (sometimes it's someone's pet cow) is turned loose in the arena. A herd of kids chases the calf around the arena, trying to grab the bills.

At the **J. H. Rodeo,** held in Driggs, Idaho, and Pinedale, Wyoming, two unlucky calves have ribbons tied to their tails, while 50 to 100 kids ages 4 to 11 chase the calves to capture the winning ribbon. J. H. Rodeo is held at the fairgrounds on Snow King Avenue, (307) 733-2805. Kids from ages 5 to 12 can get wild and woolly at the **Livingston Roundup Rodeo** when they compete in a mutton-busting contest. Each contestant tries to ride a sheep for eight seconds before the buzzer goes off to signal the end of the ride. Most kids get a mouthful of rodeo arena dust, but the ones who stay on win prizes. Check the Annual Events chapter for more rodeo locations and times.

S IS FOR SKIING

Steep slopes and beautiful bunny hills at ski areas around Yellowstone await your arrival. All offer extensive kids' programs with snowboard and ski instruction for all ages and abilities. Equipment rentals are also available

at these ski meccas: **Big Sky Resort,** Big Sky, Montana, (406) 995-5000, (800) 548-4486; **Moonlight Basin Lodge,** Big Sky, (406) 993-6000; **Bridger Bowl,** 15795 Bridger Canyon Rd., Bozeman, Montana, (406) 586-1518, (800) 223-9609; **Red Lodge Mountain Resort,** Red Lodge, Montana, (406) 446-2610, (800) 444-8977; **Jackson Hole Mountain Resort,** (307) 733-2292, (888) 333-7766, just to name a few. (Check out the Winter Sports chapter for additional information.)

T IS FOR TRAINS

From the Yellowstone Express to the Northern Pacific Railroad freight train, a group of Livingston, Montana, collectors has meticulously gathered major Rocky Mountain landmarks, constructed towns, and laid elaborate tracks that wind through tunnels and across rivers. The first Tues and Sat of each month from July through Sept, these train buffs invite the public to marvel and relish in their running miniature train collections in the basement of the **Livingston Depot Center.** Admission is free. Also look for the annual collectors gathering in Jan. Call (406) 222-0850 for more information.

If you're in Nevada City, Montana, you can check out the fully restored **1910 Baldwin Steam Locomotive,** and the kids can take a ride on a smaller, gasoline powered version that goes back and forth between Virginia and Nevada Cities. Visit www.virginiacitymt.com.

U IS FOR UNDERGROUND CAVES

You and your kids will marvel at the stalactites and stalagmites jutting out of **Lewis and Clark Caverns State Park** near Three Forks, Montana, (406) 287-3541. You'll learn about resident bats and the formation of this geological wonder on a 2-mile guided tour available Memorial Day through Labor Day.

V IS FOR VIRGINIA CITY, MONTANA

The gold rush days will seem real in this historic mining town with its old buildings and boardwalks. You can peek into store-fronts and houses from the Wild West days and ride the narrow-gauge railroad 3 miles to Nevada City—where several preserved old buildings still stand. Go to **Boot Hill** and check out the gravestones of the Plummer Gang. Play the nickelodeons in the **Bale of Hay Saloon,** and don't miss the melodrama by the **Virginia City Players**—you don't get to throw tomatoes, but you do get to cheer, boo, and hiss with the rest of the audience. Don't forget a stop at the town's famous candy store, too, where you can buy homemade fudge and taffy as well as other popular confections.

W IS FOR WHITE-WATER RAFTING

One way to stay cool and take in some of the area's most spectacular scenery is to hit the rivers. The Gallatin, Madison, and Yellow-stone Rivers in Montana and the Shoshone and Snake Rivers in Wyoming all have big white-water rapids. Local guides make the promise that you will not leave the raft with dry clothes. In Gardiner, Montana, **Yellow-stone Raft Company,** (800) 858-7781, will take you and your folks down the scenic Yellowstone River (the longest undammed river in the Lower 48)—and if your timing is just right, you may be able to attempt the 6-foot standing wave in Yankee Jim Can-yon. For a little tamer perspective, talk your

parents into an easy float down 13 miles of the Snake River outside Jackson, Wyoming, with **Teton Expeditions,** (800) 700-7238. With the Teton Mountains towering over you, this trip is bound to be memorable. But if you want to get back to the wild part of the Snake, set up a river run with Jackson's **Mad River Boat Trips,** (800) 458-7238. Their experienced guides will teach you about how to "read" the water as you navigate the Big Kahuna rapid. If you vow to wear your life preserver, maybe your parents will let you go down the Gallatin River to meet the challenge of House Rock and its field of rap-ids with **Geyser Whitewater Expeditions,** (800) 995-4989, near Big Sky, Montana. Gey-ser also offers zipline tours, sure to give any kid the thrill of a lifetime.

i Mountain Sky Guest Ranch, south of Livingston, Montana, is renowned as a family vacation haven. The extensive kids' program includes day hikes, nature crafts, clowns, swimming, and trail rides. Call (406) 587-1244 for more information or res-ervations.

X IS FOR X-ING OFF PICTURES

Page eight of your Yellowstone National Park Junior Ranger Activity Paper has a checklist of animals to help you keep track of all the creatures you see in the park. The paper is for kids 8 to 12 years old, but the park has papers for younger kids, too. At the end of your park visit, you can turn in your activity paper. If you've done everything required, you become a Junior Ranger and get a patch to prove it. In order to qualify you must attend at least one ranger-naturalist program, view a visitor center or roadside exhibit and tell about it, take a walk on a park trail, read and understand the Junior Ranger pledge, and understand six basic park rules. You must also complete a certain number of pages of your activity paper. For $3 you can buy one of these at any one of the visitor centers in Yellowstone National Park.

Y IS FOR YELLOWSTONE BUDDIES

This children's environmental education program in Yellowstone National Park teaches kids about volcanoes, Yellowstone's bird population, geysers, and other environmental issues in the four regions of the park through storytelling, games, nature crafts, and hikes. The two-hour segments are offered at Old Faithful, the Grand Canyon of the Yellowstone, Mammoth Hot Springs, and Yellowstone Lake.

Classes focus on a theme each session: earth, wind, fire, or water. The cost is $20 per child and includes a "buddy busy bag" with activity books, pins, patches, and postcards. The program is designed for 7- to 12-year-olds. Sessions are available twice a day at 9:30 a.m. and 2:30 p.m., June 15 to Aug 15. There are eight different courses offered throughout the park, each ending with kids taking the "Buddy Pledge" to protect the environment for future generations. For more details about the **Yellowstone Buddies Children's Program,** call Xanterra Parks and Resorts at (866) GEYSERLAND or (307) 344-7311.

The Teton Public Library has many events for kids, including preschool storytime every Thursday from 10:30 to 11 a.m. A journal-making class and a teen snow-sculpture contest are two examples of monthly events popular with older kids, and the library also hosts art and photography exhibits on a regular basis. The library is located at 125 Virginia Lane, and you can check the schedule by calling (307) 733-2164.

Z IS FOR ZIPLINE

Here's your chance to fly! The zipline at **Big Sky Resort** takes you soaring through the mountains and forests above the base of the ski area. Take a leap from the specially designed platform, your arms and legs completely free, and zip down the cable for the ride of your life. For children ages 3 and older (and their parents) it's $59 per ride. Call (406) 995-5769 or visit www.bigskyresort.com.

FISHING & WATER SPORTS

Yellowstone Country's waters include vast mountain lakes, roiling rivers, and tiny, meandering trout streams. From blue-ribbon fishing to windsurfing, waterskiing, and white-water rafting—you can choose just one thing or do them all. Either way you'll find that our area has a bounty of recreation opportunities on the water.

In this chapter we highlight some of the most talked-about spots and some of the local treasures. If an area is famous for its angling, we'll tell you a bit about regulations and the best equipment to use to catch those wily fish. If it's white water, we'll focus on typical water conditions for that area. If it's open to motorized craft, we'll tell you about boat ramps and other essentials. At the end of each region's description, look for listings of fishing guides, floatboat outfitters, powerboat tours, and equipment rental. With this information we hope to give you a jumping-off point; when you get out here, you will find your own resources as well.

Change in Rocky Mountain weather is an ever-present factor for any outdoor pursuit, so remember to prepare for a wide range of conditions. Even if the forecaster predicts sunny skies and warm temperatures, come prepared for snow—you never can tell out here. Bring along extra supplies and dress in layers so that you can easily adjust to the daily temperature fluctuation. Use our write-ups and your own experience as general guidelines only. You should always obtain current information about an area before you set out.

For up-to-date info, call area sporting-goods stores and outfitters. Park rangers, the Fish, Wildlife and Parks Department, and the USDA Forest Service can provide most of the information you'll need to plan your excursion. (Look for contact numbers in the Resources chapter.)

THROW IN A LINE

Talk with anyone who has fished in Yellowstone Country and you won't hear stories about the one that got away, but how many he or she caught. The region's streams yield astounding catches. On the most popular stretch of the Yellowstone River, by Sulfur Caldron in the park, catches of 50 to 60 trout a day occur regularly. That's because these fisheries are comparatively free of pollution and serious habitat degradation. With underwater hot springs flowing into many area rivers originating in Yellowstone National Park, fish thrive on the added nutrients and food sources encouraged by the warmer water. It helps keep fish metabolic rates and temperatures higher in winter cold and supports aquatic vegetation for prime habitat. Also, the region's heavy snows act as reservoirs, feeding into streams from spring to fall to keep water levels up and temperatures cooler during summer months—key factors for fish to survive the heat.

Because the climate throughout Yellowstone Country is similar, so is the fishing—but each stretch of water has its nuances. The waterways are linked within the ecosystem, giving each stream, mountain lake, and fast-flowing river a unique role in the big picture. This means you will find many of the same fish in this region. Trout are the mainstay of Rocky Mountain waterways, and you will largely encounter the same species of fish throughout this region: cutthroat, brown, brook, bull, rainbow, and lake trout, as well as grayling and mountain whitefish. Cutthroat, the only native trout species, are so named for the red slash under their throats. The other species were introduced mostly by government agencies beginning in 1890. A few, such as chub, sucker, and shiner, were planted inadvertently by bait anglers dumping unused live minnows into rivers and lakes.

As far as fishing lore, each state offers a distinct experience for both the expert and novice. In Yellowstone National Park you might go after some of the mightiest native cutthroat trout in legendary Yellowstone Lake, where they grow up to 18 inches long. In Idaho's impossibly clear waters look for the red-bodied kokanee salmon. Within Grand Teton National Park, the lake trout are big enough to tip your canoe on Jenny Lake, where the fish can weigh as much as 30 pounds. Montana's famed fisheries are home to great numbers of big, tricky browns, while Wyoming's secret is its hefty brookies.

Each state has its own set of fishing regulations and licenses. Generally, everything you'll need to get your rod on the river can be found at local sporting-goods stores or in the parks at visitor centers and ranger stations. Check out the Resources chapter for regional fishing guidebooks.

Trout Protection

Anglers should pay special attention to fishing regulations within Yellowstone National Park, as the National Park Service recently began to focus on protection of native trout species. Most Yellowstone Park fishing is catch and release, but the exceptions may change on different waterways for nonnative lake trout, brookies, browns, and rainbow trout. Water levels and temperatures are also factors, so don't forget to check for emergency closures or restrictions, particularly in July and Aug.

FISHING OUTFITTERS

Hiring an outfitter won't guarantee that you'll catch a fish, but it will make the logistics of your fishing easy. Local guides have the insider expertise and can take you where the fishing is hot while cluing you in on what the fish are eating. They know the regulations, so you won't mistakenly end up on the wrong side of the law. Plus, most guide services supply transportation to and from the fishing area, a boat, meals and drinks, and sometimes even equipment. Expect one day of guided fishing in Greater Yellowstone to cost between $200 and $400 per person (plus tip). Package deals that combine lodging or group rates are common.

RIVER OUTFITTERS

A local guide's knowledge of the river is a great asset, but even better is how simple he or she will make your time on the water. The outfitter provides most of the gear—boat, life preservers, food, water, transportation, and expertise. You just bring the sunglasses and the sunscreen. Whether you opt for a scenic river trip or heart-plunging white water, you can count on local guides and their gear to be reliable. Many companies pride themselves on their guides' knowledge of local history, flora, and fauna. Rates vary depending on the length of your trip, shuttle distance, and other factors, but generally you can expect to spend between $200 and $425 per person for a one-day float trip (about three or five hours on the water, including lunch). Some shorter trips can cost $100 per hour.

A word of caution: Floating is not allowed on rivers within national park boundaries.

RATING RIVERS

In the descriptions that follow, we refer to the international rating scale for rivers. It provides a general idea of a river section's difficulty. Remember, these ratings change as water flows rise and fall throughout the year. The difficulty of a section also depends on the craft and your ability to maneuver it.

Wading anglers can use this scale also, as it gives an idea of water turbulence and gradient. A Class IV, V, or VI river will be mostly or entirely turbulent and will likely be very steep. Most of the region's best fishing rivers are rated I to III.

YELLOWSTONE NATIONAL PARK

Within Yellowstone National Park's 3,472 square miles are 800-plus miles of broad

---

River Rating Scale

- **Class I** (practiced beginner): Easy-moving water with small or no waves.

- **Class II** (beginner to intermediate): Regular waves, fast current, unobstructed rapids; may require some maneuvering.

- **Class III** (intermediate to advanced): Large waves and obstacles; maneuvering required; clear route exists, but may not be obvious.

- **Class IV** (expert): Large, chaotic waves; maneuvering difficult but not required; route often not obvious; clear route may not exist; scouting recommended.

- **Class V** (expert with previous Class IV experience): No beginners onboard; scouting strongly recommended; most people choose to portage.

- **Class VI** (expert with previous Class V experience): No beginners or intermediates onboard; extremely dangerous; most people choose to portage.

---

rivers and smaller backcountry streams, and 175 lakes. The sheer variety leaves enough water for any level of angler. Experienced anglers often seek the calm waters of the Firehole or Gibbon River, where advanced fishing skills are necessary. Less-experienced anglers can fulfill their trout goal at Yellowstone Lake or the Buffalo Ford stretch of the Yellowstone River.

To fish Yellowstone you should know the water and have the right gear. Grab a set of regulations and a permit, which you can find at any fly shop or sporting-goods store in Yellowstone's gateway towns. Anglers age 16 and older must buy a fishing permit. You can fish for three days for only $15, seven days for $20, or spend $35 for a season permit. Permits are available at ranger stations, visitor centers, and convenience stores. Children under 16 can fish without a permit if they are fishing with an adult with a permit, or they can obtain a free permit that can be signed by a responsible adult. Most fishing in Yellowstone National Park is catch and release. Humans are at the end of the food chain out here, and wildlife—the grizzly, otter, mink, pelican, osprey, eagles, and others—prey on fish as a mainstay in their diets.

Generally Yellowstone National Park's fishing season begins on the Sat of Memorial Day weekend and continues through the first Sun in Nov. For complete information on park fishing, we suggest you pick up a set of regulations. Write the Chief Ranger's Office, P.O. Box 168, Yellowstone National Park, WY 82190; call (307) 344-2107; or visit **www.nps .gov/yell/planyourvisit/fishing.htm.**

Yellowstone is not exactly a boater's paradise, only because access is limited within the park. Be advised that with the exception of the Lewis River channel between Lewis and Shoshone Lakes, there's no boating on Yellowstone National Park rivers, and limited motorized boat access is permitted on park lakes. Motorized boats are allowed on Yellowstone and Lewis Lakes. Nonmotorized vessels, except float tubes, are permitted on all lakes except Sylvan, Eleanor, and Twin Lakes, as well as Beach Springs Lagoon.

All vessels, including float tubes, require permits with a sticker displayed. You can pick up motorized and nonmotorized boat permits at the park's south entrance, the Lewis Lake Campground, Grant Backcountry Office, Bridge Bay Marina, and the Lake Ranger Station. For nonmotorized boat permits only, you'll have to go to the Bechler Ranger Station, the park's west or northeast entrance, or the backcountry offices at Canyon, Old Faithful, and Mammoth Visitor Centers. An annual motorized permit costs $20, while a seven-day permit costs $10. For nonmotorized boats an annual permit costs $10 and a seven-day permit costs $5. For information about scenic lake cruises and boat and slip rentals, call the Bridge Bay Marina, (307) 344-7311.

Yellowstone Lake

In the blink of an eye Yellowstone Lake can change from glassy calm to churning treachery. At 20 miles long and 14 miles wide, this inland ocean is rimmed with layers of mountain ranges. Though it is popular with boaters and anglers, the waters of this lake are so frigid that swimming is discouraged even on the hottest Aug day. With an average depth of 140 feet, the water of this 89,000-acre lake is so cold (41 degrees on average) that hypothermia can set in within 20 minutes should heavy winds swamp or capsize your boat. These are important facts to know. Be sure to check current water and weather conditions at the visitor center or ranger station before heading out onto the lake.

Fishing

When Yellowstone was designated as a national park, more than 40 percent of its waters had no fish—including Shoshone and Lewis Lakes, the Firehole River, and Firehole Falls. Early park managers transplanted fish and produced hatchery fish, and introduced nonnative species to new waters. By

Bridge Bay Boat Rentals

For a true lake experience, try renting a private boat from the **Bridge Bay Marina** on Yellowstone Lake. Choose from a 22-foot Grady White or a 34-foot Shoshone, which can each hold up to six people and be on the lake for as many as 12 hours. You can use the boats for fishing or sightseeing; rates range from $152 to $1,152. You can also rent motorized rowboats per hour or overnight, or if you just want a quick trip, you can take an hourlong Scenicruiser ride for $14.25 for adults, $9 for kids 2 to 11.

Yellowstone Lake is also home to the notorious lake trout, which dwell in deep water. Although these abundant fish are big and fun to play once you hook them, they are considered the scourge of Yellowstone. Lake trout prey on cutthroat and currently threaten to offset the balance of the park's ecosystem since cutthroat are food for key species like grizzlies, pelicans, and eagles. Catch and release is the norm within Yellowstone, but if you catch a lake trout, please keep it and turn it in to the ranger station (there are no harvest limits on lake trout). Thanks to efforts such as gill netting of lake trout, the wild cutthroat population is still at a healthy level. Yellowstone Lake is the gauge of fishery health throughout the park, and though it is heavily fished, so far so good.

Powerboating

All but 13 miles of the 110 miles of Yellowstone Lake's shoreline are accessible by powerboat. There are two boat launches: one at Grant Village near the campground and another at Bridge Bay Marina operated by **Xanterra,** (307) 344-7311. Most people seem to opt for either riding with Xanterra or renting one of its boats. Each summer Xanterra hosts 5,000 anglers on guided lake trips and another 15,000 who tour the lake on one of the hourlong scenic cruises. These cruises run five to seven times a day from the first week in June to the last week in Sept.

Shoshone Lake

At 80,000-plus acres, Shoshone is the second-largest lake in the park. All 7 miles of this backcountry lake are protected wilderness. This deep, icy lake is accessible by trail, boat, or canoe from Lewis Lake (see below). Although getting here isn't easy, the payoff

the middle of the 20th century, there were more than 310 million stocked fish; stocking no longer occurs in Yellowstone. About 40 lakes contain healthy fish populations today, and 50,000 anglers hit Yellowstone's fisheries each year.

Those seeking consistent action for cutthroat in the 15- to 17-inch range head to legendary Yellowstone Lake. Since cutthroat trout live in shallow waters, most people fish from shore between Sedge Bay and Grant Village. Check out the inlet streams, especially during spawning time in June. One of the secrets of the lake, however, is that you'll catch more fish when you're out in a boat. This could simply be because there is less competition combined with the fact that you can cover more miles. Regardless, because of unpredictable winds and storms, fishing from a boat on Yellowstone Lake shouldn't be taken lightly.

comes in the form of watching undisturbed wildlife, such as moose and sandhill cranes. According to Yellowstone Park historian Lee Whittlesey, Shoshone Lake had six different names before park superintendent P. H. Norris christened it in the 1870s after the Shoshone Indians who sometimes visited the lake during summer months.

Fishing

Shoshone boasts large brown and lake trout along with some good-size brook and cutthroat trout. But the best fishing opportunities here are in the fall when the huge old lake trout come to spawn in the shallows.

Floatboating

If you plan on canoeing or sea kayaking to Shoshone Lake, you should begin on the south shore of Lewis Lake near the campground and then travel down the Lewis River Channel. Inside the heavily forested channel, it is calm and protected from the regular winds of both lakes. You'll pass gorgeous rock formations. Depending on the time of year, water conditions could be high enough to warrant a wet suit and good shoes to cross the river on foot while you pull your boat. It's hard work but worth it once you get to Shoshone Lake to explore its fragile Shoshone Geyser Basin (there are more than 70 geysers here) and surrounding wilderness. There are several nice gravel beaches for camping along the eastern shore.

Lewis Lake

The third-largest lake in the park, Lewis Lake is 12 miles from the south entrance of Yellowstone. At the southeast end is a campground and boat launch. At the opposite end is the mouth of the Lewis Channel, which connects to Shoshone Lake.

Fishing

Lewis hosts mainly brown trout but is also sprinkled with lake and brook trout. There's roadside access as well as a boat-launching ramp—an important element, since the best fishing often results from a boat on this lake. High winds and rough water can make it dangerous to canoe on this lake, so you might opt to fish from the safety of the shoreline. If you're canoeing, float tubing, or kayaking on this 2,000-plus-acre lake, hug the shoreline even if you're headed up the Lewis River Channel to Shoshone Lake.

Floatboating

Just off Lewis Lake you can enjoy a rare privilege. The Lewis River Channel is the only stream in Yellowstone that allows canoes or kayaks. The 3.5-mile stretch of water drains from Shoshone Lake, so from Lewis Lake boaters must haul their craft up the river using ropes in order to enjoy the trip downriver later. Water in the channel is high in June, and bear activity is still a concern until early July, but by Aug the channel is knee deep and peaceful.

Powerboating

Along with Yellowstone Lake, Lewis Lake is the only other lake in the park where powerboats are permitted. Morning is the best time to enjoy calm waters and sunrises reflecting off the lake.

✳Firehole River

With its source at tiny Madison Lake, south of Old Faithful on the north side of the Continental Divide, this is one of America's most famous rivers. It meanders gently through Yellowstone for 35 miles before tumbling through the canyon leading to Madison Junction. Wandering through the Midway and Upper Geyser Basins, the Firehole is fed by thermal springs that warm its waters throughout the year, making it popular with both anglers and swimmers, as well as lazy bison, which are often seen soaking their feet in its waters. Mountain man Jim Bridger told folks this river ran so fast downhill that it was hot at the bottom.

Fishing

It's fly fishing only on the Firehole, and though it's not written anywhere, it may as well be experts only, too. The fish are wily in this stream and aren't fooled easily. Veteran guides suggest the use of tiny flies to catch this river's crafty ones. Look for feisty browns around 15 inches and 17-inch rainbows. What's great about this river is that, unlike most of the other park streams, which aren't in peak fishing form until late June or July, the Firehole is in gear when the park opens in late May. No fishing is permitted from Old Faithful to Biscuit Basin.

Gibbon River

The Gibbon flows for 38 miles from Grebe Lake to its confluence with the Firehole at Madison Junction. Its cascading route passes through the Norris Geyser Basin and through Elk Park and the Gibbon Meadows until it plunges over Gibbon Falls. The Gibbon is accessible via the Madison–Norris Road, which parallels most of its length.

Fishing

A 5-mile stretch of water winding through Gibbon Meadows is home to some big browns and good-size rainbows. The water here can be deceptively deep. Be aware that from Gibbon Falls downstream to the Fire-hole, the river is restricted to fly fishing. The upper river, from Grebe to Elk Park at Norris

Geyser Basin, has small brook trout and rarely caught grayling. Fishing is best at this river during early summer and early fall.

Slough Creek and the Lamar River

Stake your claim in the Slough Creek Camp-ground the night before so that you can get on the river by dawn—this is the fly fisher's mecca. Conditions on this stream are rarely crowded, since it covers so much terrain. From the campground, trails lead to a series of three meadows through which Slough Creek creeps along until it tumbles to its next sleepy slither and at last into the Lamar River in the northern portion of the park.

The Lamar River, famous as the site where the reintroduced wolves were released in 1995, coasts along for 66 miles before rushing through the Lower Lamar Canyon and dumping into the Yellowstone River near Tower Junction. The Lamar Valley is rimmed by the Absaroka Range to the east and offers supreme opportunities for wildlife watching. It's also one of the last streams to clear from spring runoff, and it muddies easily after heavy rains. For best results fish here in late summer. We recommend the Little Lamar River and Cache, South Cache, Soda Butte, Amphitheater, Flint, Cold, and Miller Creeks. If you feel discouraged at first, be aware that the Lamar can be moody, so move around until you find fish.

Fishing

Hidden in the pools, glides, riffles, and side channels of Slough Creek, you'll find the world-famous cutthroat trout (as big as 24 inches). Fishing for the cutts is strictly catch and release. Both Slough and Lamar offer easily accessible meadow fishing. The season runs from Memorial Day through Oct 31.

GRAND TETON NATIONAL PARK

The Tetons jut up from glacial lakes and divide Wyoming and Idaho with a sheer granite wall. If there is anything that makes being on the water more dramatically scenic or breathtaking than these mountains in Grand Teton National Park, we haven't found it. Unlike Yellowstone, Grand Teton does not require its own fishing license. Generally fishing rules are the rules of Wyoming, with a few special restrictions. Just be familiar with park fishing regulations, which you can pick up at Moose Village Store, Signal Mountain Lodge, Colter Bay Marina, Flagg Ranch Village, and many locations outside the boundaries. A one-day, nonresident Wyoming fishing license costs $14. Nonresident children younger than 14 may fish without a license, as long as they're accompanied by an adult with a valid fishing license.

Permits are required to float your boat in the park's lakes and rivers. You can buy craft permits at Craig Thomas Discovery and Visitor Center year-round; in summer you can get them at Colter Bay and Flagg Ranch visitor information centers and at Buffalo and Signal Mountain ranger stations. A one-week, nonmotorized permit costs about $10. A season permit costs $20. Motorized permits cost about $20 for one week and $40 for the year. Motorized craft larger than five horsepower must display a state registration sticker. Grand Teton and Yellowstone National Parks honor the other's permits, although Yellowstone requires that those with Grand Teton craft permits check in at a ranger station.

Scenic paddling is mostly what you'll experience in Grand Teton, since there really is no white water here. Kayaks, canoes, and quiet craft allow you to observe wildlife easier and possibly get closer than in a louder

boat. The park's lakes and waterways give you the opportunity to leave busy roads and experience a side of the Tetons you might otherwise miss.

Leigh and String Lakes

The square, black top of Mount Moran stands ominously over Leigh Lake. Its deep, glacial waters butt up against the mountain and are not accessible by road. To get here you must paddle the shallow, wandering length of String Lake (accessed along an offshoot of Teton Park Road) until you reach a portage on a short but hilly trail. You can also get here on foot to fish the shore via a short hiking trail. The trail into Leigh continues about halfway around its perimeter. Numerous attractive backcountry campsites sit along the trail near the lakeshore.

i Most of Yellowstone is off-limits to bait fishing, but Panther, Obsidian, and Indian Creeks are reserved for bait fishing by children under age 11.

Fishing

Since Leigh Lake is generally more difficult to reach, it sees less fishing and boating traffic than any other lake in the park. Like Jenny and Jackson Lakes, the chilly, deep water is home to massive lake trout, a few brookies and browns, and stocked cutthroat. The fishing here is better compared with shallow String Lake. The lake is open to anglers all year. The limit is six fish per day, although size limitations do apply.

Floatboating

Unlike placid String Lake, Leigh's deep waters are known for sudden winds kicking up rough, choppy waves. Because of this, most boaters hug the shoreline. One of the more popular canoe trips on Leigh takes you from the put-in after the portage from String to the base of Mount Moran. Most climbers looking to conquer Moran paddle this 2.5-mile one-way trip. There is also a trail leading to the foot of the mountain.

Jackson Lake

Grand Teton's largest lake is also its most popular. The average depth here is 400 feet, and the lake offers miles of shoreline and numerous islands that are good for exploring. Spanning 31 square miles, Jackson is a natural lake formed by glacial runoff five million years ago, but it wasn't always this big. The dam at its southern end—built for farmers' irrigation purposes—increased its size. Be sure to make reservations for one of the several backcountry sites along the shore. Call in advance: (307) 739-3602.

Fishing

Although fishing is great any time on Jackson Lake except in Oct, when it's closed to fishing, ice fishing has become increasingly popular. It's easy to access the lake from several points along the shore and any one of the three marinas. The ideal time to fish is in the spring and fall. During summer months the fish go deep and are harder to catch. You may hook cutthroat here. The limit is six fish per day. Other regulations, including size, may apply.

Floatboating

With high winds likely to whip up an unexpected storm, most paddlers hug the shores on Jackson Lake. Access to the lake is good, so you have many options for paddling trips. One popular route begins at Spalding Bay and takes you to Moran Bay, on the

secluded, roadless side of the lake. Hikers like to paddle across the northern arm of the lake from Lizard Creek Campground to access hard-to-reach backcountry trails. Because of Jackson Lake's popularity, you might not get that wilderness experience you're looking for, particularly on weekends. Powerboats hauling water-skiers, sailboats, and sailboards compete with one another on sunny summer days.

Powerboating

Jackson Lake's three marinas offer everything you need to make your powerboat experience on the water memorable. You can rent boats, hire a guide, and buy gasoline and groceries at both **Signal Mountain,** (307) 543-2831, and **Colter Bay,** (307) 543-2811. **Leek's Marina,** (307) 543-2494, offers limited services. Of the lakes in Grand Teton National Park, only Jackson, Jenny, and Phelps allow motorized traffic; there is no public access to Phelps Lake. Only Jackson Lake allows sailboats, water-skiers, and personal watercraft.

Jenny Lake

Necklaced by a rolling trail, Jenny Lake is considerably smaller and quieter than Jackson Lake. Its 2 square miles lie at the base of Mount Teewinot, where a ferry shuttles backcountry hikers and climbers to trailheads. This lake is open to the public throughout the year.

i Jet Skis and other personal watercraft are not allowed on any waters of Yellowstone or Grand Teton National Parks.

Fishing

Big fish like deep water, and Jenny Lake has that. The lake trout here are fabled to weigh as much as 40 pounds. To hook the biggies you'll probably need to get into a boat. There are several acceptable boat-launch areas on the lake and a marina on the southeast end. Motorcraft with more than 10 horsepower are not allowed on this lake. For shore fishing, the trail encircling the lake makes it easily accessible. You may catch a few cutthroats, browns, and brookies. The limit is six fish per day, although other restrictions may apply. Ice fishing is also popular on Jenny Lake.

Floatboating

To get the best from boating on Jenny Lake, we recommend getting up early and paddling out to the middle to see the sun come up over the Tetons and their image reflecting off the dark, glacial waters. The best launching point is at the lake's East End boat dock at South Jenny Lake.

Powerboating

Jenny Lake allows small watercraft with motors less than 10 horsepower. No personal watercraft, sailboats, or sailboards are allowed.

Fishing and Boating Outfitters

Whether it's gear, a boat, or local knowledge, hiring a guide will be worthwhile. Expect a daylong guided fishing trip to run between $250 to $300 per person. Floating in Grand Teton National Park means the Snake River. The long, meandering river is pretty tame, with almost no white water except in Alpine Canyon. Most float trips will be calm, scenic ones, unless you opt for white-water rafting down the canyon. Expect float trips to take between three and five hours and cost around $60 for an adult. Extras such as Dutch-oven dinners or private boats will cost more.

ADVENTURE SPORTS
Dornan's at Moose
(307) 733-3307
www.dornans.com
These folks rent stable canoes and kayaks for beginner boaters, anglers, and families. Their boats are intended for lake floating, not for the Snake or any other river. The full-day rate for a canoe is around $50. The shop is closed during winter months.

BARKER-EWING SCENIC TOURS
Moose
(307) 733-1800, (800) 365-1800
www.barker-ewing.com
Providing scenic raft tours in the park since 1963, this company is considered an old-timer. Trips run from Deadman's Bar to Moose, a 10-mile float on Class II water. Some trips include a gourmet cookout. Trips run June through Aug and begin at $60 per person.

FLAGG RANCH FLOAT TRIPS
John D. Rockefeller Jr. Memorial Parkway
(307) 543-2861, (800) 443-2311
www.flaggranch.com
Flagg Ranch offers both scenic and white-water trips on the Snake above Jackson Lake. The river is smaller and less traveled than other major rivers. Both Class III white-water and Class I and II scenic trips are available starting at Moose Junction or from a meeting point in downtown Jackson, respectively.

GRAND TETON LODGE COMPANY
Colter Bay Village and Jackson Lake Lodge
US 89, Moran
(307) 543-2811, (800) 628-9988
www.gtlc.com

Regular fishing boats depart at flexible times from Colter Marina if you want to catch a ride and fish Jackson Lake for giant lake trout without planning the logistics. You can also rent a boat or aluminum canoe for the day. Arrangements for watercraft and the ferry on little Jenny Lake can also be made here. Guided fishing trips require advance reservations. Scenic floats leave every morning and afternoon from Colter Bay and Jackson Lake Lodge. Some Snake River float trips include picnic lunches or dinners at Deadman's Bar. Transportation is provided for the scenic 10.5-mile float. Colter Bay also runs four regularly scheduled scenic cruises of Jackson Lake daily. Its most popular cruise includes breakfast or dinner on Elk Island.

SIGNAL MOUNTAIN LODGE
Teton Park Road
(307) 543-2831
www.signalmountainlodge.com

Perched on the shore of Jackson Lake, Signal Mountain Lodge offers daily guided fishing and scenic trips. If you don't need a guide, you can rent your own fishing boat here. Canoes and oar boats are available for $17 per hour. Signal Mountain also rents fishing skiffs with outboard motors and offers scenic trips on the Snake below Jackson Lake Dam. Reservations are suggested. If you feel like a scenic cruise of the lake on your own, pontoon boats and deck cruisers can be held for groups of 8 to 10 people. Deck cruisers rent for $99 an hour or $649 for the day. Guest buoys and other services for boaters are available, and pontoon boats and runabouts can also be rented.

JACKSON HOLE, WYOMING

It is no secret that Jackson Hole has legendary skiing, but with so much attention focused on those Teton Mountains, sometimes the area's waterways are forgotten You should be able to guess by location alone that this region just on the edge of Grand Teton National Park is a fishing and boating paradise. Wyoming fishing regulations apply throughout Jackson Hole. You can pick up regulations and other fishing information at the local office of the **Wyoming Game and Fish Department,** 360 North Cache St., (307) 733-2321.

Green River

About an hour's drive east of Jackson, the Green River meanders along the flats between the Wind River and Salt River Ranges. Only a stone's throw from Jackson's summer crowds, the upper Green's wide oxbow turns and fast-moving straights make this an off-the-beaten-path river. Most people put in at the Warren Bridge on US 191/189, 20 miles north of Pinedale.

i Wyoming's Game and Fish Department holds the Wyoming Cutt Slam in which anglers try to catch the state's four native cutthroat trout—Yellowstone, Colorado River, Snake River, and Bonneville—from their original drainages. The challenge was started in 1998 to help anglers learn more about Wyoming's cutthroat subspecies.

Fishing

After the spring runoff, this river tends to clear about two weeks before other area fisheries. You can expect to catch Snake River cutthroat, brookies, browns, and rainbows. If you're a fly fisher, the Green is well known for its gray drake hatch in early July. You can float this river early in the season, but there is also plenty of shore access. On the north side of the highway, a Bureau of Land Management road runs along the river for about 10 miles and offers a dozen access points.

Floatboating

The wide stretches of the Green River are ideal for canoes and wooden fishing boats. You might want to leave that rodeo kayak strapped to the roof of your vehicle, however, since there is virtually no white water to be found on this river. But if you are in the mood for a scenic float, this is your river. With views of the Wind River Mountains to the north and the smaller Salt Range to the south, you can't go wrong.

Hoback River

The Hoback River runs rocky and shallow through 43 miles of sagebrush. It livens up a bit for boaters when its pace quickens in the canyon until it crashes into the Snake River at the bottom of Jackson Hole. US 191 runs parallel to this shallow stream and provides easy access. Otherwise much of the river is bordered by private land. This fact keeps Hoback somewhat isolated compared to the bigger Jackson-area rivers.

Fishing

Although fishing is not as good here as on some of the more famous waters, the scenery more than makes up for it. If a little peace and quiet are what you yearn for, this is the river for you. This small, rocky stream is best fished from shore or by wading. You can fish all year on this water. Most people focus on the pockets of water in the lower section above the confluence with the Snake, where they find cutthroats and brookies.

Floatboating

This river is narrower and shallower than its cousin the Snake, but the boaters who

frequent Hoback like the challenge. Akin to the Snake River's Alpine Canyon, the 12-mile stretch of water between the Granite Creek put-in and the Hoback Junction takeout is popular with kayakers and really brave white-water canoeists. Although the rapids are a steady Class II and III (during spring runoff it's a solid Class III river), logjams add to the difficulty of this section of water. You can shorten or lengthen your trip by using lower put-in points or the lower takeout at Astoria Hot Springs on the Snake.

Snake River in Alpine Canyon

This is no isolated river float. Alpine Canyon on the Snake River is the Jackson area's white-water expressway. You'll see enough raftloads of tourists in this stretch of the Snake to fill several buses. Jackson residents stop here after work to get a couple hours of hole riding and wave surfing in with their kayaks. It may be overused, but it is a fun spot with legendary rapids known as Lunch Counter and the Big Kahuna (in spring they can reach a Class IV rating).

Mostly you'll see rafts, white-water canoes, and kayaks in this part of the river. It is an expert and intermediate waterway, so play it safe and study the water. The put-in is called West Table, and the takeout is Sheep Gulch.

Fishing & Boating Outfitters

**BARKER-EWING JACKSON HOLE
  RIVER TRIPS**
45 West Broadway
(307) 733-1000, (800) 448-4202
www.barker-ewing.com
This company has a solid regional reputation as a fine outfitter. For scenic floats, Barker-Ewing guides will take you through

the Snake River's South Park area. When it comes to white water, Alpine Canyon is a thrill a minute in a raft or white-water canoe. The best is a combo scenic/white-water trip combining these two stretches of the Snake.

HIGH COUNTRY FLIES
185 North Center St.
(307) 733-7210
www.highcountryflies.com
Since 1974 this fly shop and guide service has been floating down the Snake River near Jackson, the New Fork, and the Green River to the south. You can also fish the famous waters in Yellowstone National Park. High Country can offer instruction and even arrange for casting, entomology, knot tying, and playing and releasing sessions with a fish on your line. Trips are catch and release only. A full-day guided trip for one or two anglers starts at $400.

JACK DENNIS SPORTS
50 East Broadway Ave.
(307) 733-3270
www.jackdennis.com
Jack Dennis Sports is home to one of the better-known fishing guide services in Jackson. The fishing celebrity opened his fly shop and guide service here in 1967. His guides can take you to the rivers and lakes of Yellowstone National Park, to the remote holes of the New Fork, the Green, and through the Upper Snake River. Through an Idaho outfitter, you can also book trips on eastern Idaho's South Fork of the Snake, famed for its native cutthroat fishing. Besides organizing the heralded one-fly trout derby, Dennis also offers seminars and fly-casting instruction. A $475 daily cost is standard for a float trip with two people.

✳JACKSON HOLE WHITEWATER
650 West Broadway Ave.
(307) 733-1007, (800) 700-7238
www.jacksonholewhitewater.com
This raft company has been voted a local favorite again and again. The scenic/white-water combination trip is popular. You'll meander along the Upper Snake for a sleepy but beautiful 8 miles before reaching the legendary Alpine Canyon for a fast set of rapids. Along the float, guides will give you information on the area's geology, history, and wildlife; they will make you lunch, too. A seven-hour trip costs $110 for adults, $90 for children.

MAD RIVER BOAT TRIPS
1255 South US 89
(307) 733-6203, (800) 458-7238
www.mad-river.com
If it makes you feel more comfortable, rental wet suits are washed and dried after each use at Mad River Boat Trips—but that's just one of the perks. They also offer a free tour of the Mad River's River Runners Museum, where you can learn about the roots of rafting. But the best thing after jamming down the rapids of Alpine Canyon is the lunch or barbecue dinner they'll serve you at the end of the line.

WESTBANK ANGLERS
3670 North Moose–Wilson Rd.,
Teton Village
(307) 733-6483, (800) 922-3474
www.westbank.com
Outdoor clothing, reels, rods, flies, and waders won't necessarily make you a better angler, but you can still buy the stuff here. You can also arrange fishing adventures for nearby Flat Creek and the Upper Snake in Jackson Hole, the South Fork of the Snake,

and the Firehole, Gibbon, Madison, and Yellowstone Rivers—but not all in one day. Half-day, full-day, and overnight trips are available throughout the region.

Craft Rentals

LEISURE SPORTS
1075 South US 89
(307) 733-3040
www.leisuresportsadventure.com
If you feel like you can hit the lakes, rivers, and streams on your own but don't feel like lugging your gear, this is the all-purpose stop for you. During summer you can rent rafts between 12 and 18 feet long (around $115 per day). You can also rent Coleman canoes and inflatable kayaks as well as wet suits, waders, and just about anything else related to boating.

RENT-A-RAFT/JACKSON HOLE OUTDOOR CENTER
Lewis Landing
10925 US 89, Hoback Junction
(307) 733-2728
www.rentaraft.net
Rod Lewis has been in the river business for decades. Now from his riverside location at Hoback Junction, he rents Achilles and Hyside rafts. Lewis's staff can also rent you a trailer or help you load your rented raft. They will even shuttle you up to the Hoback or down to the Snake. Other services here include innertube, sit-on-top, and inflatable kayak rentals.

✴SNAKE RIVER KAYAK AND CANOE
155 West Gill Ave.
(307) 733-9999, (800) 529-2501
www.snakeriverkayak.com
This is the kind of place where you can go crazy buying all the gear to start you

kayaking or canoeing and take lessons at the paddling school. Even in winter you can practice your rolls and rowing technique in the indoor training pool. The 45,000-gallon pool is 12 feet deep, equipped to simulate a 4 mph current, and is a much more forgiving place to practice than the chilly rivers and lakes around Jackson. Besides operating a paddling school and water-sports shop, these folks rent canoes, inflatable kayaks, paddle and oar rafts, and sea kayaks. Rafts rent for about $120 a day. You can rent a canoe for $50 per day.

SOUTHWESTERN MONTANA

Some of North America's most renowned fishing holes are in Montana—the Yellowstone, Madison, and Gallatin Rivers and many secret spots in between. The list of blue-ribbon fisheries is so long that we can't cover enough here to do it justice. One guarantee is that no matter what your ability or experience, there is good fishing to be found.

Make no mistake, folks take their fishing seriously in these parts. The teeny town of Ennis is so identified with angling that as you enter you will see a larger-than-life bronze statue of a fisherman casting his line across the highway and a sign reading HOME OF 640 PEOPLE AND 11 MILLION TROUT. You might find enough anglers on the water to match the trout population one-to-one in the more popular areas, such as Ennis's Madison River and Paradise Valley's stretch of the Yellowstone, but there are countless other stretches of water to explore. Any fly-fishing shop can tell you about the hot spots and the more-out-of-the-way spots as well, so use local retailers as resources.

But the fish aren't the only thing jumping out here. If you like to water-ski, windsurf, and boat, read on to find out about Ennis, Dailey, and Hebgen Lakes and great paddling water, too. The good thing about southwestern Montana waters is that they are very accessible—you can be on any one of three different rivers within a 45-minute drive out of Bozeman. If you're visiting and need equipment, we've listed several sources for renting gear.

Ennis Lake

When locals say "Let's go to the beach!" they mean Ennis Lake. A short drive west of Bozeman, this lake covers about 3 square miles. It is a haven for water-skiers and sailboarders from June through Sept. Formed in 1905 when Montana Power Company built a dam on the Madison River at the head of Bear Trap Canyon, the lake has slowly been getting shallower because of silt deposits from the river. The good thing about this is that it keeps the water warmer, a boon for recreationists. High winds sweep in from the Madison Valley and off the Spanish Peaks to create ideal windsurfing conditions on most afternoons. Spectators congregate at Sandy Beach, on the north side of the lake.

Most of the lake is surrounded by private property, but there is one primitive public campground on the west end and another one along the river's channels south of the lake. The area has enough room for about 10 sites and has a vault toilet; there's an informal boat launch at each site. The channel site, however, is used more as a takeout since the shoreline downstream is entirely bordered by private homes. The private property aspect of Ennis Lake makes this more of a day-use area, but that doesn't mean you can't have fun.

Fishing

Fishers troll along the lake during summer months, but the high level of motorized traffic makes the fishing pretty slim. Your chances are better during winter months, when ice fishing is popular. Look for rainbow and brown trout from the Madison River. Each spring after ice-out, thousands of trumpeter swans land on the lake and spend a few days here before flying on.

Powerboating

Near the mouth of the lake, on the north side, the Bureau of Land Management acquired Sandy Beach, which has a vault toilet and informal camping. Also on this end you'll find the **Lakeshore Lodge,** (406) 682-4424, which offers a boat ramp and a marina for guests. They also rent small motorboats for fishing.

Hebgen Lake

Located 8 miles northwest of West Yellowstone, Hebgen offers some of the finest stillwater fishing in the state. That's what it's known for, but you'll also see waterskiing, windsurfing, and sailing out here. Formed in 1915 by the construction of a Montana Power Company dam, Hebgen is 16 miles long, with 57 miles of shoreline, most of which is public land managed by the USDA Forest Service. This means there are very few private homes or services around the lake, and that makes it seem kind of remote.

You can reach the water via three Forest Service boat ramps at Lonesomehurst and Rainbow campgrounds and at an informal launch on the north shore. Four private resorts also have launch sites they'll let you use for a minimal fee.

Fishing

Big fish don't necessarily live in big-name rivers. While the famous monikers of the Madison, the Yellowstone, or the Gallatin River draw the crowds, other top-notch Montana fisheries go practically unnoticed. Hebgen Lake is one of those. "It's the best brown trout lake in Montana," says Dick Greene, outfitter and owner of Bud Lilly's Trout Shop in West Yellowstone.

Three "arms," the Madison, Grayling, and South Arm, supply the lake with water and offer excellent fishing areas. This is primarily a trout fishery supporting an abundant population of Eagle Lake rainbows and brown trout that average 16 to 17 inches. Greene says the biggest he's caught was a 23- to 24-inch brown.

Hebgen is open all year, but without a doubt the lake is renowned for its summer "gulpers." On any given day an angler might encounter pods of trout rising, eager to inhale mayflies and other prolific insects. Anglers tell stories of how the fish make an almost audible gulping sound as they grab the fly off the top of the water. But they also caution that gulper fishing is probably the most difficult because you have to figure out which direction the fish are swimming.

One of the most popular times of the year to fish Hebgen Lake is at ice-out in late Apr or early May. The water temperature begins to rise after a long winter, and the fish become more active. This is a fantastic time to strip streamers like the woolly bugger, kiwi muddler, and zonker. Both browns and rainbows can be spotted cruising the shoreline for prey at this time.

Important hatches during the summer months include the tiny trico, the larger Callibaetis mayfly, and the caddis. On a perfect day an angler could fish the trico hatch early

in the morning, catch the Callibaetis emergence at midday (the parachute Adams is an effective imitation), and finish off the day witnessing the explosive strikes of the caddis hatch. Though these hatches are fished best with a float tube or a boat, shoreline anglers can still get in on the action.

When the weather begins to cool in the fall, Hebgen's resident browns grow restless and start congregating to make their annual spawning journey up the Madison River into Yellowstone National Park. It is then, from Oct to late Nov, that many die-hard streamer anglers try their hand at one of the lake's big browns. Fishing is tough at this time of year. Expect foul weather and long days while on the quest for a trophy. Fly selections at this time include egg-sucking leeches, large sculpin patterns, and other ostentatious streamers.

Floatboating

With so much public land encircling Hebgen Lake, there are ample opportunities to see undisturbed wildlife as you cruise along the shore in a sea kayak or canoe. The more sheltered areas of the Madison and Grayling arms are where the deer, elk, and moose hide, especially in the early morning or near dusk. At certain times of year you might spot black bear and all kinds of waterfowl as well. In the afternoon, when hot winds usually kick up, sailboats and sailboarders speckle the lake from July through Sept.

Powerboating

On warm days powerboats, scenic cruisers, and houseboats zoom around the lake. There are three marinas on Hebgen's north shore: **Kirkwood Ranch Motel,** (406) 646-7200; **Yellowstone Holiday Resort,** (406) 646-4242, (800) 643-4227; and the **Happy**

Hour Bar, (406) 646-5100. The **Madison Arm Resort and Marina,** (406) 646-9328, is on the south shore. Each rents slips, sells gas, and rents watercraft ranging from rowboats to speedboats and party pontoons.

✳ Cliff and Wade Lakes

Take a hint from Mother Nature and follow her sharpest anglers—the bald eagle and osprey—up to the chill, glassy waters of Cliff and Wade Lakes in the Beaverhead-Deerlodge National Forest. Nestled in cool mountain slopes at 6,400 feet, these icy sister lakes are a well-guarded treasure. Located a mere 18 miles northwest of Hebgen Lake, Cliff and Wade are serene, spring-fed lakes with a no-wake speed limit and secretive fish. But more than that, these jewel-colored pools offer amazing scenery and fun camping spots near the water.

Although the lakes are busy with campers over national holidays, the rest of the time they are almost untouched. Cliff and Wade Lakes are accessible from May 15 through Nov 1 for most of us. The die-hard angler, however, can make the 5-mile trek on snowshoes or skinny skis to cast a solitary line into a hole on pristine Wade Lake in deep winter months.

Fishing

Wade Lake is the better of the two and the kind of spot that the regulars don't tell just anyone about. The past state record for the largest brown trout caught here was set in 1966: a 29-pound Loch Laven brown. The wild rainbow and Eagle Lake trout found here grow fat off year-round hatches in good weed cover.

"The water clarity is the greatest challenge," says Dave Schmidt, owner of Wade Lake Lodge and fly shop. "The key to catching

them during the day is to fish with really long, thin leaders." With the spring filling Wade at a steady 51 degrees Fahrenheit, the Callibaetis and blue dun hatches start early and continue through Sept. Unrivaled hopper fishing starts up in July and Aug. Bring the pheasant tail nymphs, sheep creeks, and dragonfly nymph imitations along. With its constant clear water, Wade is almost always fishable.

Cliff Lake is larger at 750 acres, but also deeper and not quite as fishable. Here the rainbows, browns, and sparse cutthroats are smaller due to a harsher habitat.

Floatboating

The no-wake rule on these tiny mountain lakes makes for peaceful boating. The lakes are deep and not very big, but the sheer pristine atmosphere makes it a relaxing place to paddle a canoe or kayak. Since most of the camping sites lie on the north and south shores of Wade and the north shore of Cliff, you can paddle to uninhabited sides for a quiet picnic lunch.

Madison River

From the border of Yellowstone National Park to the confluence of the Jefferson and Gallatin Rivers at Three Forks, the Madison River covers more than 100 miles. The river flows through a wide valley coming out of the park, through ranchlands and canyon with mountain ranges rising up on either side. It is a fly-fishing paradise, usually packed with guided boat trips from mid-June through Sept. The stretch between Ennis and Three Forks is the most popular, and along these banks you might see moose or even some black bears during certain times of the year.

The best access points for this river are Quake Lake, Hebgen Lake, Slide Inn, Lyons

Bridge, McAtee Bridge, and Varney Bridge, along with a host of other public accesses. US 287 parallels the river from Yellowstone to 40 miles past Ennis.

Fishing

There is arguably no western river more popular or more famous than the Madison, according to expert fishing guides around here. The big river supports an amazing number of trout and an even more amazing number of trout fishers. The Madison River has a variety of characteristics and water types, insect hatches, and moods. You could fish any 1-mile section of the river for a year and still not know it fully.

Unlike many other productive trout fisheries, the Madison lacks many of the usual trout haunts, including the deep pool. There just aren't many deep pools or much still water on the rushing Madison River. The banks aren't cluttered with roots, rocks, or moss. Still, the angler needs to look for any slower water available, any current seams, behind and in front of boulders, in the back eddies, against the banks, in the braided channels, and in the riffles. Many local anglers believe the riffles are the only type of water on the river. This sweet, shallow river has good, solid hatches of mayflies and caddis throughout the year and excellent dry-fly fishing after runoff.

The most famous (read: most crowded) time of year to fish a hatch is in late June and early July as anglers chase the salmonfly hatch. If you catch the hatch—many locals have tried and failed for years—then it is indeed an experience to last a lifetime. Salmonflies are as long as your index finger and clumsy. They sputter along in the air and then splash into the stream, when one, maybe two, trout streak from their hidden lies to grab the insect with a heart-stopping slash.

They do the same for #2 Sofa Pillows, and they cause the same cardiac arrest. To imitate these large insects, any number of dressings will suffice, including the Sofa Pillow, Stimulator, Bird's Orange, McSalmonfly, and Madam X, but check in with the local fly shops for their creations to imitate the salmonfly. Some of the best fishing on the Madison is in the spring and fall when the crowds clear.

The Madison faced some tough times in 1999 and 2000 when whirling disease robbed the great river of several classes of rainbow trout. In one stretch the Madison River lost about 95 percent of its rainbow trout population. Since then, efforts from biologists have effectively confined the disease, and the Madison has nearly recovered its fish population.

The trout in this mighty stream are plentiful and often finicky, sometimes requiring match-the-hatch angling from an increasingly sophisticated fishing crowd. But part of the charm of the river is that it is many things to many people. For trout cover, the Madison has pocket water, riffles, eddies, undercut banks, boulders, underwater structure, side channels, braids, beaver ponds, and more. Typically the river has movement and is rarely slow, meaning that the fish have lots of well-oxygenated water and resulting energy. Don't be surprised when these trout take enough line off the reel to go into the backing and cause your palms to sweat. The average-size trout here is somewhere between 13 to 17 inches, probably closer to 13, though many go over 17 inches. There are some biggies in this river, but if you nab a rainbow it is catch and release only. You can keep two brown trout less than 13 inches.

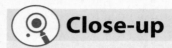 **Close-up**

Paradise Valley Spring Creeks

When the rivers are running high and muddy, the crystalline spring creeks in Montana's **Paradise Valley** are ideal for anxious anglers who are ready to start the season off right.

"The spring creeks offer the best fishing there is this time of year, because they aren't affected by runoff," says George Anderson, owner of the Yellowstone Angler in Livingston.

Located a few miles south of Livingston, these spring-fed streams, known as **Armstrong, Depuy,** and **Nelson Creeks,** are celebrated for their crystal-clear water and abundant but finicky wild trout. Meandering at their own sweet pace almost parallel to the wide, raging waters of the Yellowstone River, the spring creeks make up only a few scant miles of pristine fishing before joining the river. But in that stretch of water there are countless challenges for both the expert and the novice fly fisher.

According to Anderson, the key is to "match the hatch." Since the spring creeks consistently maintain a moderately warm 50- to 60-degree temperature year-round, the insect hatches are fat and frequent. But with this comes a savvy rainbow, brown, or cutthroat that will accept only the finest imitation, cast with precision.

"What you have is an ideal habitat with a food source that fosters an increased fish population," Anderson explains. "The spring creeks have 10 times the number of fish per square mile compared to the Yellowstone."

Though the spring creeks are heralded by experts, even the best angler can get frustrated without the right equipment. Long leaders, fine tippets, and specific flies are essential for success on these tricky streams. Rods in the 3- to 5-weight range and reels spooled with a floating line are considered standard.

Spring hatches generally consist of midges, blue-winged olives, and pale morning duns. Accurate representations of these insects in #16 to #20 sizes are effective. Wet-fly selections for late summer should include small pheasant-tail nymphs, sowbugs, scuds, San Juan worms, brassies, and midge larva patterns. Fished with weight and an

Waders should be prepared for the constant pressure exerted on their legs from the heavy current. It pays to be on your toes when wading the river, as some places can be slippery or tricky. You can wade between high-water marks of the stream, but you may not trespass on private land above the water line nor gain access to the river by crossing private land. From Reynolds Pass Bridge to Varney Bridge, there is a catch-and-release, artificial-flies-and-lures-only regulation. There are other regulations along the river on a smaller scale, so check

the rulebook from the Montana Fish, Wildlife & Parks Department.

Floatboating

Mostly what you'll see on the Madison are fishing drift boats and recreational rafters. The river is floatable except for the stretch below Slide Inn all the way to Lyon Bridge and from Ennis Bridge to Ennis Lake, where no boats are allowed, only wading anglers. One of the most popular float areas is below the confluence of the West Fork of the Madison. The sight of drift boats and rafts

indicator in the deeper runs, these flies can be quite productive and offer beginners an excellent opportunity at landing a finicky spring creek trout. The average fish is between 14 and 16 inches long, with some up to 20 inches.

As the weather warms in June and July, the emergence of sulphur duns, midges, pale morning duns, and caddis flies offer a continued food source and terrific surface activity for the dry-fly fisher. Ants are effective as well and are a good option if you can't seem to match the current hatch.

Aug and Sept provide prime terrestrial fishing as hoppers become a staple in the trout's diet. Imitations work well when fished tight along the grassy banks. Oct and Nov continue to provide consistent fishing with midges and blue-winged olives. Woolly buggers may also fool a few fish when stripped through the deeper runs.

For the hardy angler the winter months still provide solid fishing when weather permits. Though some surface action does take place, most fish are caught below the surface with midge larvae, sowbugs, and small nymph patterns.

Beyond their reputation as famous wild trout fisheries, the spring creeks are a prime spawning ground for the Yellowstone's trout. The record floods of 1996 washed the Yellowstone over the fragile banks of Depuy and Armstrong Creeks, ruining that essential habitat. Through careful planning and reconstruction, a dike was designed to divert the river away from the creeks. As a result, these special fisheries have made a strong comeback.

"It was important to the entire ecosystem to reroute the Yellowstone after the flooding," says Anderson.

The spring creeks are privately owned and require a fee in order to fish. Certain rules apply, such as fly fishing only, as well as catch and release. A valid Montana fishing license is necessary. For information on current fishing conditions, be sure to contact a fly shop in the Bozeman or Livingston area. For reservations call the following numbers: Dupuy's (406) 222-0221; Armstrong's (406) 222-2979; and Nelson's (406) 222-2159.

queuing up in the morning at launches is mildly comical with so many people milling around, but this is a big river and can handle all its fans.

Beartrap Canyon below Ennis Lake is an undiscovered treat. This stretch of the Madison is filled with treacherous rapids and deep pools, followed by slower water. On the slow parts you can enjoy the steep canyon walls. The water isn't deep enough for sporty kayakers, but it is perfect for a fun and scenic river run in a white-water canoe.

Gallatin River

Even if the Gallatin River wasn't ranked a blue-ribbon fishing stream, it would be rewarding just to walk along its stony banks, wade waist deep into a slow green eddy, or float on its steady currents. The fact that this river parallels US 191 doesn't even take away from its beauty; in fact, it makes the Gallatin very accessible for fishing, boating, and camping.

Fishing

Parts of Robert Redford's movie *A River Runs Through It* were filmed on this river, and when you experience the way the sun filters through the trees onto the rippling, swirling, glistening water through Gallatin Canyon, you'll understand why.

But fishing the Gallatin is not all Hollywood glam and glimmer—it's the real thing. Generally this is a wader's stream, although you need to be wary of deep holes and fast currents. Some of the holes here are very tricky and can be reached best if you are casting from the shore.

Just barely over the boundary into Yellowstone, the Gallatin braids into a series of channels flowing through a wide, green meadow. (We've never been through this area without spotting a moose.) The fishing in these channels is for lightweight rods only, and if your touch is just right, you might catch a pretty little cutthroat. Just outside the park is the confluence of Taylor Creek, which largely dictates downstream fishing conditions based on whether it is running clear or muddy. You'll find rainbows, browns, and hatchery grayling from Taylor Creek all the way through the Gallatin Valley until the Gallatin joins with the Madison and Jefferson Rivers outside Three Forks.

In Montana the Gallatin is fishable year-round, but the park closes for the winter. You must release grayling, but you can keep up to five trout, with one longer than 18 inches allowed. In Yellowstone it's catch and release for cutthroat, with a two-fish limit on rainbows and browns.

Floatboating

Whether you are looking for wild rapids or a relaxing float, the Gallatin has it. The legendary stretch of white water frequented by a half-dozen local rafting guides and groups of kayakers is House Rock and the subsequent field of rocks following it. But from the put-in at Moose Flats, you'll find plenty of medium rapids to frolic in as well. This 13-mile stretch of water is scenic and fun. Although the rapids rank between Class II and IV, by mid-summer there are some slow sections where you can take quick plunges off the side of your boat to cool off. Most people take out at Storm Castle Creek about 2 miles after House Rock. If you opt not to go through House Rock, you will want to take out at the large landing area on river left just before the 35 mph bridge (as insiders call it because the speed limit is posted right on the bridge), or you'll get pulled right into fast water.

Yellowstone River

The venerable Yellowstone is a river that has always gotten good press. It became famous as the thoroughfare of the Lewis and Clark Expedition. Both of Robert Redford's movies *A River Runs Through It* and *The Horse Whisperer* filmed scenes along this stream, but most of its fame comes from being the largest undammed river in the lower 48 states. For the many ranchers and farmers who live along its banks, the Yellowstone is a life-source for their businesses.

From its source in the high mountains of Wyoming, through Yellowstone National Park, into Yellowstone Lake, over the Grand Canyon of the Yellowstone, into the serene Paradise Valley of Montana, and finally out onto the prairie past Billings, this river crosses some of our country's most rugged terrain. Its 678-mile course is wide, long, and swift up to where it finally merges with the Missouri River in North Dakota.

Fishing

The Yellowstone River is the most popular river in Yellowstone National Park for fishing. There is some exquisite angling within the park, particularly above Fishing Bridge. Those 16- to 24-inch cutthroats are available only from July until Oct, while the rest of the Yellowstone is open year-round. The 30-mile stretch of water from Paradise Valley through Livingston and on to Sheep Mountain is famous for sport and scenery.

Because of the distance between access points, most anglers float this section and do the majority of their fishing from a boat, occasionally getting out to cover areas where islands divide the river and create more interesting water. Some high banks near Mallard's Rest access house-deep pools that hold plenty of fish, particularly cutthroat. There are a few creeks that dump into the river, and their mouths provide attractive areas to find fish: Big, Dry, Six Mile, Fridley, and Mill Creeks all flow into the river.

You should be careful in one area along this stretch of the river. About midway into the float, there is an area that has some underwater hazards, but they are clearly marked with a sign. Also look for an irrigation ditch off the river on the left side: It resembles a channel, and some anglers have mistakenly floated down this ditch, only to be surprised by a small dam, which can put a damper on a day's floating. Otherwise there is no water that can be considered difficult or dangerous in this section, and any type of craft, from canoes to drift boats, will have no trouble navigating it.

Floatboating

Outside the park the Yellowstone River becomes a very tame, snaking stream. But for rafters, canoeists, and kayakers the rapids

in Yankee Jim Canyon will get your heart pounding. During spring runoff you could meet up with a 6-foot standing wave in the canyon. Most boaters do their best to skirt around it. To get in on the white water, most people put in at Gardiner's Queen of the Waters access and float the 16-mile stretch to Carbella access. This Class III section is frequented by a lot of river outfitters.

From Carbella through Livingston the river flattens out and is a popular scenic float. With the stately Absaroka Range sweeping into the flats of Paradise Valley, you'll see why. On a clear day you can see the far-off Crazy Mountains to the north. Keep your binoculars out along this float for bald eagles, which like to nest in the high cottonwoods lining the Yellowstone, and it's almost a guarantee you'll see deer on the shore among the willows.

Quite a few kayakers put in after work at the Ninth Street Bridge and skim down about a half mile to a sweet set of rapids to play before the takeout downstream at Mayor's Landing. But if you are boating upriver, locals warn about the currents around Carter's Bridge just before Livingston. Because the river hits the bridge at an angle, kayakers and canoeists can be pulled into the bridge supports. Navigating this stretch of river is for experienced paddlers only. Numerous people have lost their lives here in the high waters of the spring runoff.

Fishing Outfitters

The great thing about fishing is that it is something that can be a family affair or a solitary pursuit. With the number of fishing outfitters located in southwestern Montana, you should have no problem finding someone to set you up for your first angling experience or to fine-tune your lifelong love. During peak fishing months (July through Sept), guides are booked up months in advance.

Make the best of your time out here and contact an outfitter ahead of time to make a reservation for your trip. The rates quoted for each listing are from 2010 and include guide service, transportation, lunch, and beverages for the day. Also, in case you didn't realize it, tipping your fishing guide is standard. According to area guides, the average tip is between $40 to $100 a day per person.

Big Sky

*EAST SLOPE OUTDOORS
US 191
(406) 995-4369

Long-time Big Sky local Dave Alvin (known as Super Dave to most) has operated East Slope since 1986. Located just across from the Gallatin River, the Orvis-endorsed shop has an exceptionally knowledgeable and friendly staff. East Slope offers guided trips and whatever tackle you might need for your fishing trip. In the winter, you can return to East Slope for ski rentals, or to fish the Gallatin's icy waters when nobody else would want to venture out.

GALLATIN RIVERGUIDES
US 191
(406) 995-2290
www.montanaflyfishing.com

Owner Betsy French opened this Big Sky fly shop in 1981. Affordable casting clinics are held behind the shop at the two-acre pond, which is set up with a casting platform and target rings, not to mention some hefty rainbows. The shop employs eight guides, almost all of whom have at least five years of experience fishing southwestern Montana's waters. Fishing the Madison and Gallatin Rivers, as well as Yellowstone National Park, they

also do overnight trips on the Beaverhead and Missouri Rivers. A day of guided walk-and-wade fishing costs $360 for two people. A float trip costs $450 for two people.

Bozeman

THE BOZEMAN ANGLER
23 East Main St.
(406) 587-9111, (800) 886-9111
www.bozemanangler.com

Owners Rod and Pam King have a marriage bound by fish, water, and traveling all over the world in search of both. The couple runs guided fishing trips primarily on the big local streams: the Gallatin, Madison, Yellowstone, and Missouri. They offer fishing classes throughout the year, with topics ranging from a women-only fishing clinic to the entomology of Montana streams. Their standard day float, walk/wade, or float tube trips (includes tube and fins) for one or two anglers begin at $450 per day. Bozeman Angler also offers an overnight horse-pack trip in Yellowstone.

Gardiner

PARKS' FLY SHOP
202 Second St.
(406) 848-7314
www.parksflyshop.com

This landmark local shop has been around since the 1950s. Owner/guide Richard Parks took over the business from his father. Parks is a Yellowstone National Park fishing expert—he knows every riffle, hole, and hatch on park waters. He'll take you to other areas, too, of course, and he guides on all the big rivers. He does much of the guiding himself but also works with independent outfitters. A float trip or walk/wade trip starts at $375 for one angler.

Livingston
DAN BAILEY'S FLY SHOP
209 West Park St.
(406) 222-1673
www.dan-bailey.com
Outfitting fly fishers since 1938, Dan Bailey's Fly Shop is a downtown anchor in Livingston. Whether it's equipment or information, they can help make your next fly-fishing trip a memorable one. The shop is a great source not only for gear but also for river reports, maps, fly patterns, and news on local hatches. Bailey's guides have access to backyard rivers, such as the Big Horn, Missouri, Madison, Gallatin, Boulder, Big Hole, Beaverhead, Ruby, Jefferson, and Yellowstone. A one-day float trip is $400 for one angler, $425 for two people, and $525 for three fishers, including lunch. License, special fishery rod fees, and gratuity are separate costs. Check out Dan Bailey's online catalog for unique gear.

GEORGE ANDERSON'S YELLOWSTONE ANGLER
US 89 South
(406) 222-7130
www.yellowstoneangler.com
World-famous fly fisherman George Anderson could be your trusty guide if you plan to drop in at the Yellowstone Angler. Anderson grew up fishing, and his passion for the sport grew into his profession. He has fished all over the globe and is best known as the personality for ESPN's *Fishing the World* program. He and his five full-time guides love to share their expertise with other anglers, but Anderson is a real showman with a fish story for every occasion.

His shop is located just south of Livingston and is a full-service store. Yellowstone Angler guides have exceptional expertise in their home waters on Paradise Valley's Yellowstone River and spring creeks, but they also travel as far as the Big Horn River and offer equal knowledge in other area streams. A one-day wading trip for one person costs $400; two people, $425; three people, $525. A float trip for one person is $400; two people, $425; three people, $575. There may also be additional rod fees on private lakes or creeks.

SWEETWATER FLY SHOP
5082 US 89 South
(877) 628-FISH
www.sweetwaterflyshop.com
That Sweetwater is a newcomer to the retail fly-shop scene in Montana doesn't mean the proprietors are novice anglers. Born and raised in Montana, the Vermillion brothers have a lifetime of experience fishing Yellowstone and its surrounding waters and have run an international fly-fishing travel business, Sweetwater Travel Company, for more than 15 years. Professional guides have experience on local Depuy, Armstrong, and Nelson spring creeks, on 120-plus miles of Yellowstone River, as well as on the multitude of waters in Yellowstone National Park. Sweetwater offers a variety of trips with variable rates. Additionally, certified casting instructors on staff regularly work with anglers of all skill levels.

West Yellowstone
BUD LILLY'S TROUT SHOP
39 Madison Ave.
(406) 646-7801, (800) 854-9559
www.budlillys.com
Bud Lilly no longer owns this little shop, but the new owners are pretty effective at maintaining his household name and reputation in the fishing and guiding arena. If you don't

want to lug your own gear, your guide will be able to provide all the essentials plus the extras for your trip. You can choose from eight knowledgeable, full-time guides who can direct you through regional fisheries from waters inside Yellowstone to equally famous rivers outside the park. Rates for float trips and walk/wade trips vary based on the number of anglers to a guide, but a 1:1 ratio begins at around $385. Discounts for groups; call for details. Bud Lilly's is open year-round.

ℹ There are a lot of angler's guide-books on the market, but *Tightlines,* an annual fly-fishing forecast to Rocky Mountain waters, is unbeatable. Expert angler Greg Thomas researches and reports current conditions with an honest voice. The guide is available in Orvis-endorsed fly shops, lodges, and many other locations in Idaho, Montana, and Wyoming.

JACKLIN'S FLY SHOP
105 Yellowstone Ave.
(406) 646-7336
www.jacklinsflyshop.com
Expert angler Bob Jacklin and his shop in West Yellowstone has become a fly-fishing institution. Look for the many books, signature rods, and flies from Jacklin, as well has his DVDs. Running a full-service fly shop and guide service, Jacklin is a noted conservationist and member of the Fly Fishing Hall of Fame. His most recent claim to fame is the catch of a lifetime on June 16, 2006—a 10-pound, 30-inch brown trout on the Madison River. It was arguably the largest fish ever caught on that famous river. Jacklin offers guided trips on Yellowstone and Montana waters. Rates vary during the season and depending on the region.

Floatboat Outfitters

✳GEYSER WHITEWATER EXPEDITIONS
47200 Gallatin Rd., Gallatin Gateway
(406) 995-4989, (800) 914-9031
www.raftmontana.com
Located on US 191, just south of the Big Sky turnoff, Geyser Whitewater Expeditions may be the only river runner to offer horseback-riding combination rafting trips. It's a great way to see Gallatin Canyon off the beaten path. They also run half- and full-day river trips on the Gallatin River.

MONTANA WHITEWATER
US 191, Gallatin Gateway
(406) 763-4465, (800) 799-4465
www.montanawhitewater.com
Bill Zell and his fun-loving group of guides may seem a little crazy at first glance, but they are solid white-water experts. They run half- and full-day white-water and scenic floats on the Upper and Lower Gallatin River. They also offer trips on the Yellowstone River.

WILD WEST RAFTING YELLOWSTONE
Outpost Mini Mall (Headwaters Angler)
US 89, Gardiner
(406) 848-7110, (800) 862-0557
www.wildwestrafting.com
Wild West Rafting caters to family river trips. Their experienced guides will lead you down the Yellowstone River through gentle or rough water and in some cases, a little of each. They also offer horseback-riding packages.

YELLOWSTONE RAFT COMPANY
406 Scott St., Gardiner
(406) 848-7777, (800) 858-7781
www.yellowstoneraft.com
In business since 1978, Yellowstone Raft Company is based in Gardiner. They offer

full- and half-day trips down Yankee Jim Canyon on the Yellowstone River. Ask about their guided fishing trips, too.

Floatboat Rentals

NORTHERN LIGHTS TRADING COMPANY
1716 West Babcock, Bozeman
(406) 586-2225, (406) 585-2090
www.northernlightstrading.com
Not only is this the place to rent rafts, canoes, kayaks, and windsurfing boards, but it's also Bozeman's all-around outdoor outlet. With the oldest outdoor store in town, owner Mike Garcia can tell you how he has watched the recreation scene in southwest Montana blossom. There are discounts for multiday rentals. You must leave your credit card for a deposit; in the event that the raft is lost or damaged you may be charged between $1,000 to $4,000. When you return to the shop with the raft intact, they return your card uncharged. Northern Lights also rents water-sports accessories, such as paddles, wet suits, dry bags, life preservers, and helmets. This is a great place to find used equipment listed on the ad board in the entryway.

RUBBER DUCKY RIVER SERVICES
128 Mount Baldy Dr., Livingston
(406) 222-3746
www.riverservices.com
This little rental shop is easy to miss, behind the railroad tracks across Livingston's main thoroughfare. They rent inflatable kayaks, sit-on-top kayaks, rafts, canoes—all things boating. They also offer guided trips on the Yellowstone and shuttle services for rentals. Rates for an afternoon raft rental start around $100 for an eight-person boat.

EASTERN IDAHO

With so much hype focused on the area of Sun Valley, this little corner of Idaho doesn't get the attention it deserves. But seasoned anglers and boaters daydream about the kind of water in the Targhee National Forest on the border of Montana and Yellowstone National Park.

Quiet, lazy rivers, raging rapids, serene lakes, or a fun-filled day of waterskiing—that's the Targhee. Fishing is very popular here and requires a state license. The Island Park area is world renowned for its excellent stream and lake fly-fishing opportunities. Other parts of the forest can provide more solitude and similar successes. Game fish include rainbow, eastern brook, brown, and cutthroat trout; kokanee salmon; and whitefish. Rafting, kayaking, and canoeing are popular sports in the Island Park Ranger District on the North Fork of the Snake River.

For anglers it's a good idea to hire a fishing guide to help you enjoy your time in the area. There are enough nuances to fishing here to make it challenging even for experts. If you don't opt for guided fishing trips, get the skinny on area conditions at the fly shop where you purchase your license. You can also call the **Idaho Fish and Game Department** at (208) 525-7290, or check out the website: www.fishandgame.idaho.gov. Boaters and paddlers should be aware of unique conditions resulting from dams and irrigation systems on regional waterways.

Henry's Fork

The Henry's Fork of the Snake River is one of the most highly regarded streams in the nation for trout fishing and wildlife watching. Though silting, logging, cattle grazing, and the construction of dams has troubled this area in the past, the Henry's Fork has shown an uncommon resilience. It winds across the Island Park Caldera at a slow, steady pace, casting a golden light across the otherwise plain landscape. Cornered by two reservoirs, it rages through Cadillac Canyon before coasting another 100 miles downstream to join the South Fork of the Snake River. Together they form the Snake River and meander through Teton Basin in shallow but swift Class I or II waters.

Fishing

You'll see the big, fighting rainbows of the Henry's Fork jumping out of the stream before you even have a chance to wet your line. That's what this river is known for, along with lots of brown trout, a few brookies, cutthroat, and cutt-bows (the hybrid rainbow-cutthroat), as well as several species of salmon. The fish are abundant but hard to catch because the Henry's Fork is both shallow and narrow.

Winding and riffling its way through the Island Park Caldera, access to this famous river is good for the sections outside of canyons, where wading, bank, and drift-boat fishing are popular. There are many fishing accesses along the water, since Big Springs Road/ID 47 and US 20 run along much of its length.

Fishing regulations are complex and strict on the Henry's Fork, since it sees such high use by recreationists and agriculture. For instance, Box Canyon to Riverside Campground is catch and release only, Big Springs National Waterway allows no fishing, and Harriman State Park is fly-fishing only. Check the regulations at a ranger station before you set out on the water.

Floatboating

The clear water and mild temperatures along this narrow waterway aren't just for fish. Rafting, kayaking, and canoeing are popular sports in the Island Park Ranger District on the North Fork of the Snake River. This river offers challenges for paddlers with intermediate skills. Put in at Island Park dam; take out at Last Chance. Dams, large falls, and irrigation canals present hazards along stretches of the river, so paddle with care.

Put-in is at Last Chance for paddlers with advanced skills, and takeout is at Hatchery Ford. Another put-in is at Grandview Campground, with a takeout at Warm River. This section demands "advanced-plus" skills and a large raft, and the launch is described as "poor." Find out about other access areas from the Ashton, St. Anthony, or Island Park Ranger Stations.

Henry's Fork, Big Springs Water Trail

This National Scenic Water Trail was the first one established by the Forest Service. From the cool, clean source of Big Spring, this water tumbles over smooth-washed pebbles for a 5-mile stretch of unhampered aquatic wilderness. It's a fine scenic float for beginners and offers a great opportunity to view wildlife. You're likely to see bald eagles, ospreys, and kingfishers all diving and vying for fish as long as your arm.

To protect the health of this mini-ecosystem, fishing is not allowed on the Big Springs Water Trail, so the only way to catch a fish is by taking a picture (don't worry, you'll get so close to some fish that you won't even need a zoom lens). Expect to spend about four hours on this stretch of water if you just plan to float with the current. The route is easy to navigate. Put in at the sign on Big Springs Road/ID 84 and take out at Mack's Inn.

Henry's Lake

In the shadow of the Targhee, Centennial, and Gravelly Ranges, Henry's Lake stays relatively cold all year, but that doesn't take away from its beauty or its popularity with anglers and wildlife. You can watch bald eagles soar above this tempestuous mountain lake. At its narrowest the lake is 2 miles wide, but it expands to 4 miles wide and stretches 5 miles in length. Although it is a natural lake, it was expanded by a dam and is known for sudden winds that cause high waves.

Fishing

Henry's Lake is an angler's paradise and a haven for trophy-size trout. Mostly it's the cutthroat (both wild and stocked) that break the records, but you can also look for rainbow, cutt-bow (the rainbow-cutthroat hybrid), and brook trout. You'll find the cutthroat near the shoreline in the shallows, and most people cast for them from a boat or float tube. Since most of the lake is surrounded by private land, there isn't much access to shore fishing. In Aug the lake's tributaries open to fishing except for Hatchery Creek. The limit is two fish, and you must stop fishing once you catch your limit. You can fish Henry's Lake from Memorial Day to Oct 31.

Floatboating & Powerboating

Unpredictable winds and cold temperatures keep most paddlers off Henry's Lake. For the same reason, most powerboats, sailboats, and personalized watercraft avoid this lake as well. In fact, Henry's Lake is pretty much

for anglers in motorized boats. Everyone else gravitates to nearby Island Park Reservoir (described below).

Island Park Reservoir

Of the two large lakes in this area, 8,400-acre Island Park Reservoir is the powerboater's hangout. Its twin, Henry's Lake, draws more anglers because of its cold, often choppy waters. Neither lake attracts many rafts, canoes, or kayaks, since maneuvering across and around these large bodies of water is a lot of work. But camping, picnicking, and hiking are all accessible around Island Park Reservoir's heavily forested shores. Anglers catch brook, cutthroat, and rainbow trout as well as coho and kokanee salmon. There are only two boat ramps on the lake.

Fishing Outfitters

HENRY'S FORK ANGLERS
3340 US 20
(208) 558-7525, (800) 788-4479
www.henrysforkanglers.com
Mike Lawson was born in this area and has fished here his whole life. He writes for fly-fishing magazines and presents lectures on the sport during the off-season. But when rainbows are biting on the Henry's Fork, he'll be fishing. Mike and his guides also offer trips on the Madison, Firehole, Gibbon, Yellowstone, and Gallatin Rivers in Yellowstone National Park, as well as on Island Park Reservoir. A full-service fly shop is on the premises. A full-day summer guided float trip is $490 for up to two anglers.

WORLDCAST ANGLERS ISLAND PARK
3350 US 20
(208) 558-7068
www.worldcastanglers.com

With locations in Island Park and Victor, Idaho, as well as Jackson Hole, WorldCast can set you up on just about any area river, including the Henry's Fork. Rooted in the groundwork laid by founders Vern and Joe Bressler, the WorldCast Anglers guide staff prides itself on creating fly-fishing experiences that will last a lifetime. Full day float and wade trips run about $485 for two anglers, while the popular two-day, 26-mile overnight float trip on the South Fork of the Snake runs $1,695 for two—including meals and lodging in a deluxe tent camp complete with a private chef.

Craft Rentals

MACK'S INN RESORT
US 20, at Mack's Inn in Island Park
(Henry's Fork Landing)
(208) 558-7672, (208) 558-7272
www.macksinn.com
This is the place to come to rent rafts and canoes to float the tranquil Big Springs Water Trail. For $29 to $70 you'll get a boat, life jackets, and a ride to the put-in. Reservations are a good idea. Mack's Inn is at the junction of the Henry's Fork and US 20 (you can't miss it). It also rents watercraft by the hour for paddling around the immediate vicinity. The staff will drop you and your rental boat at the Big Springs boat dock to begin your two- to three-hour float back to Mack's.

NORTHWESTERN WYOMING

The rivers and lakes near Cody in northwestern Wyoming may not get the same press as other regions, but that doesn't mean there isn't an abundance of water to explore here. The fishing is good, the water is clean, the rivers are swift and scenic, but what else would you expect so close to Yellowstone

National Park? Although we've listed only one lake here, there are many in the area. Ask at a local fly-fishing shop for more details.

North Fork of the Shoshone River

President Teddy Roosevelt called this slice of Wyoming the most scenic 50 miles in the United States, but he wasn't the first to discover it. Buffalo Bill Cody himself used the area for his early Yellowstone National Park tours, and before him, explorer John Colter traveled down this river. With its red rock spires standing sentinel over a steadfast stretch of wild river, it's no wonder the North Fork of the Shoshone has carved its way into western history. US 20 parallels the river for 40 miles between Pahaska Tepee and Buffalo Bill Reservoir.

Fishing
When hungry bears roust from hibernation in spring, they know where to go for fine fishing—the North Fork of the Shoshone. If that isn't proof that there are fish in this stream, then nothing is. The North Fork is easily accessed and holds good-size Yellowstone cutthroat, rainbow, browns, and brookies.

Because so many small tributaries run into the North Fork, you have the chance to fish several different streams. The Grinell, Clearwater, Sweetwater, Elk Fork, and Eagle Creek all offer good fishing. The North Fork is not a big river, but it is deep. One of the deepest areas on the river is below the reservoir, although it's hard to access. The limit here is three fish, with only one bigger than 20 inches.

Floatboating
This narrow river is wrought with logjams, frequent downfalls, and surprise drops. It's

an experts-only kind of river, and even they only run the upper stretches. Spring runoff raises water levels to Class V on some rapids and then quickly down to Class III and IV later in the year. The North Fork is frequented by local commercial raft companies, which guide clients down the 12-mile stretch from Rimrock Ranch to just below the Buffalo Bill Reservoir. Early in the season is the time to take this trip; otherwise the water mellows out late in the summer.

Shoshone River

You can count nine rapids on the Shoshone River from Demaris Hot Springs to Corbetts Crossing. That's what makes this route a commercial rafting mainstay from early spring until late summer. But the truth is, this stream is used more for irrigating Bighorn Basin than for recreation. Sure, some daring kayakers put in just below Buffalo Bill Dam and traverse the hairy rapids for the next 4 miles, but for the most part everyone else stays on the tamer stretch of river downstream. It's those 11 miles of water that bring visitors and local boaters out to enjoy Class III waters for the season.

There is no real fishing of note on this river, although there are cutthroat, rainbow, and brown trout in there somewhere. The river's many small diversion dams (used for irrigation) don't bode well for fish.

Clarks Fork of the Yellowstone River

From high in the Beartooth Mountains, the Clarks Fork carves its way down through Sunlight Basin along a route used by Chief Joseph when his Nez Perce band fled from US troops in 1878. That's just the recent history of this river. Along its scenic 140-mile route, it traverses through some of the world's oldest mountains down into Wyoming and back up into Montana. You can see the Clarks Fork from the Chief Joseph Scenic Byway between Colter Pass to Crandall Creek.

Fishing

The Clarks Fork of the Yellowstone isn't that easy to get to, and perhaps that's just what makes fishing here so satisfying. You may not see another person fishing here for the whole day you're on the water. From the Montana-Wyoming state line to Crandall Creek, you'll find a 16-mile stretch of water winding through a high mountain, forested valley. Most of the fish are cutthroat, but you'll also see browns, rainbows, and good-size brookies. The Upper Clarks Fork has mostly rainbows, with a few brook trout and browns; the lower area has about the same, but with a few grayling as well. Fishing regulations vary greatly depending on what part of the river you plan to fish. Check with the Wyoming Game and Fish Department or local fishing shops for details.

Floatboating

There is one 5-mile stretch of challenging water on the Clarks Fork through one of Wyoming's most beautiful canyons. But the going is hard and for expert paddlers only because of a treacherous Class V rapid at the end of the canyon. A few local rafters and kayakers brave this stretch of water. The rest of us head for the breathtaking views on the next 12 miles of water where the Red Rock River joins the Clarks Fork. From here you can cruise at an easy pace with views of the Beartooth Mountains and imagine yourself as an early explorer to this spectacular land.

Family Fishing

Here are a couple wonderful sites for family fishing recommended by the Idaho Fish and Game Department.

East Harriman Fish Pond is ideal for vacationers in the Island Park area who are interested in a simple fishing trip. The pond is stocked with trout, and bait fishing is allowed.

Island Park Reservoir is a large lake on the Henry's Fork; it is stocked with rainbow trout, brown trout, and kokanee salmon. Fishing is very productive in the summer from a boat, but bank fishing can also be fun. During fall and spring months, many people fish near the dam.

Buffalo Bill Dam Reservoir

Feeding water onto the once-dry lands of Bighorn Basin, the Buffalo Bill Reservoir plays an important role in northwestern Wyoming. Unfortunately the frigid waters and high winds on this lake keep most everyone away except anglers and sailboarders. In the 1980s Buffalo Bill Reservoir made it on *Outside Magazine's* top-10 list of national windsurfing lakes. A hearty core of sailboarders put the place on the map and decided to share it with the world by organizing a three-day national windsurfing event—and for the first time in anyone's memory, the wind did not blow on this lake tucked into the pretty North Fork Canyon. And so the story goes that Buffalo Bill Reservoir remains the best-kept windsurfing secret in Wyoming.

Fishing

This is a lake that can be all things to all different kinds of anglers, from trolling with bait to matching the hatch for fly fishers. Either way, you'll be fishing for some seriously big lake trout, rainbows, browns, and cutthroats. The legendary lake trout have been found up to 30 pounds, the rainbows as high as 12 pounds, while the browns and cutthroats average around 6 pounds. Chinook winds make for poor ice-fishing conditions here in winter, causing unevenly frozen, or "rotten," ice.

i So far inland, who would guess that Yellowstone Country is also home to an avid windsurfing and kiteboarding population? Look for information on the gusty waters of Dailey Lake, south of Livingston, Montana; Ennis Lake, west of Bozeman, Montana; Buffalo Bill Reservoir, east of Cody, Wyoming; and Jackson Lake in Grand Teton National Park.

Fishing Outfitters

NORTH FORK ANGLERS
1107 Sheridan Ave., Cody
(307) 587-7274
www.northforkanglers.com
Operating out of its store on Cody's main thoroughfare, North Fork Anglers not only has a full-service fly shop with hand-tied flies customized for the area, but also offers a range of guided fishing trips in and out of Yellowstone National Park. In tune with fishing conditions, Tim Wade and his guides weigh your needs and capabilities with area conditions to personalize your experience on area fisheries. In addition to weeklong horsepack trips combined with fishing in summer and fall, Wade offers trips in Yellowstone, the

Shoshone National Forest, the North Fork of the Shoshone, and the Clarks Fork. A basic float trip on an area river starts at $400 for up to two anglers.

TWO RIVERS EMPORIUM
211 West Pine, Pinedale
(307) 367-4131, (800) 329-4353
www.2rivers.net
In addition to the standard guided trips, fly-fishing school, and casting lessons, Mike Haul's outfitting and guide business offers unique lake-fishing packages for anglers. He has acquired access to Faler Creek, a private lease that fishes like a spring creek and meanders through a private ranch on the outskirts of Pinedale. With a nice cross-section of trout species—which include rainbow, cutthroat, cutt-bow (a cross between rainbow and cutthroat), and big, feisty browns—it produces some wonderful trout in the 18- to 24-inch category. Rod fees start at $250.

Inquire about Two Rivers' Wyoming Cutt Slam package, which takes anglers on an expedition in search of Wyoming's four cutthroat subspecies in their native range in Wyoming. Guides bring clients to remote locations for each different fish, take measures to present a clear photo of the catches to a Wyoming Game and Fish fisheries biologist for species verification, provide information on date and location of catch, and ensure that a certificate of completion is sent to clients.

Floatboat Outfitters

RED CANYON RIVER TRIPS
1374 Sheridan Ave., Cody
(307) 587-6988, (800) 293-0148
Red Canyon River Trips is the only local rafting company to offer guided trips on the Clarks Fork of the Yellowstone River, and that's something you won't want to miss. The views and history down this 12-mile stretch of water are unbeatable. They also offer floats on the Shoshone River Canyon and the North Fork of the Shoshoe outside of Yellowstone Park. Rafting rates range between $20 and $30.

WYOMING RIVER TRIPS
233 Yellowstone Hwy., Cody
(307) 587-6661, (800) 586-6661
www.wyomingrivertrips.com
For more than 25 years Rick and Ron Blanchard have been guiding family rafting trips on the rivers around Cody. They offer five different raft and kayak trips during the season. Four of them, including an inflatable kayak trip, are on the Shoshone River. The fifth is on the North Fork of the Shoshone. Clients return year after year to float with Wyoming River Trips. Their experienced guides enjoy sharing the freedom of wild rivers with visitors. You can find them in two locations: the Holiday Inn complex on Sheridan Avenue and on the Yellowstone Highway west of Cody. Most trips cost between $27 and $55 per person, between $22 to $35 for children under age 13.

HIKING & OUTDOOR RECREATION

On the surface Greater Yellowstone's regions appear similar: mountains, forests, valleys, and rivers. But the people who populate its regions have many differences in politics, upbringing, occupation, and lifestyle. It's safe to say, however, that the outdoors is our great unifier. Whether it's hiking or hunting, horseback riding or mountain biking, rock climbing or golfing, there's plenty of room for everyone to pursue his or her own version of getting outside.

In this chapter we share some of the popular pursuits that showcase a whole different side of Yellowstone Country. What you'll find here is only a glimpse of what is out there; the rest is for you to discover in your own way.

Learn more about your choice of outdoor recreation in guidebooks for the region and detailed information on specific areas. Falcon publishes a series of hiking guides for the Greater Yellowstone region, including *Hiking Yellowstone National Park, Best Easy Day Hikes Yellowstone, Hiking Grand Teton National Park,* and *Best Easy Day Hikes Grand Teton.*

HIKING

Each year millions of visitors flock to Yellowstone National Park. Tangled in crowds at popular attractions and hung up in traffic jams along park roads, few realize what they are missing just beyond the pavement. With only 3 percent of this huge park accessible by roads, they are missing a lot, perhaps even the essence of Yellowstone itself. You can access the rest of the park along more than 1,000 miles of designated, marked trails. Grand Teton National Park offers an additional 200 miles of trails. The seven national forests in the region add to this bounty, with hundreds of miles of footpaths into their wilderness. The Gallatin, Bridger-Teton, and Shoshone National Forests alone combine some 6,300 miles of designated trails.

Both hiking and backpacking are popular in the area, but here we have primarily included day hikes throughout the region. Most are well traveled and easily accessed. This is a good place to begin your forays into the Yellowstone Country wilderness.

Going into the backcountry should not be undertaken lightly. It requires knowledge of area geography, first-aid skills, map and compass reading, and survival skills in case of an emergency. It's best to go with a seasoned hiker, take an outdoor class, and read about the area you plan to explore.

From this chapter we hope you will discover the beauty of Yellowstone Country away from roads, traffic, and crowds. There is a lot to see and experience, and the possibilities are endless.

Yellowstone National Park

MOUNT WASHBURN

Picking out just one superlative hike from among Yellowstone's 1,000 miles of trail is no simple feat, but the Mount Washburn Spur Trail is a pretty safe choice. Starting from the Glacial Boulder trailhead in the Canyon area, this trail follows the north side of the awe-inspiring Grand Canyon of the Yellowstone on the Seven-Mile Hole Trail before climbing steeply up the east face of Mount Washburn for a 12-mile, one-way trek. This option is not for poorly conditioned hikers. Less ambitious hikers can reach Washburn via the more heavily trafficked trails that begin at Dunraven Pass and the Old Chittenden Road (recommended trailhead), both off the Tower–Lake Road, for shorter round-trip hikes of 6 miles and 10 miles, respectively. Whichever route you choose, this hike offers an amazing breadth of high-country wildlife, midsummer wildflowers, and views.

A large herd of bighorn sheep summer near the summit; yellow-bellied marmots and red foxes are also common. On a clear day the 10,243-foot peak offers views all the way to the Gallatins, Absarokas, and Tetons, along with panoramas of the Grand Canyon of Yellowstone, Hayden Valley, and Yellowstone Lake.

RIDDLE LAKE TRAIL

South Entrance Road

Rolling hills and meadows splashed with wildflowers are the main attractions along the 2.3-mile hike to Riddle Lake. You can cruise along this well-maintained trail without seeing another hiker. Be on the lookout for wildlife, because this trail is prime habitat for moose and grizzly. In fact, you'll find this area is often closed through the month of June and possibly into July due to grizzly sightings.

Once you reach the lake, walk around to the north shore for a majestic view of Mount Sheridan's 10,308-foot peak and the colorful Red Mountain Range. Peaceful little Solution Creek flows from the lake. Riddle Lake was named during the 1870s, by the way, when it was believed that a lake existed in this area containing major drainages to both oceans. Once the actual location of the Continental Divide was determined, however, the "riddle" was solved, and the creek flowing from the lake was the "solution." Although you'd never know it from the easy terrain on this hike, the Continental Divide is only another mile to the southeast.

Start from the South Entrance Road, about 4.3 miles from Grant Village. The trailhead is plainly marked for this moderate 7-mile round-trip hike.

✳SHOSHONE LAKE

Old Faithful–West Thumb Road

Yellowstone's largest backcountry lake offers an unspoiled destination for wildlife watching, fishing, and camping or as a remote picnic spot. Head out on the DeLacy Creek Trail, which begins from Old Faithful–West Thumb Road about 8 miles east of Old Faithful. Look for moose along the trail, especially as you cross the wide meadow where the creek flows for about 3 miles down to the lake.

Once you get to Shoshone Lake, you'll see fine gravel beaches and great views of the surrounding mountains. Eleven campsites circle this lake, and you'll find a ranger cabin near the Lewis Channel. If you plan to stay overnight (permit required), you might want to add a little side trip to your stay with the 7-mile trek from the lake up to Shoshone Geyser Basin. This is one of the park's most impressive geothermal areas, and from the lake you can find a loop trail to access it.

Grand Teton National Park

HIDDEN FALLS AND LAKE SOLITUDE
Near Jenny Lake Visitor Center

There are two ways to get to the refreshing mists of Hidden Falls. You can either hike the 2.5-mile trail around Jenny Lake or ride the ferry straight to the trailhead. If you take the boat, you'll shave this quintessential Grand Teton day hike down to 2 miles round-trip.

From the East Shore boat dock, the climb to the falls is pretty steep, although you gain very little elevation. Since most Grand Teton hikes begin at 6,800 feet, unless you head out on a longer hike, you're not likely to get much higher than a few hundred extra feet. This trail brings you quickly to Hidden Falls, where you will no doubt encounter a flock of other hikers (with the ferry departing every 20 minutes from 8 a.m. to 6 p.m. every day from June through late Sept, this can't be avoided). However, don't let the crowds dissuade you, because the falls are impressive and the view from Inspiration Point (another half mile up the trail) is fantastic. From there you will get a bird's-eye view of Jenny Lake, Jackson Hole, and the Gros Ventre Range.

To make this a more strenuous day hike, assuming you're in good physical condition, you can also travel to Lake Solitude. This deeply carved glacial lake lies another 7.6 miles from the boat dock through Cascade Canyon. The canyon is a classic U-shaped glacial cut, and well named. An enormous volume of water rushes down the canyon, dropping violently in chute after chute. Lake Solitude, at 9,035 feet, is a spectacular setting for viewing Teewinot, Mount Owen, and the Grand Teton. This is a popular area for both people and bears—you're likely to catch a glimpse of a black bear from afar.

You can pick up maps at the Jenny Lake Ranger Station or at the trailhead. Remember that the last ferry across Jenny Lake leaves the trailhead at 6 p.m., so time your hike accordingly or you will add another 2.5 miles to your return trip.

i In Grand Teton National Park, most of the trails begin at 6,800 feet and gain elevation. If you're unaccustomed to high altitudes, take it slow and give yourself extra time. Carry plenty of water and extra clothes, and always let someone know where you are going and when you will return.

PHELPS LAKE OVERLOOK
Moose–Wilson Road

You'll find that there is no such thing as a middle-ground hike in Grand Teton National Park. Most trails are either extensive overnight treks or easy day hikes. Phelps Lake Overlook is the latter and a perfect jaunt for the whole family. The 2-mile, round-trip hike gently gains 400 feet as it climbs to a scenic overlook of the fourth-largest lake in the park and the portals of Death Canyon. This well-used path travels quickly through forests and lush wildflowers fed by snowmelt and springs. The walking path begins at the Death Canyon trailhead, accessed off Moose–Wilson Road.

SKI LAKE TRAIL
Off WY 22, west of Wilson

A short, moderate 2.3-mile walk along a path sprigged with wildflowers will lead you to the crystal-clear waters of Ski Lake. You'll get all the rewards of high-mountain hiking without much work. Along the way you can relish great views of Jackson Hole and the Gros Ventre Range. At the 1-mile mark, the trail forks at the expanse of two sprawling meadows. The right fork heads up to Phillips Pass, which is another 3 miles up. Even though this trail climbs to the crest of the Tetons, most of the hiking is moderate. Much of this is because the trailhead starts out at such a high elevation. This is a popular starting point for hikers connecting with the Teton Crest Trail—a trail that traverses the length of the mountain range.

The left fork trail continues to the lake, following the outlet stream of Ski Lake. Ski Lake is a beautiful lake jewel tucked right up against the peaks. As you walk around it, you will notice that its bottom quickly drops out of sight. The deepest part is up by the mountain. Another view of the lake can be seen with a bit more effort by taking the side trail that climbs up the north side of the lake.

Find the trailhead from Wilson by driving 4.5 miles west on WY 22 toward Teton Pass. Watch for the sign for Phillips Canyon. Pull off the road there and into a parking area on the left (south) side. From the parking area, walk across the highway and up the jeep road for about 0.3 mile. The sign for the trailhead is on the left.

STRING LAKE TRAIL
North Jenny Lake Junction
If you're the kind of hiker who needs a treat at the end of the line, String Lake Trail is for you. The lake is perfect for swimming and a favorite with families because of the easy 3.5-mile round-trip walk. On top of that, you'll see nice views of the Tetons from pleasant little picnic areas lining the shallow mountain lake.

From the trailhead, walk around the lake clockwise along a gentle rolling path through a dense lodgepole pine and Douglas fir forest. The trail soon forks; the left route takes you around Jenny Lake to Hidden Falls. Take the right fork and continue around String Lake. On the west side of the lake, the trail begins to climb and distance itself from the lake, giving hikers a nice view of the lake and valley. About a quarter of a mile past the rocky area the trail passes an avalanche zone. Evidence of past snowslides down the slopes of 11,144-foot Rockchuck Peak will be obvious. Here all the trees have been swept clean off the mountainside almost to the valley floor. The tremendous power of avalanches can be seen in the effects on the trees and rocks. Fortunately for hikers, the danger of avalanche is long gone by late spring. Snow often covers this stretch of the trail into early summer. If snow is present, be careful with your footing as you cross.

The trail continues to climb until it comes to another fork. The left fork goes up Paintbrush Canyon, a very strenuous hike into the heart of the Tetons. Take the right fork. From here the trail goes downhill to cross a footbridge over the Leigh Lake outlet. Head left to pick up the Leigh Lake Trail or right to return to your vehicle and the picnic area.

Hiking here is good from May through Oct. To get to the trailhead, drive 14 miles north of Jackson on US 89 to Moose Junction. Turn left (west) and drive 11 miles to the North Jenny Lake Junction and turn left (west). Drive 2.5 miles to the String Lake picnic area and park at the first parking lot near the footbridge.

✳SURPRISE LAKE AND AMPHITHEATER LAKE
South Jenny Lake Junction on Teton Park Road
For a strenuous day hike, the trip up to Surprise Lake and Amphitheater Lake is

outstanding. Starting from Lupine Meadows, the trail begins with an abrupt hill. The whole route is a steep but well-switchbacked climb gaining almost 3,000 feet in elevation over just 4.8 miles (one-way). The cool air floating off the creek paralleling the trail and, of course, the reward of these two jeweled mountain lakes at the end make it worthwhile. Along the way you'll get a panoramic view of Jenny, Taggart, and Bradley Lakes.

The trailhead is at Lupine Meadows. Find it by turning onto an unpaved road a mile south of the South Jenny Lake Junction. About 1.5 miles in, you'll see a parking lot and a restroom marking the trailhead.

Southwestern Montana

Big Sky
GARNET MOUNTAIN LOOKOUT TRAIL
Off US 191, north of Big Sky
The Garnet Mountain Lookout Trail begins at the Forest Service horse pasture at the mouth of Squaw Creek. From there it gains 2,000-plus feet of elevation, but the trail is moderate and well maintained. Along this 4-mile climb you'll see a section of the trail that parallels the path of a recent avalanche, giving you an opportunity to view the results of this natural phenomena. Most of your jaunt keeps you low in Gallatin Canyon until you get to the lookout cabin at 8,245 feet. From there you will have terrific views of the surrounding area, including the Gallatin Range, Hyalite Peaks, and the Spanish Peaks, with 25 summits topping 10,000 feet. The lookout is no longer manned; all fire detection on the Bozeman-Gallatin District is now done with aircraft. The Garnet Mountain Lookout is one of many Forest Service cabin rentals available to the public through the Gallatin National Forest Ranger District and can be reserved in advance at www.recreation.gov.

To get to the trailhead, follow US 191 south of Bozeman for 25 miles to the Squaw Creek Ranger Station. Follow Squaw Creek Road 132 south for approximately 1.5 miles to the trailhead.

Bozeman
HISTORY ROCK TRAIL
Hyalite Canyon
This easy day hike is ideal for getting acclimated to the Rocky Mountains. The 1.2-mile trail up to History Rock gently rises from 6,550 feet to 7,000 feet. History Rock is a limestone outcropping with dates, initials, and inscriptions carved by early settlers and many more recent visitors. From the trailhead the path follows History Rock Creek through stands of Engelmann spruce and lodgepole pine. It is a nice walk for the entire family.

From Bozeman take Nineteenth Avenue due south for 7.5 miles to Hyalite Canyon Road milepost 62. Proceed south for 9.7 miles to the History Rock turnoff. The turnoff is on the west side of the road just 1 mile north of Hyalite Reservoir.

SACAJAWEA PEAK AND HARDSCRABBLE PEAK TRAIL
Off Bridger Canyon Road, west of Bozeman
The long, bumpy drive up to Fairy Lake Campground, where the trailhead for this hike begins, will be worthwhile once you see the view from the top of Sacajawea Peak. This 2-mile, one-way trail sounds short, but you'll be huffing and puffing with the altitude gain of 2,065 feet to the summit. Most of the trail switchbacks through part of a snowfield and then a long stretch of boulders up the steep slope to Hardscrabble saddle. At this point the trail divides: To the

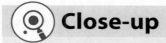 **Close-up**

Three Forks of the Missouri

From his vantage point atop a limestone cliff, Meriwether Lewis observed the "three noble streams" in a sweeping view of the vast valley basin ringed by snowcapped mountain ranges. Lewis and Clark named the three rivers the Jefferson, the Gallatin, and the Madison for the three heads of state who played key roles in the Louisiana Purchase and the expedition itself.

". . . an essential point in the geography of this western part of the Continent," Lewis wrote in his journal on July 27, 1805.

A natural crossroads, the Three Forks was a meeting place for Indian hunting parties and early fur trappers. Five years previous to the expedition, the Minatari had captured Sacagawea near the area. A few years later several expedition members returned to the Three Forks, where John Potts and George Drouillard were killed in separate incidents with the Blackfoot and a naked John Colter made the famous 5-mile run for his life.

By 1822 the Three Forks was trapped out. Several settlements established in the 1860s failed to thrive, but the coming of the railroad brought permanent residents to the area with the founding of the town of Three Forks in 1908 (west of Bozeman off I-90).

Today the Three Forks of the Missouri is a National Historic Landmark and is central to 560-acre Missouri Headwaters State Park.

---

left is the summit of Sacajawea Peak, just a few hundred yards up the trail, and to the right is 9,561-foot Hardscrabble Peak about 2 more miles up. If you feel up to it, you can stand atop two mountains on one hike. Hardscrabble is at the very edge of the Bridger Mountains and offers a closer view of the Shields Valley.

The trail on the back side is hard to follow at times, as it gets lost in the rocks. But there is only one way to go, and that is up. Along the way you'll enjoy an excellent view of the Crazy Mountains, the Shields River Valley, and the Bridger Range from most points along the trail. The 9,665-foot Sacajawea Peak affords a good view of the Gallatin Valley, with refreshing, cool winds drifting up from the valley. Have a seat in one of

the grassy areas and recover from the climb while you take in the view.

This trail is accessible summer through fall. From the Bozeman city limits, take MT 86 (Bridger Drive) for approximately 24 miles to Forest Road 74. Turn west and continue for 7 miles to Fairy Lake Campground. The trail begins at the campground, and adequate parking is available. The road to Fairy Lake is rough and is not recommended for trailers or large campers.

There are other trails in the area as well. In fact, this is the starting point for the annual Bridger Ridge Run, a 21-mile race along the jagged spine of the Bridgers that ends at the "M" trailhead off Bridger Canyon Road.

Livingston

✳PINE CREEK FALLS AND LAKE

Off East River Road, south of Livingston

From Pine Creek Campground, this popular trail begins in the cool forest of the western Absaroka Range and traverses pleasantly for a mile to lovely little Pine Creek Falls. This portion of the trail is popular with families because it is relatively easy, despite a rocky ascent just before the falls. From the trailhead to the falls, you'll see quite a few other hikers, but beyond that the numbers thin. So does the air, as the trail grows steeper on its way to a 3,406-foot elevation gain up to Pine Creek Lake at 9,062 feet. But you will be rewarded for your travels with an astounding view of Mount McCowan and a dip in the chilly glacier water of the lake.

This 5-mile hike up to the lake is a popular overnight trip for backpackers, but it's also a satisfying 10-mile day hike if you begin in the early morning. About 3 miles up the trail you will need to ford Pine Creek, which can be spooky if the water is high during spring runoff. But later in summer the creek is tame and poses little danger. There are several rocky areas on the trail, but plenty of shade for when the summer temperatures begin to soar.

From Livingston take US 89 south to the Pine Creek turnoff to East River Road (about 5 miles) and continue to the tiny hamlet of Pine Creek, where you will turn right (south) and drive about 1 mile until you see the brown Forest Service sign for Pine Creek Campground. The drive up to the trailhead alone is invigorating, with its views of the broad, sweeping Paradise Valley and the Absaroka Range.

RAMSHORN PEAK

Off US 89, south of Livingston

Ramshorn Peak is one of the easier peaks to hike in Paradise Valley. This hike originates in Tom Miner Basin, one of the richest and most diverse wildlife drainages in North America. Geologically, the basin also has an amazing petrified forest. Petrified wood is scattered all about; just remember that you need a permit from the Forest Service to collect any. It is best if you just leave it all there for others to appreciate.

Access the trailhead at the end of Tom Miner Basin, which is 38 miles south of Livingston off US 89. The well-established trail climbs steadily through open terrain for the first half of the hike, taking you up to Buffalo Horn Pass. Once at the pass, take the northerly trail, which takes you to the top of the peak. You are now walking on the crest of the Gallatin Range, with excellent views to the west of the Madison Range, with the Sphinx being particularly prominent. Every step reveals a new vista, which keeps drawing you upward to the top—until, before you know it, panoramic views unlike any other spread before you.

Red Lodge

ISLAND LAKE TRAIL TO BECKER LAKE

Off US 212, west of Red Lodge

For day hikers, the Beartooths are ringed with trailheads and a greater concentration of alpine lakes than anywhere else in the world. On the south side of the range, Becker Lake is a fairly easy yet worthy destination about 4 miles in from the Island Lake trailhead.

Starting at 9,518 feet, the Island Lake trailhead is an enduring favorite to begin this top-of-the-world hike with an elevation gain of only 200 feet. The trail winds through wildflower meadows studded with boulders, hugging the west shore of spectacular Island

Lake en route to Night Lake at only 1 mile into your trek. From there you will reach Flake Lake at the 2.5-mile mark and then Mutt and Jeff Lakes less than a mile farther up the trail.

Once you arrive at Becker Lake, you'll be dazzled by the sheer cliffs rising from its west shore and 11,409-foot Lonesome Mountain to the north. Becker is not on official maps, but the lake is easy to find. Cross the small stream between Mutt and Jeff, traverse the rock field, and then climb the small hill in front of you for your first views of Becker. The terrain, vistas, and distance make this a popular camping destination for families. Island Lake Trailhead is at the end of the marked Island Lake Campground Road, located off US 212, approximately 25 miles east of Cooke City and 38 miles west of Red Lodge.

Eastern Idaho

Teton Valley
✳TABLE MOUNTAIN
Off Ski Hill Road from Driggs

This popular trail allows you to be engulfed by the dramatic Teton Range. When you finally crest the 11,106-foot summit of Table Mountain, you can lie on top of its warm flat granite and bask in your accomplishment. To get there you will traverse a well-worn but rocky trail, with an elevation gain of 4,000 feet over 12.5 miles (round-trip) and a hearty scramble the last hundred yards to the top. But once you're up there it's just you, the thin mountain air, and the spine of the Tetons spanning across the border between Wyoming and Idaho. You'll need lots of water on this hike, and it won't be enjoyable unless you are in good physical condition.

To get to the trailhead, turn right from Ski Hill Road, which leads to Grand Targhee

Ski and Summer Resort, onto a dirt road marked with a sign for Teton Campground. Drive 5 miles to the trailhead parking area at one end of a Forest Service campground.

Northwestern Wyoming

Cody
CLARKS FORK TRAIL
Off WY 296, 55 miles northeast of Cody

With nearly 2.5 million acres of some of the most raw and rugged country in the lower 48 states, the Shoshone National Forest offers endless opportunities for hiking. One of its most breathtaking areas is the Clarks Fork of the Yellowstone River, which starts high above Cooke City, Montana, and runs into Wyoming before slipping back into Montana to converge with the Yellowstone River near Billings. Early on its way just south of Cooke City, the river runs through narrow granite gorges, its waters plummeting over frequent waterfalls that make the river itself virtually impassable.

Eventually it opens into a broader valley with long stretches of smooth water, but here the river is only teasing. Again the gradient steepens and the stream carves the Box, the sheer-walled canyon that earned it Wild and Scenic status. You can see solid granite walls towering 1,200 feet above the river in a spectacular gorge from the Chief Joseph Scenic Byway. Hikers can get a better view from the north side trail. The trail along the north side of the Clarks Fork is great for anything from a long day hike to several days of camping. Along the way you will encounter spectacular canyon vistas and varied ecologies.

The trailhead starts about 5 miles from where the Chief Joseph Highway (WY 296) turns off to US 212. The Hunter Peak Campground of the Shoshone National Forest is on the left, and the trailhead is on the left just before the campground. Hikers out for the day can explore the land along the Clarks Fork Canyon rim. For 8 miles the trail gently wanders through the benchland above the river.

If you're an experienced backpacker out for a few days, you can descend to the canyon bottom. The trail drops down just beyond Table Creek and follows the canyon bottom for a couple of miles to Thief Creek. Beyond this stream the path climbs and heads farther east along the high benches above the river. From here you can retrace your route to Hunter Peak Campground or, if you have arranged transportation, keep going. The one-way hike ends at the Morrison Jeep Road, about 8 miles beyond the ascent from Thief Creek. The jeep road is on the north side of the river. Hikers can also be picked up on WY 296, but beware of the river crossing to the south side. It can be harrowing, and local Forest Service officials should be consulted before planning the ford.

The Clarks Fork Trail offers a great wilderness experience that relatively few hikers have discovered.

i Increasing numbers of outdoor recreationists have significantly impacted America's wildlands. Please help minimize impact on our wilderness by practicing these principles: Plan ahead and prepare; travel and camp on durable surfaces away from water sources; properly dispose of waste; leave what you find; minimize campfire impacts; and be considerate of other visitors.

HORSEBACK RIDING

There is no image of the West with longer staying power or greater reach than the cowboy. Modern-day rodeos preserve the cowboy's ways and traditional garb, while our imaginations preserve his heroism. And what would a cowboy be without a horse? If you long to experience Yellowstone Country on horseback, there are hundreds of outfitters in the region who will be happy to oblige.

Outfitters offer varying lengths of trail rides as well as multiday pack trips, and none of it will be like anything you've seen before. Cowboy wannabe or not, there is something energizing about sitting in the saddle, hearing the leather squeak in rhythm to your horse's gait, the scent of sage and mountain air in your nostrils. Your eyes will soak up the electric colors of wildflowers along the trail, and the view of skyscraping mountains will seem somehow closer than when you are just walking on your own.

We're not saying the view is better sitting on the back of a horse. But one thing is certain: By horseback you will see this

---

East Rosebud

The Beartooth Mountains' Beaten Path, also known as the **East Rosebud Trail**, is a remote but popular trans-Beartooth route begins at the East Rosebud trailhead at 6,208 feet (near Roscoe, Montana) and tops out above 10,000 feet before descending to the Clarks Fork trailhead. The trail gets its name from the large number of hikers that travel it each summer. The 26-mile one-way route traverses close to 20 alpine lakes and offers an intimate look at these rugged mountains.

country from a new perspective. Rates for horseback rides range between $15 and $20 per hour. Most stables prefer that you make a reservation. Outfitters and dude ranches have a wide range of rates depending on the length, location, and activities of your horse-pack trip.

What follows is a sampling of area outfitters. There are so many operations out here, it's impossible to list them all. We suggest you contact the Outfitters and Guides Association in the appropriate state to obtain more details.

Yellowstone National Park

XANTERRA PARKS AND RESORTS
Mammoth Hot Springs
(307) 344-7411
www.travelyellowstone.com
From Mammoth, Roosevelt, and Canyon Village, Xanterra offers daily one- or two-hour trail rides throughout the summer. These are slow and easy rides along gentle, scenic trails. The horses know the routine well enough that all you need to do is enjoy the view. Wranglers lead you and sometimes as many as 24 other riders along a loop nearby, talking about area history and wildlife. Roosevelt Lodge also offers stagecoach rides five times a day. Children must be 8 years old and 48 inches tall to ride; children age 11 and younger must be accompanied by someone age 16 or older. For a more extensive trip through the park, look into packages offered by area outfitters and dude ranches. Several dozen area outfitters offer pack trips through Yellowstone.

Grand Teton National Park

COLTER BAY VILLAGE AND JACKSON LAKE LODGE CORRALS
(307) 543-2811
www.gtlc.com
Operating from two locations, the Grand Teton Lodge Company offers a variety of trail rides within the park. You can choose from breakfast rides, evening campfire rides, and wagon rides. All last one to two hours and are led by a wrangler. Reservations are recommended.

Thorofare

A popular ride for operations near Jackson, Wyoming, is the **Thorofare**—the route from Yellowstone's southeastern corner north to the tip of Yellowstone Lake's Southeast Arm. It was used for centuries by Indians to get from Jackson Hole to points north, and by mountain men and trappers during frontier days. The scenery is spectacular:

Thousands of elk summer here, and in the distance the crags of the Absarokas rise to the east and the Wind River Range is to the south. These days the Thorofare is one of the largest, most remote expanses of wilderness in the Lower 48.

Standard one-hour rides are about $20; two-hour rides are about $50.

*SCOTT'S JACKSON HOLE TRAIL RIDES
Teton Village, WY
(307) 733-6992, (307) 739-2753
www.jhtrailrides.com
Located near the Moose–Wilson Road entrance to the park, the Scott family offers one- and two-hour trail rides into Grand Teton National Park. The entrance sees less traffic than other park roads and is convenient for quick trips offering wonderful views of the Tetons. The Scott family has been guiding horseback rides throughout Jackson Hole since the 1960s.

Jackson Hole, Wyoming Area

JACKSON HOLE OUTFITTERS
P.O. Box 117, Grover, WY 83122
(307) 654-1506
www.jacksonholetrailrides.com
This is not just a trail ride around the barn and back; it's an all day adventure through some forgotten wilderness. Cowboy Maury "Jonesy" Jones books only small groups of five or less. Groups meet in Alpine, 35 miles southwest of the town of Jackson, at 9 a.m., load the horses in a horse trailer, climb in the Suburban or pickup, and drive a few miles up Greys River to a trailhead. The riding is easy, but the mountain scenery is fantastic; the group stops frequently to take pictures and stretch, and to have lunch, before heading back down the trail to return around 5 p.m.

YELLOWSTONE OUTFITTERS
P.O. Box 1149, Afton, WY 83110
(800) 447-4711
www.yellowstoneoutfitters.com
Ride for two hours, or take all day in the Teton wilderness. Yellowstone Outfitters will provide the guides and the food to keep you going on your trip. They run short trail rides

and weeklong excursions throughout the Bridger-Teton National Forest and Teton Wilderness Area. For a taste of the Old West, you can step back in time on a covered wagon trek through Teton country. The wagons look and feel authentic (all but the rubber tires, which are thankfully shock absorbent) as they bump and roll along the remote dirt roads.

Southwestern Montana

Big Sky
CANYON ADVENTURES
47200 Gallatin Rd.
(406) 995-4450, (800) 520-7533
www.montanacanyonadventures.com
Fun and knowledgeable wranglers lead you through the Gallatin National Forest during the summer months. One-hour, two-hour, and combination riding and rafting packages are available. Depending on the weather, Canyon also offers spring and autumn rides through Gallatin Canyon. Owner Ed Hake grew up in the canyon and knows the area extremely well. Rates begin at $36 per person for the hourlong scenic ride.

JAKE'S HORSES
US 191
(406) 995-4630, (800) 352-5956
www.jakeshorses.com
Jake and Katie Grimm have been running guided pack trips and trail rides in Big Sky since the early 1980s. They offer multiday packages in Yellowstone and throughout the Gallatin National Forest. From the corrals in Gallatin Canyon you can saddle up for an all-day fishing and riding trip to a nearby lake or hit the trail for just a couple hours. The shorter, one- or two-hour rides are $37 and $57 per person, respectively, and will take you along the foothills of the Spanish Peaks

and eventually give you a vantage point to take in the gorgeous view of 11,000-foot Lone Peak. Three- to four-hour rides and weeklong pack trips can also be arranged.

Livingston
CHICO HOT SPRINGS LODGE AND DAY SPA
1 Chico Rd., Pray
(406) 333-4933, (800) HOT-WADA
www.chicohotsprings.com

Even if you are not a guest at the resort, you can start here with a trail ride (and soak in the hot springs, too). Diamond K Outfitters can share their horse sense with you. They also arrange multiday pack trips in Yellowstone. You can arrange for rides as short as 30 minutes or as long as a day. The shortest ride, which is great for kids younger than 12, takes you up a well-trod path to a small trout pond above the resort. Just before the trail heads into the trees, you will have an outstanding view of Paradise Valley all the way to the Crazy Mountains. Longer rides take you through Emigrant Gulch and to cool, cascading Emigrant Falls. Chico also offers summer wagon rides that include lunch or dinner. A one-hour ride is $35 per person, $55 per person for two hours.

i If you are interested in leasing a horse for a long trip during hunting season, a weekend family ride, or even for the whole summer, Montana Horse, Inc., is the place. With more than 300 head of horses, they offer quality stock for all different riding abilities and will deliver your horse to you. Call (888) 685-3697 or visit www.montana horses.com.

Eastern Idaho

Teton Valley
BAGLEY'S TETON MOUNTAIN RANCH
265 West 800 South, Victor
(208) 787-9005, (866) 787-9005
www.elkadventures.com

The Bagley Ranch has been in operation since the late 1800s, raising sheep, hay, grain, and potatoes, with a small dairy. Over the years it changed from sheep to beef cattle, and today it is still a working ranch with beef, dairy, hay, and grain. The fourth generation has diversified by adding elk to the operation. Enjoy views of the Big Hole Mountains on the west side of beautiful Teton Valley and close-up views of these majestic animals from horse-drawn wagon rides in summer and horse-drawn sleigh rides in winter. The herd consists of more than 100 bulls, cows, and calves. A one-hour ride is $35 per person; a two-hour ride is $55 per person. They also offer wagon rides through the National Elk Refuge herd from mid-Apr through Nov—$9 for age four and up; children age three and under are free.

BEARD OUTFITTERS
Tetonia
(307) 576-2314
www.beardmountainranch.com

Born and raised in the Teton Valley, the Beard family guides trail rides by the hour or by the day from their family ranch at the base of the Tetons. Beard is licensed to take trips into the Bridger-Teton National Forest and Yellowstone National Park. His family also offers commercial elk hunting trips from the ranch in fall and winter. Half-day and full-day trips are offered, beginning at $85 per person.

Northwestern Wyoming

Cody

BILL CODY RANCH

2604 Yellowstone Hwy.

(800) 615-2934, (307) 587-6271

www.billcodyranch.com

Located 26 miles from Cody and 26 miles from the east entrance of Yellowstone National Park, Bill Cody Ranch is in the heart of Wyoming's legendary cowboy country. Riding here is a pleasant way to enjoy the majestic beauty of the Shoshone National Forest and the area surrounding Yellowstone National Park. This dude ranch offers trail rides and fishing/riding trips to the public as well as to ranch guests. Utilizing more than 14 different mountain trails, the wranglers keep groups smaller than usual. Two-hour rides are about $50 per person and four-hour rides with lunch are $80; longer rides with an outdoor cookout meal and overnight trips are also offered.

PAHASKA TEPEE RESORT

183 Yellowstone Hwy.

(307) 527-7701, (800) 628-7791

www.pahaska.com

Buffalo Bill Cody's famous lodge is accessible to Cody and to Yellowstone National Park. Several favorite trails in the Shoshone National Forest bring you high on a mountainside or in a lush mountain meadow within 30 minutes. An early-morning ride is a great time to see the wildlife, or plan on an early dinner and go for an evening ride. Two-hour rides are $50 per person; all-day rides are about $150.

"Cabin Camping"

The USDA Forest Service maintains more than 120 cabins and lookout towers in some beautiful and breathtaking spots throughout the region. Open to the public, these facilities are reasonably priced, between $25 to $60 per night for a minimum of four people. Some are remote and require a bit of hiking, but others are so accessible that you can drive up to the front door. The cabins range from very sparse to charming, but all are equipped with table, chairs, woodstoves, and bunks. Some have electricity, but for most you must bring your own drinking water. Most lack indoor plumbing, but in exchange for roughing it a little, you can have a mountain retreat all to yourself. For a free *Recreational Cabin and Lookout Directory*, contact a Forest Service office in Idaho, Montana, or Wyoming. Currently all cabins can be reserved through www .recreation.gov.

For Further Information

IDAHO OUTFITTERS AND GUIDES ASSOCIATION

P.O. Box 95, Boise, ID 83701

(208) 342-1438

www.ioga.org

**MONTANA FISH, WILDLIFE & PARKS
DEPARTMENT**
1420 East Sixth Ave., P.O. Box 200701,
Helena, MT 59620-0701
(406) 444-2535
www.fwp.mt.gov

**MONTANA OUTFITTERS AND GUIDES
ASSOCIATION**
2033 Eleventh Ave., #8, Helena, MT
(406) 449-3578
www.montanaoutfitters.com

**WYOMING OUTFITTERS AND GUIDES
ASSOCIATION**
P.O. Box 2650, Casper, WY 82602
(307) 265-2376
www.wyoga.org

HUNTING

Hunting is the very thread that connects humans to this tapestry we know of as Yellowstone Country. Even the prehistory of this land, unearthed by archaeologists and paleontologists, tells us of the Clovis people who tracked big-game animals across the land bridge from Asia to Yellowstone. Those people, like the Plains Indians after them, were subsistence hunters who utilized every scrap and bone and tooth of elk, bison, or bear for food, shelter, and clothing. The very act of pursuing an animal and killing it was embedded in their cultural and spiritual practices as their sacred connection in the circle of life. Later the plentiful prospects for fur trade and for hunting the bounteous bison attracted trappers, businessmen, and eventually settlers. Though without the same reverence for the hunt, those who came here before us relied on the abundant wildlife.

The ritual is still a popular practice throughout the Rocky Mountain area, although not permitted within national park boundaries. In Yellowstone Country we hunt for sport, for trophy, for food, and even as a rite of passage. Hunters travel from all over the world to hunt the region's big-game animals: mule deer, white-tailed deer, elk, antelope, bighorn sheep, mountain goat, Shiras moose, black bear, and mountain lion. They also come for unparalleled upland bird hunting, in search of wild turkeys, geese, ducks, pheasants, and grouse.

i If you are experienced in the backcountry, to truly experience the Tetons, nothing is better than backpacking the Teton Crest. The full route is 39 miles, from Teton Pass on WY 22 south of the park to String Lake, just north of Jenny Lake. A good option is to take the aerial tram from Teton Village and hike to Marion Lake for the first night and then pick up the Crest Trail. Marion Lake has limited campsites, which require a permit.

For some, hunting is even a means to taste and smell and feel the wilderness that we have become so separate from in these modern times. Although today's supermarket society isn't dependent on the meat, fur, or feathers gained from a kill taken in the thick forests, the snow-covered foothills, or the boggy wetlands, hunting is special for some people. Perhaps it is a way to reconnect with the history, nature, and wildness of this land.

The practice of hunting and what is hunted can spark the fire of discord within communities. It has often been the source of conflict, as many people believe that the

HIKING & OUTDOOR RECREATION

practice of hunting trophy animals such as bighorn sheep, mountain lions, and bears is a barbaric way to appreciate nature. Advocates argue that it is man's "natural right." For the state agencies that regulate hunting, it is a management tool used to keep herds and flocks and land in a healthy balance.

Throughout our region the hunting regulations and seasons vary drastically, often changing from month to month within a calendar year. For this reason we have listed fish and wildlife departments for Montana, Idaho, and Wyoming, as well as the guides and outfitters associations to assist you with details on hunting. By far the most popular animals hunted are elk and deer, because they are prolific in this region.

IDAHO FISH AND GAME DEPARTMENT
600 South Walnut, Boise, ID
(208) 334-3700
www.fishandgame.idaho.gov

IDAHO FISH AND GAME DEPARTMENT, UPPER SNAKE REGION
1515 Lincoln Rd., Idaho Falls, ID
(208) 525-7290

IDAHO OUTFITTERS AND GUIDES ASSOCIATION
P.O. Box 95, Boise, ID 83701
(208) 342-1919, (800) 49-IDAHO
www.ioga.org

MONTANA FISH, WILDLIFE & PARKS DEPARTMENT
1420 East Sixth Ave., P.O. Box 200701, Helena, MT 59620
(406) 444-2535
www.fwp.mt.gov

MONTANA OUTFITTERS AND GUIDES ASSOCIATION
2033 Eleventh Ave., #8, Helena, MT
(406) 449-3578
www.montanaoutfitters.com

WYOMING GAME AND FISH DEPARTMENT
5400 Bishop Blvd., Cheyenne, WY
(307) 777-4600
http://gf.state.wy.us

WYOMING OUTFITTERS AND GUIDES ASSOCIATION
P.O. Box 2650, Casper, WY 82602
(307) 265-2376
www.wyoga.org

MOUNTAIN BIKING

Mountain biking is just another way to access what Yellowstone Country has in abundance: trails. From harrowing summer routes that scream down area ski runs to lazy, rolling trails along rivers or through residential areas, there is plenty to do. In places such as Jackson, Wyoming; Big Sky, Red Lodge, and Bozeman, Montana; or Driggs, Idaho, you'll find a counterculture of bikers who test themselves regularly on their area's most challenging trails.

Outside Yellowstone and Grand Teton National Parks is where you'll find most of the mountain biking action. Just like hiking or horseback riding, your bike can take you to the far reaches of wilderness that you might otherwise miss from the paved roads. What follows is general information on surrounding areas, as well as listings of bike shops that sell or rent gear. The local bike shop is probably your best resource for getting the scoop on mountain biking hot spots. Generally you'll find bike rentals by the hour, half day, and full day, ranging from $15 to $75.

Yellowstone National Park

Although snowmobilers can access thousands of miles of trails in Yellowstone, off-road biking is very limited here. Largely what you'll find are short jaunts of only a few miles on old spur roads or utility roads. For specific bicycle trails in Yellowstone National Park, check out the "Pedaling Yellowstone National Park" Close-up in the Yellowstone National Park chapter.

Touring park roads via bicycle is very popular in spring or fall when there is less traffic. Many cyclists even choose to brave the crowds along Yellowstone's frighteningly narrow roads in summer. If you are determined to see Yellowstone on two wheels during summer months, try to travel early in the morning or in the evening when traffic is lighter. It's a good idea to install side mirrors on your helmet and to pack extra provisions, since full-service rest areas are far apart. Bicycle entrance fees are $12 in Yellowstone.

A multi-use pathway runs from Dornan's in Moose to South Jenny Lake. The 8-mile paved route also includes a spur trail to the Craig Thomas Discovery and Visitor Center, and is popular with pedestrians and cyclists.

Grand Teton National Park

Grand Teton, like Yellowstone, is not the best location for technical biking. Other than a 7-mile loop on Shadow Mountain's gravel road, no off-trail biking is permitted in the park. If you're tired of seeing the national parks framed by your windshield, you can cruise on your bike around Jenny Lake and Antelope flats. Both are paved 15- and

12-mile rides, respectively, and offer outstanding Teton views. Bike passes cost $12.

ADVENTURE SPORTS
Dornan's at Moose
(307) 733-3307
www.dornans.com
Ride in style on the newest models of Diamondback, Cannondale, Giant, and Marin, for rent or sale. Dornan's staff can provide area maps and ideas for rides to suit your skill and fitness levels. They'll also supply a shuttle if you are renting gear.

Jackson Hole, Wyoming

An abundance of old logging roads and hiking trails throughout Jackson Hole provide fun two-lane routes or challenging single-tracks. One popular but strenuous technical loop is the 18-mile-long Cache Creek ride, which goes up Cache Creek Road, becomes single-track, and includes a steep ascent and matching technical descent. You return to Jackson on Game Creek Road.

For a more leisurely ride, try the Elk Refuge's dirt road, accessed from Broadway in Jackson. You can travel the road for as long as you like across rolling hills and head back to town whenever you feel like it. The route is popular with runners and bikers during summer months, though you'll see an occasional vehicle here, too.

For information on bike/pedestrian paths within city limits, contact **Friends of Pathways in Jackson,** (307) 733-4534.

THE EDGE SPORTS
490 West Broadway
(307) 734-3916
www.jacksonholeedgesports.com
With more than 200 rentals from mountain bikes, road bikes, and cruisers to choose

If You Can Ski On It...

For a quick-fix day of mountain biking, look at ski areas. Most are on USDA Forest Service land. Wide roads gently switchback up, allowing for leisurely excursions with kids or novice riders. Or for a fast, furious downhill experience, take the chairlift or gondola up the mountain and ride back down. At Grand Targhee Resort, a ride-all-day pass for the high-speed quad with a bike costs $20. Ride the gondola at Teton Village for $10 (advanced and expert riders only) or the Big Sky Resort chairlift all day for $30. Most rides run from June through Sept.

from, you should be able to find something to suit your needs. This shop's experienced staff offers advice on the best local trails and tips on technique. You'll find area trail maps and bike accessories here, too.

HOBACK SPORTS
520 West Broadway
(307) 733-5335
www.hobacksports.com
Fat Tire Tours operates right out of this outdoor store. They can treat you to guided mountain biking adventures to the National Elk Refuge or the more formidable descent on the back side of Snow King Mountain (you take the tram up the ski hill) on a single-track trail. You can also pick up local trail maps and rent Specialized, Trek, and Voodoo performance mountain bikes, including full-suspension bikes.

WILSON BACKCOUNTRY SPORTS
1230 Ida Dr., Wilson
(307) 733-5228
www.wilsonbackcountry.com
The advice here is free, but you'll have to pay for the bikes. You can rent or buy a bike and ride out the front door to the base of Teton Pass, where you'll find a bunch of loop trails that climb and crest to mountain vistas. Bike repair is also available.

Southwestern Montana

Big Sky
It's safe to say that Big Sky would not exist if it weren't for Big Sky Resort. This means that most of the residents live here to ski, and in summer (when they are not day-dreaming about winter) they hit the trails on two wheels. Mountain biking in the Spanish Peaks and Gallatin Canyon is not beginner terrain. What you'll find up the popular Bee-hive Basin or Storm Castle Creek Trails are steep ascents and fast, rocky downhills for the technical biker. But for the great amount of energy you exert on these types of rides, you will be rewarded with the freedom of the sun on your face, wind in your hair, and 360-degree mountain views. Ask about specifics in local bike shops.

GRIZZLY OUTFITTERS
11 Lonepeak Dr., Town Center
(406) 995-2939
www.grizzlyoutfitters.com
Grizzly Outfitters offers a bike-rental package to suit your skill and fitness levels. Owner Ken Lancey is a seasoned mountain biker with a wealth of knowledge about area trails. Grizzly offers reduced rates for kids. Get the summer trail map for specific rides in Big Sky.

Bozeman

The Bozeman area offers such an abundance of mountain biking trails that you could take a different one every day of the summer for five years. From the Hyalites to the Bridgers, you'll find easy access to trails suitable for all levels and abilities. Traversing the switchback road of Bridger Bowl ski area is a local favorite for its prolific wildflowers and views of the neighboring Crazy and Absaroka mountains. For strenuous, all-day rides head to Hyalite Reservoir. But if you just want to get in a quick after-work cruise, join the rest of this outdoorsy population on the miles of trails that secretly meander through town.

For more information on Bozeman's Main Street to Mountains trail system, contact **Gallatin Valley Land Trust** at (406) 587-8404.

Bozeman-based Beartooth Publishing puts out the best multi-use maps in the region. The full-color, easy-to-read topographic maps include trails for hiking and biking, as well as Forest Service roads, campgrounds, picnic areas, and fishing access sites. Maps cover individual mountain ranges or a specific geographic area, and are printed on waterproof, tear-resistant plastic. Look for them in most of the area's outdoor shops.

BANGTAIL BICYCLE AND SKI
137 East Main St.
(406) 587-4905
www.bangtailbikes.com
Owner Chris Saboda won't tell you how to ride, but he can tell you where to go and the right kind of bike to get you there. This veteran cyclist has logged enough miles to travel every trail in the county and then some. Bangtail specializes more in road biking but also offers mountain bike rentals, trail maps, and local expertise.

CHALET SPORTS
108 West Main St.
(406) 587-4595
www.chaletsportsmt.com
Open since the early 1980s, Chalet Sports has seen the population of mountain bikers explode over the years. The crew of veteran recreationists can outfit you with top-of-the-line bikes from Cannondale, Giant, and Specialized. They offer experience to go with the gear, so be sure to ask about area trails and buy the trail map to go with the advice you get.

✳SUMMIT BIKE AND SKI
26 South Grand Ave.
(406) 587-1064
This is the place to come for the inside scoop on area mountain biking. Through the spokes of bicycle wheels hanging from the ceiling of this shop, you might get a glimpse of a staff person who can tip you off to where the single-tracks are plentiful but the crowds are not. This tiny shop does a lot of bike repairs and offers this year's Diamondback, Trek, Kona, and Cannondale bikes for rentals. You can also buy clothing, repair kits, and other accessories.

Livingston

Because the surrounding Absaroka, Crazy, and Gallatin mountains are so steep, there are not a lot of biking trails to choose from around Livingston. Many local cyclists drive the distance over to Bozeman's Gallatin Valley to access loads of trails there. But the great thing about the few challenging rides around Livingston is that you will more than likely have them all to yourself.

A popular trail from town can be accessed off Swingley Road about 1 mile north of Livingston. Pedal along this wide

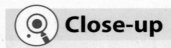 **Close-up**

Bear Safety

Yellowstone Country is also bear country, and whether you are a mile from a heavily traveled trailhead or a day's walk into the backcountry, you should be prepared for an encounter with bears.

Each year area newspapers report unnerving entanglements between bears and humans, including horrific maulings, unfortunate bear killings because of aggressive behavior, and many near misses where recreationists escape unhurt. This makes it sound as though the country is crawling with bears, but in fact the vast majority of visitors will never see a bear at all. There is always the possibility of a chance encounter, however.

Experts say the best weapon against bear attack is knowledge. So read up on grizzly and black bear behavior, and learn to respect them and their territory. **Be alert**—look for bear signs such as tracks, droppings, or diggings. **Be noisy**—talk, sing, clap your hands, or attach "bear bells" to your gear. **Be social**—a bigger group makes more noise and looks more formidable than a single person. Travel between 11 a.m. and 3:30 p.m., when wildlife is likely to be bedded down. **Stay on trails,** as bears tend to avoid them during the day because they know humans travel there. If you smell something dead or see a carcass, **steer clear.** It could be a grizzly food cache—even black bears will aggressively defend a kill. If you see a bear cub, know that its mama is somewhere nearby and **back off.** Avoid bringing pungent foods or smelly deodorants, perfume, or lotion.

More and more people are also carrying pepper spray when they are in bear country. It works as a bear repellent when sprayed in the face and eye area. The high-powered pepper spray comes in a canister that works from 10 to 15 feet away (but who wants to get close enough to try it?) and has proved to be an effective tool in the event of an attack. It is, however, no substitute for **caution** and **knowledge.**

If you do encounter a bear, Yellowstone National Park officials recommend **backing away slowly, talking quietly** to the bear, **refraining from sudden movements,** and **avoiding eye contact** with it. A bear can outrun you, so don't run for a tree. Black bears, young grizzlies, and even some adults can climb trees. If you are actually attacked by a bear, most authorities recommend **playing dead** by dropping to the ground, putting your knees to your chest and your hands behind your head. Usually a bear will swat and bite a couple of times before running off. Don't move from that position until you are positive the bear is gone.

Before you venture into the backcountry, it's a good idea to check with the appropriate ranger district or forest service office (check the Resources chapter) for information on trail conditions and information on bear activity. When you are in the backcountry, be sure to set up camp at least **100 yards away** from your cooking and food-storage site. Store your food by **hanging it from trees,** and don't store any food in your tent.

dirt road until you see the Forest Service sign marking the Livingston Peak trailhead. From there the road narrows and begins to climb up the trail, traversing private land, and finally becomes single-track. Most of this 20-mile ride is forested single-track along the rocky rim of a small drainage that dips and dives in through the Absarokas. It is an intermediate to advanced ride with a lot of technical maneuvering once you get to the trailhead.

For a pleasant beginner to intermediate ride, try Emigrant Falls. This short, 6-mile out-and-back trail begins about 5 miles past Chico Hot Springs Resort and takes you to a gentle, cascading waterfall. You'll ride up the old logging road beside Emigrant Peak for most of the way and take the left fork in the road along a tree-covered single-track for the last half mile.

TIMBER TRAILS
309 West Park St.
(406) 222-9550
It's hard to miss this hip outdoor shop at the edge of the historic district—there is a bicycle mounted on the rooftop. Owner Dale Sexton is a do-everything kind of outdoorsman, and his store reflects that. But as the only shop in town renting mountain bikes, this is the place to go for local knowledge and expertise on what equipment you will need out on local trails. Wed during summer a bike club meets here for a weekly ride.

YELLOWSTONE GATEWAY SPORTS
1106 West Park St.
(406) 222-5414
Specializing in camping and fishing gear, locally owned Yellowstone Gateway Sports is tucked into a strip mall on the edge of historic Livingston. Look for the huge Pamida sign; this sporting goods store is in the building to the left of the chain store. The staff here is knowledgeable about area hikes, river conditions, and hunting regulations

Red Lodge
The slick-rock formations west of Red Lodge are only one of the features that has turned this into a mountain-biking haven. The town hosts its annual Fat Tire Frenzy in July, attracting mountain bikers from around the country. This event offers a criterion and cross-country race.

Even if you are not ready to start competing, there are enough trails around Red Lodge to accommodate any level, from beginner to expert. Willow Creek and Upper and Lower Red Lodge Creek Roads—both west of town off MT 78—are ideal for family rides, while a more challenging ride can be found along the Silver Run trails, where a series of interconnected loops allows you to choose from rides of different lengths along the West Fork of Rock Creek. For technical, single-track riding, try the Greenough Lake Trail along the Main Fork of Rock Creek. Ask for details and trail maps at local outdoor shops.

HELLROARING CYCLE AND SKI
105 West Twelfth St.
(406) 446-0225
The crew at Hellroaring will point you in the right direction for mountain-biking adventures around Red Lodge and give you information on the annual Fat Tire Frenzy races held here each July. They'll also rent you the latest Trek, Cannondale, and Diamondback bikes for any of your rides. This shop is the hub for area trails.

West Yellowstone

The trails you'll find around West Yellowstone are mostly flatland routes through forests or around lakes. This is a boon for beginning riders or families. One of the more popular courses is the system of ski trails bordering town. This 40-kilometer trail system loops around rolling hills and through timber for a pleasant, not-too-challenging ride.

Additionally, the local chamber of commerce organizes two races each year: One in early Oct is in the park; the other, in Apr, goes past Hebgen, Wade, and Henry's Lakes, over Targhee Pass, and back into West Yellowstone.

*FREE HEEL AND WHEEL
40 Yellowstone Ave.
(406) 646-7744
www.freeheelandwheel.com

If you need an energy boost before pedaling around West Yellowstone, get a jolt of caffeine from the lively espresso bar in this store. You can also rent Trek and Specialized mountain bikes with accompanying gear. Owners Melissa Alder and Kelli Sanders have been running the shop since 1996 and can suggest the best biking routes for you—easy or hard. They occasionally organize a women-only ride from the shop during summer months. Located just half a mile from Yellowstone's west entrance, the store is a home base for cyclists heading through the park.

Eastern Idaho

Teton Valley

On your mountain bike you can crisscross Teton Valley's wildflower-washed meadows, endure excruciating climbs for close-enough-to-touch views of the Grand Teton, or test your technical skills on a lift-assisted downhill along the ski runs at Grand Targhee Ski and Summer Resort. The possibilities are limitless here in this vast outstretch of land on the back side of the Tetons.

For starters, try the Horseshoe Canyon area west and northwest of Driggs, where you'll find three good beginner or intermediate rides. The Big Challenge trail is single-track with few obstacles, so it's suitable for intermediates. The trail begins as a gravel road, becomes double-track, then narrows to single-track. The first part of this 12.5-mile ride is uphill; the downhill is fairly steep but not technical. Enjoy good Teton views and heavily forested sections.

The Grand View Point ride is a bit longer. It takes off from the end of Packsaddle Road. Since it's mostly double-track, some beginners may enjoy this ride as well, but they may find themselves walking parts of the climb. You'll ride through forest and wheat field and stop for panoramic views of the Snake River Plain and the Teton Range.

The Horseshoe Canyon loop itself is a good beginner ride. It starts where Packsaddle Road ends. Cross the cattle guard and simply pedal up the Forest Service road. More difficult trails branch off for more experienced riders.

i For easy riding in Teton Valley, look for the paved path that connects the towns of Victor and Driggs. Built in 1997 by the state of Idaho along an old railroad corridor and parallel to ID 33, this 7-mile path provides a safe route for bicyclists and pedestrians between the two largest towns in the valley.

PEAKED SPORTS

70 East Little Ave., Driggs
(208) 354-2354, (800) 705-2354
www.peakedsports.com

Peaked is the valley's Schwinn headquarters in summer. The shop rents mountain bikes, and the price includes helmet, extra tube, seat pack, pump patch kit, and advice about where to go. Two-hour, four-hour, per-day, and multiday rates are available. You can rent standard performance Schwinn models and even a bike trailer to haul the kids in. And since many rides are a drive out of town, Peaked Sports rents bike racks to mount on your vehicle.

Northwestern Wyoming

Cody

With a thick network of trails around Cody, mountain bikers can coast or climb. Favorite fat-tire haunts include numerous trailheads from the North Fork of the Shoshone River and Carter Mountain south of town. For the latter ride, locals have a friend shuttle them to the top so that they can coast down through the trees, across streams, and over meadows. You can also try the trail by the remnants of the Heart Mountain Relocation Center, west of town off US 120.

ABSAROKA BIKEFITTERS

2201 Seventeenth St.
(307) 527-5566

Not only does the knowledgeable staff rent mountain bikes, they know every good trail or road in the area. Because of this their shop has become the hub for cyclists in the area. They offer mountain guides to personalize your cycling experience in and around Cody.

GOLF

Winter in Yellowstone Country makes for a short golf season. But when there's no snow on the ground, you'll be pleasantly surprised with the options you'll find out here. Municipal courses, some pleasantly mature, others relaxed and funky, allow you to play for prices that may surprise you—some are as reasonable as $15. The region's resort towns are home to award-winning courses (with the higher greens fees you might expect). Greater Yellowstone courses often make use of the lovely mountain scenery to enhance the beauty of their courses.

Jackson Hole, Wyoming

JACKSON HOLE GOLF AND TENNIS CLUB

5000 North Spring Gulch Rd.
(307) 733-3111
www.jhgtc.com

The Teton Mountains aren't the only thing that gets national press in Jackson. *Golf Digest* ranked this set of 18 holes among the top-10 resort courses in the country. Course designer Robert Trent Jones II knew this course had to be world-class. Among other challenges, he built water hazards on 11 of 18 holes. Each hole provides excellent views of the Teton and Gros Ventre mountain ranges. This public course is just 2 miles outside of Jackson. The par 72 course is rated 72.5 with a slope of 126 from the championship tees. It measures 7,168 from the white tees. Greens fees range between $65 and $190 depending on the season and time of day. The club has undergone a $15 million improvement project.

*TETON PINES RESORT AND COUNTRY CLUB
3450 North Clubhouse Dr.
(307) 733-1733
www.tetonpines.com

If playing a round of golf in the shadow of the Tetons isn't impressive enough, then you should know that Arnold Palmer designed this course, which was built in 1987 and is located just 6 miles west of Jackson off Teton Village Road. In 2004 *Condé Nast Traveler* ranked it ninth in its "Top 100 Golf Resorts in North America and the Caribbean." Teton Pines is open to the golfing public in summer; in winter it is transformed into a snaking course of cross-country ski trails. The 18-hole par 72 course is rated 75 with a slope of 137 from the gold championship tees. It measures 7,412 from the white tees.

Please wear spikeless shoes; a few complimentary pair are available for use. Greens fees are between $65 and $160, depending on the season and day. Lodge guests receive a discount. Lessons are available for $125 per hour. Reservations are necessary.

Southwestern Montana

BIG SKY RESORT
Meadow Village, Big Sky
(406) 995-5780, (800) 548-4486
www.bigskyresort.com

When you hit the ball across the fairway on this course, you are apt to startle the resident moose, deer, or elk. While this is not a destination golf course, it's hard to beat it for setting. Nestled within the Spanish Peaks, the original 9-hole course designed by Arnold Palmer has been expanded to 18 holes. Located in the Meadow Village, it is owned by Big Sky Resort. The pro shop has a complete line of golf rentals. During peak

season, 18 holes are $59, 9 holes $40. The twilight rate is $32, after 5 p.m.

BRIDGER CREEK GOLF COURSE
2710 McIlhattan Rd., Bozeman
(406) 586-2333
www.bridgercreek.com

Voted one of Montana's top-10 golf courses by *Golf Digest,* Bridger Creek sits on the edge of town along the foothills of the Bridger Mountains. At the clubhouse you'll find a pro shop with space for catered gatherings and cart rentals. Greens fees for 9 holes are $21 weekends and $19 weekdays. For 18 holes, the fees are $31 and $33. Bridger Creek is open from Apr 1 to Nov 1.

RED LODGE MOUNTAIN RESORT GOLF COURSE
828 Upper Continental Dr., Red Lodge
(406) 446-3344
www.redlodgemountain.com

Besides the sheer beauty of the Red Lodge Mountain Golf Course's location, you'll also find a challenging set of 18 holes. Three tree-lined streams flow through this golf course at the base of the Beartooth Mountains. The first half of the course offers a formidable par 3 on the sixth and eighth holes. The back nine holes weave through trees and over hazards. Built in the mid-1980s, Red Lodge Mountain Resort bought the site in 1995. After your game you can enjoy the views from the clubhouse. This course is open from Apr to early Oct. The Red Lodge Golf Academy offers regular two-day clinics for all levels from May through Aug.

Eastern Idaho

TARGHEE VILLAGE GOLF COURSE
Stateline Road, Driggs
(208) 354-8577
www.targheevillage.com

If you need a diversion from mountains, rivers, and valleys to get that golfer's fix, then this low-key 9-hole golf course nestled below the beautiful foothills of Targhee National Forest in secluded Teton Valley could be the thing for you. Fees to play 9 holes are $18; it's $24 for 18 holes. Golf carts are an additional $6 per person per 9 holes. From Jackson, follow WY 22 through Wilson and over Teton Pass to ID 33, then turn east onto 200 South or Ski Hill Road and follow the signs.

Northwestern Wyoming

OLIVE GLENN GOLF AND COUNTRY CLUB
802 Meadow Lane, Cody
(307) 587-5551
www.oliveglenngolf.com

Golf Digest ranked Olive Glenn as the fifth-best golf course in Wyoming. On top of that, this 18-hole course offers a beautiful view in every direction. This 72-par course also has a fully staffed pro shop and clubhouse and offers club and cart rental. Many Wyoming Golf Association events are held at Olive Glenn each year. Greens fees are $70 for 18 holes, $40 for 9.

WINTER SPORTS

After the hustle and bustle of the summer season is over, a chill starts to set in around the Yellowstone region, which can mean only one thing: Winter is in the air, and snow is on the way. And from Nov to Apr, that's all people seem to talk about. You hear it in the coffee shops and on the radio and read about it in the local newspapers. Though it both elates folks and irritates them, the subject of snow won't go away. After all it's winter in Yellowstone Country, and winter here revolves around snow.

OVERVIEW

For adventure seekers, winter in Yellowstone means downhill and cross-country skiing, snowmobiling and snowboarding, and dog-sled and sleigh rides. For others it means relaxing in a thermal hot pool in the middle of the woods or simply soaking in the hot tub while the kids are busy skiing. Either way, there is plenty to do when the cold sets in and the flakes are falling.

Winter is perhaps the most beautiful time of year. Snowcapped mountains stand against bright blue skies. The cold air turns rivers into frozen landscapes. Elk and moose come down from the high country and frolic in the valleys. Snowbank-lined streets give towns a magical charm not felt any other time of the year. It can be quiet and peaceful.

It can also buzz with the excitement of winter visitors. Snowmobiles invade West Yellowstone, legally cruising on snow-covered streets headed for the hundreds of miles of trails that surround the town. Ski slopes in Montana and Wyoming are dotted with jubilant locals and eager visitors, hoping to catch one of the region's renowned powder days. Still others come by ski, snow-coach, or snowmobile to see two of our finest national parks under the white shroud of winter. It sounds cliché, but this time of year Yellowstone Country is a veritable winter wonderland.

Bring your warmest clothes when you visit during winter. Near-zero temperatures are not uncommon, even during the day, and nighttime can be brutally cold, especially in the higher elevations. The flip side of this is that temperatures can warm up into the 40s and even 50s—which seems like summer to us—drawing people outside of their homes in a pre-spring frenzy. Generally daytime temperatures will be in the 20s to 30s with nighttime lows between 0 and 15 degrees Fahrenheit, but subzero temperatures are not uncommon. The important thing to remember is that in Yellowstone Country, if you don't like the weather, just wait about 15 minutes. It's bound to change.

If you plan on visiting Yellowstone or Grand Teton National Park during winter, be sure to read the respective chapters in this book about what shuts down and when roads open and close. Otherwise, enjoy the frosted scenery of what are sure to be some of the prettiest sights you'll ever see.

WINTER SAFETY TIPS

Winter in Yellowstone Country is serious stuff. Simply driving your car can be hazardous, as road and weather conditions can change instantly. Always call for road reports and carry emergency gear with you at all times. Remember, help can be far away and cell phones don't always work. Carrying extra clothes, blankets, flashlights, food, and water is a good and safe idea.

If you're venturing out into the backcountry, exercise extreme caution. The best advice is to be prepared for anything. You should always travel with a partner and let someone know where you are going and when you expect to be back. Check with rangers if you'll be in one of the parks or in a national forest. They will always be happy to tell you what conditions are like where you are planning to go. Carry emergency gear, and don't get in over your head. Hire a guide if you don't know what you are doing.

Hypothermia is extremely dangerous but can be prevented with the right knowledge. Carrying a backpack containing extra layers of clothing, food, water, and waterproof matches or a lighter is a must, as it could be days before someone may rescue you if you or your partner is hurt. Learn to recognize the symptoms of hypothermia: drowsiness, numbness, confusion, and frostbite. This means your body's core temperature is dropping and must be warmed immediately. Drink plenty of liquids, stay dry, snack frequently, and wear warm layers.

Wind in cold weather can cause frostbite in a hurry, usually signaled by numbing in the extremities and whitening tissue. Your face will be especially susceptible, so cover it immediately when the wind picks up.

Avalanches are another concern to backcountry travelers in Yellowstone Country.

Backcountry use is up, and snow conditions are a popular winter subject around these parts. Even if you are not an expert on avalanches, there are several basic things you can do to prevent yourself from being put in a situation where an avalanche could occur. Snowmobilers and backcountry skiers should be especially alert, but anyone who travels in terrain steeper than 25 degrees should pay attention.

Again prevention is the key, and understanding snow conditions is the primary method of prevention. Luckily there are avalanche centers in the Yellowstone region that list daily snow conditions and forecasts. Calling one of the numbers given below is the first step, but it's no substitute for getting educated about avalanches.

Here are a few other basic rules to help you out:

- Avoid steep terrain after heavy snowfall or prolonged high winds. Most avalanches occur on slopes between 30 and 45 degrees, and wind deposits significantly increase the load on buried snowpack.

- Try not to cross steep slopes. If you must, do so one at a time and dig a snow pit before crossing to examine layers and slide conditions. Grainy, sugary snow anywhere in the snowpack is bad, since heavy snow deposits can cause this underlying snow to slide under pressure. Travel on ridges away from cornices.

- Notice the terrain and any previous slide activity. You can usually spot where avalanches typically occur.

- Carry and know how to use an avalanche transceiver, shovel, and probe—they could save your life.

- Examine the snowpack during your activity. Check for a "whoomp" sound while walking, indicating collapsing snow, and take notice of the snowfall rate, buried layers, and type of snow on the ground.

If you are caught in an avalanche, try to keep calm and remember what to do:

- If you are on a snowmobile, get away from your machine.
- Fight to stay on the surface and try to "swim" toward the safety zone on the side of the slide.
- As you come to a stop, try to make an airspace around your face with your hands. This will give you more time if you are buried.
- If you are a survivor, watch the victim carefully and try to spot where he or she was last seen. Probe downhill from there. Keep searching and do not leave the victim. Most buried victims don't survive past 30 minutes.

In the Bozeman area, the **Gallatin National Forest Avalanche Center** covers a large area and gives daily advisories before 7 a.m. during the winter season. For the mountains near Bozeman, Big Sky, Cooke City, and West Yellowstone, you can call (406) 587-6894. You can also get advisories on the center's website: www.mtavalanche.com.

Near Jackson Hole, you can call the **Avalanche Hazard Forecast Hotline** at (307) 733-2664 for updated information, or you can visit www.jhavalanche.org.

DOWNHILL SKIING

Montana

BIG SKY RESORT
1 Lone Mountain Trail, Big Sky
(406) 995-5000, (800) 548-4486
www.bigskyresort.com

Big Sky is Montana's largest ski area, with 3,800 acres of skiing on three mountains

---

Safe Driving

Driving around Yellowstone Country in winter takes special care. Generally there are three main rules to follow: visibility, common sense, and patience. First, see and be seen. Keep headlights, taillights, and windshields clean. Leave plenty of room between your vehicle and those around you, and drive defensively. Test the road for traction. Give yourself extra time to travel. Being in a hurry on icy roads can get you and others into trouble. Only drive as fast as road conditions allow, and leave the cruise control off. Finally, be prepared with road and weather information before you set out on your trip, and it's always a good idea to carry emergency gear. Call (800) 226-7623 or 511 for Montana road conditions, (307) 772-0824 for Wyoming, and (888) IDA-ROAD for Idaho.

---

and more than 150 trails served by 16 lifts. Big Sky is built around Lone Mountain, an 11,166-foot pyramid-shaped peak that you can actually go up to and come down. A 15-passenger tram was installed in 1995, whisking skiers to the steep, rocky summit and giving Big Sky a whopping 4,350-foot vertical drop. The ride alone is worth it, as you can watch expert skiers descend the wild Big Couloir from the window. You can opt to return on the tram if you're not feeling up to testing your skills. Technically there is no easy way down from the top, although the black-diamond Liberty Bowl can be tackled by most advanced intermediate skiers.

The skiing at Big Sky, which usually lasts from mid-Nov until mid-Apr, is nothing short of fantastic. Whether you're a seasoned veteran or a willing first-timer, there is enough terrain to keep you riding different trails each day of your visit. Advanced skiers will find rocky chutes and steep bowls off the Challenger double chair, the Lone Peak triple chair, and the Tram, as well as excellent glades off the Ramcharger and Thunderwolf quad chairs. Explorer and Southern Comfort are excellent beginners-only lifts, while the trails off the Swiftcurrent quad will test advanced beginners through expert skiers. The snow falls often here, to the tune of 400 inches a year, so conditions are usually soft and fun for all levels. The Dakota lift offers access to the runs on the south side of Lone Peak, including the fun trees of the Bavarian Forest. There are usually two terrain parks available at Big Sky, although their location seems to change from year to year. You can find food in the Mountain Village base area and at the base of the Iron Horse chairlift on the north side of the mountain, as well as at the top of the Ramcharger quad. Nightlife isn't something Big Sky is known for, but there are plenty of après-ski activities going on after the lifts close. You'll also find live music in many of the bars in Mountain Village. For more information, see the Big Sky chapter in this book.

Big Sky has a Euro-western flavor and a relaxed atmosphere. Most people come here to get away from some of the busier ski areas in the West, and they find Big Sky a quiet, out-of-the-way gem that they return to often. Much of it is upscale, with world-class restaurants, boutiques, and accommodations, but Big Sky can also be done on a budget. Either way, it is a great way to experience all that Montana has to offer.

Full-day lift tickets are $81 for adults, $61 for juniors ages 11 to 17 or college students. Kids 10 and younger ski free. You can buy tickets online at a slight discount. A Biggest Skiing in American ticket for Big Sky and Moonlight is $95. Rental and instruction are available; the ski area is located 43 miles south of Bozeman on US 191.

BRIDGER BOWL
15795 Bridger Canyon Rd., Bozeman
(406) 586-1518, (800) 223-9609
www.bridgerbowl.com
Bridger Bowl is Bozeman's local ski area and is located 16 miles north of town on MT 86. Bridger offers an excellent combination of terrain, atmosphere, and value, and it is a great spot for families, hard-core skiers, and snowboarders alike. The resort sits on the east side of the Bridger Mountains below a long ridge and offers more than 71 runs on 2,000 acres and 2,700 vertical feet. There are eight lifts that serve a variety of terrain, including open bowls, glades, chutes, and groomed trails. Bridger is well known for the 350 inches of light, fluffy powder, what the locals call "cold smoke," that falls each year.

Beginners will want to stick to the lower mountain, serviced by the Virginia City double chair and the quad chair at the base, while experts can find great runs from every chair. The Bridger double chair travels farthest up the mountain but not all the way to the top of the ridge. Advanced skiers with an avalanche beacon, shovel, and partner are allowed to hike the remaining distance to access some of the best terrain in the West. Check with the ski patrol shack at the top of the Bridger lift if you are a first-timer up the ridge.

The Schlassman's lift opens up some of Bridger's best terrain. Skiers and boarders

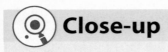 **Close-up**

Altitude without the Attitude

The big ski resorts of Yellowstone Country are among the best in the world. But if you want to get away from their big crowds and big prices, there are many smaller ski areas that make great day trips from wherever you are staying in our region. Taking a trip to one of these has many advantages. First, you'll be away from the hustle and bustle of resort towns. These small ski areas are often located in out-of-the-way smaller towns that don't depend on dollars from the ski area. Second, you'll be able to see more of the beautiful country that surrounds the Yellowstone region without having to go too far. These small ski areas are bargains. They are great for families, offer plenty of bang for the buck, and are an unforgettable off-the-beaten-path adventure.

If you are staying in the Bozeman area during the winter, you have a few options. The first is **Discovery Ski Basin,** (406) 563-2184, www.skidiscovery.com, located about two hours west of Bozeman near the old mining town of Anaconda. Discovery has a vertical drop of 1,300 feet and more than 40 runs, evenly divided among beginners, intermediates, and experts. The lift on the back side serves some of the steepest terrain in the state. All-day tickets are $35, half that for kids and seniors. Rentals and instruction are available. Nearby Fairmont Hot Springs, (800) 332-3272 or www.fairmontmontana.com, is a popular place to stay while skiing at Discovery.

Showdown, (800) 433-0022, www.showdownmontana.com, about two hours north of Bozeman on US 89, offers 34 trails and a 1,400-foot vertical drop. There's also a half-pipe and terrain park for snowboarders, and more than 240 inches of snow falls here each year. Full-day tickets are $35.

About 90 miles south of Jackson on US 191, you'll find **White Pine Ski Area,** (307) 367-7222, www.whitepineski.com, a bargain at only $40. The 9,500-foot summit produces outstanding views of the rugged Wind River Mountains, the Continental Divide, and 11-mile-long Fremont Lake.

Kelly Canyon Ski Area, (208) 538-6251, www.skikelly.com, is located 26 miles from Idaho Falls. It offers 640 acres and 26 trails of skiing and snowboarding with a 1,000-foot vertical drop. There is a terrain park with a halfpipe, and lessons and rentals are available. Kelly Canyon is one of the few areas around that offer night skiing (every day except Sun), and it is open every day at 9:30 a.m. Lift tickets are $35.

Another small Idaho ski area is **Pebble Creek,** situated just outside the city of Pocatello and about three hours from Jackson Hole. There are 54 runs spread out over 1,100 acres, and the vertical drop is an impressive 2,200 feet. From the top of the Skyline chair, advanced skiers can access the vast, challenging backcountry of the Caribou-Targhee National Forest, while freestylers can enjoy the terrain park served by the Aspen lift. Rentals and lessons are available, and lift tickets are $38. Check it out at www.pebblecreekskiarea.com.

Sleeping Giant Ski Area, (307) 587-3182, near Cody, reopened in the winter of 2009–10 and is a journey back in skiing history. Originally opened as the Red Star Camp in 1936, the family friendly Sleeping Giant is one of the oldest ski areas in the country. A new chairlift and a magic carpet for the kids have been added, and full-day lift tickets are only $29. There are 180 acres of skiing and a small terrain park, a nice day lodge with restaurant and rental shop.

must have an avalanche beacon to ride this lift. There are no named runs in the Schlass-man's area, just acres and acres of untouched powder.

You can grab a bite at the Deer Park Chalet halfway up the mountain or at the base lodge cafeteria. In the base area, Jimmy B's is the après-ski hot spot, offering great burgers and sandwiches, and FaceShots features occasional live music. The often sun-drenched patio at the base lodge is also a great spot to relax after a day on the slopes.

Lift tickets are $47 for adults, $16 for children (age 5 and younger free), and complete rental packages start at about $25 a day. Lodging packages are also available.

i **Dress warmly and bring extra clothes while exploring the parks during winter. Daytime temperatures often hover near zero, occasionally reaching into the 20s, and subzero temperatures are common at night. The lowest temperature ever recorded in Yellowstone was 66 degrees below zero in 1933.**

✳MOONLIGHT BASIN
1020 Montana Hwy. 64, Big Sky
(406) 993-6000
www.moonlightbasin.com
Developed in the 1990s, Moonlight Basin is one of the country's newest ski areas. It offers breathtaking terrain, short lift lines, and excellent service (complimentary hand warmers every time you ride up the mountain). An adult day pass is $58, and a junior day pass (ages 11 to 17) is $49; children 10 and younger ski free. A Biggest Skiing in America lift ticket, which allows skiing at Big Sky and Moonlight, is $95.

The northerly exposure ensures the best snow conditions in Montana (an average 400 inches of light, dry powder each year helps, too). Offering 2,000 acres of skiable terrain, there are challenges for beginners, long winding cruisers, and some truly hair-raising steeps and chutes, as well as groomed cruisers and powder stashes that last for days.

Riding the Six Shooter six-person high-speed chairlift accesses the broadest range of Moonlight's runs, from the beginner-level Lazy Jack that gently swoops down the mountain back to the main lodge or down the bomber black diamond Runaway. The Derringer and Pony Express chairlifts serve easier and learning terrain. The Lone Tree quad offers access to some good powder in Stillwater Bowl and Obsidian, and the resort's longest cruisers—Horseshoe, Trembler, and Lookout Ridge—are also found off this lift. For some excellent gladed runs, try Marshal, Big Tree Cutoff, and Broken Heart.

The Headwaters area—served by a double chair—allows intrepid skiers to hike along a mile-long ridge and descend down a variety of steep chutes. You can also drop into Big Sky Resort at the top of the Headwaters chair if you have a Biggest Skiing in America ticket.

In the winter of 2005–06, Moonlight opened one of the longest lift-served runs in North America. The North Summit Snowfield, accessed with a Biggest Skiing in American ticket, allows skiers to take Big Sky Resort's tram and drop off to Moonlight's north side of the mountain—via an experts-only, 4,150-foot run. It's like skiing down from the top of the world. Those interested need to check in at the Moonlight ski patrol shack at the top of Lone Peak and must carry avalanche rescue gear.

The newly built Madison base area is where you will find the rental shop, ski school, and a lodge that serves lunch and dinner. There is also a small lodge and restaurant at the base of the Pony Express lift.

RED LODGE MOUNTAIN
P.O. Box 750, Red Lodge, MT 59068
(406) 446-2610, (800) 444-8977
www.redlodgemountain.com
Red Lodge is a medium-size mountain perched at the foot of the Beartooth Mountains, a vast alpine plateau with more peaks above 10,000 feet than any other place in the country. Although Red Lodge is only about an hour from Cooke City and the northeast entrance to Yellowstone, the section of US 212 that connects the two is closed during winter. You can access Red Lodge only from the east from Billings or northeast via I-90 and Columbus.

Once you get there, you won't be disappointed. The mountain offers 2,400 vertical feet of skiing spread out over 1,600 acres in the Custer National Forest. There are more than 70 trails, with 15 percent for novices, 55 percent for intermediates, and 30 percent for experts. Snowmaking covers 40 percent of the trails, and the area receives an average 250 inches of snow per year.

Advanced skiers should head for the top of Nichols Peak (9,390 feet) via the Cole Creek quad chair to access some recently developed terrain, which includes the Headwaters glades area and a few double-black-diamond runs. The Grizzly Peak double chair also hits some great expert terrain, like the West and East Park glades and the Buckin' Chute. The middle of the mountain is reserved for novice skiers, and there are some great green runs off the triple chair in the base area. Some fun intermediate

cruisers can be found near the Palisades quad chair.

The best time to ski Red Lodge is toward the end of the season, when the Beartooths see most of their snow. It is a great mountain for all abilities, and the quaint, western town of Red Lodge is a unique and fun place to stay. The shop-lined Main Street is a nice example of small-town Montana. Lift tickets are $49 for adults and $42 for juniors (13 to 18). Children ages 6 to 12 pay $19; 5 and under ski free.

Wyoming

GRAND TARGHEE SKI AND SUMMER RESORT
Ski Hill Road, Alta
(307) 353-2300, (800) 827-4433
www.grandtarghee.com
Only one word can accurately describe the Grand Targhee skiing experience: powder. With an annual snowfall total of more than 500 inches, this somewhat undiscovered resort proudly proclaims that it gets its "Snow from Heaven, Not Hoses." It's light, fluffy, and plentiful.

Targhee is located 42 miles west of Jackson Hole, over the steep and winding Teton Pass. The pass may close during inclement weather, so call ahead. The mountain is located in Wyoming, but you will go through Idaho and the rustic town of Driggs before getting there. If you arrive early on a powder day, head directly to the summit on the Dreamcatcher quad chair and pick a trail and go. You won't believe how effortlessly you float in the feathery powder. Advanced skiers will want to stick to Dreamcatcher, the Blackfoot chair, and Sacajawea, the new high-speed detachable quad on Peaked Mountain, which access all the intermediate and expert terrain on the mountain. The only beginner runs are serviced by the Shoshone quad chair at the base area.

Targhee's long season often gets the jump on Jackson Hole and is one reason even Jackson locals make the one-hour drive over the pass to ride powder all day. It isn't as steep as Jackson Hole, but who cares when there is a foot of fresh powder? Typically the season runs from mid-Nov until mid-Apr.

There are 2,000 acres of terrain at Targhee and 2,200 vertical feet of skiing. Only 300 acres are groomed, however, leaving the trail busting to you. If you have some extra cash, you can pay about $399 (includes lunch) for a day of incredible snowcat powder skiing on more than 1,500 additional acres. The quaint base area has a variety of great lodging, restaurants, shops, and services, including a full-service rental and repair shop. Lift tickets are $69 full day and $59 half day (12:30 p.m.), which is a bargain for the fresh tracks you're likely to get. Juniors (ages 6 to 12) ski for $39, and kids age 5 and younger ski for free. Multiday rates are available.

JACKSON HOLE MOUNTAIN RESORT
3395 West McCollister Dr., Teton Village
(307) 733-2292, (888) 333-7766
www.jacksonhole.com
Jackson Hole is one of the premier ski destinations in the world, where skiers and snowboarders come for a real western experience—spectacular snow and friendly folks amid the cowboy charm of a small, vibrant town. The ski area is located in Teton Village, about 10 miles from the town of Jackson, at the base of 10,450-foot Rendezvous Mountain. The original aerial tram was discontinued at the end of the 2006 season, and a new, larger tram was installed in the winter of 2008–09. Skiing all the way down will give you a leg-burning 4,139 feet, one of the tallest continuous vertical rise of any ski resort in America. There are 2,500 acres of it to choose from.

Jackson Hole is truly an expert's mountain, as 50 percent of the inbounds terrain is marked advanced or expert. The resort's open-gate policy adds another 2,500 skiable acres and access to numerous bowls, glades, and peaks. This terrain is for skiers and snowboarders with knowledge and possession of avalanche safety and rescue equipment.

Much of Jackson's inbounds expert terrain is accessed by the tram and the Sublette quad chair, as well as the Thunder quad. The Hobacks offer powder turns, and the gnarly Corbett's Couloir is one of the best-known expert-only runs in the world. If you're just beginning or are an intermediate, don't be discouraged by Jackson's steeps, because there is plenty for you, too. The Bridger gondola, the Casper Bowl triple chair, and the Après Vous quad chair offer confidence-building intermediate terrain and fun, long runs. Beginners and first-timers will want to stick to the Teewinot quad, which serves the only green runs on the mountain.

It can take days to explore all of Jackson Hole's terrain, but the time spent is well worth it. Mountain hosts lead complimentary orientation tours for intermediate-level skiers daily at 9:30 a.m. from the Mountain Host Building. Advanced riders can also hire a guide from the Jackson Hole Ski and Snowboard Guide Service by calling (307) 739-2663.

The Jackson Hole Nordic Center, (307) 739-2629, offers 17 kilometers of groomed trails at the base of Teton Village. Jackson Hole gets an average 400 inches of snow every winter, making the skiing and snowboarding here unforgettable. Lift tickets are

$91 for adults full day during peak season. Juniors (age 6 to 14) ski for $55, and kids 5 and under ski free. Call the snow report at (307) 733-2291 or (888) DEEP-SNO. Look for discounted season lift ticket rates during the first few weeks of the season and from mid-Mar to the end of the season.

SNOW KING RESORT
400 East Snow King Ave., Jackson
(307) 733-5200, (800) 522-5464
www.snowking.com

Snow King—founded in 1939—was Wyoming's first ski area, and it's affectionately called the Town Hill by Jackson locals. While the Jackson Hole Ski Resort may get all the attention from the skiing world, a ski trip to Jackson wouldn't be complete without spending a day at Snow King. It's also the home of King Tubes, a tubing park adjacent to the resort hotel. Tubing rates are about $16 for one hour for adults, $13 for those 13 and under.

Minutes from Jackson's town square, Snow King offers 1,571 vertical feet of skiing—and most of it is vertical. The ski area has some of the steepest lift-served terrain in the country, with numerous double-black-diamond runs off the Summit chairlift, including Bearcat, Upper Exhibition, and Belly Roll. The Rafferty chair and surface tow are perfect for beginner skiers, and the Cougar chair serves the middle of the mountain and most of the ski area's intermediate terrain.

Snow King is a popular and convenient spot for locals who just want to get a few runs in, and it therefore offers two-hour tickets ($22) for those wanting to spend lunch hour on the slopes. There is also a terrain park and half-pipe, and night skiing from 4 to 7 p.m. Tues through Sat. Full-day adult lift tickets are $42, and $32 for a half day. Tickets for junior skiers 14 and

younger are $32 for a full day and $22 for a half day. Night tickets are $20 for adults and $15 for juniors. If you want to stay on the mountain, you can choose from more than 200 hotel rooms and condos, and you'll get a discounted rate on lift tickets.

CROSS-COUNTRY SKIING & SNOWSHOEING
Yellowstone National Park

Yellowstone's 2.2 million acres provide hundreds of miles of trails. From groomed-track skiing to backcountry touring, Yellowstone is a cross-country paradise with breathtaking winter scenery, abundant wildlife, and plenty of snow. There are cross-country trails in all areas of the park, including Old Faithful, Tower, Mammoth, Northeast, and Northwest.

Remember that only the road from Mammoth to Cooke City is open during winter and all other areas must be accessed by snowcoach, snowmobile, or skis. Conditions can change rapidly, so be prepared by carrying extra clothes and emergency gear, even if you are sticking to groomed trails. All unplowed roads and trails are open to cross-country skiing and snowshoeing, and a permit is required if you want to camp in the backcountry. There are many more trails than listed here, so check at the visitor centers for detailed maps and information.

i **Yellowstone National Park offers many ranger-led programs during winter. Snowshoe walks begin in West Yellowstone and Mammoth and focus on the park's winter ecology, wildlife, and geographic features. Stop in at one of the visitor centers or check the winter edition of *Yellowstone Today,* which you receive when you enter the park.**

NORTHEAST REGION

There are many trailheads along the open road between Mammoth and Cooke City. The Tower Fall Trail begins at Tower Junction and follows an unplowed road for 2.5 miles to Tower Fall. There are great views of the Yellowstone River Canyon, and you may run into bald eagles, bison, or bighorn sheep. From the fall you can continue along the 5.5-mile Chittenden Loop Trail or return the way you came.

Advanced skiers should try the 6-mile Bunsen Peak Trail, reached by taking a snow-coach from Mammoth to the trailhead. The trail is steep in spots and has some sharp turns, but it gives you splendid views of the Gallatin Range and Gardiner River Canyon.

The Blacktail Deer Creek/Yellowstone River Trail begins 7.5 miles east of Mammoth and is 12.5 (one-way) miles long. It is a great trail to spot wildlife, including bison, elk, deer, and coyotes. The scenery isn't bad either, as broad meadows give way to high, snow-covered peaks.

The Upper Terrace Trail gives you great views of the steaming lower terraces. If you've seen these in the summer, imagine them surrounded by a white blanket of snow with steam rising all around. The trail is 1.5 miles, follows Upper Terrace Drive, and starts right in Mammoth. Remember to stay on the trail, as the ground around thermal features is very unstable.

NORTHWEST REGION

There are several excellent trails leading from US 191 south of Big Sky into the park. There is no gate or entry fee here, and trailheads are located at pullouts on the side of the road. At milepost 20 you'll find the trail to Bighorn Pass, which follows the Gallatin River for a while and can be a great spot to watch for elk, eagles, moose, and coyotes.

The Fawn Pass Trail leaves at milepost 22 and goes through timber and meadows after crossing the Gallatin River. It hooks up with the Big Horn Pass Trail after about 6 miles. Specimen Creek, another favorite, is located at milepost 27. This enjoyable trek follows the creek as it gradually rises through forest and meadows. Look for elk, moose, and petrified trees on the exposed ridges above you.

A nice trail with great views of high peaks and open meadows is the Bacon Rind, which begins a few miles south of Specimen Creek on US 191. The trail begins in the park and then goes back into national forest-land, following a drainage ditch for 5 miles of gentle open terrain. Look for numerous 9,000-foot peaks as the trail climbs.

A well-kept secret is Telemark Meadows, located on the west side of US 191 at milepost 18. As the trail gains elevation you can test your telemark powder turns on a variety of gentle to steep slopes while enjoying great views of the Madison and Gallatin Mountains.

OLD FAITHFUL AREA

Part of the beauty of skiing in Yellowstone Park is the numerous thermal features you will encounter. Gone are the crowds of summer, and you will feel like you have the park to yourself. The contrast between the cold snow surrounding the geysers and hot pots and the rising steam is breathtaking. The Lone Star Geyser Trail is no exception. This moderate 9-mile trail begins at Old Faithful Lodge and takes you past Kepler Cascades and alongside the Firehole River to the geyser. The geyser erupts about every three hours from a 12-foot-high cinder cone. Advanced skiers can return via the Howard

Eaton Trail, but it is steep and should be skied with caution.

The 8-mile Fairy Falls Trail is another favorite. Hop on a snowcoach from Old Faithful Lodge to the trailhead and follow the signs. The trail winds past spectacular ice-encrusted waterfalls and through burned trees. You can head back to the lodge by following the snowcoach road to the Biscuit Basin Trail, which will take you past the scenic Upper Geyser Basin, Morning Glory Pool, and Geyser Hill.

Grand Teton National Park

Grand Teton has about 40 miles of ungroomed skiing and snowshoe trails that are among the most popular in the region. It's hard to blame skiers for flocking here, as the views alone are worth it even if the skiing is crowded. Snow isn't usually a problem, as an average of 4 feet falls even in the lowest elevations. Trails range in difficulty to suit novice and advanced skiers.

Skiing and snowshoeing are not limited to marked trails, and to get away from some of the crowds it may be necessary to explore the park on your own. If you choose this route, make sure the area you are planning to ski in isn't closed. Check with the Craig Thomas Discovery and Visitor Center upon entering the park, and while you're there pick up any one of several good maps.

Only marked trails will be described here. Generally tall flags stick out of the snow, allowing you to follow the markers after a fresh snowfall if previous tracks are covered.

JENNY LAKE TRAIL

This trail—great for any level of skier—provides some of the best views in the park. The 9-mile trail starts at the Taggart Lake parking area and heads north along Cottonwood

Creek, climbing slowly through wide meadows with panoramic views of the Tetons. You'll skirt the base of the range until the Jenny Lake Overlook, where you'll hope you still have fresh batteries in your camera. The return trip is mostly level, taking you back to the parking area.

Snow Hikes

Grand Teton National Park provides free, ranger-led snowshoe hikes several times a week from late Dec to Mar. The 1.5-mile tours include talks on snowshoeing history and winter life in the park and take about two hours. The hikes, reserved for adults and children age eight and older, leave from the Craig Thomas Discovery and Visitor Center and snowshoes are provided. Dress warmly and wear warm footwear. Reservations are required, and you can make them by calling (307) 739-3399.

SIGNAL MOUNTAIN

If you're feeling confident after the Jenny Lake loop, try this 10-mile round-trip that takes you to the top of this popular peak. Start at the end of the road near the Signal Mountain Lodge, then ski south along a snowmobile trail until you see the Signal Mountain Road heading up to the east. The climb to the summit is a gradual 4 miles, and you'll be rewarded with outstanding views across the valley of the entire Teton Range, as well as the icy Snake River on the valley floor. The return trip is a blast—downhill all the way to your car.

Montana

B BAR GUEST RANCH
818 Tom Miner Creek Rd., Emigrant
(406) 848-7523
www.bbar.com

This full-service guest ranch lies in a beautiful basin bordering the northwest corner of Yellowstone National Park and provides 30 kilometers of groomed trails for all skill levels. This newly renovated property is just 26 miles from Gardiner, Montana. The B Bar is open only in the winter from mid-Dec until the end of Feb, and trails are open to the public on weekends from 9 a.m. until 4 p.m.

BOHART RANCH
16621 Bridger Canyon Rd., Bozeman
(406) 586-9070
www.bohartranchxcski.com

Bohart Ranch is an outstanding facility offering 29 kilometers of groomed and tracked trails with spectacular views of the Bridger Mountains. Trails are groomed for diagonal and skating techniques, and there is a biathlon range, rentals, lessons, snacks, and a warming hut. Bohart Ranch is located just north of the Bridger Bowl ski area, 16 miles northeast of Bozeman on MT 86. Daily rates are $15 for adults, $8 for kids ages 7 to 12. Kids 6 and younger and adults age 70 and older are admitted free. No credit cards accepted.

LINDLEY PARK
East Main Street, Bozeman

This beautiful Bozeman park has a 1.5-kilometer loop trail that winds its way through huge trees, rolling hills, and flat meadows. It's a popular local spot when there is snow, usually from Nov until Apr. A small sledding hill here is also a popular gathering place. Lindley Park is located on the south side of East Main Street as you are heading out of town toward I-90.

✳LONE MOUNTAIN RANCH
P.O. Box 160069, Big Sky, MT 59716
(406) 995-4644, (800) 514-4644
www.lmranch.com

Lone Mountain Ranch is a full-service winter vacation resort with 90 kilometers of groomed, tilled, and tracked trails for all skill levels. Trails are groomed for traditional skiing and skating. Portions of the trails meander through the Gallatin National Forest, and the views of Lone Mountain and the surrounding peaks are nothing short of incredible. Lone Mountain Ranch was named by *Mountain Living* and *Snow Country* magazines as the top cross-country ski resort in the western United States. Don't worry, you don't have to be a guest at the ranch to ski. Full-day ($20) and multiday rates are available. See the Big Sky chapter in this book for details on the resort, including lodging, dining, and other activities. Also ask about ski tours into Yellowstone Park.

RED LODGE NORDIC CENTER
P.O. Box 1668, Red Lodge, MT 59068
(406) 425-0698
www.beartoothtrails.org

The Red Lodge Nordic Center is located 2 miles west of the town of Red Lodge on MT 78. It offers 15 kilometers of groomed trails, rentals, instruction, snacks, and snowshoe rentals. Trails range from open meadows to rolling loops through aspen trees. A day-use fee of $5 is charged to help maintain the trails.

WADE LAKE RESORT
963 US 287 North, #1, Cameron
(406) 682-7560
www.wadelake.com

This small resort—elevation 6,300 feet—is located 30 miles west of West Yellowstone on Wade Lake, part of a designated Montana Wildlife Viewing site. There is little development around this area, except for the five small cabins and main lodge, which must be accessed by skis from the parking area during winter. The 35 kilometers of groomed trails as well as miles of backcountry areas cover lakeshores, riversides, aspen groves, rolling hills, and old-growth fir forests. Winter cabin rates range from $100 to $150, depending on number of people and duration of stay.

YELLOWSTONE EXPEDITIONS
P.O. Box 865, West Yellowstone,
MT 59758
(406) 646-9333, (800) 728-9333
www.yellowstoneexpeditions.com
Yellowstone Expeditions offers backcountry cross-country skiing tours from the Yellowstone Yurt Camp near the Grand Canyon of the Yellowstone in Yellowstone National Park. The main camp consists of two large, heated yurts where guests eat and socialize before heading to bed in private, heated tent cabins—large, sturdy canvas structures. Four-, five-, and eight-day tours are offered, with trips to the Rim of the Canyon, Mount Washburn, Cascade Creek, and backcountry hot-spring pools. Snowcoaches transport guests to and from West Yellowstone and to the trailheads for the daily tours. The yurt camp also includes a sauna and shower. Package excursions include ski guides, all meals, lodging, and transportation. Backcountry snowshoe excursions are also offered. The camp accommodates only 10 guests, so this is a great way to see parts of the park that few get to see in the winter. Prices range from $900 to $1,500 per person.

Gallatin National Forest Trails
This immense forest has hundreds of miles of groomed and backcountry trails. Some trails are described below, but for more information contact the forest headquarters at 3710 Fallon St., Bozeman, MT 59718. Phone is (406) 522-2520, or check out the informative website: www.fs.fed.us/r1/gallatin.

BEAR CREEK ROAD
More than 6 kilometers of easy, groomed trail skiing takes you up through the tall timber above Gardiner. For information, contact the district ranger in Gardiner at (406) 848-7375.

BOZEMAN CREEK TO MYSTIC LAKE
To get to the trailhead of this 10-mile (one-way) moderate, uphill route, follow South Third Avenue from Bozeman to Nash Road. Head west on Nash and make a left onto Bozeman Creek Road. The trailhead is 1 mile south from there. Climbing from 5,220 to 6,550 feet and ending at the Mystic Lake Ranger Station, the trail provides expansive views of the Hyalite Range. You can combine this with the New World Gulch Trail to make a nice loop, although this makes the route steeper and much more difficult.

RENDEZVOUS SKI TRAILS
More than 35 kilometers of trails groomed daily begin at the intersection of Geyser Street and Obsidian Avenue in West Yellowstone. Trails, which range from easy to difficult, are open from Dec 1 through Mar 30 and provide great snow and scenic beauty. Day passes are $8, season passes are $40, and family season passes are $75. All are available at the West Yellowstone Chamber of Commerce, (406) 646-7701; the Hebgen Lake Ranger District Office, (406) 646-7369;

and several ski shops in town. It's no accident that these trails are among the finest in the country, as many of the top national teams in the world use them as training grounds. Groomer Doug Edgerton was the chief of grooming for the cross-country and biathlon trials of the 2002 Winter Olympics in Salt Lake City. Find out more at www.rendezvous skitrails.com.

i If you are skiing at Jackson Hole and want to take a break from the slopes, a naturalist-led snowshoe hike is complimentary with your Alpine or Nordic lift ticket, snowshoes included. Call (307) 739-2753.

Wyoming

GRAND TARGHEE SKI AND SUMMER RESORT
Ski Hill Road, Alta
(307) 353-2300, (800) TARGHEE
www.grandtarghee.com
Grand Targhee is about an hour west of Jackson and offers 15 kilometers of groomed tracks and fresh powder that accommodate skating and classic skiing styles. Adult passes are $10, seniors and children pay $6. Group and private lessons are available.

JACKSON HOLE NORDIC CENTER
Teton Village
(307) 739-2629
www.jacksonhole.com
This full-service Nordic center lies at the base of Jackson Hole Mountain Resort and offers 17 kilometers of professionally groomed trails as well as rentals, instruction, dog-sledding trips, snowshoe tours and rentals, guided backcountry nature tours, and more. A full day is $14. You can also transfer your downhill lift ticket for a Nordic pass, so you can ride the lifts in the morning and skate in the afternoon. And 10 kilometers of trails are open to your four-legged friend. The center is open daily 8:30 a.m. to 4:30 p.m.

Idaho

✳HARRIMAN STATE PARK
US 20, Island Park
(208) 558-7368
Although Island Park is a snowmobiling hot spot, skinny skiers can visit Harriman and avoid the sled traffic. No snowmobiles are allowed here, and 15 kilometers of groomed trails await you. The easy Ranch loop takes skiers past the historic Railroad Ranch, along the north side of Silver Lake, and back to the main trail. You can stop in at the Jones House warming hut to thaw out by the fire. Look for trumpeter swans in the park's open water. There are several other trails to choose from after this good warm-up. Thurman and Silver Lake loops are moderate and the more difficult Ridge loop has a few steep hills.

You can rent a pair of skis at the **Last Chance Texaco,** (208) 558-7399, just north of the park. Call the **Island Park Ranger District,** (208) 558-7301, or the **Ashton Ranger District,** (208) 652-7442 for more information and ski conditions.

Cross-Country Skiing & Snowshoeing Rentals

Yellowstone National Park
XANTERRA PARKS AND RESORTS
Mammoth
(307) 344-7901
You can rent skis and snowshoes from the park's main concessionaire, Xanterra, at Mammoth and Old Faithful. Full-day ski touring packages are about $18.50, $12 for a half day. Full-day snowshoe rentals run around

$15, $10 for a half day. Instruction is available, and children 12 and younger get a 20 percent discount on any package, rental, or lesson. Xanterra also offers guided ski tours from Mammoth and Old Faithful.

Montana

BANGTAIL BICYCLE AND SKI
508 West Main St., Bozeman
(406) 587-4905

Bangtail—named after a mountain range northeast of town—has the largest selection of Nordic equipment in Bozeman, and the shop rents cross-country skis for $12 a day. Skis with metal edges (telemark) run $18 a day and snowshoes are $10. (The shop also rents bikes in the summer.)

BUD LILLY'S
39 Madison Ave., West Yellowstone
(406) 646-7801

You can rent a pair of cross-country skis at Bud Lilly's Ski Shop for $15 per day, and showshoes are available for $12 per day.

COOKE CITY BIKE SHACK
US 212, Cooke City
(406) 838-2412

Visit Bill Blackford for cross-country and telemark skis, as well as snowshoes and backcountry accessories. Nordic skis are $10 a day, telemark skis are $18, and snowshoes are $10. Every third day is half price. If telemarking is your thing, Blackford will take you by snowmobile to Daisy Pass, where you can choose a variety of ascents or ski right back down to town. The 2,500-foot run is epic—powder conditions and glade skiing through the burned trees of the 1988 Yellowstone fires. The Bike Shack also has a nice selection of topographic and other maps. Ask about the cozy yurt accommodations.

FREE HEEL AND WHEEL
40 Yellowstone Ave., West Yellowstone
(406) 646-7744
www.freeheelandwheel.com

You can rent all kinds of skis at Free Heel and Wheel, including touring, skate, and classic styles. Standard cross-country packages start at $20 a day, or $8 per hour if you're running short on time. The shop also rents snowshoes for the same price.

GRIZZLY OUTFITTERS
Town Center, Big Sky
(406) 995-2939
www.grizzlyoutfitters.com

Grizzly Outfitters rents cross-country skis for $18 and snowshoes for $15 a day, with reduced rates for multiday rentals. Grizzly Outfitters also rents bikes in summer.

NORTHERN LIGHTS TRADING COMPANY
1716 West Babcock St., Bozeman
(406) 586-2225
www.northernlightstrading.com

The friendliest staff in town will rent you a pair of Nordic skis for $20 a day. Snowshoes are also available. The staff is full of tips on where the best skiing is and how to get there.

THE ROUND HOUSE SKI AND SPORTS CENTER
1422 West Main St., Bozeman
(406) 587-1258
www.roundhouse-sports.com

The Round House offers Alpine and Nordic ski rentals in town and at their location at the base of the Bridger Bowl ski area, (406) 587-2838. Nordic ski packages are $12 a day, as are snowshoes. Snowboards are also available, and both shops offer waxing and tuning.

Wyoming
GRAND TARGHEE RESORT
Ski Hill Road, Alta
(307) 353-2300, (800) 827-4433
www.grandtarghee.com
The ski resort rents full cross-country packages for around $30 for a full day. Lessons are available, and there are 15 kilometers of groomed tracks around the resort.

✳SKINNY SKIS
65 West Deloney Ave., Jackson
(307) 733-6094
www.skinnyskis.com
As its name implies, this is Jackson's skinny ski headquarters. The shop rents touring, telemark, and skate skis as well as snowshoes. Prices are $15, $25, $18, and $12, respectively. The Skinny Skis staff is very knowledgeable about trails in the area, so ask around for some helpful hints. Also pick up a copy of *Trailhead*, an area magazine published twice a year that will lead you in the right direction.

i Even on vacation it's fun to have some adult time away from kids. Most ski areas in the region have children's programs on the mountain. Whether it's ski school, private lessons, or a child-care center that takes them out to build a snowman, there's something fun and engaging for your child in Yellowstone Country.

SUNLIGHT SPORTS
1251 Sheridan Ave., Cody
(307) 587-9517
www.sunlightsports.com
Cody's oldest sporting-goods store rents cross-country gear for $8 for adults, $5 for kids ages 8 to 13, and $3 for kids age 7 and

younger. You can also rent snowshoes for $9 a day.

TETON MOUNTAINEERING
170 North Cache St., Jackson
(307) 733-3595, (800) 850-3595
www.tetonmountaineering.com
This full-service skiing, climbing, and mountaineering shop rents cross-country skis and snowshoes for $10 a day.

Idaho
YÖSTMARK MOUNTAIN EQUIPMENT
285 East Little Ave., Driggs
(208) 354-2828
www.yostmark.com
This is one of the Teton Valley's finest shops, specializing in telemark and backcountry ski gear. You can rent Nordic equipment for $20 per day and snowshoes for $15 per day. Call for prices and availability of telemark and snowboard rentals.

DOGSLED TOURS

ABSAROKA DOGSLED TREKS
Chico Hot Springs, Pray, MT
(406) 333-4933, (800) 468-9232
www.extrememontana.com
Veteran musher Mark Nardin runs these tours from the historic Chico Hot Springs, located 30 miles south of Livingston in the beautiful Paradise Valley. The difference here is that you get to drive. You'll get a "Mushing 101" lesson, then you'll hit the trail up the Mill Creek drainage of the Absaroka Range. Half-day treks with a picnic lunch run $225, and two-hour treks are $110. A full day of mushing, complete with a steak and trout lunch, is $300. The season usually runs from Thanksgiving to Easter, and reservations are required. If you can't get enough, sign up for a three-day rookie training session, usually held in Dec.

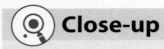 **Close-up**

Snowshoe Heaven

Not comfortable on a pair of skinny skis? Looking for something to do after you drop the kids off at the ski hill? **Snowshoeing** is an easy and inexpensive way to take care of both problems.

With the advances in snowshoe design and construction over the past years, the sport of snowshoeing has exploded in popularity. Gone are the heavy, wooden frames of the past (although you'll see them hanging in many lodges and homes throughout the area). They have been replaced with lighter, more durable materials such as aluminum and plastic.

The great thing about the sport is that it is perfect for all ages and abilities. If you can walk, you can snowshoe. The shoes may feel slightly clunky at first, but you'll get the hang of it in a few steps. The free-heel design of today's snowshoes make for easy walking or even running.

Not surprisingly, Yellowstone Country is the perfect place to strap on a pair and head out for an adventure. Basically any trail that you can hike during summer becomes a snowshoe trail in winter. You don't have to worry about grooming—your snowshoes will plod through the deepest snow. Check national forest trail maps for snowshoeing opportunities.

Both Yellowstone and Grand Teton National Parks abound with trails for both skiers and snowshoers. Most Nordic centers described in this chapter offer snowshoe rentals and instruction. In addition, many outdoor shops in Bozeman and Jackson offer rentals for $5 to $10 a day. Some folks like to rent poles, which give your upper body a workout and allow you better balance going up and down hills.

Snowshoeing is just another way for you to see our beautiful area in winter. Go ahead, give it a shot. The opportunities are limited only by your imagination.

CONTINENTAL DIVIDE DOGSLED ADVENTURES
P.O. Box 84, Dubois, WY 82513
(307) 739-0165, (800) 531-6874
www.dogsledadventures.com
Besides the usual full- and half-day trips, Continental Divide offers the mother of all dogsled adventures: three days of guided dogsledding in the rugged and snowy Wind River Range. Experienced musher Billy Snodgrass will assign you a team of dogs and give you a basic course in sled control, commands, handling, harnessing, feeding, and care of your dogs—yours for three days.

Nights are spent in the warm, cozy yurt or backcountry lodge, where you'll feast on a hearty meal and get a good night's rest. Optional cross-country skis and snowshoes are available at the rest stops for those who want more diversions.

This multi-day tour (about $2,000 per person) includes transportation to and from Jackson, instruction, meals, and expedition sleeping bags. If that sounds like too much, full-day trips ($270) take you back to Brooks Lake Lodge, and half-day trips ($180) as well as two-night (about $1,500) and overnight (about $700) are available.

JACKSON HOLE IDITAROD SLED DOG TOURS
P.O. Box 1940, Jackson, WY 83001
(307) 733-7388, (800) 554-7388
www.jhsleddog.com

Jackson Hole Iditarod veteran Frank Teasley hosts your adventure here, where you'll mush through the Bridger-Teton National Forest. Meals, transportation, and extra clothing are provided, and you can learn how to mush your own team. Full-day trips leave at 9 a.m. and return at approximately 4:30 p.m. A full-day trip will take you back to Granite Hot Springs, where you can warm up by taking a dip in the natural spring. After you dry off, you'll be served a lunch of trout or steak. Frank has been the recipient of the Iditarod's Leonard Seppala Humanitarian Award for the best-cared-for team, so you know you're in good hands. He also finished sixth in the race in 1991.

SPIRIT OF THE NORTH SLED DOG ADVENTURES
P.O. Box 1321, Ennis, MT 59729
(406) 995-3424, (406) 682-7994
www.huskypower.com

Spirit of the North offers half-day trips beginning at 9:30 a.m. and 1 p.m. seven days a week; make reservations at least one day in advance. Adults (age 13 and older) pay $125, children ages 7 to 12 are $80, and children age 6 and younger travel free. Groups of four or more get a 10 percent discount. You'll get hands-on instruction before you and your huskies set out from the Moonlight Basin Ski Resort in Big Sky. The trail affords great views of Lone Mountain and the Spanish Peaks. There is also a location in West Yellowstone, where riders are $150 per person for those age 13 and older.

SNOWMOBILING

For many winter visitors, Yellowstone Country is best enjoyed by snowmobile. And why not? Our region offers endless miles of groomed and backcountry trails, big powder-filled basins, and high-alpine ridges. There are places that you can get to only by snowmobile, and when you get there and see the view you'll realize why this powder playground is so popular.

Snowmobiling in the West is unlike other places. Because of the powdery, often steep terrain, sleds are bigger and more powerful and use longer tracks and wider skis. These "powder sleds," as they're called, are what you need if you intend to go off-trail and head for the hills. And if you decide to do that, be prepared with avalanche knowledge and equipment. Every year snowmobilers die in Yellowstone region avalanches, and in most cases those deaths could have been prevented. This chapter has some basic information, but it's best to take a class and read up on proper procedures.

If you just intend to stick to the trails, a "trail sled" is what you need. These are often more comfortable on bumpy trails and usually have more room for two. These sleds are big and powerful, too, but aren't made for deep powder or climbing hills.

The town of West Yellowstone is recognized as the snowmobile capital of the world. Streets that are paved in summer become snow-covered byways in winter. It's one of the few places you can actually drive snow machines on the roads. You can find hundreds of miles of trails—perfect for novice and advanced riders—beginning right from your hotel parking lot.

Allowing snowmobiling within Yellowstone and Grand Teton National Parks has been a controversial topic. Businesses and towns surrounding the parks say their economies will crumble if snowmobiles are banned from the two national parks. Proponents of the ban argue that the parks are for people and animals, not loud, polluting machines, and that towns and businesses will survive because park trails make up only a fraction of the terrain found in Yellowstone Country. In 2002 plans were announced to allow snowmobilers in the park in reduced numbers and on quieter, cleaner machines. In 2004 National Park Service officials agreed on an interim winter-use plan to allow limited numbers of snowmobiles and snowcoaches. Visitors who tour the parks on snowmobile must have a guide and ride environmentally friendly machines (see "Quieter and Cleaner Snowmobiles" above). A permanent plan is scheduled to be put in place by the winter of 2011–12, but as of 2010 the winter-use plan was being challenged yet again. Go to www.nps.gov/yell/ for complete details.

Pay attention to the signs and rules while riding. Both Yellowstone National Park and the Gallatin National Forest have a 45 mph speed limit, and you must stay on the trails while in the parks. Never approach wildlife on a snow machine, and always give animals the right of way.

You must also have a valid driver's license to drive in the national parks. You'll see why, as the trails can be crowded and often seem like highway driving. Hand signals and other rules apply. Read the literature handed out at the entrances for further rules and regulations.

Whether you stick to the trails or head for the hills, snowmobiling is a great way to experience the winter splendor around our region. The list below is only partial. Check forest ranger stations and visitor centers for complete maps and information.

Two things to keep in mind: If you're bringing your own sled registered in another state, you don't need to display a Montana registration. If your sled is unregistered, a nonresident, temporary-use permit is required. You can get one by contacting the Montana Fish, Wildlife & Parks Department at (406) 444-2535. You can also get statewide snowmobiling information by contacting the Montana Snowmobile Association, Box 4714, Missoula, MT 59806, or Travel Montana at (800) 847-4868 or www.visitmt.com.

Montana

Big Sky Area
The area south of Big Sky on US 191 is a mecca for thrill-seeking snowmobilers. Buck Creek Ridge is one of the most popular spots, and the trailhead is found just across from the Rainbow Ranch. The trail winds 19 miles up the Buck Creek Ridge Road to excellent snow play areas on the ridge. The trail passes alongside the Lee Metcalf Wilderness boundary and offers great views of two of our favorite mountains, the Helmet and the Sphinx—easy to pick out on the horizon because of their namesakes. The trail is marked but ungroomed, and watch out for cornices on the main ridge.

Another great trail can be found by taking the Taylor Fork Road, which is about 18 miles long, west from US 191. The road leads to a trailhead with ample parking, and the trail goes past the Wapiti Forest Service cabin into the Carrot and Sage Creek Basins. There are plenty of powder play areas, and this fun trail can occupy an entire day. Check the conditions of the Taylor Fork Road, as it is not plowed and heavy snow could make it impassable. If it is, you can park at the junction of the road and the highway.

There's one other trail to mention—the

Big Sky Trail, an iffy, ungroomed trail from Bozeman to Big Sky for experienced riders only. Many riders say that there's not really a trail at all, just parts that aren't well connected, and it's not worth searching for it.

Quieter & Cleaner Snowmobiles

These days all snowmobiles that enter Yellowstone and Grand Teton National Parks must be of the four-stroke variety, which offer cleaner emissions and less noise. These machines are deemed Best Available Technology (BAT) by the National Park Service, and every major manufacturer now makes these available. The current winter-use plan allows for 318 snowmobiles into Yellowstone, and as of this writing these numbers are expected to remain the same until a permanent solution is expected for the 2011–12 winter. Additionally, all trips within both parks must now be commercially guided by a licensed park concessionaire, many of which are listed later in this chapter. All approved concessionaires can be found on the Yellowstone National Park website at www.nps.gov/yell.

Bozeman Area

You have to drive a little bit to get to the trails here, but they are worth it. About 22 miles north of town on MT 86 just past the Bridger Bowl ski resort, you'll find the Brackett Creek parking area. Taking the Brackett Creek Trail

west into the north Bridger Mountains will lead you to numerous play areas with jaw-dropping views of this small, rugged range. Stay alert on the trail, since skiers and hikers also use the sledding hill about 0.75 mile in. Highmarking is popular in the big bowls here, but be aware of avalanche danger. This trails system links up with the popular Fairy Lake Trail, which can also be accessed by driving another 6 miles past Brackett Creek on MT 86. This scenic trail looms beneath Sacajawea Peak, the highest in the range at 9,466 feet.

The Olsen Creek area is another popular spot. This is found a few miles south of the Bridger Bowl ski area on MT 86. The parking lot is on the west side of the road, and you'll have to cross the highway to get to the trail.

The trail, which is a Forest Service road during summer, climbs steadily for about 4 miles to a wide-open area on top of a ridge. From here you can continue north or south on the ridge, toward Skunk Creek Road or Jackson Creek Road, respectively. You'll see numerous powder-filled meadows along the way. Contact the Gallatin Valley Snowmobile Association at (406) 763-4387 for more information about Bozeman and Big Sky area trails.

Cooke City

Cooke City calls itself a community of about "80 people, dogs, moose, and an occasional bison," and in winter the old mining town is an isolated place. Except, of course, for the hundreds of snowmobiles that pass through daily on their way to some of the best riding in the state. So good, in fact, that both Yamaha and Arctic Cat use the area as a test site.

The best thing about Cooke City is the easily accessible, high-elevation trails. Heading east out of town toward the Beartooth Highway (closed in winter) opens up numerous possibilities, including the popular Daisy Pass Road. The trail heads north through the burned trees of the 1988 Yellowstone fires, switchbacking up to 9,345-foot Daisy Pass. From there choose your powder play area or continue on the trail down into the basin below the pass. Other trails include Lulu Pass Road, Round Lake, and Henderson Mountain, and the trail system connects with 50 miles of groomed trails in Wyoming.

Cooke City and the surrounding area get huge amounts of snow, so avalanches are a frequent concern. Be well versed in avalanche knowledge or don't go, and pay attention on and off the trails. Call the avalanche advisory, (406) 838-2341, for detailed information on conditions. For more information on area trails, call the Upper Yellowstone Snowmobile Club at (406) 838-2212 or (406) 838-2414, or contact the Gardiner Ranger District of the Gallatin National Forest, (406) 848-7375.

Virginia City/Ennis

If you're staying in the West Yellowstone area, a drive to the old mining town of Virginia City is a worthy diversion. From west, head north on US 287 until you reach the small town of Ennis, then head west on US 287 over the pass and into Virginia City. The town, established in 1863 when gold lured early settlers into Alder Gulch, is primarily a summer destination, but its close proximity to the trails of the Gravelly Range are making it more and more popular with snowmobilers. Trails begin right from town, and you can ride on the streets. The main trail from town follows Alder Gulch through the ghost town of Summit City.

Two options exist at the Lyons Bridge trailhead off US 287. A 50-mile loop trail takes experienced riders to the spine of the Gravellys, while an easier route through Antelope Basin gives riders access to resorts at Elk and Cliff Lakes. A total of 130 miles of trails are nearby.

Contact the Vigilante Snowmobilers at (406) 843-5484 or (406) 682-7755 or the Madison Ranger District of the Beaverhead-Deerlodge National Forest, (406) 682-4253, for more information on these and other trails in the area.

✳West Yellowstone Area

If you're basing your snowmobile trip in and around West Yellowstone, you'll have 580 miles of trails at your disposal, 180 of them in Yellowstone National Park. Trails open in mid-Dec and stay open until the snow melts.

If you are snowmobiling outside the park, you're in for some incredible scenery. The nation's first designated snowmobile trail, Two Top, begins just west of town and curls its way up to the Continental Divide, passing numerous powder playgrounds along the way. When you reach the top you'll see the Tetons on a clear day.

Experienced riders should check out the wild Lionhead Loop, a steep 10-mile trail full of tricky, windblown snow. You'll get great views of the rugged Lionhead and Lower Madison Ranges, but do not take this trail unless you possess and know how to use avalanche equipment. Other nice trails include the Madison Arm Loop, the South Plateau, and the Horse Butte Trail, all of which offer inspiring vistas around every corner.

For more information and trail maps, contact the Hebgen Lake Ranger District, (406) 823-6961; the West Yellowstone Chamber of Commerce, (406) 646-7701; or Yellowstone

National Park, (307) 344-7381, ext. 2206. It's best to contact these agencies anyway to get detailed and up-to-the-minute information on trail conditions and closures.

Idaho

Island Park

Island Park is a snowmobiler's paradise, with more than 400 miles of groomed trails that spurt off in every direction. From Island Park you can access the trails in Yellowstone National Park and around West Yellowstone, as well as the trails in the Gallatin and Targhee National Forests and all the way down to Flagg Ranch on the northern end of Grand Teton National Park.

Snowmobiling is popular here because of the long season and abundant snow. The town sits at an elevation of about 6,000 feet, high enough to let the snow stick around all winter. Another reason for the popularity is that the town caters to snowmobilers. Just about every business in town can be reached by snowmobile, creating a great atmosphere for riders and making it a great place to take your snowmobiling vacation.

One of the most popular trails leads up to 8,710-foot Two Top Mountain, about 9 miles from town. This ride offers plenty for beginner and expert alike. Beginners will want to stick to the trail and then soak in the view from the top as the more advanced riders play in the powder of the many off-trail bowls. This trail can be a little crowded, with more than 80,000 sledders using it each year. Thirty miles from Island Park is Upper Mesa Falls, a flat and easy trail that ends at a 110-foot frozen waterfall, a prime example of the region's winter beauty.

Since enough snowmobilers descend on Island Park each year, there's really no need for a guide. Trails are extremely well marked, and maps are available in just about every business. For more information and trail maps, contact the Island Park Ranger District at (208) 558-7301.

Wyoming

Cody

The best bet for snowmobiling around Cody is to head to the Pahaska Tepee area just outside the east entrance to Yellowstone National Park. A groomed trail connects riders to the rest of the trails in the park, where you can ride down to Flagg Ranch, over to West Yellowstone, or up to Mammoth. Other options include taking the incredibly scenic Chief Joseph Highway (WY 296) northwest to nearly 60 miles of groomed trails and numerous playgrounds in the Beartooth Mountains. From here you can actually hook up with the trails around the Cooke City area. East of Cody you'll find the Bighorn Mountains, where more groomed trails exist.

Jackson Area

Jackson isn't exactly known as a snowmobiling mecca because you need to drive out of town to access the trails. But many feel the extra work is well worth it. You can drive to Flagg Ranch at the northern end of the park and start snowmobiling from there, but most people head south to the Togwotee Pass area to access the Continental Divide Snowmobile Trail, which runs from the Lander area up to Grand Teton and Yellowstone National Parks and on to West Yellowstone. It would take several days to ride the whole trail, so most riders head to Togwotee or the Gros Ventre River Road to access parts of the trail. You can also hop on the trail at the Grand Teton National Park RV Resort in the Buffalo Fork Valley, the Signal Mountain Lodge in Grand Teton National Park, or at Flagg Ranch just south of Yellowstone.

One popular trip with a warm ending is the 10-mile ride to Granite Hot Springs, a commercial resort with a 104-degree, natural-fed pool that beckons bathers for a relaxing dip after an invigorating ride.

Guide services are popular in these parts, mostly because you have to drive to ride, and guides are now required to ride in the park. There are a large number of outfitters, and a few offer a variety of guided snowmobile trips; there are a few rental companies as well. Whatever way you choose, snowmobiling here produces some of the most beautiful scenery in the country.

Snowmobile Rentals

Yellowstone National Park
XANTERRA MAMMOTH HOTEL SNOWMOBILE SHOP
Mammoth Hot Springs
(307) 344-7311
www.travelyellowstone.com

XANTERRA OLD FAITHFUL SNOW LODGE
Old Faithful
(307) 344-7311
www.travelyellowstone.com
You can rent sleds at Mammoth and Old Faithful for $245 for one rider or $265 for two. Children under age 12 ride free with a licensed adult. Clothing rentals are available for $21. Both locations offer Winter Getaway packages, including one-day snowmobile rental, two nights' lodging, breakfast, hot-tub rental, and ice skating.

Montana
CANYON ADVENTURES
US 191, Big Sky
(406) 995-4450, (800) 520-SLED
www.snowmobilemontana.com

This Big Sky business rents sleds from its location 1 mile south of the Big Sky entrance. Full-day rates range from $185 to $250; a half-day starts at $140. Complete clothing rentals are available for $15. Canyon specializes in guiding you to some of the best spots in the Gallatin Canyon, including Buck Creek Ridge. Guide service runs $225 per day or $150 for a half day. Trailer trips are available for larger groups.

COOKE CITY EXXON
US 212, Cooke City
(406) 838-2244
www.cookecityexxon.com
If you didn't bring your sled to this little mountain town, Cooke City Exxon has about 16 rentals from $165 to $195 per day, plus gas. You can also rent clothing and gear for $25 a day.

RENDEZVOUS SNOWMOBILE RENTALS
415 Yellowstone Ave., West Yellowstone
(406) 646-9564, (800) 426-7669
www.snowmobileyellowstone.net
Owner Randy Roberson has three generations of Yellowstone hospitality behind Rendezvous, where you'll find eight different models of Polaris sleds for rent. Prices range from $99 to $169, depending on what kind of machine you want. All of them have hand warmers, and Rendezvous gives discounts to Big Sky skiers. They also offer a $25-per-person transportation package from Big Sky to West Yellowstone, so you can spend more time on the trail. Clothing is also available for rental.

TWO TOP SNOWMOBILE RENTAL
645 Gibbon Ave., West Yellowstone
(406) 646-7802, (800) 522-7802
www.twotopsnowmobile.com
Serving Yellowstone snowmobilers since 1966, Two Top offers four single-rider and

four double-rider Polaris sleds. Prices range from $119 to $189. If you're staying in Big Sky, Two Top has some great specials. Just tell owners Dave and Jamie McCray, "I saw you at Big Sky," and you'll get $10 off. Clothing is available for $15 per day.

YELLOWSTONE TOUR AND TRAVEL
P.O. Box 410, West Yellowstone, MT 59758
(646) 9310, (800) 221-1151
www.yellowstone-travel.com
This full-service travel agency is affiliated with three hotels in town (Holiday Inn, Three Bear Lodge, and Big Western Pine) and specializes in multi-day bed-and-sled packages. Price depends on how many people you have, what kind of sled you want, and where you want to stay. They start at around $470 per person for two days and three nights. You'll get complimentary tickets to the Grizzly and Wolf Discovery Center (see the Attractions chapter) and a prime rib dinner as well.

Wyoming
JACKSON HOLE SNOWMOBILE TOURS
515 North Cache, Jackson
(307) 733-6850, (800) 633-1733
www.jacksonholesnowmobile.com
Jackson's oldest snowmobile company offers a variety of tours throughout the region. In Yellowstone National Park enjoy beautiful scenery, abundant wildlife, and the excitement of watching Old Faithful erupt. Togwotee Mountain Pass offers majestic mountain views and an adventurous ride through deep powder fields. Or try a day of off-trail riding followed by a relaxing soak in the Granite Hot Springs pool. Day trips into Yellowstone or other areas start at $269. Multiday trips along the famed Continental Divide Trail are also available.

Tour by Snowmobile

First time on a snowmobile? Several companies around the region offer guided tours. **Grand Teton National Park Snowmobile Rental,** (800) 563-6469, offers half- and full-day trips to Togwotee, Jenny Lake, Old Faithful, and more. Rates start at $79 per person. Togwotee Snowmobile Adventures offers Yellowstone, Gros Ventre, Granite Hot Springs, and Greys River day tours out of Moran, Wyoming. Call (866) 278-4245 or visit www.togwoteelodge .com. **Best Adventures,** (800) 851-0827 or www.best-adventure.com, offers snowmobile tours of Yellowstone for $269. **Backcountry Snowmobile Adventures,** (800) 924-7669 or www.backcountry adventures.com, has tours in the Gallatin National Forest and Yellowstone National Park from West Yellowstone.

Idaho
TETON VALLEY ADVENTURES
250 Buxton, Driggs
(208) 354-2233
www.tetonvalleyadventures.com
Teton Valley Adventures offers day trips through Yellowstone National Park for a close-up view of bison and Old Faithful. Convenient Teton Valley snowmobile trips are also offered. Enjoy a full-day excursion to Mesa Falls, Cave Falls, and the Big Hole Mountains. Transportation is provided. Yellowstone National Park tours include equipment, clothing, shuttle service, and entrance fee to the park for $250; tours take 10 to 14 hours. Local tours in the

Teton Valley begin at $220 per person. Snow-mobile rentals start at $125.

OTHER ACTIVITIES

HIGH MOUNTAIN HELI-SKIING
Jackson, WY
(307) 733-3274
www.heliskijackson.com

A day of heli-skiing with High Mountain consists of six runs and up to 15,000 feet of skiing. Two Bell 407 helicopters transport you to terrain south of the Jackson Hole ski resort, including all the Snake River and Palisades mountain ranges and portions of the Hoback, Teton, and Gros Ventre Ranges. Groups consist of five clients and one guide. The day rate is $1,050 per person. Terrain runs from intermediate to expert, and skiers and snowboarders are grouped accordingly. You should be at the advanced level and be able to link parallel turns if you want to give it a try. Fat powder ski rentals are also available. High Mountain's offices are located in downtown Jackson at 945 West Broadway in the Hillside Plaza.

KING TUBE TUBING PARK
Snow King Resort, Jackson, WY
(307) 734-TUBE

Some people can't ski, but everyone can tube. A rope tow lift takes you to the top of Snow King's tubing park and then you glide down the lanes on provided inner tubes for an exhilarating and slippery ride. Hours are Mon through Fri from 2 to 8 p.m. and weekends from noon until 8 p.m. Adults pay $16 per hour, $21 for two hours. Kids pay $13 and $18, respectively.

i If you plan on spending more than a week in and around the parks, or if you visit the area more than once a year, think about getting a season pass. An annual pass good for most US national parks and recreation areas is $80. If you're age 62 or older, a one-time $10 fee gives you lifetime access to all national parks.

Ice Climbing

This is a popular sport in Yellowstone Country, as winter temperatures allow for excellent ice conditions from around Thanksgiving (sometimes much earlier) through Apr. Good waterfall ice can be found in several spots, and challenging mixed routes exist for those who have the skills. If you just want to give it a try, several opportunities exist for guided excursions.

If you're staying in the Jackson area, try **Exum Mountain Guides,** (307) 733-2297, www.exumguides.com, in Grand Teton National Park, which offers everything from introductory lessons to winter ascents of a major peak. Ice-climbing areas include Death Canyon, Lake Louise, Torrey Canyon, and the Dubois area 90 miles east of Jackson. Rates are around $260 for one person, $180 each for two climbers. **Jackson Hole Mountain Guides,** (307) 733-4979, www.jhmg.com, has been leading Teton adventures since 1968. The company's acclaimed school offers an introductory ice-climbing class for $170.

The center of the ice-climbing universe in Cody is **Bison Willy's Ice Climbing Bunkhouse,** (307) 587-0629, www.bisonwillys.com, where diehards gather each winter to explore the area's excellent routes. You'll find information about the latest conditions here and tips on where to find the best ice. You can also register for the annual Waterfall Ice Round Up, held during Feb, where there's plenty of beer, food, and entertainment to go around. Also try **Sunlight Sports** at (888) 889-2463 for information on where to go.

The Bozeman area offers several ice-climbing opportunities, including waterfall-filled Hyalite Canyon. When you get to town, stop by **Northern Lights Trading Company,** (406) 586-2225, or **Barrel Mountaineering,** (406) 582-1335, for information. The staff at both of these establishments will answer questions about ice climbing in the area. Both locations also rent harnesses, ice tools, and crampons. **Montana Alpine Guides,** (406) 586-8430, www.adventure montana.com, also offers guided ice climbs around the area.

Ice Skating

BEALL PARK
North Black and Villard Streets
Bozeman, MT
A popular north-side city park, the ice rink here is large and accommodates plenty of recreational skaters and a few games of pickup hockey or broomball. It's open from noon to 10 p.m. on weekdays and 10 a.m. to 10 p.m. on weekends.

BOGERT PARK
325 South Church Ave.
Bozeman, MT
This covered rink is reserved for hockey after 4 p.m., so check the schedule posted at the rink for recreational ice-skating times.

Yellowstone Education

If you're going to be in the area for a while, take a course at the **Yellowstone Association Institute**, a nonprofit field school operated in conjunction with the National Park Service. Winter courses are held at park hotels and the Lamar Buffalo Ranch—a campuslike setting with heated guest cabins and a common building with bathrooms, classrooms, and showers. Courses run a minimum of two days and include Wilderness First Aid, Exploring Yellowstone on Snowshoes, Wolf Watching in Yellowstone, Snow Tracking, and Exploring Yellowstone's Winter World on Skis. The institute also offers lodging-and-learning packages with rooms at Mammoth or Old Faithful. Complete program information can be found at www .yellowstoneassociation.org or by calling (307) 344-2294.

HAYNES PAVILLION
Gallatin County Fairgrounds
Bozeman, MT
Bozeman's newest covered rink, built with the help of the Bozeman Amateur Hockey Association, allows recreational skating and hockey. The fairgrounds are located on Tamarack Street, between North Rouse and North Seventh Avenues.

MAMMOTH HOT SPRINGS HOTEL
Mammoth Hot Springs
Yellowstone National Park, WY
(307) 344-7311

WINTER SPORTS

If you're staying in Mammoth, you can skate on this flooded rink outside the hotel. Skate rentals are available by the hour or day.

SNOW KING CENTER ICE RINK
100 East Snow King Ave., Jackson, WY
(307) 733-5200
www.snowking.com
This big indoor rink at the Snow King ski area is open from Aug through Apr and has skate rentals, snacks, and beverages on-site. Public skating sessions, which cost around $6, are regularly scheduled during the week. A less expensive session is available on Sat, but call ahead as the rink hosts many other activities.

SOUTHSIDE PARK
West College and South Fifth Avenue, Bozeman, MT
This rink is on the south side of town near the university and is open from noon until 10 p.m. on weekdays and from 10 a.m. to 10 p.m. on weekends. Recreational skating and hockey are allowed.

VICTOR J. RILEY ARENA AND COMMUNITY EVENTS CENTER
1400 Heart Mountain St., Cody, WY
(307) 587-1681
www.rileyarena.com
All the pleasure of ice skating inside a temperate facility is available from mid-August to mid-March. Skate rentals are available at the arena for $3.

Appendix

LIVING HERE

In this section we feature specific information for residents or those planning to relocate here. Topics include real estate, education, health care, and much more.

RELOCATION

Yellowstone Country has an intangible allure. The simple greatness of so much space free from development and crowds is impressive. But the sky, the mountains, and the rivers have nothing on the hospitality and friendliness of the people out here. We have been wrapped up in the magic that this area casts upon us, and it's a pleasure to share it with you. If you can't get enough of our area and are considering relocation or a vacation home, the listings that follow will help you get started.

Although the landscape dominates our culture, this is also a place where people are interested in the arts, education, and community. In this chapter we cover real estate markets, adult education opportunities, medical facilities, and retirement information. The Resources chapter has information about area chambers of commerce. Request a relocation packet (for a fee) from the town of your choice.

REAL ESTATE MARKETS

Not since the gold rush and homesteading days has there been such a clamoring for land in Yellowstone Country. This time the treasure is mountain views, riverfront getaways, and estates on rambling acreage. Greater Yellowstone is one of the fastest-growing regions of the West. Part of that is good marketing, part of it is just luck, most of it is location. Tagged by *Outside* magazine as the "Last Best Place," southwestern Montana communities have been booming since the early 1990s. World-class skiing, shopping, and celebrities (Harrison Ford and Mel Gibson, for example) buying real estate have showcased Jackson Hole, Wyoming, and subsequently its neighboring communities. Blue-ribbon fishing in Idaho's Island Park region has made it a hotbed for second homes. Regardless of the source of the region's growth, it's happening. Many of the markets are inflated by high-end second homes, but there are still great deals to be

found out there. Whether you are buying to invest, to relocate, or to retreat, you can find your dream property.

What you will see in Yellowstone Country are wide-open spaces, jagged mountains, cascading streams, and quaint western towns, but the magnitude of this beauty shrinks as more people move in. As a result, Greater Yellowstone communities grapple with drawing lines to preserve the scenic beauty and wildlife habitat of our land without setting limitations on newcomers. City and county planning meetings are brimming with zoning issues, development proposals, and new plans to incorporate growth as well as open space. It's not easy to find a balance, but bit by bit, towns are finding their own way. Many communities, such as Jackson Hole, Wyoming, and Bozeman, Montana, have formed land trusts to save wildlife migration corridors, view sheds, and farmland within their area. Basically, private land owners agree to set aside property under a conservation easement, forever forfeiting their rights to develop or subdivide the designated land. Currently more than 500,000 acres of land are managed under conservation easements. There are real estate companies and brokers who work with this specific goal in mind, but you can also ask the Realtor of your choice for more information on conservation easements.

In this chapter we've briefly described property markets in communities. You'll find real estate publications—with their lists of local agencies—in the Resources chapter.

Bozeman, Montana Area

With a population of just under 40,000 people, Bozeman is one of Montana's fastest-growing cities, and houses are springing up all over the town and the surrounding Gallatin Valley. Because of this, downtown housing costs have soared to the point where most working-class families have to look elsewhere. On Bozeman's more desirable south side—historic homes close to downtown and the university—it's possible to find small, two-bedroom homes beginning at $250,000. Larger homes are harder to find, and many go for upwards of $450,000. The north side of town is where you'll find bargains, if you like to fix up and add your own charm. This section of town is actually older, more industrial, and eccentric. Many folks can find a house that needs lots of work and put their own imaginative touches into it. Still, it's nearly impossible to find a house under $200,000 within city limits, and the cost of housing in Bozeman is consistently around 20 percent above the national average.

The cost of living is swelling in Bozeman and surrounding areas. The local economy is largely supported by agriculture, but tourism and the high-tech industry are strong forces. With low wages (the average annual per capita personal income is about $26,000) and job shortages prevalent here, affordable housing is a controversial topic right now. Most new construction is taking place on the west side Bozeman, where subdivision after subdivision sprawl over former farmland, and they are made up of a combination of single-family homes and town houses. Generally prices in these neighborhoods start at around $250,000, on average. Upscale housing can be found all over, especially in the Bridger Canyon, Springhill, and Sourdough areas—anywhere on the outskirts of town.

Naturally, people look to the surrounding area. Belgrade, the fastest-growing town in Montana, is 8 miles west of Bozeman along the Interstate and has benefited the most from Bozeman's skyrocketing housing costs. Houses here are significantly cheaper—the average cost for a three-bedroom home in 2008 was about $250,000—while residents still enjoy all the amenities of the surrounding area. The prices drop even more the farther west you go, toward Amsterdam, Churchill, Gallatin Gateway, Three Forks, and Manhattan.

On the other hand, communities like Big Sky and Ennis are appealing for vacation properties and are more expensive. The median home price in Big Sky was about $550,000 in 2009.

Gardiner and Cooke City, Montana

As the original entrance to Yellowstone, growth in Gardiner is limited by the surrounding national forest and park boundaries. However, this fact is principally what keeps the town from losing its real western character.

Most people who move to Gardiner come for the proximity to Yellowstone (only 5 miles from Mammoth Hot Springs) because they work there or soon will. There is a small pocket of people who also choose Gardiner for recreational retreats or second homes, but these residents are generally north of town through Yankee Jim Canyon. Within Gardiner, homes are not often available and land is scarce. You'll find riverfront property with a modest two acres jumping as high as $500,000, but acreage in Yankee Jim Canyon is nearly impossible to find. In 2010 a two-acre parcel of land 5 miles outside of town was listed at $137,900.

Through Yellowstone National Park and up to 7,500 feet, available real estate in Cooke City is also less common. The tiny town is isolated by winter snows from Oct to June and hosts a strong skiing and snowmobiling business during that time. But it is during summer months when the town's population balloons from 90 to 300 and floods with tourists. It's not an easy place to live, nor is it an easy place to find property to buy. The steep mountains, designated wilderness, and other federal lands make Cooke a limited land market. When something does come up for sale, the price tends to be inflated. A one-third acre lot within the city limits was listed at $145,000, while a 4,400 square-foot log home was $795,000.

i Montana is one of the nation's major producers of log homes. Two types of house logs are made here—hand hewn and machine lathed. Twenty percent of the log houses produced here stay in Montana.

Livingston, Montana

Though it is only 25 miles east of Bozeman, this tiny old railroad town bursts with growing pains yet has managed to maintain its easy small-town feel. With a population of around 7,500, easy access to mountains and rivers, and close proximity to Bozeman, Livingston is charming and ideally located.

The real estate market in Livingston is divided into two different worlds: town and the valleys. In Livingston proper you can still find reasonably priced small historic homes for around $200,000. Town offers the sweet conveniences of provincial life—with the post office, restaurants, shops, and schools all within walking distance. The community has a rich arts culture and is home to many painters, writers, and actors.

Land prices get crazy outside of town. The region includes the ever-popular Paradise Valley to the south, the Shields River Valley to the east, and the Boulder Valley to the southeast. Newsman Tom Brokaw and actors Michael Keaton, Dennis Quaid, and Meg Ryan have planted roots here and put the area on the high-profile map. Add Hollywood exposure to breathtaking scenery and boundless recreation opportunities, and you've got a pretty nice package. Expect to pay at least $35,000 per acre, and don't expect to find your ideal property easily. The influx of second-home residents has scooped up the larger parcels over the past 15 years, so now prime pieces of land with more than 20 acres rarely come up for sale. A one-acre parcel with river access listed for $139,500.

Red Lodge, Montana

Red Lodge sits at the base of the massive Beartooth Range as it tumbles to the valley floor and stretches out into the expanse of Montana prairie. Two golf courses, a ski mountain, and access to wilderness, Yellowstone National Park, and a major airport within 60 miles are just a few of the things that make this Montana town so appealing. With a population of around 2,500, the small-town western flavor of Red Lodge is pervasive and real. It is a place that feels undiscovered, a little sheltered, a little too quaint.

You won't find bargains here, where few residential homes come on the market and outlying acreage goes for top dollar. In 2010 a golf course lot listed for about $90,000 and a 2,500 square-foot cabin on two acres listed for $549,000. Smaller downtown homes can be found priced in the $200,000s. There are still some good deals out there, but million-dollar estates are creeping up around town.

Cody, Wyoming

Views of mountains and prairie instead of traffic jams are what Cody promises. Look a little deeper and you'll see a town deeply rooted in its heritage and quietly standing at the forefront of western culture. These undercurrents shine when locals talk about town founder Buffalo Bill Cody and the famous Buffalo Bill Historical Center. You'll also find quality medical and educational facilities combined with boundless recreational opportunities.

Growing steadily, Cody offers a business-friendly atmosphere with no corporate state income tax, no inventory tax, and no franchise tax. Local industries include oil/mining, tourism and related tourist services, irrigated farming, livestock/ranching, gypsum, mining, logging/lumber mill, hunting/outfitting, and western furniture manufacturing.

The housing market is varied to service the population of about 9,000 people. In 2010 the average listing price was $443,000 and the median household income was just over $47,000.

i The largest employer in Cody, Wyoming, is West Park Memorial Hospital.

Jackson, Wyoming

Jackson is one of the premier places to live in the West, if you can afford to live here. The price of the average home has skyrocketed to more than $2 million, and you'll be hard pressed to find a place near town for less than $400,000. Even townhomes and condos are pricey, but if you are considering living here for only part of the year, that may be the best option. That way, perhaps you could make some money back on daily or weekly rentals during the busy tourist seasons.

For these reasons many people are finding out about Jackson's equally impressive surrounding small towns. On the east side of Teton Pass, these include Alpine, Pinedale, Bondurant, Thayne, and Afton. The west side of the pass—Idaho—is also booming. Driggs, Tetonia, Victor, and other Idaho towns are capturing many of those who can't quite afford to live in Jackson proper but still want to be in the shadow of the Tetons.

Idaho

The scenic stretch of Idaho—from the famed fly fishing of Island Park to bustling Driggs and Victor in the heart of Teton Valley—is a growing group of communities bolstered by the influx of second homers on the fringes and by Jackson commuters in the small towns. This area has seen tremendous growth due to the high cost of living "over the pass" in Jackson. The treasure of nearby Grand Targhee Ski Resort is an attraction, as are the other outdoor opportunities in the region. Teton Valley is the mecca of seed potato farming, but as the new generation sells off some of the traditional farmsteads, the flat, fertile fields make for perfect new-home building sites. And the view of the Teton Mountains from this vantage isn't too bad, either. The average cost for a three-bedroom home starts at around $350,000.

EDUCATION

The Greater Yellowstone region offers a variety of educational options, from small rural elementary schools to internationally renowned universities. Not surprisingly, many studies center around the culture and geography of the area, from Montana State's Big Sky Institute—the only university-based institute entirely focused on the Greater Yellowstone Ecosystem in the United States—to the Teton Science School's ecology graduate field science program. Whether you are looking to further your academic education or just pursue a lifelong interest in a particular subject, you're bound to find an educational offering that suits your needs.

BYU–IDAHO
Rexburg, ID
(208) 356-2200
www.byui.edu

BYU-Idaho, formerly called Ricks College, was founded in 1888 as Bannock Stake Academy, developed by the Church of Jesus Christ of Latter-day Saints. Ricks became the official name in 1917, and the school became known as Brigham Young University–Idaho in June 2000. It changed from a two-year junior college into a four-year institution with the affiliation of BYU. With an enrollment cap of 12,500 students, the college offers 40 majors within nine academic departments.

MONTANA STATE UNIVERSITY
Bozeman, MT
(406) 994-2452, (888) 678-2287
www.montana.edu

More than 13,000 students from 50 states and 47 countries attend MSU, which offers baccalaureate degrees in 61 fields, master's degrees in 41 disciplines, and doctorates in 20. The school is becoming well known for its bioscience, engineering, and technology research.

The 1,170-acre campus is filled with trees and surrounded by mountains, and it's a nice place to stroll around. A brochure detailing a leisurely walking tour of campus landmarks and school history is available at the Strand Union Building, the main student gathering place, located on the south end of campus.

The land-grant university was founded in 1893 as the Agricultural College of the State of Montana. Its name changed to the State College of Agriculture and Mechanical Arts, then to Montana State College, and finally to MSU in 1965. In 1994 the college merged with Northern Montana College, Eastern Montana College, and two colleges of technology, so it is occasionally referred to as MSU–Bozeman.

The university contributes much to Bozeman's atmosphere, offering art, theater, music, and sports events year-round. The Exit Gallery in the Strand Union Building and the Helen E. Copeland Gallery in Haynes Hall display student, faculty, and juried art exhibits, while Reynolds Recital Hall offers a variety of recitals and concerts. Several theater companies perform in the Strand Union

Theater, and the school is also the home of Montana Shakespeare in the Parks. The Brick Breeden Fieldhouse—where many of the sports are played—hosts big-name concerts a few times a year.

The sports teams, known as the Bobcats, compete at the Division I level in the Big Sky Conference, while rodeo competition for men and women is conducted through the Big Sky Region of the National Intercollegiate Rodeo Association. Games are always competitive and fun to watch.

NORTHWEST COLLEGE
231 West Sixth St., Powell, WY
(307) 754-6111
www.northwestcollege.edu
The neighboring community of Powell, some 50 miles to the west, is closely linked to Cody. Northwest College offers two-year programs in classic arts, agriculture, and sciences. Founded in 1949 as a satellite branch for the University of Wyoming, enrollment at the residential college has grown to more than 2,000 students.

Northwest College operates Mickelson Field Station in the Absaroka Range off the Chief Joseph Highway (WY 296). This year-round research facility is used for retreats or outdoor education classes, and it includes 12 cabins and a three-building complex. Call for availability and reservations.

TETON SCIENCE SCHOOL
P.O. Box 68T, Kelly, WY 83011
(307) 733-4765
www.tetonscience.org
Located within Grand Teton National Park, Teton Science School has provided natural science education for kids and adults since 1967. Summer programs include two- to five-week residential field ecology and field

natural history courses for junior high and high school students, as well as weeklong nonresidential programs for students in third through eighth grades. A one-year, master's level graduate program in environmental education and natural science is also offered. For those visiting the park and wanting to educate themselves a little more, the science school offers up to 40 one- to four-day field seminars taught by expert instructors.

✳THE YELLOWSTONE INSTITUTE
Mammoth Hot Springs
Yellowstone National Park, WY
(307) 344-2294
www.yellowstoneassociation.org
Learn to track wolves in Yellowstone's Lamar Valley. Identify native songbirds as they migrate into Yellowstone each year. Spend a day perfecting your plein air painting technique from Artist's Point overlooking the Grand Canyon of the Yellowstone. Or practice your wildlife photography skills along Specimen Ridge.

This is only a sampling of the Yellowstone Institute's courses offered throughout the year within the park. Established in 1948, the Yellowstone Institute provides visitors with hands-on educational experiences using Yellowstone as their classroom. The Yellowstone Institute is the education arm of the park's nonprofit Yellowstone Association. Each year more than 850 students enroll in 80 different classes, with subjects ranging from geology, ecology, and history to mysteries of Yellowstone. Sounds serious, but these courses are laid back and enjoyable. They are a far cry from sitting at a desk taking notes from a dry lecture series; most of them are conducted while you are out hiking, backpacking, llama packing, canoeing, or cross-country skiing.

Based at the historic Buffalo Ranch in the Lamar Valley, courses range in length from single session to multiday. College credit is available for many classes. The wilds of Yellowstone are the classroom, but students stay at the ranch in sleeping cabins and a historic bunkhouse and use a communal kitchen. Most classes take place between June 1 and Sept 1, but some winter courses are offered as well. A complete catalog of classes comes out twice a year. Write to the institute at P.O. Box 117, Yellowstone National Park, WY 82190, for a catalog. Classes fill quickly, so don't hesitate if you would like to participate in one.

HEALTH CARE

When pioneers first settled in Yellowstone Country, doctors made house calls. It was easier then for that one caregiver to travel to patients few and far between in this desolate country. As populations grew, country doctors had to travel farther and farther to care for their patients. Eventually towns were platted and became hubs for commerce and services. The bigger, centrally located towns built medical facilities and drew patients from far and wide to their doors.

Even today great distances separate some rural towns from complete and reliable medical care. Many towns have only clinics for day-to-day health needs, while full-service hospitals are 50 to 100 miles away. Still, rural clinics are well connected with major hospitals, and you will be able to receive respectable medical assistance throughout the region.

Emergency 911 service is available in all areas of Greater Yellowstone, including the parks. The people who answer your call are highly trained individuals, many of whom are emergency medical technicians (EMTs). Except for larger towns such as Bozeman, Billings, and Idaho Falls, most emergency crews consist of volunteers. These men and women are the people who fight our fires, answer the calls for help or tragedy, and willingly put their lives on the line to ensure the safety of our area.

What we tell you in this section is where to find the hospitals and clinics and what services they provide. If you have special medical needs, it's a good idea to figure out where you'll be able to access a hospital or clinic during your trip.

IN THE PARKS

It's not too far off base to say that Yellowstone and Grand Teton National Parks' clinics administer care for unusual ailments, including embedded fishing hooks, poison ivy rashes, altitude-related cardiac problems, and burns caused by scalding geothermal features. Primarily the three park clinics treat injuries from automobile accidents. With four million people traveling on unfamiliar, narrow, winding highways gawking at roadside attractions, the parks can be dangerous.

Yellowstone's two clinics and one hospital and Grand Teton's one clinic serve park visitors each summer. Of the millions who pass through here, less than one percent need medical care, but park facilities and emergency medical services are equipped to provide assistance for minor and major injuries. Yellowstone and Grand Teton rangers have EMT status, and many are certified Wilderness First Responders, while a few of them are trained medics. We hope you won't need medical attention when you come here, but if you do, trust that you are in good, qualified hands.

Yellowstone National Park

LAKE HOSPITAL
713 Lake Village
(307) 242-7241
This tiny medical facility has the honor of being the country's only seasonal hospital. Managed by West Park Hospital in Cody (see subsequent entry), the 10-bed facility opens with a new batch of health-care professionals each May. From mid-May until mid-Sept the small staff provides 24-hour service to tourists, with one doctor at the hospital and one on call. Three and sometimes four doctors share the workload throughout the season.

MAMMOTH CLINIC
Mammoth Village
(307) 344-7965
In the dead of winter Yellowstone's Mammoth Clinic is the only medical facility within 100 miles. Built in the 1960s, it is Yellowstone National Park's only year-round clinic. The staff provides care not just for year-round park employees but also for residents of Gardiner and Cooke City, Montana. The clinic is open seven days a week between Memorial Day and Labor Day weekends, and Mon through Fri the rest of the year. Check with either the clinic or the park service for hours of operation, which vary seasonally.

OLD FAITHFUL CLINIC
Old Faithful
(307) 545-7325
Even though you might be too sick to stand outside and watch Old Faithful Geyser blow, you can still see it from the waiting room of Old Faithful Clinic. That's not the only good thing about this medical facility (built in 1996); it also offers excellent aid for basic illnesses or injuries. With a staff of nurses

and two doctors, the clinic stays busy, but walk-ins are welcome. Open intermittently and seasonally, it's best to call the Mammoth Clinic (see listing above) to schedule an appointment here.

Grand Teton National Park

GRAND TETON MEDICAL CLINIC
Jackson Lake Lodge
(307) 543-2514
This clinic is located next to the Chevron gas station at the Jackson Lake Lodge and is open daily from 10 a.m. to 6 p.m. mid-May to mid-Oct.

MONTANA
Belgrade

BELGRADE URGENT CARE
403 West Main St.
(406) 388-8708
www.belgradeurgentcare.com
Specializing in walk-in care for acute injury and illness, no appointment is needed here. The clinic offers care for the whole family, from well women's checkups to sports physicals and occupational medicine. Founding doctor Michael Layman has organized a staff of professionals who are available seven days a week. Weekday hours are 8 a.m. to 8 p.m., weekends 9 a.m. to 5 p.m.

Big Sky

BIG SKY MEDICAL CLINIC
100 Beaverhead Trail
(406) 995-2797
www.docsky.us
Dr. Jeff Daniels and his staff are the main source of care in and around Big Sky, with a slopeside location especially handy for injured skiers and snowboarders. It's a fully

equipped facility capable of handling just about any injury or illness. Hours are 10 a.m. to at least 5 p.m. daily. A second location in Big Sky's new Town Center is open weekdays during the summer and three days a week in the winter. The clinic is located at 11 Ousel Falls Rd. (406-993-2797), above the Grizzly Outfitters outdoor store. The clinic is also on call 24 hours a day.

Bozeman

BOZEMAN DEACONESS HEALTH SERVICES
915 Highland Blvd.
(406) 585-1007
www.bozemandeaconess.org

BDHS is the not-for-profit umbrella organization that owns and operates Bozeman Deaconess Hospital, Bozeman Deaconess Health Group, Hillcrest Senior Living Neighborhood, Highland Health Park, and satellite outpatient clinics. The hospital is the only one in Gallatin County, with its service area including Gallatin, Park, and Madison Counties. The center of the hospital is an 86-bed acute-care facility that provides inpatient and outpatient services and a 24-hour emergency room. Other services include day surgery, hospice care, nutrition counseling, physical therapy, radiology, and X-rays.

The Highland Health Park campus consists of three buildings that house medical practices for 125 physicians and multiple outpatient services. In 2006 an integrated Cancer Center opened to treat the ever-growing number of cancer patients in the community. Hillcrest Senior Living Neighborhood has been providing independent living for the elderly since 1963; in 2006 independent assisted-living apartments were added at Aspen Pointe. BDHS has made the decision to put capital assets into the 400

undeveloped acres it owns to help keep basic health care affordable. The first project for 78 residential cottages and bungalows in the Hillcrest Neighborhood for people age 55 and over is now underway. There is also an affiliated Deaconess pharmacy in Big Sky that is open Mon-Sat.

FAMILY DOCTORS' URGENT CARE
120 North Nineteenth Ave.
(406) 556-9740

Urgent Care offers emergency-room services seven days a week, with no appointment necessary. From allergies and colds to fractures and sports injuries, treatment is available Mon through Fri from 9 a.m. to 8 p.m. and on weekends and holidays from 9 a.m. to 5 p.m. There's an X-ray lab on-site, and Urgent Care is staffed with several doctors and nurses.

Billings

BILLINGS CLINIC
2800 Tenth Ave. North
(800) 252-1246
www.billingsclinic.com

Since it opened in 1927, this hospital has evolved from a family-oriented, 58-bed facility to a regional medical center employing more than 1,000 people. Today the 275-bed nonprofit regional clinic, hospital, and trauma center is recognized for its patient-focused care. Services here include emergency, trauma and walk-in care, family practice, internal medicine, obstetrics and gynecology, cardiology, renal dialysis, psychiatric and behavioral health services, orthopedics and sports medicine, neurology, and women's health services. Deaconess operates DEACARE/ALS, a fixed-wing air-ambulance service that uses two prop jets.

SAINT VINCENT HOSPITAL AND HEALTH CENTER
1233 North Thirtieth St.
(406) 657-7000, (800) 762-8778
www.svh-mt.org

With 15 clinics in and around Billings as part of the Saint Vincent Primary Care Network, Saint Vincent's offers progressive health care. Billings's oldest hospital has been providing care for the people of the region for over a century. With 302 beds, Saint Vincent offers a range of services, including a notable neonatal intensive-care unit, an emergency helicopter air service, cancer care, the Women's Center, and the Sports Medicine Institute. They also provide a 24-hour service called Ask-A-Nurse, which gives free healthcare information and can assist in finding a physician.

Livingston

LIVINGSTON MEMORIAL HOSPITAL
504 South 13th
(406) 222-3541
www.livingstonhealthcare.org

Livingston Memorial Hospital is a nonprofit, community-owned facility servicing an area spanning roughly 150 miles within Sweetwater and Park Counties. Built in 1995, this 45-bed facility offers 24-hour emergency care and a four-bed intensive/critical-care unit. A full-service facility, patients have access to a full lab, birth center, mammography, ultrasound, and surgery. The hospital is also known for its post-op care, with echocardiography, respiratory therapy, physical therapy, cardiac therapy, and pulmonary rehabilitation available.

Red Lodge

BEARTOOTH HOSPITAL AND HEALTH CENTER
600 West 21st St.
(406) 446-2345
www.beartoothhospital.org

The numerous rural towns between Red Lodge and Billings rely on the Beartooth Hospital and Health Center for the finest medical care. Owned by the community since 1993, this 25-bed hospital has an attached nursing home and offers 24-hour emergency care. In addition, it offers a range of outpatient surgeries, including knee surgeries, plastic surgery, mastectomies, and appendectomies. The facility includes a day-care center and a pharmacy. Obstetrics, cardiac rehabilitation, and community health education are also among the hospital's services.

Mountain View Medical Center, a private clinic across the street from the hospital, encourages appointments but will accept walk-ins.

WYOMING
Cody

BILLINGS CLINIC CODY
201 Yellowstone Ave.
(307) 527-7561

This clinic offers complete care and welcomes walk-ins during regular daytime office hours, which are 7:30 a.m. to 5 p.m. weekdays and 9 a.m. to 11:30 a.m. on Sat. After hours you'll have to head for the emergency room at West Park Hospital (see listing below).

WEST PARK HOSPITAL
707 Sheridan Ave.
(307) 527-7501, (800) 654-9447
www.westparkhospital.org

As the regional medical center for the entire Bighorn Basin, West Park Hospital provides general medical care as well as specialty care. The 153-bed hospital is also responsible for medical services within Yellowstone National Park, and patients who need more extensive care than park facilities can provide are frequently sent here. West Park Hospital has 24-hour emergency/ambulance services and the latest technology, including MRI and renal dialysis equipment. Physicians at West Park also specialize in family practice, pediatrics, general surgery, obstetrics, gynecology, internal medicine, orthopedic surgery, and urology.

Attached to the hospital is the Coe Medical Center, which accommodates 30 physicians. The 20-bed inpatient Chemical Dependency Center is one of only four resident facilities in Wyoming. West Park Hospital is the largest employer in Cody.

WEST PARK URGENT CARE CLINIC
424 Yellowstone Ave.
(307) 587-7207
This clinic encourages walk-ins seven days a week and is located in the Cathcart Health Center. Operated by the West Park Hospital, the clinic is staffed by a doctor, physician's assistants, and a registered nurse.

Jackson

ST. JOHN'S HOSPITAL AND LIVING CENTER
625 East Broadway Ave.
(307) 733-3636
www.tetonhospital.org
St. John's has provided a continuum of health-care services for the Jackson Hole and Teton County area for more than 80 years. The 108-bed hospital is a nonprofit community health-care facility and a member of the Voluntary Hospital Association, the Wyoming Hospital Association, and the Quality Healthcare Foundation of Wyoming. Comprehensive care includes 24-hour emergency services, general surgery, professional home care, sports medicine, wellness programs, and an outpatient surgical center. There is also physical therapy, a pain clinic, and the Hospice of Tetons. The hospital also includes the St. John's Living Center, a long-term care facility.

RETIREMENT

Yellowstone Country is an oasis of good, clean living with its close-knit communities, majestic mountains, open space, and clean water. Low crime and access to education, recreation, and health care make our region an appealing place to retire.

Larger towns such as Bozeman, Cody, and Jackson have strong programs for older citizens at area senior centers. They also offer ready access to medical care, which may be important for seniors with failing health. Smaller communities such as Gardiner and Ennis, Montana, or Driggs, Idaho, are quaint but may be isolating (especially in winter) because they are without organized senior programs, public transportation, or ready medical facilities.

Do your homework before you select a town for your retirement. Before you make your decision, come visit the area at different times of year. Too many people fall in love with Yellowstone Country in summer only to be jolted into the reality of long, cold, harsh winters. To get you started, here are some contact numbers throughout the region: Gallatin County Council on Aging in Bozeman, (406) 586-2421; Cody Council on Aging, (307) 587-6221; and Idaho's Region VII Council on Aging, (800) 632-4813.

MONTANA

BOZEMAN SENIOR CENTER
807 North Tracy Ave., Bozeman
(406) 586-2421
Like much of Bozeman's population, the town's seniors are an active bunch, and the Bozeman Senior Center is the place to be for many of them. Noon meals are served Mon through Fri, and a Sun dinner is served once a month. Reservations should be made for any meal. With more than 1,800 members, the center offers organized trips and has a busy social-events calendar, which includes music, dances, and arts and crafts.

Galavan—a free senior shuttle—may be the center's most valuable asset. The wheelchair-accessible bus takes passengers from around the area to Bozeman, dropping them off at the supermarket, drugstore, or

just about anyplace else. Call (406) 587-2434 for schedules and more information.

i Permanent residents of Jackson number around 9,000, but if you count part-time residents and employees, the population swells by 52,000 people during summer months and by 5,000 people in winter.

DARLINTON MANOR
606 North Fifth St., Bozeman
(406) 587-2981
Located on Bozeman's north side, the 100-unit Darlinton Manor offers apartment-style senior citizen housing with on-site management. Its convenient spot is a block away from a supermarket and is adjacent to a

partially developed city park. Utilities are included with monthly rent, and rental assistance is available.

RED LODGE SENIOR CITIZENS' CENTER
207 South Villard Ave., Red Lodge
(406) 446-1826
The Mother's Day brunch, card parties, and bingo aren't solely what bring Red Lodge's older citizens to the senior center. It's also a place to share experiences and stories about the past and present. The 150 members pay $5 for organized activities; the camaraderie is free. This volunteer-run center serves three meals a week: soup and sandwiches at noon on Wed, a full meal on Thur at 11:30 a.m., and lunch on Fri at noon.

SENIOR CITIZENS' CENTER OF PARK COUNTY
206 South Main St., Livingston
(406) 222-7195
Located at the center of town, Livingston's senior center is a gathering place and a source for information on area physicians, fitness programs, local clubs, and fun get-togethers. Started with a grant in the 1960s, the center has grown dramatically and now boasts 400 members. The board offers low-income housing for seniors by maintaining 26 apartments in the building. A staff of several part-time employees manage events and an in-house thrift store. Members pay annual dues of $7. Besides serving lunch Mon through Fri, the center offers card parties, dances, bingo, a pool table, exercise,

and a wellness center, and it publishes a monthly newsletter. Members also participate in many volunteer activities throughout the community. The facility prohibits the practice of politics or religion on the premises. It's open Mon through Sat.

WYOMING

CODY SENIOR CITIZENS' CENTER
613 Sixteenth St., Cody
(307) 587-6221
This hub for older citizens boasts a growing membership, and some say it's because the meals here are so tasty. Big on home-cooked meals shared with lots of friends and lively conversation, the Cody senior center serves up the vittles in the 200-seat dining room. A crew of volunteers operates a thriving thrift shop Mon through Sat from 10 a.m. to 3 p.m. The center offers a senior bus service as well as medical and personal services. A membership at the Cody Senior Citizens' Center is free.

SENIOR CENTER OF JACKSON HOLE
830 East Hansen Ave., Jackson
(307) 733-7300
www.seniorcenterjh.org
Stop in the Senior Center of Jackson Hole for a daily lunch if you're age 60 or older. The center asks for a $3.50 donation, and reservations are required. The center also delivers meals and provides home care, and its monthly newsletter includes a lunch menu and an activities calendar.

MEDIA

Unlike many parts of the county, print media seems to be alive and well in the Greater Yellowstone region. Although newspapers are struggling with declining circulation numbers and advertising sales, they still seem to be the primary source of local information, particularly in many of the smaller towns surrounding both national parks. You'll notice plenty of glossy magazines, too, especially in the resort towns, touting everything from real estate to restaurants. These can be great ways to find coupons, specials, and deals on just about anything. In addition, more prominent magazines like *Montana Quarterly* and *Big Sky Journal* consistently receive awards for their in-depth coverage of the people, places, and issues of Greater Yellowstone—definitely pick up one of these on your way through.

Television and radio stations can be few and far between—many will cover a large geographic area and are really only pertinent to the local population. Yellowstone Public Radio, however, covers most of the area in this book and can be an excellent source of news and information.

Lastly, believe it or not, don't expect every establishment you visit to have a website. Some of the best places in the region can be found only when you stumble upon them. That is, getting off the beaten path might end up being your greatest reward and most memorable experience.

NEWSPAPERS

In the Parks

TEEWINOT
Grand Teton National Park
Moose, WY
(307) 739-3600
When you enter the park, you'll be handed the current issue of *Teewinot*, which contains information on the park and the John D. Rockefeller Jr. Memorial Parkway. Published each summer and winter, this paper includes campground listings and information on roads, trails, attractions, wildlife, and much more. A comprehensive map details trailheads and visitor centers, and you'll also find interesting facts about the park's history,

geology, and plants. There is also a schedule of ranger-led activities, hikes, evening talks, and other programs.

YELLOWSTONE TODAY
Yellowstone National Park
Mammoth Hot Springs
(307) 344-2258
As a visitor to Yellowstone National Park, this is the first item you should pick up. This quarterly paper produced by the National Park Service includes listings and directions to all the park attractions, from Old Faithful Geyser to Uncle Tom's Trail. Campgrounds, visitor centers, and ranger-led activities are

listed here as well. This little paper gives you everything you'll need to get started on your tour of Yellowstone, but it's not just a directory. It's also packed with informative articles on topics such as ongoing research on geothermal formations at the bottom of Yellowstone Lake, wolf activity, or history.

Each year, close to one million copies of *Yellowstone Today* are handed out by the park service at park entrance gates. Originally, the paper began publication in 1974 as *Yellowstone Explorer*. It has been going strong ever since.

Dailies

BILLINGS GAZETTE
401 North Broadway Ave., Billings, MT
(406) 657-1200
www.billingsgazette.com
If Yellowstone Country could claim just one newspaper, the *Billings Gazette* would be it. With a circulation of about 50,000, Montana's largest paper covers more than 90,000 square miles, from the Canadian border to central Wyoming and from the western Dakotas to Helena, Montana. The bulk of the paper covers state and national stories, with well-done features mixed in. Most residents read the *Gazette* and their own small-town paper for a well-rounded perspective. Owned by Lee Enterprises, this daily supports bureaus in Cody, Wyoming, and in Bozeman and Helena, Montana. In addition to "Enjoy!" the regular weekly arts-and-entertainment supplement, the *Gazette* also publishes 60 special sections each year, including a tab on Yellowstone National Park.

BOZEMAN DAILY CHRONICLE
2820 West College St., Bozeman, MT
(406) 587-4491, (800) 275-0401
www.bozemandailychronicle.com

For a small paper, the *Chronicle* supplies ample amounts of regional and national news seven days a week. The morning paper—which has been voted the state's best in the past—has a circulation of about 15,000 and covers Bozeman and its suburbs—Big Sky, Belgrade, Three Forks, Livingston, West Yellowstone, and everywhere in between. Environmental coverage and issues concerning Yellowstone National Park are particularly strong. "This Week," the *Chronicle*'s weekly entertainment section, comes with the Fri issue and covers arts, music, movies, theater, and more.

LIVINGSTON ENTERPRISE
401 South Main St., Livingston, MT
(406) 222-2000
www.livingstonenterprise.com
The *Livingston Enterprise* prides itself on covering the provincial happenings within Park County, Montana. Because of proximity to Yellowstone (only 50 miles from the northern entrance), the *Enterprise* often gets the scoop on what's happening in the park. Publishing city and county news every weekday afternoon, you'll find local features mixed in with a generous dose of Associated Press stories. With a current circulation of 3,300, the *Enterprise* is one of Livingston's oldest continuously operating businesses. It first began as the *Livingston Post* in 1889 and was published from a small stone building on Callender Street, where the Blue Slipper Theatre currently operates. Today publisher John Sullivan is president of the *Enterprise*'s parent company, Yellowstone Newspapers.

Biweeklies

BELGRADE NEWS
19 East Main St., Belgrade, MT
(406) 388-5101
www.belgrade-news.com
Every Tues and Fri this biweekly newspaper provides complete news, weather, and sports coverage from Belgrade, Manhattan, Three Forks, and Amsterdam/Churchill for free. Circulation is about 4,500.

CODY ENTERPRISE
1549 Sheridan Ave., Cody, WY
(307) 587-2231
www.codyenterprise.com
Founded by none other than the legendary Buffalo Bill Cody, the *Cody Enterprise* is the town's oldest business. With a circulation of about 7,000, this paper is published every Mon and Wed afternoon. In addition to local feature articles and coverage of Yellowstone National Park issues, the *Enterprise* is heavy on local sports stories. This award-winning paper combines excellent photography with solid reporting. Locally owned by Sage Publishing.

Weeklies

CARBON COUNTY NEWS
202 South Hauser St., Red Lodge, MT
(406) 226-2222
www.carboncountynews.com
The photos and copy of the lively *Carbon County News* mirror this town's dedication to community issues. Stories on tourism, recreation, and Yellowstone Park issues make the headlines in this weekly. First published in 1907, the *Carbon County News* has a circulation of 3,000 and comes out every Wed.

COOKE CITY NEWSLETTER
P.O. Box 1011, Cooke City, MT 59020
(406) 838-2395
www.cookecitychamber.org
Published once a week, the *Cooke City Newsletter* is mailed or e-mailed directly to citizens. It offers community information from birth announcements and obituaries to job listings, city meetings, and current events.

GARDINER COMMUNITY NEWSLETTER
233 Main St., Suite A, Gardiner, MT
(406) 848-7971
www.gardinerchamber.com
Gardiner may have only 200 year-round residents, but it's not too small to have a collective voice. That voice can be heard in the *Gardiner Community Newsletter*, which hits the streets most Wed mornings throughout the year. The Gardiner Chamber of Commerce produces the two-sided legal-size paper featuring listings of upcoming events and meetings, local advertisements, and a classifieds section. It is distributed at most local businesses for free.

INTERMOUNTAIN FARM AND RANCH
P.O. Box 1800, Idaho Falls, ID 83403-1800
(208) 528-2278
This is eastern Idaho's weekly agricultural newspaper and covers news from crop statistics and hunting on private land to updates on the dairy and lamb markets. It's an important voice in the communities just on the back side of Teton Pass from Victor and Driggs out to Pocatello and Idaho Falls. Look out on the rolling fields of potatoes and wheat as you drive ID 32 to Ashton, and you'll get an idea of who reads this publication.

MEDIA

JACKSON HOLE DAILY NEWS
1225 Maple Way, Jackson, WY
(307) 733-2047
www.jhnewsandguide.com
With a circulation of 9,500, the *Jackson Hole Daily* comes out six times a week and is distributed free. It offers both locals and visitors news and information in a variety of areas—local, state, regional, national, world, sports, business, entertainment, and syndicated comics and features.

JACKSON HOLE NEWS AND GUIDE
1225 Maple Way, Jackson, WY
(307) 733-2047
www.jhnewsandguide.com
Jackson Hole News and Guide publishes this weekly newspaper every Wed, the *Jackson Hole Daily News,* and two high-quality, four-color glossy publications, *Jackson Hole Magazine: The Magazine of the Tetons,* and *Images West Art and Living in Jackson Hole,* which come out monthly. The weekly paper offers in-depth features on local issues, events, environment, and art and entertainment.

LONE PEAK LOOKOUT
P.O. Box 160123, Big Sky, MT 59716
(406) 995-7133
www.lonepeaklookout.com
The *Lookout* is owned by the *Bozeman Daily Chronicle* and is Big Sky's free source for news, sports, and features. It comes out every Thur and also includes the *Chronicle's* "This Week" arts-and-entertainment section. As the Big Sky community grows, the *Lookout* has become the loudest voice on issues concerning the resort town. It also features a calendar of events around the area.

MONTANA PARENT
Bozeman, MT
(406) 556-0364
www.mtparent.com
Montana Parent is a free magazine published six times a year and available throughout Gallatin, Park, and Yellowstone Counties. It's a wonderful resource for family-oriented events between Billings, Bozeman, and Livingston, featuring in-depth articles and essays on health, parenting, and education. Look for book reviews for all ages of readers, from toddler to teens.

TETON VALLEY NEWS
75 North Main St., Driggs, ID
(208) 354-8101
www.tetonvalleynews.net
The *Valley News* brings together the hybrid of residents in and around Driggs and Victor who have strong links to both the trendier Jackson over the hill and the slow-paced Idaho community. It features political stories regarding Teton Valley zoning issues, education, and local profiles.

WEST YELLOWSTONE NEWS
309 Canyon St., West Yellowstone, MT
(406) 646-9719
www.westyellowstonenews.com
This weekly paper has become West Yellowstone's voice and is part of a three-paper system operated by the *Bozeman Daily Chronicle.* You'll find news, editorials, columns, sports, and classifieds in the tabloid-size paper, which comes out every Thur. Look for it in racks around town, or stop by the office in downtown West Yellowstone.

MAGAZINES

BIG SKY JOURNAL
1050 East Main St., Bozeman, MT
(406) 586-2712
www.bigskyjournal.com
Published six times a year, this well-designed glossy magazine is known for excellent writing and photography. It covers the diverse culture and communities in the Northern Rockies, featuring outdoors, art, fly-fishing, and conservation issues.

IDAHO FALLS MAGAZINE
360 B St., Idaho Falls, ID
(208) 524-7000
www.idahofallsmagazine.com
This bimonthly down-home glossy features events, local profiles, travel, and fun stories related to the area surrounding the town of Idaho Falls.

MONTANA LIVING
52 Buffalo Hill Dr., Kalispell, MT
(406) 862-6489
www.montanaliving.com
Celebrating the lifestyle of Montana, this quarterly magazine offers light fare for the visitor. Features profile luxury homes, restaurants, and statewide destinations.

MONTANA MAGAZINE
P.O. Box 5630, Helena, MT 59604-5630
(888) 666-8624
www.montanamagazine.com
This glossy, photo-focused magazine has become a favorite source for local color and events around the state. It is published bi-monthly.

MONTANA QUARTERLY
2820 West College St., Bozeman, MT
(406) 587-4491
www.themontanaquarterly.com
Founded in 2005, this publication features issue-based coverage of lifestyle in Montana's changing landscape. Published four times a year, it won the award for best new magazine from the Western Magazine Association.

OUTSIDE BOZEMAN
P.O. Box 10934, Bozeman, MT 59719
(406) 582-8068
www.outsidebozeman.com
This free quarterly publication is southwestern Montana's essential outdoor resource. The magazine features maps, gear, outdoor reports and forums, books, calendar events, weather information, a fly-fishing page, a list of local outdoor clubs, and coverage from knowledgeable outdoor writers.

POWDER MOUNTAIN PRESS, INC.
189 North Main, Suite 114, Driggs, ID
(208) 354-3466
www.powdermountainpress.com
Publisher of *Teton Valley: Top to Bottom, Teton Home and Living,* and the *Jackson Hole Explorer,* this little company bridges the gap between locals, part-time residents, and visitors to the Idaho-Wyoming border towns of the Tetons.

RADIO STATIONS
Adult and Soft Contemporary

KYYA 93.3 FM, Billings, MT
KBMJ 95.5 FM, Billings, MT
KOHZ 103.7 FM, Billings, MT
KTAG 97.9 FM, Cody, WY
KMXE 99.3 FM, Red Lodge, MT
KEZQ 92.9 FM, West Yellowstone, MT

Christian

KULR 730 AM, Billings, MT

Contemporary

KCTR 102.9 FM, Billings, MT
KSCY 96.7 FM, Bozeman, MT
KZ 95 FM, Jackson, WY
KMTN 96.9 FM, Jackson, WY

Country

KGHL 790 AM, Billings, MT
KDWG 970 AM, Billings, MT
KIDX 98.5 FM, Billings, MT
KXLB 100.7 FM, Bozeman, MT
KZLO 99.99 FM, Bozeman/Livingston, MT
KPRK 1340 AM, Livingston, MT
KGST 1340 AM, Jackson, WY
KSGT 93.3 FM, Jackson, WY
KPOW 1260 AM, Powell, WY

News/Talk/Sports

KBLG 910 AM, Billings, MT
KWYS 920 AM, West Yellowstone, MT

Oldies

KKBR 97.1 FM, Billings, MT
KODI 1400 AM, Cody, WY
KWYS 920 AM, West Yellowstone, MT

Public Radio

KEMC 95.9 FM, Big Sky, MT
KEMC 91.7 FM, Billings, MT
KEMC 102.1 FM, Bozeman, MT

i Much of the region tunes into Yellowstone Public Radio, which broadcasts on FM frequencies around the area. From Thermopolis, Wyoming, to Bozeman, Montana, you can listen to National Public Radio and regional shows 24 hours a day. Call (800) 441-2941 or visit www.ypradio.org for more information.

Rock—Alternative/Classic

KRKX 94.1 FM, Billings, MT
KMMS 95.1 FM, 1450 AM, Bozeman, MT
KPRK 97.5 FM, Bozeman, MT
KBZM 104.7 FM, Bozeman, MT
KTMN 96.9 FM, Jackson, WY
KLZY 92.5 FM, Powell, WY

MAJOR TELEVISION STATIONS & NETWORK AFFILIATES

KTVQ Channel 2 (CBS), Billings, MT
KHMT Channel 4 (FX), Billings, MT
KSVI Channel 6 (ABC), Billings, MT
KULR Channel 8 (NBC), Billings, MT
KBZK Channel 4 (CBS), Bozeman, MT
KTVM Channel 6 and 42 (NBC), Bozeman, MT
KUSM Channel 9 (PBS), Bozeman, MT
KJWY Channel 2 (NBC), Jackson, WY

TIME LINE

1803—Thomas Jefferson signs the Louisiana Purchase. The United States pays France $15 million for the rights to 828,000 square miles of uncharted land west of the Mississippi River.

1805 to 1806—The Lewis and Clark Expedition passes west and east through Greater Yellowstone, missing the Mammoth Hot Springs by 50 miles.

1807—John Colter explores the area that will eventually become Yellowstone National Park.

1869—Folsom-Cook-Peterson Expedition of 1869 travels through Yellowstone, seeing geysers and hot pools. The three men return to Montana Territory with tales that many doubted.

1870—Gen. Henry Washburn and Nathaniel Langford (who later became the first park superintendent) are among the members of the official exploration party. Old Faithful is discovered and named.

1871—The Hayden Expedition, including photographer William Jackson and artist Thomas Moran, chronicle the area. Moran's paintings and Jackson's photos help convince Congress to preserve the area.

1872—On March 1, President Ulysses S. Grant signs the National Park Act, which creates Yellowstone National Park. It is the country's first national park.

1877—The Nez Perce Indians, led by Chief Joseph, pass through Yellowstone during a retreat after a series of summer battles in which they lost 300 people. The retreat is later hailed as a masterful tactical display.

1882—Gen. Philip Sheridan tours Yellowstone Park. Appalled by rampant poaching of wildlife in the park, he plants the first seeds for the Greater Yellowstone idea by promoting park expansion to encompass wildlife migratory and wintering grounds.

1883—Yellowstone National Park superintendent Philetus W. Norris persuades Congress to allocate funds to build access roads into Yellowstone. This effort establishes the road system that is known today as the Grand Loop Road.

1883—The first grand hotel, the National Hotel at Mammoth Hot Springs, is built by the Yellowstone Park Improvement Company.

1885—The Army Corps of Engineers completes Yellowstone National Park's Golden Gate Bridge.

1886—The US Army takes over Yellowstone National Park's administration.

1888—Excelsior Geyser, which erupted up to 300 feet high and 300 feet wide, is the world's largest geyser until eruptions cease in 1901.

1891—Congress passes the Forest Reserve Act, and President Benjamin Harrison creates the Yellowstone National Park Timberland Reserve, precursor to today's national forests and a key component of Greater Yellowstone.

1892—The Northern Pacific Railroad completes tracks within 3 miles of Yellowstone's northern entrance, making visits to the park more accessible to wealthy tourists.

1894—The Lacey Act is passed to "protect the birds and animals in Yellowstone National Park, and to punish crimes in said park." The act leads to the end of hunting, with heavy penalties for poaching game in Yellowstone.

1900—Approximately 9,000 people visit the park this year.

1901 to mid-1950s—The world's largest trout hatchery operates on the shores of Yellowstone Lake.

1903—President Theodore Roosevelt dedicates the Roosevelt Arch on August 24.

1904—Old Faithful Inn, the world's largest log hostelry, opens.

1905—President Theodore Roosevelt creates the USDA Forest Service and appoints Gifford Pinchot as its first director.

1915—The first automobile is allowed to enter Yellowstone.

1916—President Woodrow Wilson signs an Act of Congress on August 25, creating the National Park Service as a bureau of the Department of the Interior. Shortly thereafter, civilian superintendents are appointed, replacing the park's military overseers.

1927 to 1943—John D. Rockefeller, hoping to create Grand Teton National Park, buys thousands of acres of private land in Jackson Hole.

1929—Congress creates Grand Teton National Park, which includes only the Teton Mountains.

1941—Park officials end bear-feeding shows at Canyon. The shows, during which the bears were fed garbage, began as a way to entertain visitors during the days when the army controlled the park.

1943—President Franklin Roosevelt creates the 221,000-acre Jackson Hole National Monument.

1946—Bison are fed their last hay at the Buffalo Ranch in nearby Lamar Valley. The herd numbers more than 1,000 animals.

1950—Jackson Hole National Monument is incorporated into Grand Teton National Park.

1959—An earthquake causes considerable damage, including a rock slide at Golden Gate Bridge. The quake's epicenter is at Hebgen Lake, Montana.

1965—The number of park visitors exceeds two million.

1973—Yellowstone National Park managers institute catch-and-release fishing.

1985—Excelsior Geyser erupts for the first time in 95 years and hurls large pieces of rock into the Firehole River for 47 hours.

1988—Summer fires sweep through two-thirds of the park, the largest burn in Yellowstone history.

1995—The National Park Service reintroduces the gray wolf into Yellowstone National Park. President Clinton issues a moratorium on mining near Cooke City, Montana, putting a stop to the proposed New World Mine.

1996—Yellowstone's bison herd numbers drop to 2,400 animals, one-third of the population lost to a harsh winter and government-sanctioned slaughter to prevent the spread of brucellosis to domestic cattle.

1997—Yellowstone turns 125 years old, with an average 30,000 to 40,000 visitors each day in summer.

2000—The National Park Service and other federal agencies create a management plan for population size and disease to maintain the Yellowstone bison herd.

2002—The first geologic map of Yellowstone Lake is completed. The map reveals unusual hydrothermal and historic seismic features that will help the National Park Service protect the lake habitat and its wildlife.

2003—The trail through Norris Geyser Basin's Back Basin is closed out of concern for public safety due to eruptions from Porkchop and Steamboat (the world's tallest active geyser) Geysers.

2004—Geologists report an earthquake "swarm" in the Yellowstone Park region; 400 earthquakes are recorded over a three-day period.

2006—Montana Fish, Wildlife & Parks extends a public bison hunt with extra licenses issued to shoot bison that have left the park boundaries.

2006 to 2007—The winter-use plan is enforced, implementing strict regulations on snowmobiles in Yellowstone National Park by limiting numbers of commercially guided snowmobiles each day and enforcing the use of cleaner and quieter four-stroke machines.

2009—Montana and Idaho initiate a limited wolf hunt, citing record populations. However, a federal judge terminated the hunt before the 2010 season. Legislation is ongoing.

2010—Project begins to prepare the next long-term managing winter use in the park. Whatever decision is made will go into effect in the winter of 2011–12.

RESOURCES

REAL ESTATE & RELOCATION

HOMES AND LAND OF SOUTHWEST MONTANA
(406) 522-7800
www.southwestmontanarealestate.com
This magazine and website is a comprehensive guide to the real estate offerings surrounding Bozeman. It's published monthly and available for free at various retail and office locations around the area.

PROSPERA BUSINESS NETWORK
222 East Main St., Bozeman, MT
(406) 587-3113
www.bozeman.org
This economic development group has been operating since 1985 and answers questions individuals, businesses, and families have about the Bozeman economy.

www.homesandlandofjacksonhole.com
Online version of the free real estate magazine offering complete, up-to-date listings of homes and properties for towns within a 200-mile radius of Jackson.

www.jacksonhole.net
A cyber go-to guide for every aspect of Jackson and the surrounding areas, especially real estate listings from multiple brokers; sponsored by the Jackson Chamber of Commerce.

www.move.com
A site with lists of local real estate companies and agents, average house sales, current listings, and neighborhood and school information, plus information on rentals, the job market, and recreation by town.

www.wy-realestate.net
Wyoming Real Estate is a free multiple-listing service network of commercial and residential listings throughout the state.

REGIONAL INFORMATION
Montana
BIG SKY CHAMBER OF COMMERCE
P.O. Box 160100
Big Sky, MT 59716
(406) 995-3000, (800) 943-4111
www.bigskychamber.com

BOZEMAN CHAMBER OF COMMERCE
2000 Commerce Way
Bozeman, MT 59715
(406) 586-5421, (800) 228-4224
www.bozemanchamber.com

COOKE CITY CHAMBER OF COMMERCE
P.O. Box 1071
Cooke City, MT 59020
(406) 838-2495
www.cookecitychamber.org

GARDINER CHAMBER OF COMMERCE
P.O. Box 81
Gardiner, MT 59030
(406) 848-7971
www.gardinerchamber.com

LIVINGSTON CHAMBER OF COMMERCE
303 East Park St.
Livingston, MT 59047
(406) 222-0850
www.livingston-chamber.com

RED LODGE CHAMBER OF COMMERCE
601 North Broadway
Red Lodge, MT 59065
(406) 446-1718
www.redlodge.com

TRAVEL MONTANA
P.O. Box 200533
Helena, MT 59620-0533
(800) 548-3390
www.visitmt.com

WEST YELLOWSTONE CHAMBER OF COMMERCE
P.O. Box 458
West Yellowstone, MT 59758
(406) 646-7701
www.westyellowstonechamber.com

Wyoming

CODY COUNTRY CHAMBER OF COMMERCE
836 Sheridan Ave.
Cody, WY 82414
(307) 587-2777
www.codychamber.org

JACKSON HOLE CHAMBER OF COMMERCE
532 North Cache St.
Jackson, WY 83001
(307) 733-3316
www.jhchamber.com

Idaho

GREATER IDAHO FALLS CHAMBER OF COMMERCE
(208) 523-1010, (800) 634-3246
www.idahofallschamber.com

ISLAND PARK AREA CHAMBER OF COMMERCE
(208) 558-7755
www.islandparkchamber.org

TETON VALLEY CHAMBER OF COMMERCE
P.O. Box 250
Driggs ID 83422
(208) 354-2500
www.tetonvalleychamber.com

National Parks

GRAND TETON NATIONAL PARK
Moose, WY 83012-0170
(307) 739-3600
www.nps.gov/grte

YELLOWSTONE NATIONAL PARK
P.O. Box 168
Yellowstone, WY 82190
(307) 344-7381
www.nps.gov/yell

OUTDOOR RECREATION

Montana

GALLATIN NATIONAL FOREST
Bozeman Ranger District
3710 Fallon St.
Bozeman, MT 59718
(406) 522-2520

GALLATIN NATIONAL FOREST
Hebgen Lake Ranger District
P.O. Box 520
West Yellowstone, MT 59758
(406) 646-7369

GALLATIN NATIONAL FOREST
Livingston Ranger District
5242 US 89 South
Livingston, MT 59047
(406) 222-1892

**MONTANA FISH, WILDLIFE & PARKS
DEPARTMENT**
Region 3 Headquarters
1400 South Nineteenth Ave.
Bozeman, MT 59715
(406) 994-4042

Wyoming

BRIDGER-TETON NATIONAL FOREST
P.O. Box 1888
Jackson, WY 83001
(307) 739-5500

SHOSHONE NATIONAL FOREST
808 Meadow Lane
Cody, WY 82414
(307) 527-6241

**WAPITI RANGER DISTRICT, CLARKS
FORK RANGER DISTRICT, GREYBULL
RANGER DISTRICT**
203A Yellowstone Ave.
Cody, WY 82414
(307) 527-6921

**WYOMING GAME AND FISH
DEPARTMENT**
360 North Cache St.
Jackson, WY 83001
(307) 733-2321

Idaho

ISLAND PARK RANGER DISTRICT
P.O. Box 220
Island Park, ID 83429
(208) 558-7301

TARGHEE NATIONAL FOREST
420 North Bridge St.
P.O. Box 208
St. Anthony, ID 83445
(208) 624-3151

TETON BASIN RANGER DISTRICT
P.O. Box 127
Driggs, ID 83422
(208) 354-2312

WEBSITES

www.buffalofieldcampaign.org
A nonprofit activist group based in West Yellowstone, Montana, that opposes the hazing, slaughter, and hunting of the Yellowstone bison herd.

www.defenders.org
The official site for the Defenders of the Wildlife.

www.greateryellowstonecoalition.org
The quintessential conservation and activist group protecting the region.

www.newwest.net
A comprehensive online daily newspaper for the diverse communities of the Rocky Mountains.

www.northrock.org
The Corporation for the Northern Rockies is a nonprofit group promoting sustainable living in the West.

www.nps.gov
The official National Park Service website.

www.tetonlandtrust.org
This is a community based organization group that works to conserve agricultural and natural resources around the Teton Valley.

www.travelyellowstone.com
The official site of Xanterra, the company that operates Yellowstone lodges and resorts.

www.weather.com
Find out what your stay in our area will be like before you arrive.

www.yellowstoneassociation.org
Affiliated with the National Park Service, the Yellowstone Association is a nonprofit organization that offers educational excursions throughout Yellowstone National Park.

www.yellowstonenationalpark.com
An extensive site that informs you of lodging, dining, recreation, art, events, and shopping for Yellowstone National Park.

www.ypf.org
Yellowstone Park Foundation is a nonprofit organization that sells books, films, and programs for the purpose of raising private donations for Yellowstone.

LIVING HERE

INDEX

Performing Arts Company
of Jackson Hole, 83
Perry's RV Park and
Campgrounds, 163
Perspectives, 113
Pete's Rocky Mountain
Pizza and Pasta, 93
Phelps Lake Overlook, 260
Pickle Barrel, The, 108, 139
Pine Creek Cafe, 139
Pine Creek Campground,
136
Pine Creek Falls, 264
Pine Creek Lake, 264
Pinedale, Wyoming, 200
Pines at Island Park, The,
89
Pink Garter Mainstage
Theater, 83
Pinky's, 140
Pioneer Grill, 61
Plains Indian Powwow, 206
Playmill Theatre, 95, 193
Plonk, 108
Plum Logo, 129
Plush Pony, The, 178
Pole-Peddle-Paddle, 203
Pollard Hotel, The, 159
Pompey's Playground, 220
Ponderosa Campground,
175
Pond Skim, 204
Pony Express Motel, 87
Poor Richard's News, 113
Powder Mountain Press, Inc.,
329
Prairie Rose Northern
Plains Indian Gallery,
179
Prospector Restaurant, 156
Prospera Business
Network, 334
Proud Cut Saloon, 176

Q
Quake Lake Visitor Center,
193, 222

R
radio stations, 329, 330
Rainbow Motel, 134
Rainbow Ranch, 121, 126
Ramshorn Peak, 264
Rare Earth Store, 94
real estate, 310
recreation information
resources, 336
Red Box Car, The, 166
Red Canyon River Trips,
257
Red Lodge Ales Brewing
Co., 166
Red Lodge Chamber of
Commerce, 335
Red Lodge KOA, 163
Red Lodge, Montana, 158,
197
Red Lodge Mountain, 288
Red Lodge Mountain
Resort, 223
Red Lodge Mountain
Resort Golf Course, 280
Red Lodge Nordic Center,
293
Red Lodge Pizza Company,
166
Red Lodge Senior Citizens'
Center, 324
Red Lodge Winter Carnival,
202
Red Star, Kevin, 162
relocation, 310
Rendezvous at Red Lodge,
210
Rendezvous Bistro, 79
Rendezvous Mountain
Rentals, 69
Rendezvous Royale, 214
Rendezvous Ski Race, 202
Rendezvous Ski Trails, 294

Rendezvous Snowmobile
Rentals, 304
Rent-A-Raft/Jackson Hole
Outdoor Center, 239
Residence Inn, 100
resources, 334
retirement, 323, 324
Rexburg, Idaho, 192
Riddle Lake Trail, 259
river ratings, 228
River Rock Lodge, 121
Rock Creek Resort, 160
Rockford Coffee, 97
Rocky Mountain Roasting
Company, 97
Rocky Mountain RV Camp,
147
Roman Theater, The, 167
Roosevelt Arch, 196
Roosevelt Lodge, 48
Roosevelt Lodge Cabins,
41
Roosevelt Old West Dinner
Cookout, 48
Root, The, 113
Round Barn, The, 168
Round House Ski and
Sports Center, The, 296
Rubber Ducky River
Services, 251
Running Bear Pancake
House, 93
Rustic Inn at Jackson Hole,
69
Rustler's Roost, 95
Rusty Parrot Lodge
& Spa, 69

S
Sacajawea Park, 218, 219
Sacajawea Peak and
Hardscrabble Peak Trail,
262
Saint Vincent Hospital and
Health Center, 321

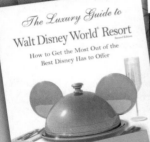

INSIDERS' GUIDE®

The acclaimed travel series that has sold more than 2 million copies!

Discover: Your Travel Destination.
Your Home. Your Home-to-Be.

Albuquerque

Anchorage &
    Southcentral
    Alaska

Atlanta

Austin

Baltimore

Baton Rouge

Boulder & Rocky Mountain
    National Park

Branson & the Ozark
    Mountains

California's Wine Country

Cape Cod & the Islands

Charleston

Charlotte

Chicago

Cincinnati

Civil War Sites in
    the Eastern Theater

Civil War Sites in the South

Colorado's Mountains

Dallas & Fort Worth

Denver

El Paso

Florida Keys & Key West

Gettysburg

Glacier National Park

Great Smoky Mountains

Greater Fort Lauderdale

Greater Tampa Bay Area

Hampton Roads

Houston

Hudson River Valley

Indianapolis

Jacksonville

Kansas City

Long Island

Louisville

Madison

Maine Coast

Memphis

Myrtle Beach &
    the Grand Strand

Nashville

New Orleans

New York City

North Carolina's
    Mountains

North Carolina's
    Outer Banks

North Carolina's
    Piedmont Triad

Oklahoma City

Orange County, CA

Oregon Coast

Palm Beach County

Palm Springs

Philadelphia &
    Pennsylvania Dutch
    Country

Phoenix

Portland, Maine

Portland, Oregon

Raleigh, Durham &
    Chapel Hill

Richmond, VA

Reno and Lake Tahoe

St. Louis

San Antonio

Santa Fe

Savannah & Hilton Head

Seattle

Shreveport

South Dakota's
    Black Hills Badlands

Southwest Florida

Tucson

Tulsa

Twin Cities

Washington, D.C.

Williamsburg & Virginia's
    Historic Triangle

Yellowstone
    & Grand Teton

Yosemite

**To order call 800-243-0495
or visit www.Insiders.com**